REBUILDING THE WORLD ECONOMY

COMMITTEE ON
FOREIGN ECONOMIC RELATIONS
OF THE TWENTIETH CENTURY FUND

The following committee has been in charge of an investigation by a special research staff, the findings of which are summarized in Chapters 1 to 12 inclusive of this volume. The Committee itself is responsible for the recommendations for action which are incorporated in Chapter 13.

REBUILDING *the*

WORLD ECONOMY

America's Role
in Foreign Trade and Investment

---

by Norman S. Buchanan

and Friedrich A. Lutz

With the Report and Recommendations of the
Committee on Foreign Economic Relations

NEW YORK The Twentieth Century Fund 1947

MANUFACTURED IN THE UNITED STATES OF AMERICA
BY E. L. HILDRETH & COMPANY, BRATTLEBORO, VERMONT

FOREWORD

EVENTS UNDERLINE more heavily every month the fact that the prosperity and well-being of the people of the United States are definitely tied to the economic state of the rest of the world. Similarly, the welfare of other nations is linked more closely than ever before with the workings of the American economy.

Recognizing that the foreign economic policies of the United States and America's role in world trade and investment are now matters of supreme world importance, the Trustees of the Fund authorized and underwrote a survey of this whole subject, the findings of which are included in this volume. Following the usual Fund practice this report is divided into two parts: one factual and analytical, the other a program for action. Chapters 1–12 inclusive, for which the research staff is wholly responsible, are designed to give the background of facts and history which is necessary to understand the issues of today. Chapter 13 contains a statement of the policies which the Fund's distinguished Committee on Foreign Economic Relations has formulated to meet these problems in the interests of the American people.

Under the chairmanship of Winfield W. Riefler, who was Minister in Charge of Economic Warfare at the American Embassy in London during World War II, the Committee is representative of the leading economic interests — business, labor, agriculture — as well as of economic science. That a group of men so diverse in their backgrounds and vocations have unanimously agreed on an action platform with sharply specific planks is proof of the vitality and promise of the democratic way of life.

It is a pleasure to record the Fund's appreciation for the Committee's generous contribution of time and effort which has borne fruit in this volume and for the outstanding work of the research staff on which the whole project has been based.

EVANS CLARK, *Executive Director*
The Twentieth Century Fund

330 West 42d Street
New York 18, N.Y.
June 26, 1947

AUTHORS' PREFACE

It is my privilege to acknowledge the authors' obligations to others. The Institute for Advanced Study at Princeton, New Jersey, facilitated our work in many ways — too numerous to mention in detail. The Institute made office space available for use of the survey staff. We also profited greatly from our contacts with the members of the Institute for the academic year 1945–1946. The members of the Economics Department — Professors Walter W. Stewart, Winfield W. Riefler and Robert B. Warren — and the many other economists who came as their guests deserve our special thanks, for we learned a great deal from them.

The text citations indicate only slightly how much we owe to the staff of the Economic, Financial and Transit Department of the League of Nations, which was also located at the Institute for Advanced Study.

We are indebted, too, to those who were kind enough to read and criticize our manuscript. Apart from the members of the Committee on Foreign Economic Relations — whose own report and recommendations are an integral part of the present volume — we wish to thank J. B. Condliffe, Howard S. Ellis, William Fellner, Margaret S. Gordon and J. M. Latiche.

The staff of the Twentieth Century Fund helped us in every possible way, often at considerable personal inconvenience. And Eileen Berryman, our secretary and research assistant, deserves more credit than I can acknowledge here for her patience and good humor amidst the trials and difficulties of joint authorship.

To all these persons and to many others we are sincerely grateful both as joint authors and as individuals.

This volume was virtually completed in June 1946 and it should be read in that light. While the final text was necessarily a joint effort, Professor Lutz took the main responsibility for Chapters 3, 5, 6, 10, 11 and most of Chapter 12, while the chief responsibility for the remaining chapters was mine.

Norman S. Buchanan

CONTENTS

APPENDIXES

TABLES

Contents

xiii

REBUILDING THE WORLD ECONOMY

Chapter 1

INTRODUCTION

THROUGHOUT HISTORY people have exchanged goods with peoples of distant areas. In biblical times caravans brought frankincense and myrrh from the East. In the Middle Ages spices, condiments and silks from the Orient enriched European monastic and manorial life. The charm and beauty of present-day Venice testify to its once thriving commerce with the Orient. The fur trade, which played such a large role in the development of the American continent, depended almost entirely on a European market. People at all times and places have benefited from the products of regions other than those in which they lived; interregional commerce has always tapped the special resources of distant areas.

The great technical improvements in communication and transport in the 18th and 19th centuries made possible a dramatic expansion in world trade. Roads, canals, railways, steamships and wireless telegraphy all contributed. They enormously extended trade between regions with unlike resources. Not only did more territories become accessible, but with cheap transport, more products of all countries could move in trade.

The remarkable growth of international trade during the 19th century was accompanied by an equally remarkable development of customs, practices and institutions. These provided an organizational structure within which people could exploit the unequal world distribution of resources. People's wants were virtually unlimited. The trick was to make goods and services available at a price at which people could buy. Highly organized commodity markets came into existence. The prices of wheat, cotton and sugar in the world market were eagerly watched in a hundred cities. People bought and sold standardized commodities by telegraph.

But such a thriving commerce required a supporting complex of financial institutions. The old money-changers with their laborious weighing and exchanging of alien coins were no longer adequate. Dis-

3

count houses, bill brokers, foreign exchange dealers and banking institutions dealt simultaneously in commodities and foreign moneys. Indeed, commodities and money were merely different sides of the same transactions. International trade and international finance developed together. By the turn of the century there was a world economy, which was fairly well organized to exploit the productive resources of the different parts of the globe.

THE WORLD ECONOMY

Every country has certain productive resources — land, capital equipment and people with various skills. These are combined to produce goods and services to meet people's needs and wants. Deprived of trade and exchange with other countries, any country would be handicapped: it could draw only on its own productive resources. The United States without foreign trade would lack tropical fruits, cocoa, coffee, nickel, tin and a host of other products of common use. Some resources superabundant in some parts of the world are lacking altogether in others. Other resources are only *relatively* more plentiful in some regions than in others. The international economic problem, therefore, is how to organize the world's resources so that they may make their utmost contribution to material welfare.

The world once had an institutional framework that served this purpose fairly well. But within the last three decades three major blows have greatly impaired its effectiveness. The first was World War I. The second was the Great Depression. The third was World War II. Each took its own heavy toll. Each left in its wake its own litter of debris. The havoc wrought by the first was not cleared away before the second struck. When at last, on September 1, 1939, the third blow fell, the international economy retained only a semblance of its onetime resilience and strength.

The international economic problem now is to build a new institutional framework within which the world's resources can again be turned to the production of goods and services for the welfare of all mankind. The reconstruction of the world economy — the problem to which this volume addresses itself — requires an understanding of the basic foundations upon which the world economy once rested. The havoc wrought by two world wars and a world depression of unparalleled severity is not easily overcome. Some of the damage is irreparable. Yet, unless the world is to disintegrate into a collection of fortresses within which each country sweats out a meager living before emerging for the next titanic struggle, the problem of international economic reconstruction must be squarely faced.

INTERNATIONAL ECONOMIC POLICY

The present international economic situation is both confused and confusing. It is not likely to evolve into a workable system by itself. Moreover, few responsible persons are now disposed to let the situation drift. People today show little faith in an inherently beneficent trend in human affairs, and almost none when it comes to international relations. The temper of the times favors a conscious policy of control as against reliance on automatic correctives.

The belief is now widespread that, within limits, public policy can effectively shape national economic and political development. But the well-intentioned policy maker faces a thorny task, because he is forced to operate with the necessarily myopic point of view of the contemporary. Historians may properly insist that today's events can be understood only in retrospect. But an economic policy for the transition from war to peace cannot wait until 1960, even though in 1960 today's problems will be seen in a clearer light. The policy maker must learn what he can from the past and use his best techniques to analyze the present. No other recourse exists.

International economic policy for any country consists of the means, methods and principles that a government chooses to use in its economic relations with other countries for the attainment of desired ends. If one of the aims of the government is a high standard of living for its citizens, then trade and exchange with other countries may be one way of contributing to that end; hence a trade policy is needed that does not prohibit exports and imports. There might be specific exceptions; for example, food imports might be restricted if the government believed it was dangerous to rely on other countries for food, even though domestic production costs were higher.

Alternatively, a government might judge that any reliance whatever on other countries for goods and services was potentially dangerous in a warlike world and so adopt an autarchic economic policy, i.e., no imports and no exports whatever. International economic policy is but a part of national policy, so far as each nation is concerned.[1]

When governments assume responsibility for economic policy as a whole, they must take some account of the relative importance of conflicting ends. One example will illustrate the point.

A country that joins in world trade must accept such adjustments in its domestic economy as are forced upon it by the rest of the world. Its membership in a group of nations having trade and financial relations with one another implies a willingness and an ability to make adjustments to shifts in demand, costs of production, etc., arising both inside and outside its boundaries. Consequently, its international economic policy must recognize this necessity for making adjustments and preserving flexibility within the home economy. If at the same time the policy makers have a responsibility for "full employment" (to use the current phrase), these changes and adjustments precipitated by developments abroad may be extremely troublesome. They may even make the maintenance of full employment nearly impossible. Full-employment policies probably are more easily carried through in a closed economy, insulated from external changes, than in one with outside trade and financial relations. Hence the policy makers may be forced to compromise in part between full-employment policies on the one hand and policies aimed at full participation in world trade on the other.

While most modern governments bear responsibility for maintaining "full employment," few, if any, of the large industrial countries have in fact an adequate program to achieve it. If a strong international trading system is to be re-established, the United States is perhaps called upon to put forth the greatest effort. High levels of steady employment and national income in the United States would go far to make an international trading system workable. Yet the United States has as yet no carefully integrated policy either to avoid a serious slump or to get out of it if one should develop. The United Kingdom is possibly somewhat more committed to a definite policy. But neither country

---

1. We may seem to imply that the "ends" or "objectives" of national policy are explicitly formulated for all the citizens to read and understand. This, of course, is not the case. The ends are not always explicitly formulated nor even more than subconsciously sensed. Nevertheless, they are always present and provide whatever sense or purpose is inherent in the policies adopted. Few Americans, for example, would find it easy to give a clear, coherent description of what they mean by national security. Yet each citizen would have a judgment as to whether a specific policy proposal was likely to contribute to or detract from American national security.

has a comprehensive program to keep national income moving in a steady upward trend.

International economic policy must deal with a number of considerations at once. It must be a compromise among various ends that, in the very nature of the case, no policy can realize completely. National political security, the attractions of an autonomous economic system and the advantages inherent in international specialization and trade — all these, and many more, inevitably go together, along with the selfish pleadings of special interests, to shape a country's international economic policy.

Moreover, a country does not frame its international economic policy in a vacuum. No country can have everything entirely its own way except through complete isolation. The actions of any one country must reckon with the objectives, power and position of other countries, upon whose economies any specific policy must necessarily impinge.

NATIONAL VS. INTERNATIONAL POLICIES

The international economic problem that now faces all countries is how to organize the world's resources for mutual benefit in a world where governments try to formulate economic policies primarily for the national welfare. Each nation has its own peculiar problems stemming from its particular endowment of productive resources, its political and geographical position and, above all, the ideological complex from which it views its own people and the world outside. Somehow these national divergencies must be harmonized within an institutional framework that evokes a more bountiful flow of goods and services from the world's productive resources than would otherwise be possible.

The problem of erecting the framework of a new international economic order has at least three aspects, corresponding to the three types of economic contact between countries. The first of these is trade and commercial policy pertaining to imports and exports; for it is only through trade that the variety of the world's productive resources can be exploited. The second is international investment, which, after all, is fundamentally a means of increasing the effectiveness and speed with which national productive resources yield goods and services. The third is currency and foreign exchange; for each national government insists upon its own currency, and special financial arrangements must be made.

These three aspects of the problem of re-establishing an international economic order within a world of national states are basically all of a piece. Although somewhat different issues are connected with each aspect, all are various sides of the same problem: how to create a workable international economic order out of the current confusion.

Chapter 2

THE RISE AND DECLINE OF THE WORLD ECONOMY[1]

THE NINETEENTH CENTURY: "GOLDEN AGE"

ECONOMIC AND political institutions alike reveal their structural foundations most clearly when they are disintegrating. When the structures are sound and in use, the underpinnings are taken for granted.

From the vantage point of the present, the foundations of the 19th century international economy are now fairly obvious. They include certain cultural and social features as well as certain institutions of a technical economic nature. Together they contributed enormously to the smooth functioning of what, in retrospect, can be labeled a world economy.

The defeat of Napoleon at Waterloo began a century of British dominance in world affairs. By 1914 there was an international economy, based on liberal[2] economic principles of British origin, and centered in London. During the century, this development was aided by, and in turn helped to create, an environment that favored its rapid growth.

A COMMON IDEOLOGY

By the last quarter of the 19th century the western world had attained a unanimity of opinion about ultimate values that persisted down to the outbreak of war in 1914. In western Europe, the British Isles, the British Dominions, the United States, and to a lesser degree in central Europe, economic and political freedom were the keystones

1. The present chapter attempts to cover much territory in a few pages. Our interest has been to emphasize the main contrasts between the 19th century world and the period after 1929. At times we have had to omit qualifications and exceptions that would be possible in a longer treatment. Specifically, we have perhaps given a more pleasing picture of the world economy in the 19th century than the full facts warrant; but this seemed unavoidable in the space available.

2. The word "liberal" is used here and elsewhere in this book in the formal, traditional sense. It connotes a whole body of economic and political doctrines associated with such names as Smith, Ricardo, Bentham, James Mill, John Stuart Mill, and others. Cf. L. T. Hobhouse, *Liberalism,* Holt, New York, 1911. In current American usage the term has almost lost specific meaning.

on which mankind confidently expected to rear new monuments of achievement. The rest of the world, in this view, was a "backward area," a "white man's burden," toward which missionaries and businessmen bore a moral obligation.

This common outlook entailed something more than a firm belief in the "obvious and simple system of natural liberty" of Adam Smith. People really believed in competition, and in the virtues and benefits of allowing individuals to pursue their self-interests. And the function of the state, they thought, was mainly to nurture the institutions of free contract, private property and individual freedom; it was not its job to meddle in economic affairs. But this seemingly general agreement went even further: it embraced modes of conduct too. Certain things were "simply not done." Not the least important phase of extending world commerce to the "backward areas" was familiarizing the natives with the intangible amenities of trade. As one writer recently said:

The written and unwritten rules of commerce were rules of gentlemanly conduct translated into the everyday language of business — just as routine diplomacy was transacted by aristocratic conventions, no matter whether its functionaries were heirs to ancient titles or representatives of the middle classes. International integration in that period arose from the fact that the liberal philosophy was dominant in all major trading countries, that a body of ethical maxims commanded universal allegiance . . .[3]

But there were dissident voices. Karl Marx and others inveighed against exploitation of the workers. Even its supporters conceded that the system had blemishes. Free trade was not universal; indeed, late in the century, protectionism was growing. Crises periodically brought ruin to many. But even crises had the virtue, some argued, of purging the economic system of certain wastes and poisons that accumulated with a too easy growth of opulence. Yet, on the whole, people believed in economic liberalism throughout most of the western world. Liberalism held values beyond mere material achievements. Freedom of enterprise, the workers' freedom of choice of occupation, freedom of consumers to choose among competing sellers and a general freedom from control and supervision by government were considered essential and important values.

Thus the doctrine of economic liberalism was not a way of interpreting *one*

3. Robert Strausz-Hupé, *The Balance of Tomorrow*, Putnam's, New York, 1945, p. 24.

area of life, while religion, personal relations, or art developed their own philosophies; rather except to maverick critics, it was the central, guiding philosophy of the period by which others must stand or fall — or in relation to which they must become unimportant.[4]

The world had a common outlook in economic and political affairs that it has not since regained.[5]

LONG PEACE

The century preceding 1914 also favored the development of a world economy because no major wars disrupted economic relations. The impact of war has been nearly disastrous in the 20th century. The century of relative peace preceding 1914, on the other hand, permitted a complicated network of trade and financial relations to spread over much of the world. Great Britain invested heavily, in the United States and in the British Dominions, in industries having a European market. Countries developing without much assistance from foreign loans also frequently found the export industries the most profitable. Economic expansion in the new countries was closely linked with world trade. Conversely, British exports of manufactures increased as the Dominions and the United States expanded economically. Side by side with this international exchange of goods a complicated financial system developed to facilitate their flow.

The long years of peace contributed to this development mainly in two ways. First, the international economy was able to grow steadily with an almost organic relationship among its several parts. A common social outlook and the acceptance of the liberal principles as axiomatic were partly responsible. Second, because there was peace, no major financial disturbances, such as wars almost inevitably provoke, disrupted the smooth functioning of the system. The financial pattern of international economic relations evolved in harmony with the flow of commodities, the development of new sources of supply and the distribution of consumer demand. The "goods side" and the financial side in the international economy tended to form a symmetrical pattern; it was not distorted by wartime intergovernmental

4. Helen Merrell Lynd, *England in the Eighteen-Eighties,* Macmillan, New York, 1945, p. 66.
5. Cf. Wilhelm Röpke, *International Economic Disintegration,* Hodge, London, 1942, Chaps. 5, 15, and *passim.*

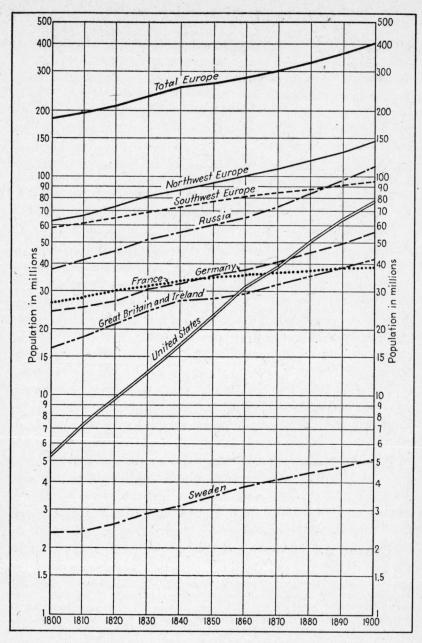

Chart 1. Growth of Population in Selected Countries, 1800–1900

Source: Appendix Table A.

12

borrowings, reparations, economic blockades or the uneven rise of prices as in war inflation.[6]

A century of peace provided a nearly organic structure of world trade and a nice harmony between finance and production. The peace, in turn, was mainly dependent upon the dominant role of Great Britain in the developing world economy: *Pax Britannica*. Britain's key position in world trade was at once a reason why it desired peace and the basis of its power to maintain it. World commerce meant seaborne commerce, and Britain was mistress of the seas.

EXPANDING POPULATION

The population of Europe more than doubled between 1800 and 1900, increasing from 187 million to 400 million. In northwestern Europe the increase was from 62.8 million to 144.4 million, and in southwestern Europe (France, Italy, Spain and Portugal) from 59.7 million to 95.7 million. And this increase took place despite heavy emigration. The population of Great Britain and Ireland rose from 16.5 million to 42.1 million; of Germany from 24.5 million to 56.3 million; of Belgium from 3 million to 6.6 million; and of France from 26.9 million to 38.9 million.

This rapid increase in population contributed significantly to the smoothness with which the 19th century world economy developed and functioned. The rates of population growth were not constant, of course, throughout the century for each country. For Great Britain and Ireland the periods of most rapid growth were from 1800 to 1830, and again from 1870 to 1880; for Germany from 1820 to 1830, and again from 1870 to 1880. For France the percentage rate of increase almost steadily diminished from 1820 to 1900 and was throughout much lower than in most other countries. The growth of population for selected countries is shown in Chart 1.[7]

6. The Franco-Prussian War ended with a levy of reparations on France, but it was paid without any noticeable disruption of international trade or finance. Perhaps this was unfortunate in so far as it gave the peacemakers at Versailles the notion that the international financial system would support any burdens they might choose to place upon it.

7. Chart 1 and the actual figures for Europe that appear in Appendix Table A are from Gustav Sundbärg, *Aperçus statistiques internationaux*, Norstedt, Stockholm, 1906. The figures in the table and given above in the text are from this source and relate to the territorial areas of the countries prevailing in 1900. We are indebted to the Institute for Population Research of Princeton University for selecting this source for us as containing the most reliable estimates available. The Sundbärg volume is, incidentally, a treasury of various comparative statistics by countries running back many years — data, in many

To link rapid population growth, a common ideology and a long interval of peace as fundamental factors in the development of the world economy in the 19th century may seem illogical. For from one point of view the increasing population was itself partly a consequence of the development of the world economy: food became cheaper and more abundant, living standards improved, death rates declined and, as a result, population increased. But, in fact, the rapid growth of population contributed to the development and smooth operation of the world economy in several ways.

Immigration

First, with the rapid growth of population in the British Isles and northwestern Europe, many people migrated to the United States, the

---

instances, that are not readily accessible.

By way of comparison it is worth observing the reported estimates of European population as a whole prior to 1800.

According to Sundbärg's estimates (Appendix Table A) total European population in 1800 was approximately 186.9 million. This is identical with an estimate reported by Quincy Wright (*A Study of War*, University of Chicago Press, Chicago, 1942, Vol. I, p. 612) on the basis of estimates by Kuczynski, Willcox, and others. Wright's table, however, gives estimates running back to 1450 and also (p. 467) cruder figures for selected years back to 400 B.C. These are reproduced here together with the percentage rate of increase in the European population by fifty-year periods since 1450 as reported in *ibid.*, p. 612.

Year	Population (In Millions)	Percentage Increase in the 50 Years Preceding the Year in Column 1
400 B.C.	22	—
0	37	—
A.D. 200	63	—
700	27	—
1000	40	—
1328	59	—
1400	44	—
1450	60	—
1500	68	13
1550	76	12
1600	87	14
1650	100	15
1700	118	18
1750	140	19
1800	187	34
1850	266	42
1900	401	51

The very marked rate of increase after 1750 and the even greater increase after 1800 are quite astounding. The interval from 1750 to 1900, in which international trade grew into an organized system, has been unique in European history. The rate of increase is, of course, currently on the decline.

British Dominions and colonial areas. But the migrations involved more than the transfer of manpower to areas of higher economic productivity. They also brought about the transplantation of economic institutions and the ideology of 19th century liberalism to new areas where they flourished with new vigor. Furthermore, the strong cultural and social ties between the "new" countries and the "old" fostered trade between them. The immigrants brought a knowledge of overseas needs, markets and sources of supply. Financial connections were maintained. This all helped to develop trade and close relations between western Europe and the areas of immigration. It was the migration of a culture as well as of persons.

Aid to Economic Adaptability

The expansion of population was even more important, however, for the adaptability it gave to the whole framework of world trade.

Any economic system based on liberal economic principles always faces the problem of adaptation to changes in buying habits and sources of supply. The consumer buys what he prefers from the cheapest supplier. Production must adjust accordingly. But this means that productive resources — labor, capital equipment and land — must be regrouped as new wants develop or as new sources of supply appear. And in a dynamic world these changes are always occurring. But a country that trades with other countries must accommodate itself to economic changes occurring not only within but also without its own borders. If cheap food is imported from abroad, domestic agriculture must shrink in relative importance. If cheaper cotton from other countries is capturing the world market, then domestic industry may be devoting too much land and labor to cotton production. If consumers prefer rayon to cotton, then cotton output must be reduced. Domestic production must be responsive to changes in international demand and supply. The distribution of employed labor and the types and quantities of capital equipment in the country must be harmonized with the pattern of consumer demand and production costs at home and abroad. In a dynamic world this means that capital equipment and labor cannot maintain the same proportional distribution among industries over the years. The problem of reallocation is always present.

But how can a rapidly increasing population facilitate this adaptation of the structure of production?

An absolute shrinkage in the quantity of capital equipment and labor employed in an industry is usually not easily achieved, especially in the short period. Laborers have family and social roots. They do not leave an industry just because the demand for its product declines. Capital equipment is, if anything, more difficult to transfer. It is often specialized: much of it consists of buildings and structures difficult to adapt to other uses.

If population is growing at a rapid rate, however, no absolute shrinkage may be necessary: the affected industry need only grow less rapidly than industry as a whole. A relative shrinkage suffices. The coal industry, for example, may decline in relative importance by simply ceasing to grow, or merely by growing at a slower pace than all industry. No withdrawal of labor or capital from the industry is then required. A rapidly growing population and a rising total output thus permit an easier adjustment to economic change; and an appropriate distribution of productive resources among industries is more easily maintained.

A rapid rate of increase in population will certainly not wholly solve this problem of keeping productive resources in harmony with alterations in supply and demand changes regardless of the degree of adjustment.[8] But throughout much of the 19th century, most such adjustments seem to have been made with comparative ease. The most serious exception was probably the reaction of European agriculture to cheap food supplies from overseas. Here Great Britain accepted the change by allowing its domestic agricultural production to shrink; but certain European countries partially avoided this by imposing tariff duties. Yet, on the whole, the 19th century adjustments were readily achieved partly because of the rapid rate of population growth.

To summarize: A common ideology and point of view on economic, political and social questions, a century of nearly unbroken peace, and a rapid rate of population growth were all conducive to the rapid growth of international trade and finance.

ECONOMIC AND TECHNICAL FACTORS

By 1914 a system of international trade and finance had evolved possessing a color, flavor and strength largely determined by the en-

8. If the decline in relative importance of an industry is sufficiently great, then a relative decline will mean an absolute decline as well.

vironment in which it was nurtured. The 19th century world, particularly in the forty years preceding 1914, possessed certain favorable economic characteristics that contributed in a high degree to the development of an international trading system and that facilitated its operation. Some of these, such as the international gold standard, related to finance and prices. Others, such as the type of capital equipment in use in the 19th century, were more technical than economic. It was a special combination of favorable factors that gave the world an international economy. Unfortunately, the 20th century heirs to this mechanism have often quite misunderstood what made it work as it did.

THE INTERNATIONAL GOLD STANDARD

If each national currency unit is defined as a specific amount of fine gold, this automatically provides fixed rates of exchange among them. These rates of exchange are simply the ratios of the pure gold content of the respective currency units to one another. So long as countries maintain free convertibility of currency into gold and gold into currency, a system of fixed exchange rates automatically prevails.[9] But the international gold standard was something more than a formal definition of national currency units in terms of physical quantities of gold.

A decision by a country to participate in the international gold-standard system meant that its domestic economy — its structure of relative prices, its distribution of productive resources, etc. — was tied to the train of world events. For if each country assigned a fixed gold content to its currency unit, and determined to maintain the designated convertibility, it had to conduct its foreign economic relations in such a way that fixed rates of foreign exchange could be maintained. The exchange rate was held fixed and other economic factors adjusted to it. Exports, imports, foreign lending and borrowing, service transactions, etc., so adapted themselves to economic change that the foreign exchange rate held unaltered.

Britain's Dominance

Just as British thought and practice provided the rationale of 19th century trade, so the international gold standard centered in the Bank

9. That is, within the limits set by the cost of transferring the amount of gold defined as the currency unit from one country to another.

of England and that coterie of private banks, bill brokers, acceptance houses and foreign exchange dealers constituting the London money market. The international gold standard without London would have appeared almost inconceivable in 1900. And, of course, this position was both cause and effect of Britain's dominance in world trade. As B. M. Anderson has written in discussing the pre-1914 position of London:

> More commodities were dealt in in London than in any other single center. There was a great community of expert students of commodities, of recognized integrity, whose grading of commodities was accepted throughout the world. There was an admirable warehouse system. There was a great body of expert speculative buyers, who knew their outlets, and who were prepared to buy, at a concession in price, almost any commodity, on very short notice. The merchants of the world trusted this machinery, and the British banks could safely trust it. They could make loans which were truly liquid loans, against virtually any commodity. The London stock market also was a wide and dependable stock market, which made readily marketable a greater range of securities than would be marketable in any other center, and which consequently made good collateral out of securities which could not serve as collateral, safely, in other financial centers. The foreign exchange of every country in the world was freely dealt in in London, and could consequently be made the basis of bank credit. What came to London became liquid, and everything came to London.[10]

In appraising currency problems after World War II this key position of London down to 1914 must not be overlooked, for it goes far to explain the effectiveness with which the gold-standard system once functioned. Indeed, some would argue that the pre-1914 gold standard was fundamentally a sterling standard; world trade was mostly transacted and financed in sterling. Certainly other countries were less rigid about gold than Great Britain. But the position of Great Britain in world commerce and finance before 1914 was pre-eminent: and sterling held fast to gold.

Its "Automatic" Nature

The international gold standard was, from one point of view, but an application of liberal economic principles in the monetary sphere. Under the protection of stable exchange rates, individuals could commit their labor and capital wherever they promised the most favorable

10. As quoted by William Adams Brown, *The International Gold Standard Reinterpreted, 1914–1934*, National Bureau of Economic Research, New York, 1940, Vol. I, p. xvii.

returns, whether at home or abroad. In so far as credit and exchange policies played a role in the gold-standard system, they were mainly based on the size of the central bank's gold reserve in each country. The central bank maintained convertibility of the currency into gold by tightening or easing credit through changes in its rate of interest in relation to the size of its gold reserve. But the central bank's gold reserve reflected the country's international economic position as shown by exports, imports, foreign borrowing and lending, etc. Hence, maintaining gold convertibility not only induced stable foreign exchange rates, it also closely linked together national economies and world trade. Currency management, such as was common after 1929, did not exist. The wisdom of maintaining gold convertibility and stable exchange rates was taken for granted. There was an international monetary system based on clear-cut rules that left little room for human discretion. In this sense it was often described as "automatic."

The international gold standard, however, is often also termed "automatic" in a different, though related, sense. We have shown that the determination to maintain convertibility makes domestic credit policy a function of a country's gold holdings. When gold reserves are dwindling, credit must be tightened. When gold reserves are increasing, credit must be relaxed. But in the absence of political and social disturbances, a country loses gold *because* it is importing too much in relation to its exports. To raise interest rates by action of the central bank will tend to depress prices and money incomes at home and so encourage exports and discourage imports. And conversely. Hence, gold drains or gold accretions tend to be self-correcting, provided the authorities keep close watch and shape their credit policy accordingly. The international flow of goods and gold is part of a self-equilibrating process of adaptation and adjustment.

The international gold standard is, of course, not the only possible arrangement by which international trade can be carried on. But in contrast to most alternative schemes, the international gold standard does emphasize the international aspects of a country's economic life. Broadly speaking, stable exchange rates, as provided by the international gold standard, are more favorable for international trade and investment than fluctuating exchange rates or stable exchange rates maintained by special controls. But there is another and even more important way in which the gold standard emphasizes the international aspects in any national economy. In a gold-standard system, monetary policy is shaped by the country's gold position, which in turn is affected by economic developments both at home and abroad. The country has, therefore, to adapt its domestic economic policy to developments in other countries. It sacrifices much of its freedom to go its own way in economic policy. As compensation, of course, the country gains from participating in a system that probably tends to maximize international specialization.[11]

FLEXIBILITY OF PRICES

If credit policy based on gold reserves is to keep the national economy in equilibrium with the rest of the world, then it must force adjustments in domestic prices. For the system to be workable, prices must be flexible and resources adaptable to alternative uses.

To prove that most commodity prices were more flexible before than after 1914 is probably impossible. Nevertheless, there are good reasons for believing that this was the fact. In proportion to all business, the volume of business carried on at "administered" prices almost certainly increased after 1914. Cartels, quasi monopolies, oligopolies and public regulation embraced a larger part of the economy than they did in the 19th century. The dictum "affected with a public interest" applies to more and more industries, and so more of the economy has been brought under the control of public authority.[12] Finally, the steady removal of wage rates from determination in the

11. In recent years there has been a tendency to emphasize only the undesirable side of membership — particularly that a country is precluded from pursuing an expansionist economic policy. Yet impulses making for depressions are not the only economic disturbances that a country may receive from other countries. More than once countries have been spared a domestic depression by favorable developments in the outside world.

The account in the text above is not intended to be either a complete description of the full logic of an international gold-standard system or a description of how it operated. Rather the aim has been to focus attention on those aspects of the international gold-standard system that seem, in retrospect, to have been most important in establishing a world economy and maintaining it in reasonably effective operation. As such we have had to omit numerous qualifications and to state bluntly cause and effect relationships that were often intricate and delicate in their operation. For a full account the reader should consult the standard works on the subject: R. G. Hawtrey, *The Gold Standard in Theory and Practice*, Longmans, Green, London, 1939; T. E. Gregory, *The Gold Standard and Its Future*, Methuen, London, 1932; Brown, *op. cit.*

12. Actually the change has not been so much that more industries are "affected with a public interest" as that the relative importance of these industries — railroads, power and light, natural and manufactured gas, water works, and urban transportation — has grown enormously.

open market has been of far-reaching importance with respect to many prices. The increasing numbers of "administered" prices presumably make for less price sensitivity and flexibility. Furthermore, there has been a steady increase in the variety of goods not directly comparable and not competing with one another primarily on a price basis. This fact would also tend to reduce price flexibility. A society that is growing wealthier means one in which there is a steady increase in the variety of products available and a diminution in competition on the basis of price alone. Producers' and consumers' durable goods, of course, are the outstanding groups of highly differentiated commodities in which price competition plays a secondary role. Turret lathes or radios from different producers do not compete only in regard to price.

The underlying reasons for diminished flexibility of prices as a whole will not be explored here. Partly the change is attributable to technical factors, partly to changing concepts of social responsibility and partly to changes in the distribution of power within society as a whole. Current attitudes on wages, for example, are a far cry from the 19th century view — shared fairly generally by plain citizens, the clergy and economists alike — that individualism, self-help and laissez faire would cure all ills. But there was some basis for this faith. Unemployment actually was less of a problem for the economy. Sir William Beveridge, after a careful examination of pre-1914 unemployment, reports that in Great Britain, "At a rate of 14.2 [per cent] between the wars unemployment was between two and three times as severe as before the first World War, most probably about 2½ times."[13]

But whatever the reasons, in the late 19th century, prices within national economies did seem to adjust sufficiently to prevent gross disequilibria from appearing in the international balance of payments.[14] Commodity exports and imports kept reasonably well in

13. William H. Beveridge, *Full Employment in a Free Society,* Allen & Unwin, London, 1944, p. 337. Appendix B of this volume contains an elaborate discussion of the probable relation between pre-1914 unemployment and unemployment in the interwar period.

14. One could argue, certainly, that in the period under discussion the number and magnitude of the adjustments that national economies were required to undertake as members of a world economy were, as a matter of plain fact, substantially smaller than those to which the world economy was subjected after 1918. For example, such a major adjustment as the inflow of cheap food from the new world in the 1880's was *not* achieved by a disappearance of European agriculture, i.e., a major shift in economic resources;

balance, with due allowance for service transactions and international lending. In the main, no great difficulty was experienced in adjusting domestic price structures to international economic transactions at fixed rates of exchange. This must mean that the price structure was sufficiently plastic to accommodate the changes forced on it, whether from inside or outside. The world economy down to 1914 was a going concern partly because these adjustments could be carried through without unconscionable hardship. That there were many hardships is common knowledge. But the adjustments were mostly accepted and made nonetheless.[15]

MOBILITY OF RESOURCES

Flexibility is not important for its own sake in an economic system based on principles of free enterprise and the private pursuit of gain. The changes in prices, if they are indeed flexible, imply changes in demand for consumption goods and for means of production, or changes in supply, or both. Money prices, what the classical economists were wont to call the "money veil," do actually shroud underlying economic relationships. Each system of price relationships implies an "appropriate" distribution of the means of production among possible employments and therefore a "correct" flow and composition of output. In a free-price economy the function of the price system is to achieve this appropriate distribution of the means of production and this correct flow and composition of output. Adjustments in prices induce readjustments in the allocation of productive factors and hence

---

but, instead, it was partly avoided by tariff protection. After 1918 (as will become clearer as our story unfolds) there were many adjustments of this magnitude, to which an equilibrium adjustment between prices and resource distribution was apparently not possible. Furthermore, the fact that capital flows in the 19th century were almost altogether from the older, wealthier countries to the newer, poorer countries gave a stability to international economic relations that has no parallel in the period between 1918 and 1939. In summary, therefore, one could argue not only that prices were more flexible and resources more mobile in the 19th century, but that the adjustments imposed on the world economy were less numerous, more gradual and of smaller magnitude.

15. It may be pointed out that wealthier economies are perhaps inherently more unstable than poorer ones because as an economy becomes wealthier a larger proportion of total output consists of "services" and of consumers' and producers' durable goods, the demand for which is both more volatile and more easily postponed. In other words, in contrasting the pre-1914 and the post-1914 economic setting one might perhaps keep in mind that the secular growth in aggregate output in the industrial countries was likely to be accompanied by greater instability because services and durable goods were becoming progressively a larger fraction of total output.

alter real output. Flexibility of prices is only a means, though not the only one, of continually reallocating the factors of production between alternative employments.[16]

In contrast to the 19th century, prices in recent years have probably become more inflexible. But what is even more important for an effective integration of a world economy is that economic resources are probably less mobile than before 1914. Diminished price flexibility means diminished pressure to shift resources to other occupations. But even where prices do change, the resistances to the transfer of resources appear to have intensified. Hence national economic adaptability to changes at home and abroad is less than it once was. Several factors seem to be responsible.[17]

16. Until comparatively recent times economists assumed that price flexibility was desirable, nay indispensable, for the operation of a free-enterprise economy. The reasons were: First, changes in particular commodity prices or prices for particular productive resources indicated the changes in consumers' preferences, in the relative scarcity of particular factors, etc., and so made the whole price system capable of adapting itself and of absorbing whatever changes might occur. Second, the very fact of price changes would diminish the actual shift of productive resources necessary to any change in the economic data (consumers' tastes, quantities of the factors, etc.) that might appear. So, for example, if rayon is preferred to cotton, then a fall in cotton goods prices will mean that fewer productive resources will have to shift out of cotton — assuming the demand to have some elasticity, though not necessarily greater than unity — than if cotton prices remain at their old level. In other words, changing relative prices were likely to minimize resource shifts necessary in response to intruding changes. This is altogether an argument having to do with *relative* prices; it is an argument from value theory and has nothing to do with changes in the price level, an average of all prices. The theory of the price level was more or less a separate compartment of economic theory, except in the work of Knut Wicksell, the Swedish economist.

More recently, especially since 1929, the desirability of price flexibility has been questioned because of the tendency it may have to generate general downward and upward movements in prices as a whole. This is not simply the old price level problem that the older economists, as we have said, kept in a separate compartment from value theory. It is rather the tendency of falling prices to generate a decline in national income and employment through, first, the adverse effect of falling prices on consumers' and entrepreneurs' expectations, thus causing a general shift in demand curves to the left without any obvious limit; and second, through the effect of falling factor prices, especially wages, on aggregate demand for commodities as a whole. Both these tendencies may lead to a *cumulative* fall in prices as a whole, which is adverse for national income and employment. This argument has most recently been advanced by Oscar Lange in *Price Flexibility and Employment,* Principia Press, Bloomington (Ind.), 1944.

An economy with extensive trading relations with other countries *at fixed exchange rates* has both these difficulties to deal with, i.e., the problem of relative prices and the problem of the price level at home compared with the level of prices in other countries. In the text above, the argument relates chiefly to relative prices and price flexibility. But in later sections the problem of the price level will come into the discussion as well.

17. Our earlier discussion (pp. 15–16) on the economic effects of a rapid rate of population growth should be borne in mind here, too.

More Fixed Capital Per Head

First in importance, perhaps, is the increased capital employed per unit of output. Economic progress goes hand in hand with an increase in the stock of real capital employed in production. As nations become wealthier, more capital takes the form of investment in factories, mines, railroads, machinery, buildings, etc. In large measure these augment productivity in the degree to which they are "special-purpose" rather than "general-purpose" capital goods. The increased efficiency in the refining of petroleum, for example, has been achieved by a greater use of highly specialized capital equipment that has virtually no alternative use. Since about 1870 there has been a succession of new industries and a continual modernization of older industries that has involved a heavy investment in plant and equipment of a special-purpose type. What does this mean in terms of mobility of resources? Clearly, the greater the proportion of fixed, specialized investment without alternative use, the lower the price of the product may fall without forcing any decline in productive capacity. Any returns over the small direct costs of production make it worth while to continue production. Firms may fail and financial claims may be scaled down, but productive capacity diminishes only very slowly. A bankruptcy reorganization of the firm may be put through, but the productive capacity continues in use.

These technical conditions markedly contrast with those in industries such as wholesaling and retailing, where the bulk of the invested capital is in inventories and accounts receivable that, at a sacrifice, can be readily liquidated and the investment withdrawn from the industry. In the 19th century a greater proportion of industry and agriculture was of this "commercial" sort. And in the international sphere, economic activity was, to a high degree, "trade" and "exchange" between regions that were unlike in their respective specialities. The mobility of capital investment — "stock," the classical writers used to call it — was sufficient to accommodate most changes that occurred. Nowadays, with heavy, specialized capital investments the mobility of capital is much reduced.[18]

18. It is an interesting speculation as to how far classical economic theory as developed from Adam Smith down through J. S. Mill and even Alfred Marshall — though here to a lesser degree, of course — implies an economic system in which adaptability is achieved through growing a different crop — oats as against wheat, for example — on the cultivable land or turning out a different textile design on the same machinery. The

Decreased Labor Mobility

Somewhat different factors have diminished labor mobility in response to economic change. For the world as a whole, there has been a virtual cessation of large-scale migration. After World War I, few countries were anxious to receive new immigrants; people could not migrate in great numbers to less crowded areas. But even within countries, peacetime labor mobility among industries has probably diminished.[19] The greater proportion of older people in the total population in most developed countries would, in itself, tend to diminish labor mobility, since younger persons are more mobile and more easily directed from declining into expanding industries. More recently, trade-union policies and unemployment insurance have also probably diminished labor mobility. Cheaper transportation as well as a reduction in the average degree of skill required to use more automatic machinery have, on the other hand, worked in the opposite direction. Possibly labor mobility (given price flexibility) has not greatly changed since the 19th century, although the writers' judgment is that some decrease has probably occurred. Since, however, price flexibility has almost certainly declined, people have not been pressed to move as much as before. Consequently, the distribution of labor among various occupations is now more likely to get out of harmony with demand and supply conditions than in the 19th century. The domestic structure of production therefore tends to be less easily adaptable to a changing world economy.

THE ROLE OF THE STATE

Finally, among the many favorable factors encouraging the growth of an integrated world economy in the long peace down to 1914, the economic role of the state takes a prominent place.

Prior to 1914, economic and political liberalism was the dominant philosophy throughout the countries important in world trade. The state did not assume responsibility for eliminating unemployment or

---

case where more and more industry takes on the character of capital investment in railroads — as in petroleum, chemicals, cement, nonferrous metals, gas and electricity works, etc., where disinvestment of fixed capital is nearly impossible — seems not to have been much examined by classical writers. In all probability this neglect, if neglect it is, arises from the fact that these difficulties were not nearly so prevalent in the 19th century as they are in the 20th century.

19. Internal migrations during World War II were enormous, of course. But this had special, even unique, features.

raising national incomes beyond the broad obligation to protect national security and to maintain an environment in which laissez faire could function. Full employment, social security, public welfare functions and state economic undertakings were activities that governments did not, in the main, have thrust upon them either by conditions or by the electorate. These were private matters that the citizen, *qua* citizen, handled or not in his own way as he saw fit. The state's role was distinctly limited. That this often resulted in enormous hardship and great suffering is not to be denied. Yet the fact is that the obligations and responsibilities of the state in economic matters were far less down to 1914 than they later became. Private enterprise had a free field in which it could pursue its own logic and laws of operation. The significance of this freedom for the particular form that the world economy assumed was great indeed.

To sum up: A long peace, a common ideology and an expanding population allowed world trade and finance to develop along laissez-faire principles between 1815 and 1914. Moreover, the international gold standard — a kind of liberal economic constitution with accepted principles, rules and procedures analogous to many political constitutions that were coming into existence contemporaneously — operated within and upon an economic framework that was fairly flexible and adaptable with respect to both prices and real resources. It was in such an environment that the "world economy" or "the international economy" — in reality a whole complicated system of trade and financial relationships existing between private persons in different countries for the exchange of commodities and services — came into existence. But the important point is that the system was intimately attached to its environment and at many points quite indistinguishable from it.

In passing the foundations of this earlier economic system in review, its substantial material achievements must not be forgotten. Both extensively between countries, and intensively within national boundaries, the degree of economic development between, say, 1850 and 1914 was astounding by comparison with earlier centuries. There were marked technical advances. Transportation and communication achieved an efficiency and reliability previously unknown. More products were available, and their variety exceeded previous experience. There was a rapid increase in population, and on the average people lived longer and at a higher standard of living than ever before.

FROM THE GREAT WAR TO THE GREAT DEPRESSION

Only some future historian will be able to discern whether the foundations of the world economy were already crumbling and its institutions atrophying in 1914, or whether the Great War loosed forces of destruction too strong for even a sound edifice.[20] In any case the war tore a gaping rent in the intricate fabric of the international economy that hasty stitching in the twenties and extensive patching in the thirties quite failed to mend.

The war of 1914–1918 elevated national governments to new heights of economic authority. Familiar views persisted, but practice changed perceptibly. The state's role enlarged despite formal obeisance to liberal principles. Because the struggle ranged groups of powers rather than single nations in contest, only state action could coordinate joint activities in the common cause. An allied shipping control was created, for example. Purchasing missions on government account were organized. Yet, strange as it may now appear, governments still relied heavily on the price system to procure what goods, services and war materials they needed. "Business as usual" expressed not only one's patriotic duty, but also an abounding faith in the transitory character of the whole episode. The potentialities of the income tax and the excess profits tax were discovered.[21] And in Great Britain and the United States, after protracted discussion, there was even conscription for war service.[22] But these, too, were treated as temporary departures from the basic principles on which the economy functioned. The long-familiar ideology persisted even though practices and external economic conditions both altered.

ECONOMIC RECONSTRUCTION AFTER 1918

The dominance of traditional views is perhaps nowhere better illustrated than in the attitude taken toward economic reconstruction after 1918. "Back to normalcy" was the slogan. Budget balancing, re-

20. At present the prevailing view seems to be that the Great War of 1914–1918 only precipitated a disintegration that was already far advanced, though not apparent, in 1914 or even earlier.

21. The income tax as a fiscal device apparently dates from its introduction by Pitt during the Napoleonic Wars. But the full possibilities of the income tax were only discovered during and after World War I.

22. It is perhaps symptomatic of the change in outlook that in World War II conscription was scarcely an issue at all in democratic countries. In 1914–1918 it was vigorously debated in terms that now seem archaic.

moval of wartime controls and a return to the international gold
standard appeared to many as the principal items on the agenda; and
if the cost of the war could be saddled upon the defeated Central
Powers, the return to normality seemed easy.

But the recuperative powers of the economy and its capacity for
effective operation, without interference from the state, apparently
diminished after 1914, or more probably, the wartime changes over-
taxed the absorptive capacity of traditional institutions. For in the
United States, after a brief boom characterized by inventory speculation and skyrocketing prices, the curve of business activity turned
steeply downward in 1920. Prices dropped sharply. Unemployment
spread. And through 1921 and part of 1922 conditions dragged along
in a highly unsatisfactory manner. Somewhat similar events took place
in Great Britain.

Continental Europe was plagued by even more serious problems.
Food and raw materials were scarce. Physical destruction had been
considerable. The revival of output was halting and tenuous. But
perhaps overshadowing all else was the persistence of budgetary deficits and mounting inflation. The old virtues of industry and thrift were
mocked by the decline in the purchasing power of money. The savings
of the laborers and the middle classes evaporated while speculators
and profiteers lived luxuriously. But the speculators and profiteers
were usually the entrepreneurs, the traditional mainspring of a liberal
economic system built on private property and the pursuit of gain.
The entrepreneurs behaved as they had always behaved: they followed the dictates of the market price mechanism, only to find themselves cursed by the populace for profiteering and blamed by governments for raising prices. With unemployment rife, entrepreneurs in
disgrace and starvation and disease widespread, the governments of
Europe were forced to the public purchase and distribution of food.
The market system could not function amid capital shortages, a shat-
tered transport system and inflated currencies. People would not
starve quietly. State action became imperative. And more often than
not, the swollen public expenditures were drawn from fresh currency
issues that served as a bellows to an already dangerous inflation. As
a recent report of the League of Nations stated:

The problem of postwar reconstruction, ignored at the time of the armistice,
did not solve itself. It was adjourned for four years and during these four years

the whole economic and social organization of many countries rotted. When it was finally faced, it had ceased to be a general problem of transition and reconstruction and had become a problem of cutting the gangrene out of the most affected areas one by one.[23]

FAILURE OF RECONSTRUCTION

The failure of traditional market forces to achieve economic reconstruction, or to restore more than a semblance of the pre-1914 world economy, had profound consequences. The common ideology was dissolving. Especially in central Europe, but elsewhere as well, people lost faith in liberal economic institutions. The charms of freedom and the beneficence of competition held little attraction for hungry people rustling for bread.[24] Many wondered if, as the Marxists had long been saying, it were not indeed a system of capitalist exploitation of the toiling masses. And in contrast to earlier times, the European denouncers of capitalism could point to Russia, where capitalist institutions had been swept away in favor of new forms geared to new ideals. People wondered if state action toward the common good might not promise more than the "obvious and simple system of natural liberty."

The major problem of economic, as distinct from political, reconstruction was never really solved. This was the problem of achieving a workable harmony between the structure of international financial claims and obligations on the one hand, and export capacities and import needs on the other.

We need not explore here the ramifications of reparations, interallied borrowings and foreign lending on private account. But it was a tangle of debits and credits running to what were then considered astronomical sums. On the other hand, import needs and export capacities as between one country and another were not what they were in August 1914. America was stronger, Europe weaker. European industry and transport had deteriorated during the war years, while European postwar import needs for effective reconstruction were

23. *The Transition From War to Peace Economy,* League of Nations, Geneva, 1943. II.A.3, p. 70.
24. The failure of economic reconstruction is, of course, not properly chargeable entirely to the mistake of leaving the task chiefly to private enterprise. The attempt by reparations and otherwise to keep Germany economically weak without reference to her prewar key position in the European economy perhaps made a restoration nearly impossible. See J. M. Keynes, *The Economic Consequences of the Peace,* Harcourt, Brace, New York, 1920.

large. Europe needed imports, but lacked exports with which to pay. And later, exchange rates depreciated faster than internal prices rose, so that the terms of trade moved against the European countries until their currencies were arbitrarily stabilized or, as in the case of Germany, collapsed altogether. Great Britain, long the center of international trade in commodities and a heavy importer, encountered increasing difficulty in finding foreign buyers for its usual exports of coal and textiles. International trade continued, but it was no longer so easy to balance debits and credits by offsetting imports against exports and against income from foreign investments. There was too great a divergence between the financial pattern and the postwar structure of needs and resources.

RECONSTRUCTION AND THE UNITED STATES

There were few serious doubts in the United States in the 1920's about world economic affairs or about the validity of the principles on which the economic system rested. The war left no deep scars. The postwar depression was soon forgotten except as an object lesson in the virtues of hand-to-mouth buying by business firms, and the country passed into an era of technical improvements and rising standards of living. Although remaining protectionist in commercial policy, the country loaned large sums abroad in Europe and Latin America. Americans were gratified by the restoration of the gold standard in England in 1925 — and at the old gold parity at that!

The task of recounting how unsuccessful were the efforts to reestablish the "world economy" of 1914 need not, fortunately, be attempted here. The story has been told often enough. One can doubtless point the finger at this or that error and, with impeccable logic, show what disastrous results necessarily followed. In any case, only the external forms of the 1914 world economy were restored, not its inherent substance and strength. When the gong sounded the close of business on the New York Stock Exchange on October 29, 1929, it signalized more than the loss of thousands of personal fortunes: it signalized the end of a superficial effort to reassemble a global economy that had been deeply scarred and damaged.

FROM THE GREAT DEPRESSION TO WORLD WAR II

The Great Depression that began in 1929 and deepened perceptibly after the international financial crisis in 1931 further weakened the foundations of the world economy. In Great Britain, even before 1929, there were rising doubts about the ability of traditional market mechanisms to keep the balance of payments in equilibrium at the old gold parity and yet avoid domestic unemployment. In the United States and Canada loss of faith came only later as prices continued to fall and unemployment mounted. The old correctives — liquidation, lower prices, wage reductions and credit restriction — were apparently unable to halt the falling curve of national income. The other British Dominions, Latin America, and raw-material-producing and agricultural countries generally, were plagued by disastrously low prices for their exports and with foreign debts. By the early 1930's these countries, along with the United States and to a lesser extent the United Kingdom, were the chief remaining strongholds of laissez faire and free enterprise. But no longer could a British Royal Commission say as in 1894:

> Many of the evils to which our attention has been called are such as cannot be remedied by any legislation, but we may look with confidence to their gradual amendment by natural forces now in operation . . .[25]

— and expect a round of applause. People in 1932 were not looking with confidence. They were looking askance at the whole system.

This dying faith in liberal economic principles was given a further blow by the apparent success attending the authoritarian regimes in Russia and (after 1933) Germany. Here there was no unemployment. The state took responsibility and bent the price system to its iron will with subsidies, quotas, state enterprise and an outburst of deficit financing. Personal freedom was at a discount, personal security at a premium.

DEPRESSION AND ECONOMIC FLEXIBILITY

The crux of the depression problem seemed to be the fundamental incapacity of economic resources and the composition of output to adjust themselves, either sufficiently or fast enough, to changes in the structure of prices and in the pattern of financial claims and obligations. A system of free enterprise relying on the price system to control and regulate production implies either that real resources are mobile enough to accommodate whatever changes prices command

25. As quoted from the Royal Commission on Labour (*Fifth and Final Report*, Pt. I, p. 112) by Lynd, *op. cit.*, p. 70.

or that the change is not great enough to require unlimited adaptability of real resources. But between 1929 and 1935, actual price variations seemed to call for enormous changes in the structure of production and the composition of output.

Especially troublesome were the chaotic capital movements that plagued national economies and foreign exchange markets prior to September 1931 when Great Britain left the gold standard, and before and after the United States devalued the dollar in 1933. These were not international capital movements bearing any relation to the long-term profitability of investment in other countries. They were inspired by the hope of short-term speculative gains and by political fears. But from the point of view of the national economies forced to adapt to them, the effects were even more drastic than if they had been huge capital movements on the 19th century model. Such capital movements as long-term commitments in undeveloped countries would at least have stimulated exports from the countries losing capital. The capital movements after 1930 were inspired by different motives. They were "hot money" that could blister an economy that had to deal with them.

While the international economy was experiencing chaotic changes — tumbling prices, flights of capital — the adaptability of labor and capital goods was becoming less, not greater, than before. There were more heavy industry, more specialized equipment and more sunk investments. The mobility of labor, certainly internationally, and probably within countries as well, had diminished. The rigidity of the economic system was greater. It became increasingly clear that national economies could not adjust to whatever changes might appear. The conviction grew that the adjustment had to be achieved on the side of prices and finance rather than, as in past depressions, by accommodating the use of resources to the financial superstructure. If farmers stubbornly produced cotton or wheat beyond home needs and export demand, then the government — for political reasons — financed them and stored the product. But this meant that fixed exchange rates and simple trade controls such as tariff duties were inadequate. In some countries it was a case of too little exports; in others of too much imports. Production was out of line with prices. But if the two could not be brought together by changes in production, then exchange rates had to give way. The balance of payments could not be kept in equilibrium at fixed exchange rates. Consequently, exchange rates became increasingly pliable, or, if they remained nominally fixed, the government limited and controlled all exchange transactions. Exchange control and quantitative trade controls became nearly inevitable when governments faced a rigid structure of production and steep changes in commodity prices.[26]

These new devices were an almost unavoidable adaptation to an inflexible structure of production. For if the structure of output does not easily adapt itself to changes in international demand at fixed exchange rates, then a country is virtually forced to adjust demand to the existing structure of production. Exchange control and quantitative trade controls restrict the consumption of imported goods; the government simply refuses to allow domestic consumers to buy as they please from abroad. Consumers' expenditure is forced away from imports and toward domestic goods. Exchange depreciation is, in a sense, only an alternative means of redirecting demand. When the rate of exchange is allowed to fall, all imported goods become more expensive, and thus less appealing to home buyers. But at the same time all exportable goods are now cheaper to foreigners, and so the volume sold abroad is likely to increase. The new controls to which many governments turned when they abandoned fixed exchange rates after 1931 were intended, fundamentally, to force adaptations in demand. Changes in domestic demand were substituted for such changes in home output as would force it into harmony with world prices.

GROWING OBLIGATIONS OF THE NATIONAL STATE

The depression following 1929 so increased industrial unemployment in the major countries as to make it the major political issue. Employment was no longer a wholly "personal" matter for each individual to solve for himself. The fully developed view that the state is

26. What matters for the problem of the distribution of real resources within a country is, of course, the structure of relative prices rather than the price level. But in a country having economic relations with other countries at fixed exchange rates the level of prices is also highly important. That is to say, cotton textile prices relative to electric machinery prices may suggest that resources should shift from textiles to electrical goods. But at fixed exchange rates the relative prices of cottons and electrical goods may be satisfactory and yet both prices (along with many others) may be too high in relation to prices elsewhere *given fixed rates of exchange*. It should also be pointed out that a change in the price level is impossible to achieve without altering relative prices as well. Not all prices are equally flexible on the rise and the decline. Hence a change in the price level will almost inevitably imply a change in relative prices too. See also footnote 16, p. 23.

responsible for establishing and maintaining "full employment" emerged only gradually. Neither the objectives nor the instrumentalities of national economic policy were ready to hand when it was reluctantly conceded that this was something more than a cyclical depression of the 19th century type. But after 1930, despite some hesitancies, the main emphasis in national economic policy shifted. It shifted from mere state responsibility for providing a laissez-faire environment to a positive state obligation to assure a minimum of economic and social security by deliberate government action. The state took, or had forced upon it, responsibility for national economic welfare. General unemployment compelled the state to have a positive economic policy.[27]

NATIONAL ECONOMIC POLICY AND THE WORLD ECONOMY

Nowadays a positive national economic policy is, perhaps, primarily directed toward achieving "full employment." Widespread unemployment certainly brings drastic checks to international trade, as the experience of the 1930's clearly shows. Consequently, in so far as governments succeed in holding national incomes on a high plane, they greatly encourage the flow of world trade.[28] Nevertheless, when governments take responsibility for a positive economic policy, in-

27. The evolution of economic policy in the United States after 1930 was fairly typical. The first reaction was that the depression must run its course, though the Federal Farm Board and the RFC antedated the election of 1932; the election was certainly interpreted as a mandate for more positive policies. Then came the NRA, partly based on the doubtful proposition that the depression was chargeable to too much competition resulting in too low prices, and the AAA as a crop restriction program in agriculture. Another attack was the strenuous reform movement in commercial banking and the related areas of security flotation and the securities markets. The idea would not easily down that in some manner (never altogether clear) some group of persons could be saddled with the responsibility for the depression. Parallel with these efforts were attempts to increase total money in the hands of the public and so raise prices from the low levels of 1932–1933. The dollar was devalued, silver purchases made mandatory, the restrictions on rediscounting almost disappeared, member bank reserves were made adjustable, and the government finally insured deposits up to $5,000. Not all these changes occurred simultaneously, of course, and they were probably not part of an over-all policy from the start. Yet their general objective was essentially the same: to raise purchasing power and prices by monetary measures. WPA, PWA, NYA, were originally means of putting people to work who were unemployed through no fault of their own. The generative effect of these programs on national income was first stressed as "pump priming." The more sophisticated analysis came only later as Keynesian doctrines spread their influence. But after five years there was no longer serious disagreement about the state's having welfare and security obligations to its citizens.

28. This problem is dealt with in greater detail in Chapters 3 and 10.

ternational economic relations may become more difficult for three reasons.

First, governments exercise authority only within their territorial boundaries. They have little control over external economic developments. But if they allow imports or exports, national economic policy is always in danger of being disrupted by developments abroad. Trading relations with other countries may limit the effectiveness of domestic economic policy. A government can decide, for example, that domestic agriculture must be supported and encouraged. But if the product is exported the government has no control over prices received abroad and hence, without special arrangements, no complete control over farmers' incomes. Similarly, attempts to take positive measures for the development of a particular home industry may be nullified if imports are not excluded or rigidly restricted.

On a much broader scale there is the conflict between an aggressive fiscal policy to achieve full employment and the danger that such a policy will disarrange the balance of payments. The government must decide how much foreign trade is worth to the nation in view of the limitations foreign trade may impose on domestic economic policy. And although one cannot be sure in these matters, the record suggests that freedom of domestic action is likely to be rated higher than the benefits of international specialization and exchange. National economic policy has perhaps a bias in favor of autarchy.

The second difficulty that may flow from government responsibility for economic policy is that ideological differences are more likely to intrude themselves into international economic dealings. Foreign trade policies are then likely to be more than the expression of narrowly economic considerations: diplomacy and trade have a tendency to get linked together. So long as private traders deal with one another only within the sphere of their immediate economic interests as traders, their ideological differences are of little moment and certainly no barrier to commerce. But an aggressive foreign trade policy may well reflect ideological convictions and even inject them into the trading relationship.

Finally, international trade, an important phase of international economic relations, will probably tend to be increasingly bilateral when government assumes responsibility for a positive economic policy. Instead of fixing general tariff rates and allowing foreign trade to pursue its own course, government is pushed by the demands of its domestic economic and political policies and its international diplomatic policies toward discriminatory bilateral agreements with particular countries. While multilateral trade agreements — agreements among several countries — are theoretically possible, the record to date discloses few. Bilateralism, however, tends to shrink the volume of world trade, not to increase it. Hence, government responsibility for national economic policy tends, in this way too, to diminish national specialization and multilateral trade.

Thus, a world in which sovereign governments assume responsibility for economic welfare, and hence for national economic policy, is not a world with strong "natural" tendencies toward expansion of international trade. Without special precautions and new arrangements, international trade more probably has a tendency to shrink rather than to expand. The 19th century world economy, linked together by indigenous ties that now no longer exist, has passed beyond recall. The problem now before the nations is how again to knit the world together economically, on the assumption that the gains from foreign trade are worth the costs.

Until 1914 the international economy was organically so integrated that prices of goods and services and the financial side of the national economies in general harmonized fairly well with the distribution of real resources and the composition of national output. Change was orderly and gradual, and in the main it was toward higher living standards within a world possessing a common ideology. Even at more or less fixed exchange rates, productive resources seemed sufficiently adaptable to accommodate the technological changes, shifts in demand and alterations in supply conditions that occurred.

World War I and the years immediately following disrupted this orderly progress and injected some highly discordant tones. The structure of needs and resources within and among countries was no longer so well adapted to the financial network as before 1914. And after 1929 these difficulties became worse from a broad international point of view. There was less and less effort toward international harmony as the bigger countries — the United States, Great Britain, Russia, France, Germany and Italy — sought their own solutions to their own pressing domestic economic problems. In 1939 when the German armies marched into Poland there was no longer anything resembling the nicely balanced world economy of 1914, in which international financial claims, domestic prices, the structure of world output and the flow of world commerce were thoroughly integrated.

Chapter 3

ANALYSIS OF WORLD TRADE

THE PREWAR world economy accommodated total imports in 1938 of $24.6 billion. In 1928, before the Great Depression, the figure was even larger, $35.5 billion. Many countries and many areas participated in this trade; it was composed of many products. What determined the participation of the various countries in this world commerce? Which countries were important in world trade, and why? In which directions — from what countries and to what countries — did trade move, and what were the reasons? What commodities and services were involved, and what was their relative importance for the various countries? What role did foreign investment play, and how did it affect world trade in goods and services?

FOREIGN TRADE AND NATIONAL OUTPUT

National output is an alternative expression for national income. The net output of any country for any period can be measured either in terms of aggregate net values produced or of total incomes earned. The two are the same thing looked at from different vantage points.

Unless a country has a special policy to restrict imports or exports (e.g., tariffs), its national output and its foreign trade are likely to be closely linked. Increasing national output means that people are producing, exchanging and consuming a larger total volume of goods and services. If no special restrictions prevail, the probability is that some of their expenditures will go for goods produced abroad. One might therefore expect imports to rise and fall according to the cyclical ups and downs of national income. For the long-term upsweep of national output over the decades, a similar, though less intimate, relationship might be anticipated.

If such a relationship is fairly probable for any one country it is fairly probable for all other countries, or for the world as a whole. For the world as a whole, imports of goods and services must equal exports of goods and services — an import into one country is necessarily an export from some other country. World imports and world exports

38

must therefore each tend to bear a fairly close relationship to world output if special factors do not intervene.

VARIATIONS IN NATIONAL INCOME AND TRADE

The cyclical parallelism between national income and imports is exemplified by the recent experience of the United States. Between 1922 and 1929, imports rose or fell with national annual income, with the exception of 1928. The ratio of imports to national income in 1922 was 5.1 per cent; in 1929 it was 5.3 per cent, which was also the average for the whole period 1922–1929. In the 1930's annual imports continued to rise and fall with national income, but the ratio of imports to national income was lower (the average was 3.6 per cent for 1930–1938). The greater decline in prices of imports than in prices of home goods, the Hawley-Smoot tariff of 1930 and other factors doubtless explain the smaller ratio in the 1930's.

American exports show a similarly close connection with American national income. The ratio of exports to national income was 6.3 per cent in both 1922 and 1929, and deviated only slightly from this value, except for 1924, in the whole period 1922–1929. After 1929 the ratio was lower (just as was the ratio of imports to the national income), with an average of 4.1 per cent; but again, year by year, American exports rose and fell with American national income.

The correlation between changes in imports and exports and changes in national income is not really surprising. Most dollar funds with which American exports are purchased are provided by American imports of goods and services from other countries. Thus, if American imports correlate closely with national income, exports will also. In a causal sense the relationship is, of course, closer between imports and national income. When national income is high the United States tends to import heavily from abroad and foreigners use the dollars so acquired to buy American goods and services. Exports, as well as imports, correlate with the cyclical swings of American national income. Probably there is a similar cyclical relation between national income and foreign trade in other countries.

World output as a whole has steadily improved over the decades. Technical progress, the accumulation of capital equipment, and certainly international trade itself, have pushed up national incomes in most countries during the past hundred years. Unfortunately, however, reliable national income data running back a century or more do not exist.[1] Consequently, international trade cannot be correlated secularly with national income by individual countries.

World Trade and Manufacturing Output

In an effort to obtain some estimate of the long-run relation between international trade and world output, Dr. Folke Hilgerdt of the League of Nations has recently compiled an index of world output of manufactured goods.[2] Manufactured goods output would not be expected to indicate exact total output. Nevertheless, the behavior of Hilgerdt's index of manufactured goods production in relation to world trade is revealing.

A comparison of Hilgerdt's index of world output of manufactured goods with an index of world trade indicates that from the late 1870's until 1914 the rising output of world manufactures was accompanied by an increase in the volume of world trade. In the interval from 1876–1880 to 1911–1913, the world's output of manufactures increased 4.2 times. World trade increased, but not so much — in manufactures 3 times, in primary products 3.1 times. (All data are corrected for price fluctuations.) Thus, world trade in manufactures increased as world output of manufactures increased, but not by the same proportions. (Charts 2 and 3 show these relationships graphically.)

The imperfect statistical parallelism between the growth of manufacturing and the growth of world trade down to 1914 is not difficult to explain. Between 1876 and 1913 industrialization was spreading rapidly. The rate of increase for manufacturing output was almost certainly more than for world output as a whole. Consequently world trade would not be expected to grow as rapidly as manufacturing. Again, many countries, for example France and Germany, raised tariffs on imports of manufactures and primary products, particularly agricultural products, and so checked the expansion of international trade despite spreading industrialization. Finally, as a country becomes wealthier, people are likely to spend a larger proportion of their income on domestically produced commodities such as houses and transportation equipment, and on various "services" that cannot enter

1. Some rough calculations will be found in Eugene Staley, *World Economic Development,* International Labor Office, Montreal, 1944, Chap. 8.

2. *Industrialization and Foreign Trade,* League of Nations, Geneva, 1945.II.A.10, pp. 132 ff.

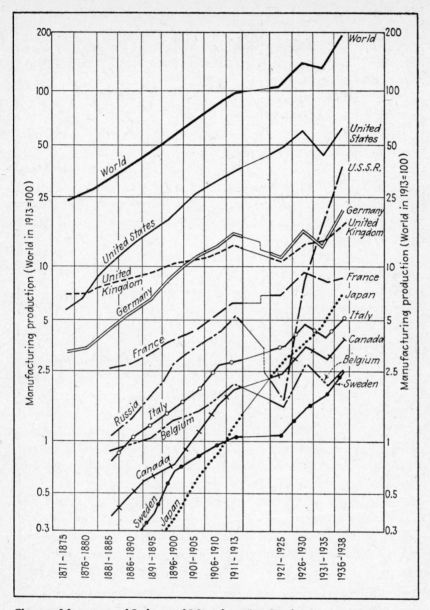

Chart 2. Movement of Indexes of Manufacturing Production, 1871–1938

Source: Industrialization and Foreign Trade, League of Nations, Geneva, 1945.II.A.10, p. 12.

Note: The ten countries together represented 87 per cent of world manufacturing production in 1913. The vertical short-dash lines in the space between 1913 and 1921 express shifts in the curves due to changes in territory after the 1914–1918 war.

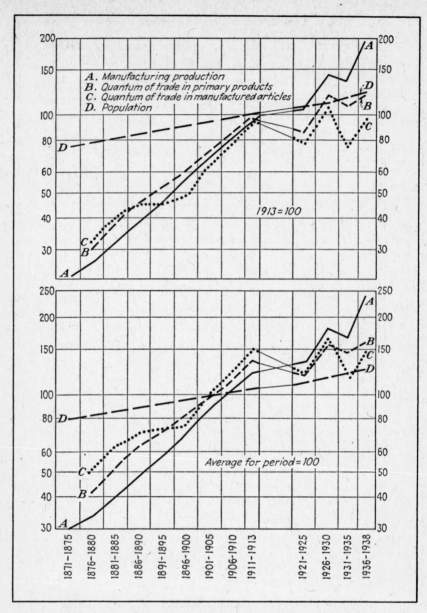

Chart 3. Movement of World Indexes of Manufacturing, International Trade and Population, 1871–1938

Source: Industrialization and Foreign Trade, League of Nations, Geneva, 1945.II.A.10, p. 15.

Note: The upper part of the diagram shows the indexes on the basis of 1913 = 100. In the lower part, the basis for each index is the average for the period 1876–1913 and 1921–1938 (56 years).

into foreign trade — such as repairs and maintenance, entertainment, vacations, laundering, cleaning, etc. Thus, even in the absence of special interference, international trade is not likely to keep pace with the secular growth of world income. The relationship between world income and world trade, though definitely operative, is less intimate in the long term than in the short.

World War I disrupted the relationship between world income and world trade. The world emerged from the war and its immediate aftermath with a smaller proportion of trade to income than in 1913. But in the 1920's the tendency of world trade to move in general harmony with world income was re-established; indeed, world output of manufactures and world trade during the 1920's moved even more closely together than before World War I.

International trade statistics for the 1930's seem to belie the proposition that world trade tends to fluctuate closely with world income. The index for world manufacturing rose by 35 per cent between 1930 and 1938–1939, probably a greater percentage rise than in world income. Compared with these increases, world trade in manufactures between 1930 and 1938–1939 actually declined 8 per cent and world trade in primary products fell 4 per cent. The explanation of this divergence lies in unstable exchange rates, currency warfare, and above all, quantitative trade controls practiced in some countries for the very purpose of becoming independent of foreign supplies.

To sum up: Changes in national income are among the prime determinants of changes in foreign trade. The changes in national output in particular countries tend to evoke like changes in their foreign trade unless commercial policy deliberately intervenes. Similarly, for the world as a whole, output and international trade show a strong tendency to move together if not deliberately checked. In the long run, however, the growth of international trade tends to lag somewhat behind world income.

NATIONAL INCOME AND PARTICIPATION IN WORLD TRADE

Subject to certain qualifications discussed below, countries with relatively large national incomes tend to share heavily in world exports and world imports. The poorer countries, by the very fact that they are poor, would not be expected to participate in world trade to the same extent as countries with large national incomes.

World trade in fact radiates from the industrialized countries. The five major industrial countries — the United States, Great Britain, Germany, France and Japan — alone took 45.4 per cent of world imports of $35.5 billion in 1928 and 43.4 per cent of world imports of $24.6 billion in 1938. They also supplied 44.6 per cent and 42.1 per cent of the world's exports ($32.6 billion and $21.9 billion respectively) in the same years.[3]

The relatively high national incomes of the industrial countries make them good customers for other countries, and their well-developed manufacturing industries make them good suppliers of exports to the less industrialized countries. But the level of the national income does not fully explain a country's relative importance as a purchaser of foreign commodities. Great Britain with a much smaller national income than the United States yet took a larger share of world imports. Britain's economy is less "balanced" than that of the United States, and so, almost by definition, more specialized, and therefore more dependent on the world economy. Britain must import agricultural products and raw materials on a proportionately larger scale than the United States, where plentiful natural resources allow profitable home production of many such products. A country's trade policy — tariffs, exchange controls, subsidies, etc. — also affects its participation in world trade. (Table 1 shows the participation in world imports and exports by continents and major countries for 1928 and 1938.)

A nation's importance as a world customer or supplier need not coincide with the importance of its foreign trade for its national economy. The foreign trade of small countries, or of countries with few natural resources, is likely to be a much higher percentage of national income than that of large countries, or those rich in natural resources. But there are exceptions, and the relationship may be complicated. The contrast in 1929 between Norway or the Netherlands and the United States in the ratio of imports to national income is striking.

3. World imports are larger than world exports because import values — except for the United States, Canada and some Latin-American countries — include transportation costs from abroad to the frontier. The figures in the text, however, are from *The Network of World Trade*, League of Nations, Geneva, 1942.II.A.3, pp. 17–18, and have already been adjusted to a comparable basis. The decline of world trade from 1928 to 1938 is partially attributable to the decline in prices over the period. If price fluctuations are eliminated, world trade in 1938 was only 9 per cent below its 1928 level, a drop that is easily explained by the increased trade restrictions imposed by many countries.

TABLE 1

INTERNATIONAL TRADE BY CONTINENTS AND MAJOR COUNTRIES,
1928 AND 1938

Continent or Country	Per Cent of World Imports		Per Cent of World Exports	
	1928	1938	1928	1938
Total	100.0	100.0	100.0	100.0
America	24.0	20.0	29.9	27.6
United States	12.4	8.9	15.8	14.2
Northern North America	3.9	3.3	4.4	4.2
Latin America	7.7	7.8	9.7	9.2
Argentina	2.3	1.8	3.1	2.0
Brazil	1.2	1.2	1.5	1.3
Europe (excluding U.S.S.R.)	53.9	55.6	46.4	47.8
United Kingdom	14.7	16.9	10.7	10.3
Germany[a, b]	9.4	9.0	9.0	9.9
France[a]	5.9	5.3	6.3	4.0
Asia (excluding U.S.S.R.)	13.6	13.7	15.5	15.2
Japan, Formosa, Korea	3.0	3.3	2.8	3.7
China (excluding Manchuria)	2.0	1.1	1.5	0.7
India, Burma, Ceylon	3.0	2.4	4.2	3.3
Netherlands Indies	1.1	1.1	1.9	1.7
U.S.S.R.	1.4	1.1	1.3	1.2
Africa	4.5	6.4	4.0	4.7
Union of South Africa	1.1	2.0	0.7	0.6
Oceania	2.6	3.2	2.9	3.5

Source: Calculated from figures in *The Network of World Trade,* League of Nations, Geneva, 1942.II.A.3. Table excludes trade in gold and silver; the figures are for "special trade."

a. The Saar was part of the French customs area in 1928.
b. Excluding Austria.

The ratio was 48 per cent for both Norway and the Netherlands and 5 per cent for the United States. (See Table 2.)[4]

Before World War II the United States was the second largest im-

4. The year 1929 has been chosen because it is the last year before the breakdown of the international trading system. Also, figures are more readily available for 1929 than for later years.

TABLE 2

FOREIGN TRADE IN MERCHANDISE AS PER CENT OF NATIONAL
INCOME, SELECTED COUNTRIES, 1929

Country	Per Cent of National Income	
	Imports	Exports
Norway	48	34
Netherlands	48	34
Denmark	46	42
Belgium[a]	45	38
Austria	45	30
Finland	38	35
United Kingdom	25	17
France	24	20
Sweden[a]	22	20
Australia	22	21
Canada	21	20
Germany	18	18
United States	5	6

Source: For the national income figures, *World Economic Survey, 1937–38,* League of Nations, Geneva, 1938.II.A.13, p. 136. For imports and exports figures, *Statistical Year-Book of the League of Nations, 1935–36,* League of Nations, Geneva, 1936.II.A.8, p. 218.

a. 1930.

porter and the largest exporter. Nevertheless, its foreign trade showed the smallest percentage relationship to national income of all the countries in Table 2. This fact has wide implications: A decline in the foreign trade of the United States is not disastrous for the American economy, but it is likely to have severe repercussions on the economies of many foreign countries of whose exports America is often the largest buyer.

COMPARATIVE ADVANTAGE AND FOREIGN TRADE

Different geographical regions specialize in different products, mainly because natural resources, capital and different types of labor skills are unevenly distributed over the globe. Regions rich in certain minerals (Bolivia in tin, Sweden in iron ore) or regions having a climate or soil particularly suited for the production of certain agricultural crops (Egypt and southern United States for cotton, Brazil for coffee, Cuba for sugar, British Malaya for rubber) will specialize in such products. Areas where labor is plentiful, in relation to capital and land, tend to specialize in lines of production using much labor and little capital equipment. Thus, Japan's major export industries before World War II (such as cotton textiles, silk and toys) were of a "labor-intensive" type. Australia, by contrast, with a small labor force in relation to land, specialized in the production of wool, which required little labor per square mile of land.

All labor is not homogeneous: there are wide differences in abilities, training and experience. Where a particular type of labor is relatively abundant, the area or country will tend to specialize in the production of commodities requiring labor of that kind.[5] This largely explains the remarkable development of the German chemical and optical industries.

What Determines Comparative Advantage

It is because of its effect on production costs that the relative abundance or scarcity of a factor of production tends to determine the type of production in a region. Factors of production that are abundant relative to demand tend to be cheap in relation to those less plentiful. Products requiring a large proportion of the abundant factor, therefore, can be produced more cheaply in that region than elsewhere. Thus, the region has a *comparative advantage* in the production of such commodities. The tendency is to export commodities having low production costs and to import commodities that the region is less well equipped to produce at low cost, that is, in which it has a comparative disadvantage.[6]

Relative production costs *within* a particular country, as determined by the relative scarcities of productive factors, do not alone determine

5. This statement should be understood as applying primarily at a particular point in time or over a comparatively short interval. Clearly, over the years labor can be trained and new skills can be developed. From a historical point of view, there is the question of how the particular labor skills to be found in any region came to be developed in the first place. But this is too large a problem to be dealt with here.

6. The principle of comparative advantage explains the specialization of production between two districts of the same country as well as the specialization among countries. National boundaries are of no importance for the specialization between geographical regions so long as wars or trade policy do not intervene. The exchange of commodities among the various parts of the former Austro-Hungarian Empire was trade among different districts of the same country before 1914 but became *international* trade after 1918. Yet this trade would have had much the same composition after 1918 as before 1914 had the successor states not erected trade barriers against one another.

a country's exports and imports. Products must move to market at a transportation cost. Actually, a complicated relationship determines "the cost of distance" within any particular country and between it and the rest of the world. It is not a simple function of geographical mileage. It depends as well upon water as compared with land transport, the volume and kind of traffic in the two directions, topography, flow of rivers, and so on. Nevertheless, proximity ordinarily encourages commerce unless trade barriers intervene. The fact that in many ways its economy is complementary and that it borders on the United States helped to make Canada the second most important export market for the United States and the most important supplier of the United States before World War II (1937). Similarly, as A. J. Brown has written:

. . . Germany's geographical position, almost surrounded by neighbors in fairly advanced stages of industrialization, has, however, also clearly played its part in bringing about this direction of specialization and trade. Among the less highly industrialized countries of Europe German exports were directed almost as much to the eastern and southeastern groups as to the western and northern — the much greater total buying-power of the latter notwithstanding. . . . Here, again, geography doubtless played an important part; the eastern countries were far nearer to Germany than to either of the other great industrial exporters; the western and northern countries were practically as near to the United Kingdom.[7]

Comparative advantage, then, must be interpreted in terms of cost at the point of ultimate delivery — laid-down cost at the point of consumption — rather than simply cost at the point of production.

Comparative advantage thus defined explains not only the composition of a country's foreign trade but to a certain extent its direction and volume. A large country has more opportunity for specialization and diversification within its own borders than a small country, and its foreign trade may therefore be less than that of the small country in spite of its higher national income.

Changes in Comparative Advantage

The comparative advantage in production of the different countries changes over the years and with it the composition of their foreign trade. Numerous examples are common knowledge. The discovery

7. A. J. Brown, "The Great Industrial Exporters," *Bulletin of International News*, March 3, 1945, pp. 213–14.

of gold in South Africa soon made gold the biggest export from the region. The opening of the American plains made for low-cost agricultural production and so increased agricultural exports in the 1870's and 1880's. Europe declined, America improved, in comparative advantage in agricultural production. After World War I Great Britain lost its long-held comparative advantage in textiles and coal as other countries industrialized. Again, the rich African copper mines developed within the last twenty years diminished the comparative advantage earlier enjoyed by Montana and Chile. In general, as industrialization spread over the world it changed the comparative advantage of different regions: more capital equipment and more skilled labor in the industrializing areas altered comparative advantage, hence altering production costs, and consequently exports and imports.

The principle of comparative advantage thus explains the relative production costs of different commodities and services in different countries at any particular time, and in the absence of bounties or restrictions, determines exports and imports. But comparative advantage is not immutable: it changes over the years, and within limits national policy can mold and shape it.

THE PRINCIPLE IN PRACTICE

World trade is often thought of mainly as an exchange of manufactured commodities for raw materials and foodstuffs. Since manufactures are exported by industrialized countries and primary products by agricultural and mineral-producing countries, the conclusion is often drawn that the exports of industrialized countries must necessarily decline as agricultural and raw-material-producing countries develop home industry. The international exchange of commodities, however, is far more complicated than any mere bartering of manufactured goods for food and raw materials. Comparative advantages cut very fine: they lead to an intensive specialization even among manufacturing countries.

The specialization of labor and exchange among industrialized countries and agricultural and mineral-producing countries is evident from the contrasting composition of their foreign trade. (See Table 3.) The foreign trade patterns of the industrial and nonindustrial countries are the reverse of each other. Manufactures dominate the exports of industrial countries. Materials and then foodstuffs follow. Raw

materials are usually a larger item than foodstuffs in imports (not for
Great Britain and Ireland), and these in turn are larger than imports
of manufactures. Nonindustrial countries, on the other hand, chiefly

TABLE 3

PERCENTAGE COMPOSITION OF MERCHANDISE TRADE,
BY GROUPS OF COUNTRIES, 1928 AND 1937

A. Foodstuffs and live animals
B. Materials — raw or partly manufactured
C. Manufactured articles

Group		Imports 1928	1937	Exports 1928	1937
Industrialized countries					
United States	A	25	29	15	8
	B	50	51	43	42
	C	25	20	42	50
United Kingdom and Ireland	A	45	40	11	10
	B	33	42	14	18
	C	22	18	75	72
Continental Europe — industrial countries[a]	A	27	23	13	11
	B	48	54	23	26
	C	25	23	64	63
Japan, Korea, Formosa	A	12	5	9	11
	B	64	74	43	19
	C	24	21	48	70
Agricultural and mineral-producing countries					
Latin America					
Mineral-producing countries[b]	A	15	11	13	9
	B	19	27	85	90
	C	66	62	2	1
Tropical agricultural countries[c]	A	24	20	80	69
	B	12	13	18	30
	C	64	67	2	1
Nontropical agricultural countries[d]	A	13	11	63	62
	B	20	19	34	35
	C	67	70	3	3

TABLE 3 (Contd.)

PERCENTAGE COMPOSITION OF MERCHANDISE TRADE,
BY GROUPS OF COUNTRIES, 1928 AND 1937

    A. Foodstuffs and live animals
    B. Materials — raw or partly manufactured
    C. Manufactured articles

Group		Imports 1928	Imports 1937	Exports 1928	Exports 1937
Agricultural and mineral-producing countries (contd.)					
India, Burma, Ceylon	A	19	15	25	30
	B	12	20	51	49
	C	69	65	24	21
Continental Europe — nonindustrialized countries[e]	A	20	13	54	43
	B	31	39	33	39
	C	49	48	13	18
Oceania[f]	A	9	8	44	45
	B	17	18	54	51
	C	74	74	2	4

Source: The Network of World Trade, League of Nations, Geneva, 1942.II.A.3.

a. Austria, Belgium, Luxemburg, Czechoslovakia, France, Germany, Italy, Netherlands, Sweden, Switzerland.
b. Bolivia, Chile, Curaçao, Ecuador, Mexico, Peru, Venezuela, British Guiana, French Guiana, Surinam.
c. Brazil, Colombia, Cuba, Dominican Republic, Costa Rica, Guatemala, Honduras, Nicaragua, Panama, British West Indies, Windward Islands.
d. Argentina, Paraguay, Uruguay, Falkland Islands.
e. Bulgaria, Denmark, Estonia, Latvia, Lithuania, Finland, Greece.
f. Australia, New Zealand and Pacific Islands.

export foodstuffs or raw materials but few manufactures. They import more manufactures than materials or foodstuffs.

Yet the whole truth is more complicated. The direction of trade flows must be considered by types of commodities as well as by total volume. Table 3 shows the relative importance of the three major groups of commodities in the foreign trade of various areas of the world in the years 1928 and 1937. It does *not* show the absolute amounts involved or the direction in which the commodities flow.

Trade Among Industrialized Nations

A sizable part of the exports of manufactures by industrialized countries is not to agricultural countries, but rather to other industrialized countries. The trade of Great Britain and Germany, in the interwar period, illustrates this point. Germany in 1928, for example, was the second most important source of imports for Great Britain, and Great Britain the second most important source of Germany's imports. First place in the imports of both these highly industrialized nations was held by the United States, also a heavily industrialized country. In short, exports of industrialized countries to each other are almost as great as their exports to nonindustrialized countries.

These exports consist not only of raw materials and foodstuffs, for which they themselves are naturally the best market, but also of manufactured commodities. Of these, more than one third stayed within the circle of industrialized countries in 1928 and 1937. As raw materials usually enter manufacturing countries at low tariff rates or duty-free while manufactured products usually bear high tariffs, the intratrade of the group of industrialized countries in manufactured products was surprisingly large. Estimates have been made of the proportion of total world trade that is an exchange of manufactured commodities against manufactured commodities.[8] The results seem to be that the exchange of manufactures against manufactures gained in relative importance between 1925 and 1931. In that interval such exchange was more than four fifths as large as exchange of manufactures for raw materials and foodstuffs. Increasing trade restrictions bore down with particular force upon trade in manufactured goods after 1931. Without extreme trade restrictions such as were characteristic of the late 1930's, the industrialization of agricultural countries need not, in so far as past experience is a guide, eliminate the export of manufactured commodities from old industrial countries. Such new industrialization will lead rather to shifts in the type of manufactured products exported by the older industrial countries. Greater specialization between countries is always possible, especially with technical progress. Some industries in a country may lose their comparative advantage in the world market, but others will take their place. Not all

8. See A. O. Hirschman, "The Commodity Structure of World Trade," *Quarterly Journal of Economics,* August 1943, p. 574; *idem, National Power and the Structure of Foreign Trade,* University of California Press, Berkeley, 1945, Chap. 7 and *passim.*

TABLE 4

PERCENTAGE DISTRIBUTION OF WORLD TRADE, 1935

		Imports			Exports	
			Manu-			Manu-
		Primary	factured		Primary	factured
Group	Total	Products	Products	Total	Products	Products
1. Highly industrial-						
ized countries	100	100.0	100.0	100.0	100.0	100.0
Intratrade	42	29.3	87.5	48.4	70.8	34.2
Trade with						
Group 2	58	70.7	12.5	51.6	29.2	63.8
2. Other countries	100	100.0	100.0	100.0	100.0	100.0
Intratrade	32	60.0	13.3	25.4	20.0	66.6
Trade with						
Group 1	68	40.0	86.7	74.6	80.0	33.4

Source: Adapted from *Industrialization and Foreign Trade,* League of Nations, Geneva, 1945.II.A.10, p. 19.

Note: The absolute figures on which this table is based represent "frontier values." The countries included in Group 1 are: Austria, Belgium, Czechoslovakia, France, Germany, Italy, Japan, Netherlands, Sweden, Switzerland, United Kingdom, United States. In Group 2 is the rest of the world.

the industries of a country can lose their competitive strength in the world market simultaneously. Technical progress alone, which continuously creates new products and improved methods of production, practically excludes this possibility.

Table 4 shows trade in both primary and manufactured products among highly industrialized nations and trade between these and nonindustrialized nations in 1935. Interestingly enough, 34.2 per cent of the exports of manufactures of highly industrialized nations were in trade among themselves, while 63.8 per cent were exported to nonindustrial countries.

Effects of Industrialization

As a country industrializes it tends to import a smaller proportion of manufactured goods and a larger proportion of primary goods. Conversely, its exports of manufactured goods tend to rise relatively to exports of primary goods. As industrialization brings a rise in total

Rebuilding the World Economy

TABLE 5

RATIO OF IMPORTS AND EXPORTS OF MANUFACTURED PRODUCTS
TO TOTAL IMPORTS AND EXPORTS, 1871–1938

	Annual Averages							
	United States[a]		Germany		Japan		Great Britain	
Period	Im-ports	Ex-ports	Im-ports	Ex-ports	Im-ports	Ex-ports	Im-ports	Ex-ports
1871–1880	38.6	14.1	—	—	—	—	13.4	88.6
1881–1890	35.8	15.0	17.3	63.8	—	—	15.0	87.1
1891–1900	30.1	17.5	13.7	65.4	39.6	20.6	16.8	83.7
1901–1910	28.9	31.5	13.0	67.8	34.8	31.5	22.6	80.6
1911–1913	26.4	28.8	12.9	68.2	30.6	54.0	18.6	80.0
1926–1930	25.0	42.7	16.9[b]	73.3	23.1	50.0	21.6	79.7
1931–1935	25.0	40.2	16.3	80.4	17.7	62.2	19.2	75.0
1936–1938	23.5	50.0	11.4[c]	82.4	19.0	72.2	16.9	73.6

Source: Figures calculated from *Industrialization and Foreign Trade*, League of Nations, Geneva, 1945.II.A.10, pp. 158, 166. The group "manufactured products" accords with the International Classification which was adopted in 1913 in Brussels. The figures are therefore comparable as between countries given in the table.

a. 1871–1932, general trade; 1871–1933, fiscal years ending June 30.
b. Post-World War I figures are not strictly comparable with pre-World War I figures because of territorial changes.
c. Average for 1936–1937.

national output, both exports and imports tend to rise absolutely as industrialization proceeds; however, industrialization alters their composition. For the United States, Germany and Japan, the percentage of manufactured goods imports to total imports shows an almost uninterrupted decline from the 1870's to World War II.[9] The corresponding rise in the proportion of imported primary products as a country industrializes is but an alternative way of emphasizing the relative fall in imported manufactured goods. The relative shift in exports from primary products to manufactured commodities is also clearly evident in the foreign commerce of these three countries. (See Table 5.)

Great Britain presents a different picture from the United States,

9. That the ratio was higher for Germany just after World War I than before is partly traceable to Germany's territorial losses after the war. In any case, the ratio again declined.

Germany and Japan. The diffusion of industrialization from England to other countries well illustrates both changes in comparative advantage over the years and the effect of these changes on the types of commodities entering into foreign trade. British imports of manufactured products showed a tendency to rise in relative importance prior to 1914. But after 1930 this tendency was reversed. This decline in imports of manufactures is probably traceable to the introduction of the British tariff in the early 1930's and is thus chargeable to conscious policy rather than to any "natural" tendency. Exports of manufactured products continuously declined in relative importance from 1870 to World War II, probably because Great Britain, having been the first country to industrialize, was bound to meet increasing competition from other countries in manufactures both at home and in foreign markets as industrialization spread. Hence, in British foreign trade, manufactures tended to increase in relation to total imports and to decline in relation to total exports. The well-known difficulties of the British textile industry in foreign markets in the interwar period reveal growing competition as other countries industrialized. Even within manufactures alone, the composition of exports changes over the years. Between 1910 and 1938, the percentage of textiles and apparel in total British exports fell from about 38 per cent to less than 28 per cent. Exports of special machinery, electrical appliances, vehicles and chemicals — most of them products of a type unknown before World War I — increased from less than 14 per cent to almost 40 per cent in 1938.[10] The relative decline in American exports of meat products and cotton manufactures and the increasing importance of new export products, such as automobiles and new types of electrical and other machinery, during the interwar period illustrate the same point with respect to the United States.

As capital and labor do not transfer readily from one industry to another, these shifts in the export trade — dictated by the change in the comparative-advantage position of industries — are often a slow and painful process. All through the interwar period, British coal and textile industries were depressed chiefly for this reason. Somewhat similar difficulties arose in the United States with respect to cotton and wheat.

10. See A. J. Brown, *Industrialization and Trade: The Changing World Pattern and the Position of Britain*, Royal Institute of International Affairs, London, 1943, pp. 59–60.

NATIONAL POLICY AND FOREIGN TRADE

The relation between domestic economic activity and foreign trade in any country can always be shaped, within limits, by purposive government action. With tariffs and bounties, governments can affect the relative prices of commodities and thus can influence the volume and composition of foreign trade and alter its relation to national income. The experience of the 1930's well illustrates the effects of commercial policy on international trade.

After 1930 national governments felt impelled to check and control their foreign trade more drastically than ever before. The devices they employed were more far-reaching in their effects at home and abroad than tariffs and bounties, which were the main instruments of commercial policy in earlier years. Three principal factors were primarily responsible for increased trade controls: first, increasing instability of economic activity after 1929; second, the apparently diminished adaptability of national economies to economic change; and third, growing political uncertainty, particularly after 1933. These three factors were interrelated and in some instances were hardly distinguishable from one another.

The traditional answer of international trade theory to the problem of rising imports or falling exports in any particular country has always been that productive resources should be regrouped into a new pattern. If other countries became more efficient producers of, say, wheat, then wheat producers at home should produce "something else" — so also with sugar, coal, textiles, machinery, or whatever. The particular products would differ in each country; but the argument, ostensibly, was generally applicable.

Yet, so great were the changes in relative prices during the Great Depression that the implied redistribution of resources among employments far exceeded what was immediately possible. The heavy overhead costs in raw materials production and the immobility of labor in agriculture precluded any immediate general readjustment of production. Yet the fact that there was a greater fall in raw material and agricultural prices than in manufactured goods prices during the depression seemed to imply that such a major shift in production should occur. But a reorganization on this scale was quite impossible: industries cannot be liquidated overnight. Moreover, there was actually no incentive to shift; manufacturing was no more profitable during the depression than the production of raw materials or agriculture. Although prices of manufactures declined less than those of agricultural products and raw materials, the volume of production of most manufactures declined more. Manufacturing was unprofitable, too. The depression was general. A mere shift in productive resources would not have solved the problem even had it been possible.

Unemployment Breeds Autarchy

To eliminate general unemployment during the depression required an increase in *total* output, not merely a change in the composition of existing production. The public authorities had to find means of overcoming general unemployment; the problem was not one of maximizing satisfactions from productive resources already fully employed. Most governments thought it obvious that the import of goods that could be made at home affected employment unfavorably. Similarly, if goods could be exported, people would be employed in their production. Most national governments concluded, therefore, that the appropriate policy was to increase exports, decrease imports. "Buy American" or "Buy British" became popular slogans to express widespread convictions about trade policy. The years after 1929 produced a multiplication of new and often bizarre controls over exports and imports. But, because exports for one country are by definition imports for another, all countries cannot simultaneously increase exports and cut imports. The end result can only be a sharp contraction in the volume of world trade.[11]

This is exactly what happened. The total volume of world trade fell not only absolutely but also in relation to world output in the 1930's. The case of Germany well illustrates both the proliferation of

11. The concept of comparative advantage and the derived theory of comparative cost were conceived in terms of the long run rather than the short run, and therefore they assumed that the problem of aggregate employment presented no difficulty. The familiar presentations of the doctrine run in terms of an opportunity-cost analysis: the argument for not producing wheat, for example, is that the same productive resources applied to corn will, year in and year out, give a larger total real income. In other words, the maintenance of acceptable levels of employment in the economy is not at issue. After 1929 numerous countries seemed incapable of providing employment for many of their citizens. It was not a question of whether they should now be employed in producing wheat or corn, but how they might be employed at all. In such circumstances the opportunity cost of putting people to work to produce products that might be imported more cheaply if full employment prevailed was virtually zero. In fact, if they were drawing public assistance in the form of unemployment benefits, etc., the opportunity cost might even be negative. Hence, *from a national short-run point of view,* the common-sense attitude of governments was not without merit.

controls and restrictions and the resulting decline in foreign trade. German exports were roughly 18 per cent of national income in 1929; by 1937 they were only 9 per cent. Imports shrank similarly. But Germany is only an extreme instance of a broad movement toward economic self-sufficiency that was apparent in many countries after 1930. In most countries foreign trade declined in relation to national income.

The intensified restrictions of the 1930's affected not only the volume but also the composition and direction of foreign trade. Indexes of duty-free imports and dutiable imports (corrected for price changes) for the United States show that free imports averaged for 1931 through 1934 roughly 40 per cent above the level of 1920; dutiable imports, on the other hand, were approximately 30 per cent below the 1920 level. In the boom year of 1937 free imports were approximately 90 per cent above 1920, whereas dutiable imports did not rise so much as 20 per cent above the 1920 level.[12]

Restrictions Distort Trade

The effects of restrictions on trade in particular commodities are well illustrated by the instance of wheat. European wheat-importing countries protected their wheat producers, partly because the latter successfully pressed for assistance and partly because the governments desired to be independent of foreign supplies for political reasons. As a result, a comparison of the two five-year periods 1922–1923 to 1926–1927 and 1932–1933 to 1936–1937 shows that the total net wheat imports of nineteen European wheat-importing countries declined from 39.9 to 25.1 per cent of their total wheat consumption.[13] In most of these countries wheat imports not only declined in relation to total wheat consumption but also in relation to total imports.

These severe trade restrictions inevitably affected the direction and composition as well as the volume of world trade. A change in composition usually implies a change in direction. If wheat imports decline in relative importance, imports of some other commodities must gain in relative importance; but the other commodities imported need not come from the wheat-exporting countries. Moreover, the restric-

12. J. Hans Adler, "United States Import Demand During the Interwar Period," *American Economic Review,* June 1945, p. 423.
13. Paul de Hevesy, *World Wheat Planning and Economic Planning in General,* Oxford University Press, Oxford, 1940, App. X.

tions of the 1930's were often highly discriminatory. The bilateral agreements of foreign-exchange-control countries tended to increase their trade with each other, at the expense of their trade with free-exchange countries. Germany's imports from six southeastern European countries, as a result of such agreements, rose from 4.5 per cent of total imports in 1929 to 12 per cent in 1938; and Germany's exports to these countries rose from 5 per cent to 13.2 per cent over the same period. Similarly, Japan's trade with countries under its domination increased in relation to Japan's total trade. (See Table 6.)

TABLE 6

SHARE OF CERTAIN COUNTRIES IN TRADE OF JAPAN AND
GERMANY, 1929 AND 1938

Trade of	Share of	Imports		Exports	
		1929	1938	1929	1938
		(Per Cent)			
Japan	Korea and Formosa	12.3	30.0	16.8	32.9
	Kwantung	6.0	1.6	4.8	13.7
	Manchuria	1.9	9.0	2.5	8.1
Germany	Six countries of south-eastern Europe[a]	4.5	12.0	5.0	13.2

Source: Review of World Trade, 1938, League of Nations, Geneva, 1939.II.A.11, p. 35.
a. Bulgaria, Greece, Hungary, Romania, Turkey, Yugoslavia.

The growth of trade within the British Empire after 1932 also illustrates the influence of discriminatory trade practices on the direction of foreign trade. The Empire preferences established under the Ottawa agreements of 1932 undoubtedly increased Great Britain's intra-Empire trade, although the maintenance of stable exchange rates within the Empire and the growth of bilateralism without were at least equally important. Whereas British imports from the Commonwealth amounted to only 30.2 per cent of Britain's total imports in 1929, they had risen to 41.9 per cent in 1938. British exports to the Commonwealth were 44.4 and 49.9 per cent of total British exports in 1929 and 1938 respectively.

The wave of restrictionism in the 1930's thus contributed to the decline in international trade, both absolutely and in relation to world output; and it forced what trade remained into channels different from those dictated by national comparative advantage. Events in the 1930's showed how deliberate national policy can reshape foreign trade within certain limits. Probably in the future, too, commercial policy will be no less important in determining the volume, direction and composition of world trade.

AMERICAN FOREIGN TRADE BEFORE WORLD WAR II

The foreign trade of the United States (or any other country) thus reflects the combined effect of the three factors just discussed — national income, comparative advantage and commercial policy. National income — its size and composition — changes along with shifts in comparative advantage. The effects of changes in comparative advantage cannot be separated statistically from the effects of changes in trade policy at home and abroad. The trade statistics show only the net result of all operative factors.

INCOME CHANGES AND TRADE

The sensitivity of American exports and American imports as a whole to changes in national income abroad and at home has already been stressed. (See p. 39.) But changes in national income do not imply an equal percentage change in all industries. The variations of incomes and expenditures by particular industries do not everywhere parallel variations in national income: some vary more, others less, than output as a whole. So also with foreign trade. Exports and imports include a wide variety of different goods and services related to particular industries in the United States and foreign countries. Hence, individual exports and imports are unlikely to be affected equally by changes in national income abroad and at home.

American exports and imports both were a smaller percentage of national income in the 1930's than in the 1920's: foreign trade fell off more than national income. Exports and imports were also absolutely smaller in the 1930's; indeed, their yearly average in value terms for 1931–1935 was less than half of the yearly average in 1926–1930. (See Table 7.)

The dollar values of exports and imports show only the net result of changes in price and in physical quantity combined. But price changes and quantity changes did not occur equally in American im-

TABLE 7

FOREIGN TRADE OF THE UNITED STATES, 1921–1938

(Indexes: 1921–1925 = 100)

| | Annual Averages | | | | | |
| | Exports | | | Imports | | |
Period	Amount	Value Index	Quantum Index	Amount	Value Index	Quan-tum Index	Per Cent of National Income
	(*In Millions*)			(*In Millions*)			
1921–1925	$4,310	100	100	$3,450	100	100	5.1
1926–1930	4,688	109	126	4,033	117	123	5.2
1931–1935	1,989	46	78	1,704	49	98	3.5
1936–1938	2,925	68	100	2,461	71	102	3.7

Source: Statistical Abstract of the United States, 1943, Bureau of the Census. Export figures exclude re-exports; import figures are "general imports" through 1933, imports for consumption thereafter.

ports and exports. Prices of raw materials and foodstuffs, both domi-nant among American imports in the two periods, fell considerably more than the prices of manufactured goods, the most important cate-gory among American exports.[14] Import quantities declined less than export quantities. This divergent behavior of prices and quantities of American exports and imports stems from their different supply and demand conditions.

To a considerable degree, American exports consist of capital goods, such as machinery, iron and steel products and automobiles. In a de-pression, the sales volume of capital goods invariably contracts se-verely. It is consequently not astonishing that the 44 per cent decline of the export volume of manufactured commodities between 1926–1930 and 1931–1935 was greater than that of any other category of commodities either exported or imported.

On the other hand, the consumption of foodstuffs — and foodstuffs are important imports — is less affected by depression. Despite re-duced incomes, consumers pare other expenditures before they re-

14. The unit value of imported crude materials for the period 1931–1935 averaged 59 per cent below that of the preceding five-year period; that of crude foodstuffs 49 per cent; whereas that of exported finished manufacturers declined by only 30 per cent.

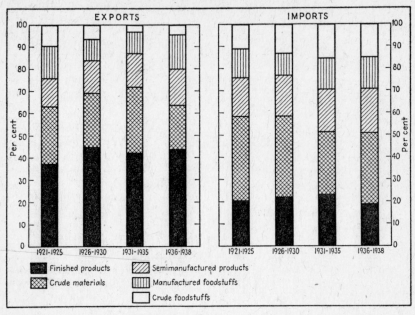

Chart 4. Composition of United States Foreign Trade, 1921–1938
Source: Appendix Table B.

duce their expenditures for food. Foods, as a class, usually have a low income-elasticity of demand.[15] This, in combination with their severe price fall, was the main reason why the physical volume of imports of crude foodstuffs declined by only one per cent between 1926–1930 and 1931–1935 and that of imported manufactured foodstuffs by only 6 per cent. (For dollar volume, see Chart 4 and Appendix Table B.)

The income-elasticity of demand for food, and hence the behavior of food imports, contrasts strikingly with that of certain "services," for example travel expenditures.

Both tourist traffic and shipping services, the most important "in-

15. The income-elasticity of demand for any product is defined as the proportionate change in quantity purchased divided by the proportionate change in income *with the price of the product remaining unchanged*. But, because the statistical data almost never contain instances where prices are constant, the loose practice has grown up of disregarding the qualifying phrase in italics. In other words, income-elasticity is now used to mean the relation between changes in quantity and changes in income with the simultaneous price changes being disregarded. Income-elasticity can be negative, i.e., a change in income produces a change in the quantity purchased in the opposite direction. So, for example, the income-elasticity of demand for bread or potatoes may be such that a fall in people's incomes means an increase in their consumption of these commodities.

visible" items in exports and imports, are extremely sensitive to business fluctuations. Expenditures by American tourists abroad declined from $483 million in 1929 to $199 million in 1933; receipts from foreigners traveling in the United States in the same period declined from $139 million to $66 million. The decline in payments and receipts from tourist traffic partly reflects the lower prices in 1933 for goods and services bought by tourists. All the same, a high income-elasticity of demand is indicated. Shipping payments declined from $509 million in 1929 to $154 million in 1933, whereas receipts declined from $390 million to $108 million. This decline was the result both of a decline in shipping and of the much lower freight rates during the depression years.[16]

COMPARATIVE ADVANTAGE, COMMERCIAL POLICY AND
AMERICAN TRADE

Changes in comparative advantage and in trade barriers in the United States and in other countries have influenced the composition and direction of American trade over the years. Between 1871 and 1938, for example, Europe declined continuously in importance as a market for American exports and as a source of American imports. (See Appendix Table F.) But this is merely another way of saying that in this interval America became an industrial nation and as such exported more finished goods and fewer foods and raw materials. An

---

16. See Appendix Table C. Before World War II the countries with the largest merchant marine were (in order of their active tonnage in international trade in 1937): the United Kingdom, Norway, Japan, Germany, United States, the Netherlands and France. These countries, owning 71 per cent of the estimated active tonnage in international trade, received 78 per cent of the world shipping receipts in 1929 and 76 per cent in 1937. Appendix Table D shows the share of the major countries in world shipping receipts and in the world's active tonnage in international trade.

The importance of a country in terms of its share in world shipping receipts does not coincide with the importance of shipping receipts for its national economy. In Appendix Table E shipping receipts are related to the national income of the principal countries concerned. In Norway the merchant fleet contributed 11.2 per cent of the national income in 1937, although Norway drew only 7.9 per cent of world shipping receipts. In Great Britain, on the other hand, which earned 37 per cent of the world's shipping receipts in 1937, the receipts were only 1.3 per cent of national income. All countries, even those with large merchant fleets, "import" shipping services in the sense that some of their commodity and passenger transport is in foreign vessels. Their *net* receipts are the difference between receipts from the "exports" and the payments arising from "imports" of transportation services. The net balance on this account was, in 1937, positive for Great Britain, Norway, Germany, the Netherlands, Japan and France, but negative for the United States, which lost ground after the early 1920's when receipts exceeded expenditures.

opposite change occurred in American imports. By the 1930's imports from Asia had surpassed imports from Europe. American tariff policy encouraged this shift by stimulating industrialization in the United States and by restricting imports of manufactures from Europe.

Examples of a decline of America's comparative advantage in certain directions are also readily available. Between 1921–1925 and 1936–1938, cotton moved from first to third place in American exports and wheat from third to ninth position. World cotton prices declined drastically during the depression. Governmental measures to help American producers raised the price of American cotton sufficiently to cut exports and to extend production rapidly in other countries (Egypt, Brazil, India) during the late depression years. By 1938 American cotton exports provided only 20 per cent of foreign cotton consumption as compared with about 47 per cent in 1928. Nevertheless, cotton was still in 1936, for the last time, first among American exports.

American wheat exports were declining even before World War I. During the postwar reconstruction period, wheat exports temporarily increased; but after the middle 1920's the downward trend in wheat exports was again resumed. The decline in wheat exports was not wholly caused by a decline in America's comparative advantage in wheat production. Economic nationalism and the fear of war abroad also played important, if unmeasurable, roles.

The change in the composition of American foreign trade has meant also a change in its geographical dispersion. The fact that Italy disappeared from the list of the ten most important buyers of American exports between the early 1920's and the late 1930's was due mainly to the fact that it bought less wheat and cotton. Italy, like some other countries, used more cotton substitutes and took various protective measures to become self-sufficient in wheat. Germany's decline in the same period from third to fifth place among American markets reflects the restrictive measures Germany took against most imports as well as its development of cotton substitutes.

As to imports, the marked increase in rubber consumption between the wars, because of the expansion of the automobile industry in the United States, pushed British Malaya from fifth place in the early 1920's to second place in the late 1930's and brought the Netherlands Indies into the first ten sources of imports. Mexico's disappearance from the first ten sources of imports by countries reflects the fall in petroleum imports because of an import excise tax after 1932 and the further development of home production. (See Appendix Tables G and H.)

In summarizing the influence in recent years of trade restrictions and shifts in comparative advantage on American foreign trade, we cannot improve on a recent statement by the League of Nations.

Economically, the United States was once complementary chiefly to Europe; but the mutual dependence of these two regions upon each other has diminished. The United States retains a big export market in Europe which in 1938 still absorbed 42 per cent of her exports (in 1928, the corresponding share was 46%, in 1906–10 about 70% and in 1886–90 about 80%). But the share of her imports derived from Europe during the twenties and thirties was less than 30%. The considerable discrepancy between imports and exports must in this case be attributed largely to the high United States tariffs which have prevented many European manufactures — particularly non-durable consumers' goods into the manufacture of which much labour has entered — from competing successfully on the United States market.[17]

THE NATIONAL BALANCE OF PAYMENTS

Trade transactions between countries are often described as if they took place in the form of barter — exports swapped for imports. Actually, of course, each export or import transaction — that is, each sale or purchase of goods and services — involves, with few exceptions, the receipt or payment of money from foreigners or to foreigners. The in-payments can be set against the out-payments and a balance of payments struck.

If the raw statistical data are available, the balance of payments for any country can be computed for any period with fair precision. Over the years, however, any country's balance of payments is likely to change. These changes and their manner of operation need to be understood in relation to the economic factors that underlie them.

AN ILLUSTRATION: THE AMERICAN BALANCE OF PAYMENTS

If, as the phrase implies, the balance of payments for the United States for any period is really a "balance," this must mean that the in-payments measured in dollars are equal to the out-payments measured in dollars when all the receipts and payments are included. A moment's reflection shows that, over any period, the total dollars

17. *The Network of World Trade*, p. 51.

surrendered to foreigners by Americans — for whatever purpose — must equal the total dollars acquired by foreigners from Americans — again, for whatever purpose. No foreigner gets a dollar without getting it from an American or from some other foreigner who already holds it. And no American pays a dollar to anyone outside the country without paying it to a foreigner. The dollars paid to foreigners must therefore always equal the dollars acquired by foreigners from Americans over any period.

More interesting are the types of transactions giving rise to the receipts and payment of dollars between the United States and the rest of the world and how these compare in size with one another. Table 8 examines the American figures for 1937. It is divided into three sections. Section 1 comprises so-called current transactions; section 2, gold movements; section 3, capital transactions.

Under section 1, Table 8 shows that in 1937 merchandise exports (receipts) exceeded merchandise imports (payments) by $265 million. This $265 million is often called the "balance of trade." The people of the United States thus had a claim on foreigners in this amount. Shipping and freight receipts and payments, however, were the other way about. Foreigners had a claim on Americans of $130 million; and, similarly, travel expenditures were greater than travel receipts. Receipts by Americans on foreign investments they owned exceeded payments to foreigners for the American investments foreigners held — and so on with the other items. Taking all the "other current transactions" in the table together, payments exceeded receipts by $296 million. This is usually called the balance of "invisible" items. As the balance for merchandise was the other way by $265 million, the *net* balance on current account was an excess of payments over receipts of $31 million. This $31 million is the result of offsetting the excess of receipts for merchandise against the excess of payments for "other current transactions."

If there were no lending or borrowing and no gold exports or gold imports, the balance of payments on account of the two groups of items under current transactions (section 1) would be an end of the matter. Correctly computed, the two would always balance. In fact, however, gold movements and capital transactions did occur. Both foreigners and Americans held gold and assets at home and abroad in one amount at the beginning of the year and in a different amount at the year's end.

At the beginning of 1937, Americans held a certain amount of gold, of bank deposits abroad and of securities representing assets abroad. Similarly, foreigners held certain deposits in American banks, securities of American companies and some gold "earmarked" as theirs in the United States. During the year, while merchandise exports and imports were being bought and paid for and when shipping services, travel services, etc., were being rendered and received, these gold and security holdings of Americans and foreigners were also changing. But if, for example, foreigners sold some of their American securities and bought American goods for export to their own country, the American export figures included these. The export figures would not, of themselves, reveal just how the goods were paid for. Hence, the full balance-of-payments account must include the gold and security transactions as well.

From the table it appears that gold imports exceeded gold exports by $1,586 million,[18] while the plus sign for earmarked gold shows that foreigners acquired gold from Americans during the year. Together these give a balance of $1,271 million.

The capital transactions are divided into long-term and short-term. Under each are two items: net flow through change in United States assets abroad, and net flow through change in foreign assets in the United States. Under each heading, capital flowed into the United States during 1937: Americans diminished their holdings of assets abroad, they repatriated capital; foreigners increased their holdings of American securities. There was an inflow on short-term and long-term account combined of $877 million. The dollars used to purchase these American securities may have come from imports or from gold sent to the United States. One cannot be sure how much of each, nor does it matter.

If thoroughly complete figures were available, the differences shown in Table 8 between the balance on current account plus or minus the net gold movements would equal the change shown on capital account. In fact, however, complete figures are not available, so that

18. The gold imports may have been used to buy American securities or goods or whatever.

TABLE 8

UNITED STATES BALANCE OF INTERNATIONAL PAYMENTS, 1937
(*In Millions of Dollars*)

Type of Transactions	Amount
1. Current transactions	
Merchandise trade	
Receipts	3,349
Payments	3,084
Balance	+265
Other current transactions	
Shipping and freight	
Receipts	236
Payments	366
Balance	−130
Travel expenditures	
Receipts	135
Payments	348
Balance	−213
Personal remittances	
Receipts	28
Payments	170
Balance	−142
Institutional contributions — net	−33
Interest and dividends	
Receipts	577
Payments	295
Balance	+282
Government aid and settlements	
Receipts	1
Payments	49
Balance	−48
Other government items	
Receipts	31
Payments	78
Balance	−47

TABLE 8 (Contd.)

Type of Transactions	Amount
Silver	
Receipts	9
Payments	97
Balance	−88
Miscellaneous adjustments and services — net	+123
Total of other current transactions	
Receipts	1,140
Payments	1,436
Balance	−296
Total of all current transactions	
Receipts	4,489
Payments	4,520
Balance	−31
2. Gold movements	
Net gold exports or imports	−1,586
Net change in earmarked gold	+315
Net gold movement	−1,271
3. Capital transactions	
Long-term capital movements	
Net flow through change in United States assets abroad	+276
Net flow through change in foreign assets in United States	+245
Balance on long-term capital movements	+521
Short-term capital movements	
Net flow through change in United States assets abroad	+45
Net flow through change in foreign assets in United States	+311
Balance on short-term capital movements	+356
Balance on all capital transactions	+877
Unexplained items	+425

Source: Hal B. Lary and Associates, *The United States in the World Economy,* Economic Series No. 23, Bureau of Foreign and Domestic Commerce, 1943, App.

we have a balance of "unexplained items" of $425 million, which is obtained as follows (in millions):

Balance on current account	$ −31
Gold movements inward — net	−1,271
	$−1,302
Net capital inflow	+877
Unexplained items (difference)	$ +425

The balance of payments for the year, all items included, balances.[19]

THE BALANCE OF PAYMENTS AND CAPITAL MOVEMENTS

By lending abroad, a country puts purchasing power over domestic commodities at the disposal of foreign countries in exchange for a promise of interest or dividend payments in the future. In the early stages of its capital exports, a capital-exporting country will therefore tend to export more goods and services than it imports: it will tend to have a "positive" balance of trade and services. If the country continues to lend capital abroad, sooner or later its receipts from foreign investments will exceed its net[20] new investment abroad. The surplus of receipts from foreign investments over new investment abroad gives the country command over foreign goods and services, and hence as its imports increase, its balance of trade and services will become "negative."

Conversely, a country that imports capital from abroad obtains purchasing power over foreign goods and will therefore at first tend to have a negative balance of trade and services. Countries of recent settlement are usually in this position. As soon as these countries reach the point where payments in the form of dividends and interest exceed current capital imports, their balance of trade and services will tend to become positive.[21]

19. Appendix Table C gives the detailed figures for the United States from 1919 to 1939.
20. I.e., the excess of capital exports over repatriation of previous investments abroad in the form of amortization payments or liquidation of foreign investments and new investments within the country by foreigners.
21. This description of the connection between transactions on capital account and the balance of trade and services implies that the causal chain runs from capital movements to the trade balance. This is not to deny that under a smoothly functioning international mechanism certain types of short-term capital movements are, like gold movements, of the "balancing" kind, inasmuch as they can be provoked by a lack of balance in all the other items in the balance of payments. Apart from these short-term capital movements,

Great Britain before World War II was the prime example of a country that had accumulated large foreign investments. Receipts of dividends and interest on foreign investments far exceeded Britain's current capital export, and this excess financed a large part of Britain's negative balance of trade. Indeed, Great Britain has had a commodity import surplus since 1854.

Before World War I the United States was a debtor country; dividends and interest payments to foreigners exceeded current new investments abroad. Consequently, the American balance of trade and services combined tended to be positive. The balance of trade — not including invisible items — was positive from 1876 to 1914, with the exception of 1888, 1889 and 1893.[22] During World War I the United States became a capital-exporting country and it continued to invest heavily abroad all through the 1920's. American receipts from foreign investment during the 1920's as a whole were just about equal to new investments abroad in the same period; the commodity trade balance remained positive as before World War I. This positive balance of trade chiefly resulted from the excess of out-payments over receipts for "invisible" items in the balance of payments. In the 1930's, capital imports into the United States exceeded capital exports because the United States repatriated part of its foreign investments, and because foreigners, for a variety of reasons, also sent capital to the United States. This excess of capital imports over capital exports, however, found its counterpart in a huge inflow of gold, and the balance of trade continued to be positive.

Before World War I the flow of capital over the world followed a fairly consistent pattern that changed only slowly, although there were cyclical swings. Some countries (the United States, the British Dominions, some Latin-American countries) were primarily borrowing countries. For the creditor countries, receipts from foreign investments only gradually came to exceed current capital exports; conversely, for the debtor countries, out-payments of dividends and interest only gradually overtook the receipts from abroad because of new borrowing. The shift of the creditor countries from a positive to a

<hr/>

it is on the whole correct to assume that financial transactions on capital account command, and the balance of trade and services obeys. See J. M. Keynes, "The German Transfer Problem," *Economic Journal*, 1929, pp. 1–7; for a recent discussion of the problem see Fritz Machlup, *International Trade and the National Income Multiplier*, Blakiston, Philadelphia, 1943, pp. 136 ff.

22. Immigrant remittances and tourist expenditures abroad contributed to this result.

negative balance of trade and services, and the shift of the debtor countries from a negative to a positive balance of trade and services, was gradual and no great difficulties arose.

World War I abruptly turned some capital-exporting countries, Germany for example, into capital-importing countries; some capital-importing countries, e.g., the United States, became capital-exporting countries. The war also left a heritage of political debts (including reparations) that, had they all been paid, would have required of many countries a violent reversal in their balance of trade.

The virtual elimination of these international political debts was followed in the 1930's by sudden capital flights provoked by political and economic fears and currency depreciation. The earlier stability in international capital flows no longer existed. Such abrupt shifts in international capital flow require equally abrupt shifts in the balance of trade and services. But *sudden* shifts from a negative to a positive balance cannot be achieved easily. Unable to adjust their trade balances to the capital flows, many countries felt they had to protect their balance of payments by special measures, such as foreign exchange control, currency devaluation, and the like.

World War II again completely changed the distribution of international financial claims. Some countries shifted from a creditor to a debtor position; others from a debtor to a creditor position. The sums involved are huge. If the new creditors attempt to withdraw their funds from the debtors within a short period of time they will put an unbearable strain on the economies of the debtor countries. This is one of the most serious problems created by World War II.

THE SYSTEM OF MULTILATERAL TRADE

The complicated system of international trade and finance that developed before 1914 was partially re-established after Versailles, but it steadily eroded after 1931. It was a system of trade and finance between the trading countries — more than 200 "countries" or statistical units, in fact — in which commodity exports, commodity imports, invisible exports, invisible imports, income from investments, and new lending and borrowing were integrated in a fairly consistent whole. Some countries had a positive balance of commodity trade. Others had an excess of receipts over payments in their invisible trade transactions. Some countries were creditors on capital account. Others were debtors. Above all else there was a high degree of specialization among different parts of the globe and a general harmony between the pattern of trade and the pattern of finance.

The system was one of multilateral trade in the sense that in the balancing of various debit and credit items against one another the many countries came together into a system whereby balances were "carried forward" from two countries to third, fourth and fifth countries before canceling themselves out completely. To a marked degree, this system of "offsetting" and "balancing" centered in the London money market. The multilateral system was the antithesis of a system of bilateral trade, which is based on the principle of pairing countries directly with one another. A recent article describes the process of offsetting balances in multilateral trade:

> The regions of recent settlement thus had a net import from the United States and, indeed from the tropics, paid for by a net export of foodstuffs and raw materials to Germany and other industrial European countries. Germany paid for her net imports from overseas by a net export to the rest of Europe; she was, of course, a net importer of primary goods and net exporter of manufactures of which four-fifths was absorbed by Europe. Other countries of Continental Europe, and particularly northwestern Europe, financed their net imports from Germany and from overseas in part by interest and dividends on oversea investments, but in part by net exports to the United Kingdom, which was a principal market for French fashion textile products, Danish bacon and butter, Swedish paper and timber, etc. It was in the form of such goods that the United Kingdom collected a large portion of the yield of her investments outside Europe and her income from shipping in oversea traffic.* Such income from tropical countries was transferred in part by net imports from the United States; on the other hand, the United Kingdom had a net export to tropical countries, as her export industry had adjusted itself to the requirements of these countries during the long period of *British capital* exports to them.[23]

* Or rather, the amount by which such yield and shipping income exceeded net capital exports to oversea countries.

The multilateral trading system was complex. Its parts had an almost organic connection with one another. It had evolved slowly through the decades and made sense only on the assumption of political tranquillity. War was alien to its inherent logic. But given the assumption of peace and orderly development, the advantages of the system of multilateral trade were great.

23. Folke Hilgerdt, "The Case for Multilateral Trade," *American Economic Review, Supplement,* March 1943, pp. 396–97.

Chapter 4

THE IMPACT OF WORLD WAR II

THE FULL implications of six years of war for international trade and international finance will become apparent only gradually. The international economic effects of World War I were perhaps not fully understood for at least a decade. But some effects of World War II are of such proportions as to be already discernible. The ordinary peacetime determinants of international trade — comparative costs, national income and national economic policy — operate through demand and supply relationships in a price and market system. But in time of war, national policy overrides all else. Immediate national security becomes paramount. Relative costs and prices play an insignificant role in comparison with more peaceful years. But wartime policies also have long-term effects for international trade and finance.

WAR AND FOREIGN COMMERCE

Modern war tends to isolate territories normally having close commercial, financial and cultural relations with each other. The emergence from quarantine reveals that numerous changes have been in progress in nearly all countries. The trading channels severed by World War II probably carried about one third of prewar international trade. From the summer of 1940 until the late fall of 1944, continental Europe was virtually isolated from the rest of the world. The outward and inward movement of goods almost ceased. The Japanese drive toward Australia similarly isolated much of the Eastern Hemisphere. The war closed customary sources of supply for long periods. It isolated large areas whose only contact was the battlefront. Such isolation inevitably dislocated international trade and forced shifts of major proportions within many countries.

WAR NEEDS AND RESOURCES

High in importance among wartime economic changes is the enormous shift that the war required in the kinds and quantities of goods and services produced in the various countries. What the American

74

economy supplied to 130 million people at peace contrasts sharply with what it had to provide when it had 11 million persons fighting with costly weapons all over the globe. What the economy drew from its own productive capacity and what from other countries to which it still had access also differed sharply in war and peace. If rubber was indispensable and the East Indies were in enemy hands, then new production had to be stimulated at home and in the Amazon Valley. Food was scarce in comparison with the demand for it; yet bananas and coffee lay unshipped in their production areas because it was more important to use shipping tonnage to send lend-lease food to the U.S.S.R. Latin-American countries cried in vain for textile machinery for which they were willing to pay cash in hand, while the United States built them airports at its own expense. Unable to obtain certain imports at any price, many countries turned to high-cost production at home. The United States fostered a steel industry in Brazil through an Export-Import Bank loan even though steel capacity at home promised to afford some surplus over peacetime domestic needs. Goods were imported at high cost on government account, not because the country had any use for them, but simply to prevent their falling into enemy hands. What was bought and sold, what moved in transport between the nations, bore the clear imprint of a world at war.

WARTIME TRADE AND MONEY COSTS

Relative costs and relative prices still determined in large measure the volume and direction of international trade in 1939.[1] But in time of war, money-cost considerations give way to military needs, and to considerations of immediate national security and strategy. What should be imported, what exported and what produced at home are questions that in time of war are unlikely to turn upon nice calculations running to several decimal places. Relative costs and prices lost their peacetime influence in determining the flow of goods and services among the nations. What occurred in the international aspects of the warring economies was all of a piece with the character of a war economy as a whole. In a modern war, large segments of economic activity are withdrawn from the control of the price system;

1. The development of newer methods of trade control, such as quotas, bilateral clearing, export subsidies, and the like, diminished the importance of relative cost considerations during the 1930's. But relative cost considerations were still the dominating causal elements in international trade before the war. They are not easily displaced.

that is to say, what is produced, in what quantities and in what places by what methods is not left to the interaction of supply and demand in the market. The flow of goods and services across national boundaries is no exception.

The diminished importance of relative costs and prices in shaping the volume and direction of trade in war implies a transfer of responsibility for exports and imports from private traders to the government. No business firm can afford to ignore the relation between costs and selling prices for the commodities it deals in. But a government at war, with the country's whole resources subject to its control, is in a different position. "Cost" and "return" to the nation as a whole are the government's concern. And when the reckoning is lifted to this broader plane, the answers are often quite different from those forthcoming from private account books and f.o.b. price quotations. By a variety of devices — direct government purchase, export and import licenses, allocation of shipping space, and so on — the control of international trade passes from private hands to government. Once relative costs and prices cease to guide economic affairs, the government has to substitute its own criteria for the dictates of the market.

These remarks concerning the effect of the recent war on the international movement of goods and services are more or less descriptive of wartime developments in both belligerent and neutral countries. The order of development and the ultimate forms of control varied somewhat from country to country. But the main shift in emphasis in foreign trade is unmistakable.

Wartime Transfers of Goods and Services

Only a small fraction of the wartime transfers of goods and services between the United States and foreign countries could be called ordinary trade or commerce. The most important were not contrived for commercial reasons and they did not move along customary trade channels. The quantities, the composition and the destination of goods shipped to other countries and received from other countries were determined by national governments. Of total American exports in 1944 of $14.1 billion, almost 80 per cent were lend-lease exports, and a high proportion of these were military items for the direct prosecution of the war. This could not be called trade or commerce in the usual sense.

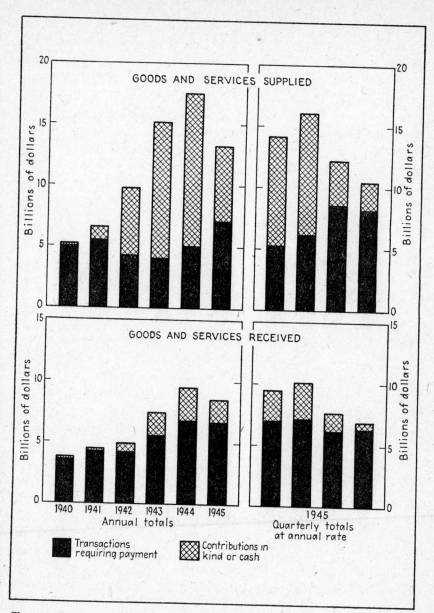

Chart 5. Goods and Services Exchanged With Foreign Countries, 1940–1945
Source: Survey of Current Business, February 1946, p. 24.

TABLE 9

LEND-LEASE AID, BY COUNTRIES, MARCH 1941 — OCTOBER 1, 1945

Country	Amount
Total lend-lease aid	$46,040,054,000
British Empire	30,269,210,000
U.S.S.R.	10,801,131,000
France	1,406,600,000
China	631,509,000
American republics	421,467,000
Netherlands	162,157,000
Greece	75,416,000
Belgium	52,443,000
Norway	34,640,000
Turkey	28,063,000
Yugoslavia	25,885,000
Other countries	43,284,000
Aid not charged to foreign governments	2,088,249,000

Source: *Twenty-First Report to Congress on Lend-Lease Operations,* Government Printing Office, 1946, p. 14.

LEND-LEASE AND THE AMERICAN ECONOMY

Between March 11, 1941 and October 1, 1945, when lend-lease operations virtually terminated, the United States supplied total lend-lease assistance valued at $46 billion. (See Table 9.) Up to July 1, 1945 the United States received from foreign countries reverse lend-lease aid valued at $6.2 billion.[2] In other words, had these been commercial operations, the American balance of payments would have shown a tremendous excess of exports over imports of goods and services. If these had been commercial transactions incurred in the ordinary course of trade, foreign countries would have owed the United States for the difference, or would have liquidated assets in this amount, or invoked some combination of the two. But these were not commercial operations at all. They were unilateral transfers incident to a common war effort. (See Chart 5.)

Of the total lend-lease aid of $46 billion furnished by the United

2. *Twenty-First Report to Congress on Lend-Lease Operations,* Government Printing Office, 1946, p. 11. Most of the facts concerning lend-lease and reverse lend-lease that follow in the present section are drawn from this source unless otherwise indicated.

TABLE 10

TOTAL LEND-LEASE AID

(*In Millions*)

Category	March 1941 to October 1, 1945 (Total Aid)	March 1941 to July 1, 1945	July to September 1945
Total aid	$46,040	$44,145	$1,895
Total charged to foreign governments	43,952	42,194	1,758
Goods transferred to foreign governments[a]	40,197	38,634	1,563
Munitions (including ships)	22,102	21,387	715
Petroleum products	2,317	2,173	144
Industrial materials and products[b]	9,689	9,210	479
Agricultural products	6,089	5,864	225
Shipping and other services	3,755	3,560	195
Other lend-lease charges	2,088	1,951	137
Production facilities in the United States	710	634	76
Transfers to federal agencies	972	815	157
Other charges and expenses	406	502	−96

Source: Twenty-First Report to Congress on Lend-Lease Operations, Government Printing Office, 1946, p. 11.

a. Includes goods consigned to United States commanding generals for subsequent transfer in the field to lend-lease countries.

b. Includes signal, chemical warfare and engineering equipment; medical supplies; chemicals, machinery, metals and minerals; and other military and war production equipment and supplies.

States, 94 per cent went to the British Empire and the U.S.S.R.: 69 per cent to the Empire and 25 per cent to the U.S.S.R.[3] China got 1.5 per cent. All other countries together received only 4.5 per cent of the total. (See Table 9.)

The $6.2 billion reverse lend-lease aid provided to the United States — chiefly in the form of supplies furnished to American troops, shipping services and construction — came almost exclusively (95

3. These percentages *exclude* $2 billion of lend-lease aid furnished by the United States but not charged to foreign governments. This $2 billion is included in the $46 billion figure.

per cent) from the British Empire. Over two thirds was from the United Kingdom alone.

Goods and services supplied under lend-lease operations embraced a wide variety of items. As one would suppose, munitions, industrial equipment and food supplies were the main components. (See Table 10.)

Wartime changes and distortions in exports show up clearly if a few specific items among American exports in 1944 are compared with prewar years. The items included in Table 11 amounted to 16 per cent of total American exports in the period 1931–1935, so that the sample is not too small. The dollar value of exports of these selected commodities is in many instances five to ten times greater than before the war. The most notable export gains were recorded in steel-mill manufactures, industrial machinery, electrical machinery and apparatus, and meat and dairy products. These gains are partially attributable to the higher wartime prices. Yet the increases are striking. For example, the industrial machinery exports in 1944, at $620 million, were more than 50 per cent of total industrial machinery production in the United States in 1939. (See Table 11.)

The general effects of lend-lease operations on American exports stand out clearly if the wartime percentage distribution of exports by commodity classes is compared with that of prewar years. In 1944, 75 per cent of total exports were finished manufactures, as against roughly 50 per cent in 1938 and other prewar years. Manufactured foodstuffs also increased sharply as a percentage of total exports, from 6 per cent to 11.5 per cent, while crude materials dropped from roughly 20 per cent to 4 per cent. These two latter changes probably reflected the scarcity of cargo space rather than a change in need. The details by commodity classes of exports for the years 1938–1944 are shown in Table 12.[4]

AMERICAN WARTIME IMPORTS

American wartime imports compared with prewar imports show no significant changes when classified by commodity groups. Prices were higher than in prewar years, with the result that the dollar value of

4. We would emphasize again that "lend-lease aid furnished" during the war years is a broader category than "lend-lease exports." Some goods purchased abroad by the United States were delivered directly to foreign countries and therefore do not appear in the export figure; similarly, shipping services furnished would not appear in the export totals. See Table 9.

TABLE 11

UNITED STATES EXPORTS OF SELECTED COMMODITIES, 1931–1944

(*In Millions*)

Commodity	Average 1931–1935	1938	1941	1944
Selected foods				
Meat products	$28.7	$ 28.4	$ 99.2	$534.6
Dairy products	6.1	6.0	83.5	260.3
Sugar and related products	6.5	7.3	10.1	32.1
Manufactures				
Cotton manufactures	36.4	45.3	117.0	219.7
Ferromanganese and other ferro-alloys	2.0	14.1	5.8	9.4
Steel-mill manufactures	24.9	51.7	173.7	243.4
Iron and steel — advanced manufactures	27.1	43.2	105.6	117.0
Industrial chemicals	18.6	25.1	63.2	131.0
Medicinals and pharmaceuticals	11.5	17.0	43.8	105.9
Machinery				
Industrial machinery	94.7	269.9	475.7	620.6
Electrical machinery and apparatus	62.6	102.1	146.3	434.4
Agricultural machinery and implements	26.7	75.4	87.6	165.3

Source: "United States Foreign Trade, 1941–44," Bureau of Foreign and Domestic Commerce, 1945, pp. 11–12 (mimeographed); and *Statistical Abstract of the United States, 1943*, Bureau of the Census.

imports increased. But the quantum index, after rising in 1941 to 143 per cent of the 1938 base, was only 104 in 1942, 119 in 1943 and 126 in 1944.[5] Imports show no increase comparable with that in exports, which were greatly stimulated by lend-lease operations. Reverse lend-lease operations are not reflected in the import figures because most of these involved goods and services supplied to the American armed forces abroad. (See Table 13 and Chart 5.)

However, the geographical areas from which the United States drew its imports during the war years were significantly different from

5. *World Economic Survey, 1942–44*, League of Nations, Geneva, 1945.II.A.4, p. 246.

TABLE 12

UNITED STATES EXPORTS BY COMMODITY CLASSES, 1938–1944

(In Millions)

Commodity Class	Amount							Per Cent		
	1938	1939	1940	1941	1942	1943	1944	1938	1944	1944[a]
Total[b]	$3,057	$3,123	$3,934	$5,019	$8,003	$12,839	$14,144	100.0	100.0	100.0
Crude materials	606	544	463	355	418	662	554	19.9	3.9	8.5
Crude foodstuffs	248	110	74	83	67	109	133	8.2	.9	2.0
Manufactured foodstuffs	184	202	166	418	925	1,550	1,632	6.0	11.5	26.0
Semimanufactures	494	598	900	777	918	1,091	1,096	16.1	7.5	16.9
Finished manufactures	1,523	1,666	2,329	3,384	5,673	9,427	10,727	49.8	75.9	47.5

Source: "United States Foreign Trade, 1941–44," Bureau of Foreign and Domestic Commerce, 1945, p. 12 (mimeographed); and *Statistical Abstract of the United States, 1943,* Bureau of the Census, p. 524.

a. After deduction of military equipment exports of $7.6 billion from both total exports and finished manufactures. See "United States Foreign Trade, 1941–44," p. 13.

b. Total figures are slightly greater than summation of columns because of "rounding off."

TABLE 13

UNITED STATES IMPORTS BY COMMODITY CLASSES, 1938–1944

(In Millions)

Commodity Class	Amount							Per Cent	
	1938	1939	1940	1941	1942	1943	1944	1938	1944
Total[a]	$1,949	$2,276	$2,540	$3,221	$2,769	$3,377	$3,871	100.0	100.0
Crude materials	576	744	1,010	1,376	1,049	1,027	1,061	29.6	27.4
Crude foodstuffs	260	290	285	376	348	584	841	13.3	21.7
Manufactured foodstuffs	310	313	277	322	274	421	521	15.9	13.5
Semimanufactures	384	486	558	724	639	677	706	19.8	18.2
Finished manufactures	417	440	408	423	457	666	741	21.4	19.2

Source: "United States Foreign Trade, 1941–44," Bureau of Foreign and Domestic Commerce, 1945, pp. 14, 15 (mimeographed); and *Statistical Abstract of the United States, 1943,* Bureau of the Census, p. 525.

a. Total figures are slightly greater than summation of columns because of "rounding off."

TABLE 14

GEOGRAPHICAL DISTRIBUTION OF UNITED STATES IMPORTS, 1939–1944

(*In Millions*)

Origin	1939	1940	1941	1942	1943	1944	1945
Total[a]	$2,318	$2,625	$3,345	$2,745	$3,372	$3,900	$4,130
American republics	518	619	1,008	977	1,310	1,600	—
Canada	340	424	554	717	1,024	1,300	—
Enemy or enemy-controlled areas							
Europe	349	136	38	4	4	3	—
Asia	510	705	782	143	6	3	—
All others	602	741	963	904	1,025	994	—

Source: *Survey of Current Business*, February 1945, p. 21, and February 1946, p. 25.
a. Total figures are slightly greater than summation of columns because of "rounding off."

those before the war. Before the war, Europe accounted for 26 to 30 per cent of American imports, Asia for 29 to 30 per cent and northern North America for 13 to 15 per cent — a combined total of 70 to 75 per cent of all American imports. Variations were minor from year to year. But Asia and much of Europe were unable to supply wartime imports for the United States.[6] Hence the sustained dollar volume of imports that continued through 1944 must have been drawn mainly from Canada and Latin America. This is clearly indicated by some partial figures recently released by the Department of Commerce and shown in Table 14.

6. Japan and southeastern Asia (rubber) were much the most important sources of American imports from Asia in the prewar years. By mid-1942 both these sources were closed.
In Europe the principal countries from which the United States drew imports before the war were the United Kingdom, Germany, France, Belgium, the Netherlands and Italy, in about that order although there were moderate shifts from year to year. During 1940 and 1941, United States imports from Europe dropped from $627 million, the 1936–1940 average, to $390 million in 1940 and to $280 million in 1941. The share of the United Kingdom rose from 23.3 per cent as an average of all imports from Europe in 1936–1940 to 48.5 per cent in 1941. (*Statistical Abstract of the United States, 1943,* Bureau of the Census, p. 537.) After 1941 total imports from Europe must have declined even more drastically and the share of the United Kingdom gained still more. But in 1944 exports from the United Kingdom to "North America" were only 50 per cent of their value in 1938. Cf. *World Economic Survey, 1942–44,* p. 254.

Imports in 1944 from the American republics were three times greater than in 1939, and from Canada nearly four times greater. Though these increases were not especially large from the point of view of the United States, they were large from the point of view of countries supplying the imports. As cheaper sources of supply are again available — for example, tin and rubber — and American import requirements revert to their peacetime composition, many of these countries will face problems of internal readjustment. Apprehensions on this score are increasingly voiced in Latin America.

WARTIME TRADE AND NATIONAL INCOME

The usual relation between national income and imports, and the usual spending of the proceeds resulting from American imports for American goods for export did not prevail during the war years. (See pp. 39 ff.) In no belligerent country, and in few, if any, neutral countries, were individuals free to buy and sell abroad as they saw fit. Export and import licensing and exchange control were standard practice in nearly all countries. Each government controlled exports and imports according to its general economic plan.

The relation between national income and exports and imports during the war further demonstrates the special character of wartime production and trade. For the United States, the ratio of exports to national income gained during the war, while the ratio of imports to national income declined. The export ratio increased from 3.3 per cent in 1938 to 8.7 per cent in 1944, whereas the import ratio decreased from 3 per cent to 2.4 per cent. (See Table 15.)

In Great Britain the change in relationship between income and exports and imports was just the reverse of what occurred in the United States: the ratio of imports to national income increased, the export ratio declined sharply.[7]

This unusual relation between national income and imports and exports underscores both the dominance of deliberate economic policy over other factors during the war, and the moratorium on the balancing of international accounts.

Production, supply and the allocation of output among competing

7. In 1938 British exports were 10 per cent of national income, but in 1943 only 2.8 per cent. Imports, on the other hand, were 18 per cent of national income in 1938 and 23 per cent in 1943.

TABLE 15

UNITED STATES EXPORTS AND IMPORTS IN RELATION TO
NATIONAL INCOME, 1940–1945

(*Dollar Figures in Billions*)

	1940	1941	1942	1943	1944	1945
National income	$77.8	$96.9	$122.2	$149.4	$160.7	$161.0
Exports						
Amount	$ 3.93	$ 5.01	$ 8.00	$ 12.83	$ 14.14	$ 9.78
Per cent of national income	5.0	5.1	6.5	8.5	8.7	6.0
Imports						
Amount	$ 2.54	$ 3.22	$ 2.76	$ 3.37	$ 3.87	$ 4.13
Per cent of national income	3.2	3.3	2.2	2.2	2.4	2.5

Source: Survey of Current Business, February 1945 and February 1946.
Note: Percentages calculated by the writers. Figures include lend-lease exports.

uses are the essential economic problems for cobelligerent countries. The "output" aspect of national income comes to the fore as the monetary aspect recedes in importance. The United States, with large productive capacity, sustained a rising ratio of exports to national income, most of these being lend-lease shipments. Great Britain, on the other hand, with a smaller productive capacity in relation to its needs, experienced a rising ratio of imports to national income. Both countries tried to maximize output, but the division of their total output between them and among the other United Nations was without regard to current balancing of the accounts as in ordinary peacetime trade.

All this was possible, of course, only on the assumption that some countries were willing to grant, and others to accept, advances far exceeding peacetime amounts. Credit advances took several forms. The United States used the lend-lease method on a large scale. But because of priorities and export licensing, dollars acquired from current American imports could not be converted by foreigners into American goods for export. Similarly, in its dealings with Empire countries, Great Britain paid for many foreign goods and services — most of them not actually imported into the British Isles — in sterling that could not be spent for exportable goods. A whole network of unsettled claims and obligations was thus created because as a result of the use of special techniques there was no attempt to balance the accounts during the war. This residue of claims and obligations constitutes one of the most acute postwar problems.

Thus during the war the usual causal chain connecting national income, imports and exports in a price and market economy was broken, leaving a remarkable carry-over of international debts that must be written off or otherwise disposed of. (See discussion in Chapter 5 on United Kingdom.)

THE WAR, COMPARATIVE ADVANTAGE AND POSTWAR COMMERCE

Many of the world's trade channels carried little commerce during the war. Changes also occurred at the terminals and junctions of these trade routes. These changes resulted only in part from the severance of customary trade flows. Even had the trade routes remained open, the war would probably have stimulated new industries in new places and forced old industries to expand in new directions. Full-scale warfare necessarily jolts national economies into the production of new commodities and into providing familiar commodities in new proportions. And when the war ends the economies do not revert to their prewar structure. There are new plants and equipment, new sources of raw materials, new synthetic products and new labor skills that were quite absent when the war began. As long as trade channels are blocked, however, these processions of changes in the various countries can march independently of one another. Only when the ships again ply the seas can the countries see how far each has traveled, and what is their new position relative to each other. The shifts resulting from World War II have been of large proportions.

All the foregoing may be summarized by stating that the war drastically shifted the comparative-advantage position of different countries and areas. As comparative advantage involves the relative plenty or scarcity of the factors of production — land, capital goods and labor — the war for the most part changed national comparative advantages by changing the quantities and types of available capital equipment and labor skills. Wartime needs and wartime isolation caused new industries to take root in new places. Already established industries were strengthened in some countries, weakened in others.

Still other countries made a good start toward industrialization. Widespread destruction of capital equipment occurred in Europe and Asia.

What emerges from the war, then, is an altered distribution of productive resources within national economies whose price structures have had little wartime connection with one another. To restore international trade on a multilateral pattern, these new national price structures and new resource patterns must somehow be reintegrated.

THE CASE OF THE UNITED STATES

The combined effect of closed trade routes and unusual war needs on national comparative advantage and hence on postwar commerce is well exemplified by the United States and rubber.

Before 1939 the United States was by far the largest national consumer of rubber. This large American import was the means of livelihood in Asia for a dense population with a low average standard of living.[8] The war not only shut off American import sources, it also increased the need for rubber. Consequently the United States was forced to turn rapidly to synthetic production on a huge scale.

In 1939 total world consumption of crude rubber was slightly more than one million long tons, of which the United States consumed nearly 60 per cent, or 600,000 long tons. But the expansion of capacity for producing synthetic rubber in the United States and elsewhere, combined with the fact that rubber trees are nearly indestructible,[9] indicates a very much larger world capacity. The geographical distribution of productive capacity will probably be about as follows (in tons):[10]

---

8. British Malaya and the Netherlands Indies accounted for about 75 per cent of total rubber exports in 1939, with Ceylon and French Indo-China together adding another 12 per cent. See K. E. Knorr, *Rubber After the War,* Food Research Institute, Stanford University, 1944, p. 2.

9. As Knorr writes: "Hevea trees are not easily destroyed. They do not burn. They would have to be cut individually, and there are hundreds of millions of them. . . . Mature rubber trees also are capable of prodigious resistance when left to themselves. Immature rubber trees in existence when the Nipponese overran these countries represented only a trifling percentage of the total acreage under Hevea cultivation. Though jungle growth may move in on fairly young trees, neglect of cultivation and general maintenance work does not harm the mature stands. In fact, a prolonged period of nontapping rests the trees and will result in flush production once tapping is resumed. . . . Smokehouses, milling machinery, and other implements that are essential to the operation of a rubber estate may indeed sustain much damage, but these constitute only a very small fraction of its physical capital and assets." *Ibid.,* p. 14.

10. *Ibid.,* p. 15.

Natural rubber

Malaysia	1,400,000	
Latin America, Africa	100,000	
U.S.S.R.	40,000	
		1,540,000

Synthetic rubber

United States, Canada	1,000,000	
U.S.S.R.	90,000	
Germany	70,000	
Other countries	50,000	
		1,210,000
Grand total		2,750,000

Against this productive capacity of 2,750,000 tons, it is difficult to forecast an average postwar demand running much in excess of 1,600,000 tons, after initial heavy demands in the postwar transition period. Even this figure may well be too high, particularly if some of the predictions as to increased durability of automobile tires, which involve the greatest use for rubber, should prove correct. Consumption will depend partly on price, and synthetic rubber will probably be more expensive than natural rubber for general purposes. But, because rubber is now regarded as a "strategic material," home production may well be fostered despite its higher cost to the consumer. Import requirements may drop substantially below prewar figures.[11]

The present plight of the world's rubber industry illustrates the kind of change that has occurred in many industries in many parts of the world. Supply and demand are quite out of balance because of wartime changes.

The war brought about a marked increase in productive capacity in many American industries. The economy not only equipped an armed force of nearly twelve million persons, but it also provided food and war matériel to other countries in large volume. All this required increased capital equipment, notably in the durable-goods industries. Postwar productive capacity will far exceed prewar capacity. On a

---

11. Synthetic rubber is not one single product but a variety of products that, to some extent, can be made to specifications. The synthetic product is said to be superior to natural rubber for some purposes, less satisfactory for others. The costs of synthetic vary not alone with the type of process but with the kind of qualities desired. Cf. *ibid., passim.*

1939 base of 100, for example, manufacturers' shipments of durable goods as a whole stood at 385 for 1944. But for electrical machinery the corresponding figure was 498, for "other machinery" 411, and for transportation equipment except automobiles — that is, aircraft and railroad equipment principally — the figure was 2,534. Such increases in output are not possible without increased productive capacity. (See Table 16.)

TABLE 16

INDEXES OF MANUFACTURERS' SHIPMENTS OF SELECTED COMMODITIES,[a]
1939–1944

(*1939 = 100*)

Commodity	1939	1940	1941	1942	1943	1944
Manufacturers' shipments, total	100	116	164	213	261	275
Durable goods, total	100	127	198	279	371	385
Iron and steel products	100	125	198	233	250	252
Nonferrous metals and products	100	121	176	213	258	273
Electrical machinery	100	129	205	276	427	498
Other machinery	100	129	207	328	408	411
Automobiles	100	130	172	172	270	310
Transportation equipment (except automobiles)	100	178	486	1,540	2,575	2,534
Nondurable goods						
Food and kindred products	100	106	134	177	194	215
Paper and allied products	100	115	151	156	167	178
Chemicals and allied products	100	113	154	173	200	210
Rubber products	100	109	156	177	282	300

Source: Survey of Current Business, February 1945, p. 22.

a. The table includes only industries where the index in 1944 stood at twice the 1939 level or higher. The raw figures are in current dollars and so the indexes exaggerate the gain in physical output.

Not all the increased capacity in durable-goods industries, of course, will necessarily be useful in peacetime. Yet, the presumption is that America's capacity to make durable goods available to the rest of the world far exceeds that of 1939. Even before the war, 43 to 47 per cent of American exports consisted of finished manufactures. Destruction of industrial capacity in Germany, Italy and Japan has been severe. Hence, the relative position of the United States as a potential supplier of finished manufactures to the rest of the world has certainly improved since 1939.[12]

American agriculture similarly underwent a marked expansion during the war years. Agricultural output, exports and home consumption all increased, though by smaller percentages than manufacturing. Great Britain drew more food imports from the United States and less from other more distant but usually cheaper sources of supply. Men in the armed forces ate more than when they were civilians. Money incomes were generally higher than in prewar years. The combined effect of all this on American agriculture is shown by the following indexes of farm marketings:[13]

		(1935–1939 average = 100)				
Farm Marketings	1939	1940	1941	1942	1943	1944
Total volume	109	112	115	128	133	140
Crops	111	109	111	123	119	124
Livestock	108	114	119	132	144	152

Some individual items, of course, have increased more than these group averages.[14] If direct military goods are excluded from the export figures, then in 1944 crude and manufactured foodstuffs combined were 28 per cent of total exports, as against 14 per cent in 1938. (See Table 12.) And, of course, *total* exports were much greater in 1944 than in 1938. But agriculture is probably not an industry in which America now has a long-time comparative advantage.[15] If foreign markets again turn to cheaper sources of supply, American agriculture may soon have to contract, with painful consequences. The general contraction of American agriculture — especially in food grains, meat animals and poultry products — once the relief phase of reconstruc-

12. This leaves out of account questions of exchange rates between the dollar and other currencies and what means other countries will have to acquire dollars for the purchase of American exports. These questions will be considered in subsequent chapters.

13. From *Survey of Current Business*, February 1945, p. 22. The rise in farmers' incomes, because of higher prices, was considerably greater.

14. The United States is now reported to be the world's greatest producer of soybeans. And, after being an importer of fats since 1915, the United States was able to export 2 million pounds of fats in 1942–1943. Karl Brandt, *The Reconstruction of World Agriculture*, Norton, New York, 1945, p. 160; see also Chap. 4 and *passim* for an interesting account of agricultural developments in various countries during the war.

15. The economic position of the United States is doubtless much stronger in manufactured foodstuffs than in crude foodstuffs: its competitive position may be such that large exports are still possible after the war.

TABLE 17

INDEXES OF THE VOLUME OF AGRICULTURAL PRODUCTION FOR SALE AND FOR CONSUMPTION IN THE FARM HOME
1938–1945

(1935–1939 average = 100)

Year	Grand Total	Crops						Livestock and Livestock Products			
		Total	Food Grains	Fruits and Nuts	Vegetables Except Truck Crops	Truck Crops	Cotton and Cotton Seed	Total	Meat Animals	Dairy Products	Poultry Products
1938	103	105	124	100	102	104	91	102	102	102	101
1939	106	107	101	111	99	106	89	106	109	102	108
1940	110	107	110	110	101	111	95	112	118	105	109
1941	113	109	131	113	100	116	83	115	118	110	116
1942	124	121	139	117	104	129	98	126	132	114	131
1943	128	114	116	107	125	124	87	138	150	113	152
1944	136	129	148	123	106	135	93	141	155	116	153
1945a	128	120	155	115	106	137	73	134	141	118	146

Source: Data for 1942–1945 supplied by Division of Statistical and Historical Research, Bureau of Agricultural Economics; for earlier years, from *Statistical Abstract of the United States, 1943*, Bureau of the Census, p. 622.

a. Preliminary figures.

tion has passed, may pose one of the most serious adjustment problems for the United States. The degree of expansion by type of product is shown in Table 17.

The effect of wartime technological developments on the volume and direction of future American trade is still unpredictable. Though inventions and improved techniques have certainly occurred on a large scale, what they mean for relative costs and prices of nonwar goods that can move in international commerce is far from clear. Technical developments, moreover, have not been confined to the United States; but whether they have been greater and more widespread abroad than at home is not yet known. What will count in international trade is not the technical developments as such, but their application to peacetime goods.

To recapitulate briefly: A world war sharply distorts the kinds and quantities of goods and services that national economies must provide; it compels economic development in the various countries to proceed more or less in isolation. The consequence is that the resumption of trade must accommodate the profound changes in costs, production facilities, tastes and needs that have accumulated during the war. The United States has experienced these changes in a marked degree.

CHANGES ABROAD AND THE PATTERN OF TRADE

The war evoked many changes abroad that will also alter world commerce. Three main developments must be recognized. First, the impossibility of international trade made home production for essential needs, particularly food and basic raw materials, mandatory in many regions. Second, the character and scope of war requirements accelerated industrialization in many areas. Third, the physical destruction and capital depletion of productive facilities, especially, but not alone, in the defeated countries, will seriously handicap some important countries in their ability to command goods and services in international trade. These three elements of the postwar trade problem interlock in a complicated manner.

Production of Food and Raw Materials

World production of food may actually have increased during the war, although not so rapidly as population. New acreage was brought

TABLE 18

WORLD FOOD PRODUCTION BY MAJOR GEOGRAPHIC AREAS AND
BY TYPE OF PRODUCT, WARTIME CHANGES

*(Average of Production in 1942 and 1943 as Percentage of
Prewar Production)* [a]

Type of Product	All Countries	North America	South America	Western Europe and North Africa	Middle East	Oceania and South Africa	Southern and Eastern Asia
Total	107	130	117	94	95	101	103
Crops	107	129	118	100	96	96	103
Cereals	106	130	104	98	99	94	102
Fruits, vegetables	109	118	130	105	87	124	104
Edible oils	123	162	297	109	66	—	109
Sugar	105	108	120	98	140	96	104
Livestock products	105	132	117	75	86	113	94
Meat, poultry, eggs	108	143	116	66	91	124	75
Dairy products	101	119	120	83	77	101	100

Source: C. M. Purves, "Wartime Changes in World Food Production," *Foreign Agriculture,* January 1945, p. 14.

a. Production measured in calories for thirty countries. The average of 1942 and 1943 is expressed as a percentage of a prewar base. The prewar average differs slightly by countries because of lack of comparable data or in order to obtain a normal period of prewar production. For most countries the prewar average is 1933–1937, 1934–1938 or 1935–1939.

The countries included in the various regions are as follows:

North America — Canada, United States, Mexico
South America — Brazil, Uruguay, Argentina, Chile
Western Europe and North Africa — United Kingdom, Eire, Norway, Sweden, Denmark, Germany, France, Italy, Spain, Tunisia, Algeria, French Morocco
Middle East — Egypt, Palestine, Turkey, Greece, Bulgaria
Oceania and South Africa — Australia, New Zealand, Union of South Africa
Southern and Eastern Asia — India, Unoccupied China, Japan

Some care is necessary in interpreting the table in order not to overlook the countries actually excluded in the various areas. Central and eastern Europe are *not* included, nor is the U.S.S.R. Moreover, the western European figures as totals fail to show the opposite tendencies in the British Isles and on the continent. The omission of Occupied China is also noteworthy. For more detailed comment, see *World Economic Survey, 1942–44,* League of Nations, Geneva, 1945.II.A.4, pp. 96 ff. But the purpose here is not to argue that people were reasonably well off despite the war, which is almost certainly false, but to emphasize the effect of the war in stimulating food production in various regions. The figures are revealing in this respect.

under cultivation and lands already in production were sown with new crops, as war and shipping difficulties closed old sources of supply. The Department of Agriculture has estimated that only in western Europe, North Africa and the Middle East was agricultural production in 1942 and 1943 lower than in prewar years. Food production in western Europe, of course, probably declined in 1944, and certainly in 1945. Elsewhere, barring serious crop failures such as recently occurred in India, food production was probably greater in 1944 and 1945 than in 1942 and 1943. Table 18 shows world food production in these years as a percentage of prewar production. The average for all foods in all countries was 107 per cent.

The initial stimulus to new food production sprang primarily from the severance of trade routes, but it was subsequently intensified as a deliberate long-range policy in many areas. The uncertainty of import deliveries, the loss of export markets, and the suffering observed in areas where locally produced food was not the rule, combined to stimulate domestic food production, even at high cost.[16] For example:

> The submarine campaign in the Caribbean and the scarcity of shipping stimulated the efforts of Venezuela, Colombia, and Ecuador to increase national production of the basic crops. These countries have not as yet been able to achieve self-sufficiency in bread grains, fats, and oils, although substantial increases have been accomplished in the production of these and a wide range of food crops.[17]

In other areas, for example Europe, the shift was from meat and dairy products to grains and potatoes, because feed imports were unavailable and because grain production allowed a closer approach to self-sustenance. Great Britain also expanded home food production during the war.

Important changes also occurred in other areas. In Egypt, cotton

16. The last factor may be the most important of all in its long-run effects. The war has driven home the grim realities of hunger and starvation. War breaks down transport within and between countries. There may be an enduring insistence that home agriculture be maintained to avoid future starvation, even at the cost of heavy subsidies. In a peaceful world, international specialization in food production may be the only sensible arrangement. But in a world where war is an ever-present danger a secure domestic food supply becomes permanently important. In England, Belgium, Norway and the Netherlands, these lessons are not likely to go unheeded. Even in the United States, where shortages have been negligible, similar ideas are often voiced.

17. John J. Hagerty, "Wartime Shifts in Latin American Agriculture," *Foreign Agriculture*, May 1945, p. 77.

production was curtailed in favor of food. The Near East generally was forced to rely more on domestically produced food and to curtail industrial crops. In India, the virtual cessation of rice imports from Burma required more domestic production of food. In 1944–1945 the acreage in both wheat and rice was estimated to have been larger than in 1943–1944.

These are expansions of acreage and production apart from those in countries such as the United States and the British Dominions, which, with Argentina, Brazil and Cuba, were normally the big food producers and exporters before the war.[18]

Whether the areas that are now more nearly self-sufficient in food will revert to their prewar dependence on imports is an open question. The British Labor Government, for example, a few days after taking office announced a program to support "home agriculture." The answer to the question of reversion, in Britain and other countries, will turn on a number of considerations, and relative production costs at home and abroad will not necessarily be decisive. If the world trend is toward national self-sufficiency, the big food-exporting countries of prewar years will have to alter their production.[19] If the trend is toward renewed international specialization, then food production must presumably shrink in high-cost areas brought into production during the war. In either case, adjustments will be inescapable.[20]

18. The changes in production in the British Dominions have been of a diverse character. The Pacific war caused heavy demands on Australia as a source of food supply for the armies in that area. But wheat acreage was curtailed while dairy production was apparently increased. As for South Africa and New Zealand, ". . . some extension of the acreage under wheat has been encouraged during the war in both countries. A notable increase in livestock numbers, with the exception of sheep, has taken place in South Africa; the upward trend (since 1937) has been particularly marked in the case of cattle. In New Zealand the sheep population at the end of April 1944 was the largest on record; cattle numbers have remained approximately at the 1934/1938 average." (*World Economic Survey, 1942–1944*, p. 114.) In western Canada, wheat acreage was curtailed in favor of hog, beef and dairy production. In some measure Canada replaced western Europe, e.g., Denmark, as a source of the United Kingdom's food supply. Cf. Kathleen O. Horton and Thomas R. Wilson, *Some Factors in Postwar Export Trade With British Empire*, Economic Series No. 39, Bureau of Foreign and Domestic Commerce, 1944, p. 30.

19. Karl Brandt (*op. cit.*, p. 280 and *passim*) has emphasized that while Nazi Germany was organizing Europe for the better production of essential products, such as food, feeds and fibers, technological improvements and organizational improvements were introduced that will have long-term consequences. In other words, the better equipment, better production methods and better seeds and breeds will remain even though German control has been destroyed. In the Danubian area, and even in Denmark, these improvements are said to be substantial. Hence these areas may now be more efficient producers in comparison with the rest of the world than they were in the 1930's.

20. Food production well illustrates the familiar proposition that the problems of the

The story of the war's effect on raw materials production is essentially similar to that of food. Europe, unable to import wool and cotton, turned to numerous synthetic fibers. Synthetic petroleum and petroleum-fuel substitutes — for example charcoal for automobiles — were pushed for similar reasons. These developments may possibly create surplus productive capacity as in rubber. Furthermore, contraction of productive capacity in industry is often less easily accomplished than in agriculture because plant and equipment are often highly durable. As it was recently stated: "Part of the prewar import market in Continental Europe, where synthetic textile production has developed rapidly during the war, may well have been permanently lost to oversea exporters of natural textile fibres."[21]

Mechanized warfare increased the production and consumption of nonferrous metals, probably far beyond peacetime requirements and often in areas where costs are high by comparison with normal sources of supply. Outside the United States, no detailed figures of recent date appear to be available on the production of nonferrous metals. Aluminum production gained in Germany and Hungary; lead in Spain and Peru; antimony in Portugal, Czechoslovakia and Bolivia; tungsten in Bolivia, Portugal and Spain; and quicksilver in Spain.[22] Postwar adjustments appear inevitable with respect to some of these commodities.

The Spread of Industrialization

Industrialization developed to an extraordinary degree in many regions during the war. Closed trade routes naturally stimulated home production of indispensable manufactures. The highly mechanized character of the war necessitated new industries in new places. Finally, the fact that the major industrial countries were at war gave new in-

---

transition from war to peace are not wholly separable from postwar problems in the longer run. In order to keep people from starving while transport is still disorganized, local food production is being pushed as a relief measure over and beyond any extension of food production that occurred in high-cost areas during the war. "Helping people to help themselves" has been announced as the guiding principle of UNRRA. But there is at least the danger that it may be exceedingly difficult to contract local food production when transport and trade routes are again usable. Vested interests take shape very quickly. Consequently, it is not at all inconceivable that the longer-run choice between international specialization and national self-sufficiency in food production will be partially fixed by the policies followed in the reconstruction period. Some of the United Nations organizations may be able to help here.

21. *World Economic Survey, 1942–44*, p. 68. The output of rayon and staple fiber in Europe in 1942 is said to have been three times the 1934–1938 average, and substantial increases are understood to have occurred since then.

22. Cf. *ibid.*, pp. 73–74.

dustries a chance to develop in neutral areas without having to struggle against foreign competition.

The spread of industrialization within the British Empire — especially in Canada, Australia, New Zealand, the Union of South Africa and British India — is likely to have far-reaching effects on the volume and composition of postwar international trade. Before the war about 40 per cent of all United States exports went to the British Empire. The Dominions and India were also important export markets for British manufactured goods. But the disruption of shipping, combined with the enormous demands for war goods, so accelerated industrialization within the British Empire that it is doubtful if India and the Dominions will either want or need industrial imports of the same type as before the war. Industrialization was already spreading in these areas before 1939. The war pushed the trend line sharply upward; and it is unlikely to recede.

The character of the industrialization achieved in the various parts of the British Empire has been shaped both by wartime necessities and by the peculiarities of local natural advantages. The production of war goods and indispensable manufactured goods, of course, had top priority. In Canada and Australia, production of iron and steel, machinery, transport equipment and chemicals grew remarkably.[23] Both countries are now apparently able to produce virtually all the machine tools they require. In New Zealand and Australia, the food-processing industries grew far beyond their prewar size because of the food requirements of the fighting forces in the Pacific war zone.[24] Although South Africa made progress in food processing and in the manu-

23. In Canada, "Steel production has doubled since the war began. New rolling and finishing mills and plate mills have been added, and steel-foundry capacity has been increased. The annual rate of steel production at the end of 1943 was over 3 million tons. The enlargement of output of alloy steels for guns, armor plate, and tools is five times as great as in 1939. Many types and sizes of steel are now produced which had to be imported before the war." Horton and Wilson, *op. cit.,* p. 27.

As to Australia, it is reported that "These industrial efforts have produced a great variety of goods, such as textiles, steel cables, tool steels, alloys, bearings, chemicals, motor and airplane parts and bodies, guns, ammunition, explosives, small arms, precision instruments, optical munitions, armored fighting vehicles, cruiser tanks, wireless sets, planes, and many others. In 1939 only five factories existed for the manufacture of machine tools, but, at the end of 1943, 100 were producing almost all types of machine tools needed in Australia. There was no mass production in heavy industries before the war, but now the steel industry, Australia's most important secondary industry, mass produces many types of steel formerly imported. Australians are using their own metals to make armor plate supplies of which were formerly imported." *Ibid.,* p. 35.

24. In Australia, it is reported, vegetable, fruit and meat canning increased fivefold. *Ibid.,* pp. 35–36.

facture of agricultural implements, its economy is still largely built around gold mining. India extended its industrial activity in iron and steel products, textiles, chemicals, engineering and railway equipment. Apart from these industries,

. . . there has been marked progress in the cement, soap, match, and paint industries. India now has 389 cotton mills, with 10,000,000 spindles and 200,000 looms. There has been good progress in the tanning industry, with particular improvement in chrome tanning. India today supplies about half its needs for glass and glassware from 101 listed glass factories. Railway wheels, virgin aluminum, tires and axles, benzol and toluol are being made for the first time. The Aluminum Co. of India expects to have an annual capacity of 5,000 tons of ingots. . . . Before the war there were about 600 engineering workshops in India, and by the summer of 1943 there were nearly 1,500, including 23 railway workshops.[25]

Industrialization outside the British Empire is perhaps less significant for postwar world trade. In the first place, it started from a lower prewar level. More important, perhaps, was the absence of any feverish necessity for direct war-goods production to stave off national disaster. And lastly, the countries that remained nonbelligerent throughout the war accounted for only a small fraction of prewar international trade. (Cf. p. 45.) Industrialization made some progress in Latin America, where the greatest gains appear to have taken place in Brazil, Mexico and Argentina. But in the main it has been industrialization for the home production of consumers' goods — textiles, leather products, food processing, simple manufactures, etc. — and not for the development of heavy industries.[26] And without heavy subsidies, through tariffs or otherwise, it is doubtful whether the new industries can survive in competition with imported goods from more highly industrialized areas.[27] Somewhat similar developments, though

25. *Ibid.,* p. 47.
26. It is reported that in Argentina workers employed in industry rose from 462,000 in 1935 to 829,000 in 1941. Over the same interval the value of manufactured products rose from 3.5 billion pesos to 6.3 billion. Since 1941 further expansion has doubtless occurred. Cf. Ysabel Fisk and Robert A. Rennie, "Argentina in Crisis," *Foreign Policy Reports,* May 1, 1944, p. 41.
27. "First a world depression, then a world war, threw the nation on its own resources and created an industry through sheer necessity. Now that the industry exists, the Argentine government will have to make a choice at the end of the war: either it must raise tariffs and diversify agriculture so that it no longer depends for its livelihood on a bilateral exchange of agricultural products for finished goods; or its infant industries might be greatly weakened, in which case the Argentine might have to fall back on an agrarian economy. Such a choice brings the industrialists and landholders into direct conflict on national policy . . ." *Ibid.,* p. 41.

on a more modest scale, occurred in the West Indies, the west coast of Africa and other areas cut off by the war from normal import sources.[28]

How all these industrial changes will ultimately affect the volume and composition of international trade cannot be foreseen. Some old markets will have dwindled because of the change in comparative advantage among countries, stemming from the spread of industrialization. But as we have stressed, natural or acquired advantage in production is not the only factor shaping international trade. National economic policy — especially commercial policy in the form of tariffs, quotas, exchange control, subsidies, etc. — also determines a country's participation in international trade. And at present, postwar commercial policy is largely an unknown factor in most countries, except for a general acceptance, "in principle," of the proposition that international trade should be encouraged.

Physical Destruction and Capital Depletion

Although the war encouraged economic self-sufficiency in food and manufactures in many regions, in others it seriously impaired manufacturing and industrial capacity. In the defeated countries and in formerly occupied territories the destruction, damage and inability to maintain plant and equipment were widespread. Germany and Japan cannot be expected to resume their prewar position in world trade for some years to come.

The reasons why industrial efficiency in Japan and parts of western Europe will not immediately regain its prewar level are fairly obvious.[29] Real capital resources — machinery, equipment, plant — will

28. As the Belgian Minister of Colonies expressed it, "In peace time the policy consisted in making Belgium and the Congo as complementary as possible; today the Congo must aim at becoming more and more self-sufficient." Grant S. McClellan, "Colonial Progress in Central Africa — Belgian Congo and French Equatorial Africa," *Foreign Policy Reports*, May 15, 1944, p. 51 and *passim*. See also Olive Holmes, "Anglo-American Caribbean Commission — Pattern for Colonial Cooperation," *Foreign Policy Reports*, December 15, 1944.

29. *The Economist* (May 26, 1945, p. 703) reports the following percentages of 1938 monthly averages in certain branches of French industry in 1944 and early 1945. The low levels of output were mainly charged to the coal shortage.

Industry	1938 Monthly Average	Per Cent of 1938 Production		
		1944 December	1945 January	1945 February
Coal (thousands of tons)	3,401	70	71	69
Pig iron (excluding Moselle district, thousands of tons)	315	10	9	10

be less efficient than before the war because they have been undermaintained, physically destroyed or stolen. For some time real working capital, in the form of raw materials and stocks with which to operate, will be too small for efficient production. Perhaps the greatest deficiency will be in transportation: harbor installations, bridges and terminals were key military targets. Until these are repaired, the industrial regions of western Europe and Japan will remain below their prewar efficiency. Moreover, the need to reconstruct their own economies will leave almost nothing for exports and hence, in the absence of foreign gifts or loans, a limited ability to import.[30]

The impaired health and morale of the people will likewise hold productive efficiency to a low level. Plant and equipment will be in poor condition, but underfed workers living in makeshift structures will not be efficient even with good equipment. Malnutrition and tuberculosis threaten many areas. The acute immediate distress of the people, coupled with their memory of the dark war years in which personal hopes, ideals and possessions disappeared, may induce lethargy and helplessness. There is no need to labor the point. The fear and sickness gripping Europeans will not yield altogether to vitamin pills and nourishing soup.

Consequently, many European countries, and Japan too, will not soon resume their prewar position in international trade. Their comparative advantage in important industries has been definitely reduced. Moreover, their position, already weakened by the war, may be further undermined by the terms of the peace. The peace is not yet written.

Industry	1938 Monthly Average	Per Cent of 1938 Production		
		1944 December	1945 January	1945 February
Crude steel (excluding Moselle district, thousands of tons)	347	16	15	17
Sulphuric acid (excluding Alsace-Lorraine, thousands of tons)	81	5	7	9
Rayon (thousands of tons)	2,333	27	25	*
Staple fiber (tons)	416	13	58	*
Footwear (index)	100	33	*	*

* Not available.

It is also reported (*ibid.*) that car loadings in February 1945 were only about 25 per cent of the prewar average.

30. Some European countries have foreign dollar balances with which they could finance needed imports for reconstruction.

But the signs increase that Germany, at least, will be partially deindustrialized. Japan may suffer a similar fate. Yet both were internationally important industrial countries. If they are deliberately relegated to a near-agrarian status, then still further readjustments will be necessary to adapt world trade to the postwar structure of international comparative advantage.

WORLD WAR II AND THE BALANCE OF PAYMENTS

It became fashionable during the war to emphasize the secondary role of finance in economic affairs. People often pointed out that no country ever lost a war because it ran out of "money." Wars are won through the effective application of real resources and manpower. This was, indeed, the proper emphasis during the war. But granted this, it would be the grossest of errors to assume that the manner in which the financial side of the war was handled does not affect the net economic position of the various countries at the war's end. Finance is handmaiden to real resources in waging war nowadays. But the financial methods employed during the war create claims and obligations that apportion income from real resources *after* the war differently from what would have prevailed had the war not occurred, or had different methods been used in its financing. As the London *Economist* recently reminded the British people:

The doctrine that what is physically possible is financially possible has been so generally accepted in wartime that it comes as a shock to be told that badly needed materials which are available on the other side of the Atlantic, and for which shipping is also available — newsprint in Canada, for example — cannot be imported for financial reasons. But there is all the difference in the world between a shortage of money of a kind that the British Government can create and a shortage of dollars, which cannot be remedied — at least not quickly — by any British action.[31]

The recent world conflict brought about a drastic redistribution among the nations of international claims and obligations. This redistribution was a direct result, for the most part, of the means by which the war was financed. From the point of view of postwar commerce the importance of this redistribution lies in the changed balance-of-payments position of the various countries. Some countries are in a stronger position than in 1939. Others are definitely weaker. As between residents and nonresidents, the distribution of the claims upon

31. July 7, 1945, p. 8.

national output is now markedly different in a number of important countries from what it was before the war.

In Chapter 3 (pp. 65 ff.) we stressed the importance of income from investments and from invisible trade items in the balance of payments. From the point of view of the balance of payments, and thus of the ability to command imports from abroad, Great Britain has suffered the most drastic weakening of its prewar position. It had to sell foreign securities — that is, claims against the annual output of foreign countries arising out of previous lending abroad. But it also had to borrow against the future by issuing to foreigners new promises to pay. Like a man with a long, costly illness, Great Britain was obliged to sell some of its gilt-edged securities and run up bills besides. Its postwar balance-of-payments position does not immediately allow it to import so much as before the war with, say, the same volume of exports. Income from investments abroad has been reduced substantially. The United States also underwent somewhat similar changes, though on a smaller scale. (The financial position of both countries is explored in detail in the next chapter.)

The immediate relevance of these changes in the international financial position of Great Britain, the United States and some other countries lies in their implications for the flow of postwar trade. Throughout the present chapter we have stressed the effect of the war on the comparative-advantage positions of different regions and countries. The war reshuffled these into a new distribution. The changes in the international financial position of the various countries are, as it were, superimposed upon these "real" changes in industrial capacity, labor skills, agricultural production, etc. Trade flows must adjust to the financial changes as well as to the real changes.

The important point to bear in mind concerning this wartime creation and liquidation of claims upon national incomes is that the prewar flow of trade and the distribution of income claims were genuinely integrated.[32] There was an intricate relationship between them. To a

32. This again emphasizes how different war is from peace, from the economic point of view. In peace, financial changes and changes in the productivity of the factors of production tend to vary in harmony with one another. In war, they often move in opposition. Thus, had the industrialization outside of the United Kingdom been carried through in peace it probably would have been accompanied by new borrowing from Britain. This would have improved Britain's international financial position. But the war set the usual relationship askew.

high degree they were not two different things but different aspects of the same thing. But the new distribution of claims that emerges from the war cannot be said to be matched by a corresponding change in comparative advantages and needs from a nonfinancial point of view. Indeed, it could well be argued that the real changes in comparative advantages have typically been almost in the opposite direction from what the wartime financial shifts would seem to require. For example, the United Kingdom's changed financial position requires that it should export more, relative to imports, than before the war.[33] But the basic wartime economic changes in the countries to which the United Kingdom might hope to export and that hold financial claims against it, have been mainly in the direction of changing their import needs and strengthening their export ability. So broad a generalization is, of course, open to numerous qualifications. Nevertheless, the basic problem remains: changes in real resources proceeded apace in many countries during the war; yet, at the same time but on a different plane, drastic shifts were occurring in the international distribution of income claims. And this new distribution of claims had no necessary relationship to the change in real resources. The wartime financial changes, combined with coexisting changes in international comparative advantages and needs, have bequeathed a tremendous adjustment problem.

33. For example, the United Kingdom is probably no more an ideal area in which to raise wheat than it was in 1939; yet, because of the war the ability of its residents to buy wheat or other goods from the rest of the world is now lower, because the United Kingdom no longer possesses its 1939 foreign investments whose income (partially) paid for wheat imports. Britain's capacity to grow wheat at home has not improved at the same rate as its ability to import wheat has declined. The financial overlay no longer corresponds with the basic factors in trade flows nearly so well as it once did.

Chapter 5

POSTWAR CLAIMS AND THE BALANCE
OF PAYMENTS

LIQUIDATION OF the international financial claims arising out of World War II requires a fundamental change in the pattern of international trade. In the final analysis, debtor countries can pay their debts only through a positive balance of trade and services; and creditor countries can realize on their foreign balances only if they import more goods and services than they export. But claims and obligations can be shifted between countries much more easily than their balances of trade and services can be harmoniously realigned. This unequal ease of readjustment between claims and trade flows constitutes one of the main difficulties in the effective reconstruction of international trade.

ADAPTABILITY OF THE BALANCE OF TRADE

A country exporting capital or repaying previously accumulated foreign debts necessarily supplies foreigners with additional purchasing power over domestic commodities. If the initial recipients of this purchasing power spend it all in the transferring country,[1] its balance of trade and services will adapt itself without difficulty. The transferring country will automatically develop an export surplus. The economy of the transferring country will not be wholly unaffected, to be sure. The foreigners who receive the transferred purchasing power will presumably buy commodities different from those the home residents would have bought with the same funds. This recomposition of aggregate demand for domestic products through transfer of purchasing power to foreigners will cause some prices to rise, others to fall. Such relative price changes will tend to shift productive resources among industries.[2] But, except in the case of very large transfers, these

1. We shall hereafter call the country transferring funds abroad the "transferring country."
2. We assume here that resources are fully utilized when the transfer of funds takes place.

shifts will not be of major proportions and the economy of the transferring country will not be seriously disturbed.

The transfer problem is fairly simple when the funds are spent directly for goods to be shipped abroad. It is likely to be more serious, however, if the initial recipients desire their own or third currencies instead of exportable goods in the transferring country. If free foreign exchange markets exist, the transfer affects foreign exchange rates first. The foreign holders of funds will exchange them for their own or for other foreign currencies. The demand for these currencies will therefore increase and their price, in terms of the currency of the transferring country, will rise; in other words, the currency of the transferring country tends toward a lower rate in the foreign exchange market. Under the gold standard, where foreign exchange rates can change only within very narrow limits, the transfer of the funds leads to a gold outflow, a deflationary pressure on incomes, prices and domestic employment.[3]

Under a "paper" standard, exchange rates can fluctuate freely. In this case a fall in the value of the currency of the transferring country, resulting from the increase in the demand for foreign currencies, cheapens domestic products for foreigners even though domestic prices remain the same, because the same amount of foreign currency can now buy more of the currency of the transferring country, and therefore more commodities, than before. Currency depreciation, while encouraging foreigners to buy domestic commodities, avoids domestic deflation and unemployment. Indeed, it may even stimulate home industry because home-produced goods may be substituted for the now more costly imports.

The above analysis must be modified for the case of the transfer of

3. As soon as the value of the currency of the transferring country has fallen in the foreign exchange market to a point where it becomes profitable to ship gold from that country to other countries in exchange for their currencies (instead of buying these foreign currencies directly in the foreign exchange markets), gold will be exported from the transferring country. (See Chapter 2, pp. 17 ff.) The central bank, losing gold reserves, will sooner or later have to take action to reduce the volume of money, with resulting deflationary pressure on domestic incomes and prices. But lower prices make domestic commodities a more attractive purchase to foreigners, and thus exports from the transferring country are encouraged. On the other hand, pressure on the price level means declining incomes and unemployment in the transferring country and hence falling imports. Expanding exports together with falling imports in the transferring country, however, mean a shift toward an export surplus. The money transfer again tends to be converted into a goods transfer. In the last analysis the funds have to be spent in the transferring country.

"inactive" balances or newly created funds. If blocked funds are released, or if a lending government sells its obligations to the domestic banking system in exchange for deposits, then the expenditure of these additional funds in the transferring country tends to raise its price level. In this instance, prices will probably actually rise as against the case where existing funds are merely transferred from nationals to foreigners.[4] Under a paper standard, if the monetary authorities in the transferring country do not deliberately offset the new money expenditure, the internal price structure will remain at a new higher level and the exchange rate at a new lower level, more or less permanently.[5]

For a paper-standard country, therefore, the transfer of newly created or previously idle funds tends (1) to lower the value of its currency in terms of other currencies, (2) to raise its domestic price level, and (3) to increase its exports to foreigners, provided that home prices do not rise as fast as the exchange rate falls. If the funds owed to foreigners are large — as is currently the case for Great Britain — and they are suddenly released and withdrawn, the results might be disastrous. For not only would there be a sharp decline in the value of the currency in the foreign exchange market and a rise in the domestic price level, but the standard of living would also fall because the sudden marked rise in exports would cut into domestic consumption.[6] For these reasons, if the sums owed abroad are very large the government will find it impossible, or at least inadvisable, to allow the free market to handle the transfer problem. Some other solution must be found.

DISTRIBUTION OF FINANCIAL CLAIMS

Almost all international debts and credits at the end of World War II involved either Great Britain or the United States or both. They are today at once the largest creditors and the largest debtors.

---

4. In the case of the gold standard, the gold outflow will be greater also.

5. The permanent level of the external value of the currency of the transferring country is likely to be above its level during the process of transfer.

Under the gold standard, the gold outflow will tend to counteract the increase in the circulating volume of money brought about by the release of formerly idle balances or by the creation of new balances. Here also, of course, the monetary authorities can, if they so desire, attempt to counteract this tendency.

6. This aspect of the transfer problem is particularly serious in a country that has not yet fully converted to peacetime production, because a given amount of funds withdrawn by foreigners will command a greater percentage of the output of "peacetime" commodities than after reconversion is complete.

An analysis of the geographical distribution of British and American foreign investments and liabilities will therefore show the creditor and debtor position of other countries as well.

GREAT BRITAIN

Great Britain's long-term foreign investments in 1938 have been estimated at as high a figure as $23 billion. Net quick external liabilities were estimated at $3.7 billion;[7] longer-term liabilities of an unknown amount would have to be included in any net reckoning.

By the middle of 1945 Great Britain's creditor-debtor position had undergone a thorough change. The war forced it to liquidate part of its long-term investments. Receipts from these liquidations amounted to $4.5 billion. The value of its remaining long-term foreign investments cannot be estimated with any accuracy. As the White Paper states:

. . . It would not be possible to give an estimate in terms of capital value of the residue to which any real significance could be attached, in view of the technical difficulties of arriving at any satisfactory basis of valuation.[8]

Table 19 summarizes Britain's international investment position as of June 1945.[9]

While Great Britain's foreign investments have decreased, its foreign short-term debts have increased roughly fourfold since 1938. In the middle of 1945 they amounted to $13.5 billion. The largest part of these short-term liabilities were to the credit of India, Iran and Egypt. Since the middle of 1945 Great Britain's foreign liabilities have increased still further. By the beginning of 1946 they may have been as much as $16 billion. This is an enormous sum. It is more than seven times the total of British exports (excluding re-exports) in 1937. It is equal to about half the reparation debt saddled on Germany in 1921. In relation to the British national income, the £4 billion short-term debt is equal to 48 per cent in 1944. Foreign creditor countries could thus claim nearly half the British national output for one year if they could withdraw their balances within one year at prevailing prices.

7. *Statistical Material Presented During the Washington Negotiations,* British White Paper, Cmd. 6707, 1945, pp. 10–11.
8. *Ibid.,* p. 10.
9. Further data on British foreign investments — by geographical areas and by types of investments — will be found in Appendix Tables I, J and K.

TABLE 19

BRITISH FOREIGN INVESTMENTS AND LIABILITIES, WARTIME CHANGES
(*In Millions*)

Region	Foreign Investments 1938[a]	Repatriations and Sales of Foreign Investments During World War II[b]	Foreign Liabilities June 30, 1945[b]
Total, all countries	$22,905	$4,500	$13,525
Sterling area	9,450	2,270	10,975
Dominions (Australia, New Zealand, South Africa, Eire)	4,605	810	1,550
India, Burma, Middle East	3,615	1,400	6,980
Colonies and other sterling-area countries	1,230	60	2,445
South America	4,705	385	1,225
North America	5,428	1,725	
United States	2,743	820	—
Canada	2,685	905	—
Europe	1,725	55	1,075[c]
Rest of the world	1,597	65	250

a. Cleona Lewis, *Debtor and Creditor Countries: 1938, 1944,* The Brookings Institution, Washington, 1945, pp. 73–74. The total of these figures is higher than Kindersley's estimates, which give the total of British foreign investments for 1938 as £3,753 million, whereas Cleona Lewis' total is £4,582 million. (R. M. Kindersley, "British Oversea Investments," *Economic Journal,* 1939, pp. 692–93.) The exchange rate used by Cleona Lewis to convert pounds sterling into dollars is $5 to the pound. Bonds are included at par value. The method of valuing stocks and properties is not always clearly shown in the source used by Cleona Lewis.

b. *Statistical Material Presented During the Washington Negotiations,* British White Paper, Cmd. 6707, 1945. In arranging the figures in the first column to fit the categories of countries given in the British White Paper, it was assumed that the term "South America" there used is identical with "Latin America."

c. Including dependencies of European countries.

The transfer of such huge amounts cannot be left to the mechanism of a free-market system without courting chaos.

THE UNITED STATES

American foreign long-term investments did not materially alter during World War II. Short-term liabilities, however, almost doubled between 1939 and the end of 1944, as shown in Table 20, so that the United States was a net debtor on short- and long-term account combined.

TABLE 20

INTERNATIONAL INVESTMENT POSITION OF THE
UNITED STATES, 1939 AND 1944

(*In Billions*)

	End of 1939[a]	September 1944[b]
Investments abroad	$ 11.4	$ 11.1
Long-term	10.8	10.6
Short-term	.6	.5
Foreign investments in the United States	9.6	12.3
Long-term	6.3	6.2
Short-term	3.3	6.1
Net creditor or debtor position of the United States		
On long-term account	4.5	4.2
On short-term account	−2.7	−5.6
On long- and short-term account	1.8	−1.2

a. Hal B. Lary and Associates, *The United States in the World Economy,* Economic Series No. 23, Bureau of Foreign and Domestic Commerce, 1943, p. 123.

b. Robert L. Sammons, "International Investment Position of the United States," *Foreign Commerce Weekly,* January 27, 1945, pp. 5 ff.

The short-term liabilities of the United States increased from $3.3 billion in 1939 to $6.1 billion in September 1944 and to $6.4 billion in October 1945. Canada and Latin America were the largest short-term creditors at the beginning of 1946, owning between them roughly 40 per cent of the total balances. The remainder was distributed among western European and Asiatic countries. (See Table 21.)

Foreign countries also acquired gold from the United States. A total of $4.3 billion in gold was held in the United States for foreign account at the end of February 1946.[10] This "earmarked gold," from one

10. Some persons would question the propriety of including "earmarked gold" without at the same time including all the gold everywhere in the world, if the purpose is to suggest the liabilities to which the American economy is exposed. We would agree that this view has some validity. But it does seem to us that, on net balance, earmarked gold already within the United States is slightly more likely to be converted into dollars than

TABLE 21

FOREIGN SHORT-TERM LIABILITIES, INCLUDING EARMARKED GOLD, REPORTED
BY BANKS IN THE UNITED STATES, BY COUNTRIES, END OF OCTOBER 1945
(*In Millions*)

Country	Amount
Grand total	$10,708.9
Total short-term liabilities	6,396.8
Canada	1,551.8
Latin America	1,097.7
Brazil	179.2
Mexico	164.3
Cuba	145.4
Panama	90.5
Colombia	83.1
Argentina	77.2
Others	358.0
Europe	2,545.0
United Kingdom	740.2
France	360.3
Switzerland	284.4
Netherlands	228.1
Belgium	195.6
Norway	182.7
Italy	62.0
Other European countries	491.7
Asia	1,007.7
Rest of the world	194.6
Gold held under earmark on account of foreign countries (end of February 1946)	4,312.1

Source: *Federal Reserve Bulletin,* March 1946, pp. 346, 302.

point of view, constitutes a "sight liability" of the United States, inasmuch as it can be spent for American commodities without notice,
by simply converting the gold into dollars. This $4.3 billion of ear-
marked gold may therefore, from one point of view, be added to the

gold held abroad. Furthermore, the attitude of the United States government toward
converting gold already within the country into dollars and toward accepting new gold
imports *ad infinitum* would probably not be identical, although this is not possible of
proof.

foreign banking liabilities. Finally, American currency of about $.5 billion held abroad[11] also belongs in the category of American short-term obligations. Total foreign short-term liabilities thus amounted to roughly $11.2 billion at the beginning of 1946. In other words, if all the foreign creditors were to liquidate their short-term funds in the United States within, say, one year, they could purchase $11.2 billion worth of American commodities, or more than three times the total commodity exports of the United States in 1937.

In appraising the position of the United States, however, several additional factors have to be kept in mind. First of all, the creditor countries are not likely to withdraw all their balances, even if they were free to do so. Part of their dollar balances are "working balances" kept to meet day-to-day inequalities between dollar receipts and payments.[12] How large these might be can only be surmised. At the end of 1938 total foreign balances in the United States amounted to $2 billion. But even part of these undoubtedly represented "hot money."[13] What part was regarded as working balances is impossible to determine. Some part of the present balances are also probably regarded as "reserves" against swollen domestic money supplies. An example is the case of Mexico.

Some further claims should be included in any complete reckoning. There is no reason for assuming that foreign countries are willing to spend on American commodities only the gold earmarked as theirs within the United States. They may use for the same purpose some of the gold they hold at home. It can be estimated that the gold holdings of foreign countries increased between the end of 1941 and the beginning of 1946 by at least $5.4 billion. This includes the increase of $2.1 billion in earmarked gold in the United States for foreign account.[14]

11. *Foreign Commerce Weekly,* January 27, 1945, pp. 5 ff.
12. The same argument applies to the sterling balances held in London.
13. That is, funds seeking "refuge" in the United States pending some clearing up of unsettled political or social conditions abroad and not for investment in the usual sense.
14. The gold reserves of the United States were, at the end of 1941, $22.7 billion; at the end of 1944, $20.6 billion; and at the end of 1945, $20.1 billion. (See *Federal Reserve Bulletin,* March 1946, p. 302.) The world production of gold between the end of 1941 and the end of 1944 is estimated at $3.3 billion. (*Letter,* National City Bank of New York, February 1945, p. 23.) In other words, gold stocks of foreign countries have, in the period 1941–1944, increased by $5.4 billion minus whatever quantities were consumed in industrial uses. No figures for the industrial use of gold during the war years

Thus gold stocks of foreign countries held outside the United States must have increased at least $3.3 billion between the end of 1941 and the beginning of 1946. Even if we suppose that foreign countries spend on American commodities no more than one half of this wartime gain in their domestic gold stocks, we must raise our previous total of $11.2 billion by another $1.7 billion in·order to obtain the total potential demand for American exports that might be turned into actual demand at reasonably short notice.[15]

Several other sources from which foreign countries may acquire dollar funds remain to be mentioned. The American quota in the International Monetary Fund amounts to $2.75 billion and the American subscription to the International Bank is $3.175 billion.[16] Furthermore, commitments (apart from the International Fund and the International Bank) have been made, or are in the process of being made, to lend to foreign countries. The American loan to Great Britain amounts to $3.75 billion. The Export-Import Bank by the end of 1945 had total commitments of $1.6 billion,[17] of which $920 million were loans to European countries. Not all of these credits had been used by the end of 1945. At the beginning of 1946, the Export-Import Bank had $1.9 billion still uncommitted.

Finally, foreign countries may draw on the long-term investments that they hold in this country. These total $6.2 billion.

The sum total, then, of the claims that foreign countries could conceivably bring against the United States at the beginning of 1946 amounted roughly to $30.6 billion, made up as shown in Table 22.

In addition to the claims shown in Table 22, noncommercial com-

are available. The quantities have probably not been large. It is highly unlikely that total industrial consumption was greater than the further decline of $.5 billion of American gold stock during 1945 plus the gold production during that year. Hence the monetary gold stock of foreign countries must have increased by at least $5.4 billion between the end of 1941 and the end of 1945.

15. Gold stocks outside the United States were abnormally low before 1939. We allow, therefore, for some rectification of this condition by assuming that, except in very unusual circumstances, no more than one half the wartime increase is likely to flow back to the United States in demand for American dollars.

16. Great Britain's quota in the Fund is $1.3 billion, and its subscription to the International Bank another $1.3 billion. But the dollars in the Fund are much more likely to be drawn upon than are the pounds sterling. As regards the subscription to the International Bank, each country has the right to veto the use of its currency by that institution for making loans to other members.

17. *Federal Reserve Bulletin,* March 1946, p. 230. There is current discussion to raise the $3.5 billion lending power of the Export-Import Bank.

Rebuilding the World Economy

TABLE 22

CERTAIN IDENTIFIABLE CLAIMS AND POTENTIAL CLAIMS AGAINST THE
UNITED STATES AT THE BEGINNING OF 1946

(*In Billions*)

Grand total	$30.6
Total claims	28.975
United States sight liabilities (from Table 21)	10.7
Long-term liabilities	6.2
Commitments under the Bretton Woods Agreements	
International Monetary Fund	2.75
International Bank	3.175
Loan to Great Britain	3.75
Unused lending power of Export-Import Bank	1.9
Estimate of United States currency abroad	.5
One half of estimated increase in foreign monetary gold stock, 1941–1945, excluding earmarked gold	1.7

mitments exist in the form of gifts and other forms of relief to European countries; all such transactions add to the drain of commodities from the domestic economy.

Not all the above claims against the United States will, of course, actually be exercised. Moreover, when assets are spent for American commodities the expenditure will be spread over a period of years. But a national balance sheet that suggests the scale of magnitude of American foreign commitments is useful and even necessary. Foreign, particularly European, countries will seek loans for imports of raw materials and consumers' goods to rebuild their economies, since they cannot at present finance imports from current exports. But the productive capacity of even the United States is limited. Claims to American commodities acquired through loans cannot be distributed freely without regard to the volume of commodities that they may draw from the American economy. In deciding on individual loans to foreign countries, American authorities cannot disregard the total amount that can be lent, and the annual rate at which the claims already outstanding are likely to be used. Moreover, they must take into consideration the long-run effects of lending. Sometime in the future the loans will be repaid; foreign countries can acquire the necessary dollars only by exporting to the United States. The American economy must therefore be willing to absorb an increasing volume of imports in the future.

Some comprehensive plan is evidently required. Lending policy must take account, first, of the capacity of the country to provide the necessary export surplus during the period in which the claims become demand for American commodities; and second, of the import surplus that the country is willing to absorb when the loans are repaid.[18]

SOLUTIONS TO THE DEBT PROBLEM

There are only two ways in which a debtor country can discharge its foreign liabilities, excluding default.[19] One is to liquidate overseas investments and use the proceeds to pay off the liabilities. In this case, investments abroad are simply canceled against claims of foreign countries on the country concerned. This assumes, of course, the existence of overseas assets. This method was used to some extent by Great Britain during the war. Securities issued by the Indian government and by private concerns in India that were held by investors in Great Britain, for instance, were purchased with the sterling credits accruing to India during the war.

But the liquidation of investments abroad cannot now contribute much to the solution of the problem of foreign indebtedness. In view of the impossibility of estimating the value of British foreign investments after World War II, it is not certain that British foreign investments would be sufficient to meet Britain's liabilities even if they were liquidated. Moreover, Britain's foreign debts are short term, while its investments abroad are long term; and most of the long-term investments are direct investments that are not readily marketable. Easily liquidated long-term investments were already sold during the war. Finally, the income from foreign investments is an important

18. A statement on the foreign loan policy of the United States was, indeed, published in March 1946. The statement was formulated by the National Advisory Council on International Monetary and Financial Problems and presented to the President. The President endorsed the recommendations and submitted the report to Congress. (The report is published in the *Federal Reserve Bulletin,* March 1946, pp. 227–31.) According to this statement the loan commitments of the Export-Import Bank from January 1946 through June 1947, which are necessary to satisfy "the most urgent foreign needs," will amount to $3.25 billion. This figure does not include the American loan to Great Britain.

19. For the purpose of the present discussion we can include under liabilities all commitments for loans to foreign countries, since these establish short-term liabilities as soon as they are made.

source of funds from which essential imports can be financed. It is therefore unlikely that Great Britain will be either able or willing to liquidate any large part of its long-term foreign investments to pay off its short-term indebtedness.

For the United States, too, total investments abroad are less than the total claims that can be brought against it; and its long-term investments are mostly direct investments that cannot be easily liquidated. Moreover, they are in private hands and have not been turned over to the government as in Great Britain. Any liquidation policy would probably require as a first step that they should be turned over to the government. In any case, the problem is not acute for the United States.

The second way of discharging liabilities to foreigners is to sell more goods and services to foreigners than are bought from them.[20] Only by this method can the debtor countries, in the final analysis, pay the bulk of their debts in the postwar years.

Can they achieve the necessary surplus in their balance of payments?

The answer obviously depends on how rapidly the claims on the debtor countries are liquidated. Great Britain clearly could not achieve a surplus on current account great enough to repay all its debts within a year.[21] Even for the United States, difficulties would arise if all the claims upon it were exercised within a year. It is possible (and in the case of the United States, probable) that the withdrawals will be so distributed that the funds can be provided by an active balance of payments on current account without special controls to postpone withdrawals or regulate their rates. If withdrawals are not properly timed, measures must be taken to harmonize them with the surplus currently achieved in the balance of payments on current account.

This can be done in various ways.

First, short-term debts can be funded, thereby reducing the debtor's annual payments to interest and amortization charges only. If this method is chosen, the long-term securities held by the creditor countries must be "blocked," that is, the foreign creditor nations must

---

20. That is, through a surplus of receipts from foreigners, from exports of goods and services and income from investments abroad, over payments to foreigners for imports of goods and services and for service charges on foreign indebtedness.

21. It is assumed throughout this discussion that British exchange rates and prices will remain at about current levels.

agree not to sell the securities in the debtor country and withdraw the proceeds. Otherwise the position of the debtor country might revert to what it was before the funding took place.

Second, through foreign exchange control, imports can be restricted and exports perhaps even increased: creditor countries can be induced to buy commodities in the debtor countries that they would otherwise have purchased elsewhere. This method tends to improve the debtor country's balance of payments with the creditor countries and the surpluses can then be used to liquidate gradually the foreign balances.

Third, it may be possible to shift the burden temporarily to another country that is in a better position to achieve a positive balance of payments. A country obliged to repay short-term debts, for instance, may borrow abroad on long-term account and use the funds to reduce its short-term debts. The burden of achieving a positive balance of payments then falls temporarily on the country making the long-term loan. When the long-term loan has to be paid back, the borrowing country will have to achieve an export surplus on commodities and services.

Finally, all these methods can be combined.

A somewhat more detailed discussion of the British case will illustrate these possible solutions.

The Case of Britain

Great Britain's difficulties with respect to the balance of payments do not stem solely from its large short-term debts. Certain other factors also contribute: Britain's income from overseas investments, which financed a large part of its prewar imports, has considerably decreased; net shipping receipts have also declined because of wartime shipping losses and increased competition from a greatly enlarged American merchant fleet. On the other hand, particularly heavy imports — much greater than before the war — will be necessary to restore a peacetime economy.

These strong pressures on Britain's balance of payments arising from the deficiency of receipts over necessary payments clearly do not permit any extensive repayment of foreign-owned balances during the transition period. The British government has estimated that, quite apart from the repayment of war and postwar debts, the volume of British exports will have to increase by 50 per cent if Britain is to import at its prewar volume and pay as it goes. If some provision is made for the repayment of these debts, for an increase in imports over the prewar level and for certain other special needs, Great Britain's postwar exports would have to be 75 per cent above the prewar level.

PARTIAL CANCELLATION AND FUNDING OF STERLING BALANCES

Some of the sterling balances might be canceled with, of course, the consent of the creditor countries. The British seem to have a good case on moral and economic grounds for suggesting at least partial cancellation. Blocked balances arose mainly because Great Britain bore a large part of the war effort for the whole British Commonwealth, for example by meeting the costs of defending India. Fairness would suggest that part of the burden should be assumed by the beneficiaries.[22] The economic argument would emphasize that prices in India and Egypt, and indeed in all the countries of the Middle East, rose during the war far more than prices in Great Britain. In India and Egypt, the price level in 1945 was more than three times as high as in 1939, whereas the rise was only 60 to 70 per cent in the United Kingdom. (Cf. Table 23, p. 140.) Despite these disparities, exchange rates between these countries and the United Kingdom remained unchanged throughout the war. This disparity between prices and exchange rates means that British wartime expenditures in those countries were credited in pounds sterling to the receiving countries — India, Egypt, Iran, etc. — at an exchange rate that considerably undervalued the pound sterling. How persuasive these arguments may be in negotiation is conjectural; and how large total cancellations may be no one can now say.

The remaining sterling balances beyond those canceled by negotiation may, in large part, be funded into long-term obligations by agreement with the creditor countries. This would reduce the annual debt payments to the stipulated interest and amortization charges. We have already analyzed this possibility on page 116.

22. The member countries owning the sterling balances contributed, of course, to the war effort inasmuch as they agreed to postpone their imports; they were willing to devote part of their resources to the war effort without obtaining immediate payment in the form of commodities. The political side of the problem — the lack of enthusiasm for the British Commonwealth on the part of India, and to a lesser degree of Egypt — should not be entirely overlooked in appraising the "fairness" of a partial cancellation of the sterling balances.

RETENTION OF FOREIGN EXCHANGE CONTROL IN THE STERLING AREA

The terms of the American loan to Britain in July 1946 presumably force Britain to terminate the "dollar pool" by July 1947. Had Britain been able to retain the dollar pool, it could have forced more British exports on sterling-area countries. Acceptance of the loan provisions means that sterling receipts from current British imports from sterling-area countries must be made freely convertible into dollars after July 1947. Furthermore, for non-sterling-area countries, exchange control must also be terminated by July 1947, unless the American government should agree to a later date.

Yet, the full consequences of the British loan agreement can be appreciated only against the background of Britain's position before the loan was approved. The "dollar pool" and Britain's bilateral payment agreements with countries outside the sterling area need to be understood to appreciate the changes that the loan will bring.

The countries in the sterling area agreed at the beginning of the war to pool their foreign exchange resources, especially dollars. Each member also agreed to purchase only "essential" supplies from the United States for which Great Britain allocated the dollar resources from the pool. Only occasionally, as in the agreements with Egypt[23] and Iraq,[24] did a member country obtain a flat annual sum of "hard"[25] currencies from the pool. Egypt was granted an amount of £10 million for 1945. Each member was responsible for its own program of American purchases. Only in so far as interallied agencies — such as the Combined Shipping Adjustment Board, the Combined Production and Resources Board and the Middle East Supply Center — determined purchases to be made, was there a central control of the use to which dollars might be put.

These arrangements might have been continued throughout the transition period if the American loan had not permitted an alternative solution of Britain's foreign exchange problem.

At early 1946 exchange rates, the pound sterling was greatly undervalued by some sterling-area countries. Some readjustment is unavoidable, unless the countries with now overvalued currencies achieve

23. *Egyptian Foreign Exchange Requirements for 1945,* Egypt No. 1 (1945), British White Paper, Cmd. 6582.

24. *Iraqi Foreign Exchange Requirements for 1945,* Iraq No. 1 (1945), British White Paper, Cmd. 6646.

25. I.e., currencies hard to obtain. Apart from United States dollars they include Canadian dollars, Swiss francs, Swedish kronor and some others.

lower domestic prices or unless British prices rise substantially. A higher pound sterling would probably not seriously reduce British exports to sterling-area countries for the time being; imports, including British goods, are urgently needed. A higher rate of exchange for the pound sterling would allow Great Britain to obtain its same imports from these countries in exchange for a reduced physical volume of exports; the terms of trade would move in favor of Great Britain.[26]

An outright upward revision of the sterling rate would encounter objections from other sterling-area countries. But there are other methods. For example, Great Britain, probably in order to keep Egypt and Iraq in the sterling area, recently granted Egypt and Iraq a fixed quota of "hard" currencies from the dollar pool. But in addition it allowed these two countries further allotments of "hard" currencies, provided that the commodities "needed" by Egypt and Iraq were more than 10 per cent higher in price within the sterling area than in "hard" currency countries. In other words, so long as the prices of these commodities are not more than 10 per cent higher within the area than outside, Egypt and Iraq must buy any further imports over their fixed "hard" currency allowances from members of the sterling area, for example Britain. From the point of view of Great Britain this is a substitute, given certain specific conditions, for a limited rise in the pound sterling exchange rate vis-à-vis Egypt and Iraq.

PAYMENT AGREEMENTS WITH COUNTRIES OUTSIDE THE STERLING AREA

Prior to the American loan to Britain, countries outside the sterling area were linked with the United Kingdom by payments agreements. The United Kingdom has concluded such agreements with Belgium, Holland, France, Sweden, Denmark, Turkey, Finland, Czechoslovakia, Switzerland and Greece. The first of these postwar agreements was made with Belgium in October 1944 and it set the pattern for many of the others.[27] The Belgian agreement fixed the rate of exchange between the Belgian franc and the pound sterling at 176.625 Belgian francs per pound sterling.[28] This rate is not to be

26. The burden of Great Britain's debts would, however, not be reduced, since the debts are expressed in terms of pounds sterling.

27. *Monetary Agreement Between the United Kingdom and Belgium,* Belgium No. 1 (1944), British White Paper, Cmd. 6557.

28. Or 2.28 American cents as against 16.58 American cents in December 1939.

altered except after mutual consultation. The Bank of England promised to furnish the sterling required by residents in the Belgian monetary area for such payments to residents in the sterling area as are permitted under Belgian exchange control regulations. Similarly, the National Bank of Belgium promised to sell francs to residents of the sterling area for purchases in the Belgian monetary area. An upper limit of £5 million was set on the balances the Bank of England and the Bank of Belgium could accumulate with each other.

The limits to the accumulation of balances in the central banks are set at different levels in other agreements. In countries having special import needs because of war damage — for instance Belgium and France — Great Britain has granted them credit by allowing its balances abroad to accumulate. But in other cases Great Britain may temporarily run into debt; that is, the other countries will leave balances in England. For instance, the agreements with Denmark and Sweden are expected to result in the accumulation by Danish and Swedish central banks of balances in the Bank of England. Britain will be the borrower. As *The Economist* said:

. . . there is little doubt that in the initial period — as is also true of trade with Sweden — it is Britain who will be the debtor. The Danes, in other words, are prepared to carry sterling until British exports of manufactured goods can expand to liquidate the debt.[29]

The agreement with France (which expired February 1946 and was renewed in a complicated form in April 1946) and the agreements with Turkey and Finland and Greece differ substantially from the rest.[30] However, for present purposes an elaborate analysis of these agreements is unnecessary.

29. August 25, 1945, p. 276.
30. The agreement with Finland stipulates that payments from residents of the sterling area to Finns are to be made into a "Finnish account" that then can be used by the Finns to purchase in Great Britain. In other words, all transactions between the two nations are carried on in pounds sterling. The British authorities in view of the Finnish inflation were apparently not prepared to carry Finmarks. A similar arrangement was made in the British-Turkish agreement. In the British-French agreement of March 1945 the British government promised to open a credit of £100 million to France and France a credit of fr.20 milliards to Great Britain. These ceilings can be raised after joint consultation. Special, rather complicated arrangements were made to settle any outstanding balance at the end of February 1946. (All these arrangements have been issued as British White Papers: the Finnish agreement under Cmd. 6664, the Turkish agreement under Cmd. 6632, the French agreement under Cmd. 6613.) The Greek agreement provides for a British stabilization loan to Greece. (Cmd. 6733.)

Great Britain thus linked non-sterling-area countries to sterling by special bilateral agreements. None of these agreements, of course, provided Great Britain with dollar exchange. But some of them, such as the Belgium agreement, provided that gold be set aside for the Bank of England whenever its balance in the foreign central bank exceeded the limit set in the agreement. This is "earmarked" gold for the account of the Bank of England that Great Britain can export. Apart from such possible gold accumulations, the agreements opened up sources of supply from which imports could be obtained without dollars.

Such agreements, as well as the pooling of dollars by the sterling-area countries, are excluded under the Anglo-American Loan Agreement. Yet Great Britain concluded, as late as September 1946, a four-year treaty with Argentina in which Argentina agreed to a partial freezing of her sterling balances. In case of a deficit with the sterling area she could dispose of them for an amount equivalent to the deficit, but only in the sterling area. This treaty led to a diplomatic exchange between Washington and London. The British government finally assured the American government that there would be no repetition of such provisions in future trade agreements.

THE AMERICAN CREDIT TO BRITAIN

In December 1945 the governments of the United States and the United Kingdom reached an agreement,[31] approved by Congress in July 1946, whereby the United States promised to extend to the United Kingdom a line of credit of $3.75 billion, to be drawn upon at any time between the effective date of the agreement and the end of 1951.[32] The total borrowings under this line of credit that are outstanding at the end of 1951 are to be amortized in fifty annual installments. The interest rate on the loan is 2 per cent, to be paid on the amount outstanding on the first of January of each year.[33] Interest is to be waived

31. *Financial Agreement Between the Governments of the United States and the United Kingdom, Dated 6th December, 1945, Together With a Joint Statement Regarding Settlement for Lend-Lease, Reciprocal Aid, Surplus War Property and Claims,* British White Paper, Cmd. 6708. (Reproduced in Appendix 2.)

32. The agreement also settled the obligations of Great Britain arising from lend-lease, reciprocal aid, the acquisition of surplus property, etc. The net sum due from the United Kingdom to the United States on this account was fixed at $650 million.

33. The first interest payment is to be made on the amount outstanding on December 31, 1951. This reduces the effective rate of interest below 2 per cent, of course.

if the income of the United Kingdom from exports, plus its *net* income from invisible current transactions, is, on the average over the five preceding calendar years, less than the average annual amount of British imports during 1936–1939 (set by agreement for this purpose at £866 million), due allowance being made for price changes in these imports; and provided further that the British government finds a waiver necessary in view of the state of the exchange markets and the level of its gold and exchange reserves. Waiver of interest is not permitted in any year unless payments in that year on foreign-owned sterling balances are reduced proportionately.

The government of the United Kingdom also agrees to terminate exchange controls immediately after July 1946 for (a) payments or transfers in respect of products of the United States permitted to be imported into the United Kingdom, or other current transactions between the two countries; or (b) the use of sterling balances to the credit of residents of the United States arising out of current transactions. Only when the International Monetary Fund, under the Bretton Woods Agreements, declares the dollar a scarce currency can the United Kingdom reintroduce foreign exchange control for dollar payments after July 1946. The United Kingdom, furthermore, promises that one year after the agreement takes effect, sterling receipts from current transactions of all sterling-area countries will be made freely available in any currency area without discrimination; in other words, the "dollar pool" will be dissolved by July 1947.

At the same date, foreign exchange control is to be terminated for current transactions with other than sterling-area members unless a later date is agreed upon after consultation. The United Kingdom, however, cannot invoke Article XIV, Section 2, of the Bretton Woods Agreement on the International Monetary Fund without the approval of the government of the United States. This clause precludes the United Kingdom from continuing foreign exchange control on current transactions during the transition period unless the American government agrees.[34]

As to British-blocked balances, the agreement stipulates: *First,* that the provisions for the removal of foreign exchange restrictions do not apply; in other words, the United Kingdom can continue to block

34. The Bretton Woods Fund Agreement is discussed in the following chapter.

sterling balances in existence in July 1946. *Second,* that the United Kingdom will attempt to reach an agreement with countries holding these balances whereby part of the balances are to be released at once, another part by installments over a period of years beginning in 1951, and a third part is to be canceled. *Third,* that the United Kingdom agrees not to use dollars supplied by the American loan to repay its short-term debts to other countries.

In addition to the loan from the United States, Great Britain has received a loan of $1.136 billion from Canada. Total new funds at its disposal therefore amount to about $5 billion.

The advantage of the American loan both for the United States and Great Britain is that it will enable Great Britain, the largest participant in international trade before World War II, to return to multilateral trade at an earlier date than would otherwise be possible.[35] The alternative for Great Britain would have been to retain the "dollar pool" arrangements and to increase trade within the sterling area.[36] The American loan reduces the need to intensify trade within the sterling bloc. Foreign exchange control within the sterling area would have tended to direct trade into channels different from those that would develop under a free-exchange system.[37] A reversion to a world-wide multilateral system would have been more difficult.

The loan cannot be expected to enable Great Britain to drop immediately and completely all quantitative controls: nondiscriminatory quantitative controls are still possible. Only if the amount lent were large enough to take care of any conceivable deficit in the British balance of payments in the transition period could the United Kingdom give up all quantitative controls. The length of the transition, however, will be determined largely by the speed with which British industry can develop sufficient exports to finance Britain's current import needs and, *in addition,* to cover the excess of interest and amortization charges on foreign debts (assuming that the sterling balances are funded) over current income from British foreign investments. The speed with which British exports can be increased will depend on the adaptability of British industry to changing world demand. The old

35. Political aspects of the loan are outside the scope of this study.
36. That is, to follow the course described on pp. 119 ff.
37. The members of the sterling area are important customers for each other even under multilateral trade. But a system of foreign exchange control for the area intensifies these trade relations beyond what they would be under multilateralism.

British export trades, particularly coal and textiles, are likely to face a continuation of the downward trend in foreign demand for their products. British export industry will have to shift to new products, with expanding markets abroad, for which Britain can hope to hold a comparative advantage — for example, electrical and other machinery, vehicles, chemicals, etc. How much time this process of reorganization and adaptation to new conditions will require cannot be foreseen. The American loan provides a "breathing space." It is gratifying to note that British exports in the second quarter of 1946 were already a full 100 per cent of the 1938 volume.

The provision of the American loan agreement relating to removal of foreign exchange control must not be interpreted to mean that Great Britain is committed to an immediate removal of all quantitative trade controls. Import licensing can be retained even though foreign exchange control has been abolished. By controlling the transactions that give rise to payments in foreign currencies, instead of controlling these payments themselves, Great Britain can achieve the result of foreign exchange control without its use. The loan agreement, however, stipulates that quantitative import restrictions must be administered on a nondiscriminatory basis. But exceptions to this rule are permitted. Moreover, *if the American government agrees,* Great Britain can invoke Article XIV of the Bretton Woods Agreement on the International Monetary Fund, which allows Britain to retain foreign exchange control in the transition period.

Even though Great Britain may not use the American credit to liquidate blocked balances, it facilitates their reduction. For dollar balances obtained through the loan diminish the pressure on other British foreign assets. Thus, more of them will become available for the reduction of blocked balances. The American loan also enables Britain, of course, to increase its imports during the five years 1946–1951. During this breathing spell — in which British export industries must gain new and larger markets — Britain's standard of living will therefore be higher than it would be without the loan.

The British have some fear that the increase in exports required to provide for current import needs, to meet interest and amortization payments on the American and Canadian loans and to reduce blocked balances cannot be achieved. The necessity of raising the standard of living above its wartime rigor, together with the political implications of not accepting the loan, were important reasons why Parliament approved the agreement despite certain misgivings. Undoubtedly, however, there was some genuine sentiment, especially "official" sentiment, in the United Kingdom for returning, if possible, to a multilateral system.

THE AMERICAN PROBLEM

The financial claims that foreign countries hold against the United States, either as short-term creditors or as recipients of long-term loans, may amount, as we have said, to as much as $30 billion. If half this amount is withdrawn within the next three years,[38] foreign countries could demand American commodities and services at an annual rate of $5 billion. Other things being equal, the United States would have to achieve an export surplus of this amount.

Although the figure of $5 billion is about 40 per cent greater than total American merchandise exports in 1937, the sum is not beyond American export capacities. In 1944, for example, the American export surplus was more than $10 billion. The export problem, however, cannot be discussed without reference to prices. During the early transition period, prices have tended to rise with most of the wartime controls removed. Increased spending for consumers' goods is perhaps the most obvious factor. Higher wage rates leading to higher production costs are probably more important in the long run. If before the pent-up domestic demand is satisfied, foreign countries use their American balances to purchase American commodities, inflationary tendencies will be strengthened. Although a rise in prices reduces the physical volume of goods that foreign countries can buy with their dollars and thus reduces the real burden of foreign dollar claims upon the American economy, few informed persons would advocate a rise in the American price level for this reason. If foreign-owned dollar balances and newly created loans are not to be inflationary, their expenditure must be so staggered as to minimize their inflationary potentialities. This problem is not likely to solve itself without the aid of conscious policy. Inflationary forces may later give way to deflationary forces. If the foreign balances could be liquidated then, they would help to sustain national income.

38. A sum roughly equal to this country's sight liabilities (including earmarked gold), plus the increase in foreign gold stocks, plus the British loan.

When internal prices are unstable, when war-incurred financial liabilities have to be liquidated, when international trade bears small semblance of normality, when many countries impose foreign exchange control, and when loans are made not by individuals seeking the highest yield on their investments but by governments, partly for political reasons — in a time such as this it may be advisable for the United States to regulate withdrawals of foreign funds. The total new loans to be granted must be decided upon as well as the timing of the withdrawal of these and already existing foreign liabilities. And both these factors must be related to internal business conditions. More funds can and should be released when business slackens than when business is booming. The liquidation of existing balances and fresh lending would then serve as one instrument among others for combating depressions in the United States.[39] Unfortunately, however, the need for dollars in many countries is too urgent for loans to wait on an American slump.

39. The problem of the repayment of foreign loans is discussed in Chapter 8.

Chapter 6

FOREIGN EXCHANGE RATES AND THE BALANCE
OF PAYMENTS

MANY COUNTRIES will be obliged to retain foreign exchange control or quantitative trade controls in the transition period. Great Britain's foreign debts, large import needs and loss of income from foreign investments and shipping will force it to retain quantitative import controls for some time to come. Many other countries, such as France, Belgium and Holland, also require large imports but cannot yet export in payment. Therefore, they too must retain foreign exchange control for several years. Even though foreign exchange rates are controlled in the transition period, occasional adjustments may well be necessary. The existing structure of foreign exchange rates shows clearly that many currencies are at present overvalued or undervalued. This has important economic consequences. Once the transition period is past, the whole problem of how international accounts are to be settled and cleared reappears. The International Monetary Fund agreed upon at Bretton Woods is intended to serve this purpose. Consequently, this longer-run problem will be discussed in the context of the Bretton Woods Fund Agreement.

THE TRANSITION AND POST-TRANSITION PERIODS

To visualize what kind of world economic structure will emerge from the transition period is nearly impossible. The transition interval is customarily identified, vaguely, with the time required for countries to reconvert from war to peace production, and in the case of those countries whose productive resources and equipment have been damaged or destroyed by military action, with the time needed to "reconstruct" their economies. But when is an economy "reconstructed"? Comparisons with prewar conditions do not always offer valid criteria. The economies of France or Belgium after the "transition period," for example, will almost certainly be very different from what they were in 1939. The transition period will be shorter in some countries than in others; it will obviously be longer for most European countries than for the United States.

Defining "Transition"

Any attempt to define the transition in terms of physical reconstruction overlooks the financial side of the problem. Great Britain, for instance, will not be back to "normal" until it has solved its debt problem and brought its balance of payments into equilibrium without the aid of foreign exchange control, import licensing or continued borrowing. The Bretton Woods Fund Agreement — which in principle aims to restore free-exchange markets and multilateral trade — nevertheless recognizes that many member countries may need to continue foreign exchange control for some time. Accordingly, on the financial side, the transition period might be defined as the time required for the world to get back to a multilateral trading system and free-exchange markets. But even this definition is not wholly satisfactory. Some countries, such as Russia and those in the Russian sphere of influence, probably do not intend to introduce a free-exchange market. And there is no certainty that in the foreseeable future all other countries will either desire or achieve a return to free-exchange markets and multilateral trade.

The system of world trade has now been so thoroughly disrupted that the difficulties of reopening trade channels are far greater than after the first world war. Moreover, there was then fairly general agreement among the nations (with the exception of Russia, then neither politically nor economically important) about the kind of international trading system that should prevail. But this consensus had vanished even before 1939, and may not reappear.

The eastern European countries are likely to adopt a system of state-controlled foreign trade; and their economies will probably be oriented in the future toward Russia, instead of Germany as before 1939. The volume and composition of their foreign trade will in this case differ sharply from what they were before the war: supplies of raw materials and food from eastern Europe will not be available for western Europe to the same extent.

Reorientation of Markets and Supplies

Germany, which in the prewar years was the most important industrial country on the European continent, will be considerably weakened if the Potsdam Agreement is carried out. What it will export and import will not be wholly decided by the market but partly by the occupying powers. Germany will neither supply so many industrial products to the rest of Europe nor be so important an export market for other countries as before 1939. In 1938 Germany supplied 9.9 per cent of world exports and took 9 per cent of world imports; 63 per cent of its exports went to continental Europe and 49 per cent of its imports came from continental Europe. In the same year, continental Europe (excluding Germany) imported 19 per cent of its imports from Germany and sent 20 per cent of its exports to Germany.[1] If Germany is no longer to be a major industrial nation, the other European economies must radically transform their economic structures. They must develop new markets and sources of supply. Furthermore, they must fill at least part of the gap left by the partial deindustrialization of Germany.[2]

As the location of natural resources cannot be changed and as industrial skills can be developed only gradually, this process of compensating for the lost German production, and of shifting markets and sources of supply, must at best be slow. Because Europe is integral to the world economy, non-European countries will also feel the repercussions of this slow process of adaptation. If Japan — also important in the trade of several countries, including the United States — should also be deindustrialized, the emergence of a reintegrated world trading system would be even further postponed.

This reorientation of markets and sources of supply probably means that free-exchange markets, at which the Bretton Woods plan ultimately aims, can be attained only after some new and relatively stable pattern of world trade has emerged. This means a pattern of world trade from which there are only minor deviations from year to year, so that no wide gaps occur in the balance of payments requiring larger amounts of gold and foreign balances than are available to the coun-

1. These figures are calculated from the tables of Annex III in *The Network of World Trade*, League of Nations, Geneva, 1942.II.A.3.

2. A large part of the burden arising from the decline in the total volume of European production would, of course, be borne by Germany in the form of a lower standard of living, but not all of it. Specialization of labor among nations mutually increases standards of living. If an important country ceases in large part to participate in international trade, the other countries will lose the advantage of the specialization of labor between themselves and the first country.

tries concerned. Until a country has achieved some such stability in its balance of payments it is not likely to discard direct trade controls. It could do so only if it were willing to allow the external value of its currency to fluctuate freely. Such a policy is manifestly incompatible with the ideal of stable exchange rates, which, despite the provisions for exchange rate adjustments, is basic to the entire Bretton Woods plan.

The first task is to analyze the problem of foreign exchange rates in the transition period, when restrictions on imports through foreign exchange control and import licensing will still continue in many countries.

The Equilibrium Rate of Exchange

The rates of exchange between any country's currency and currencies of other countries necessarily affect its exports and imports of goods and services. A fall in the exchange rate of the pound sterling — when a dollar, for example, costs more in British currency than it did before — makes British goods and services cheaper for foreigners and foreign goods and services more expensive for the British. The fall in the exchange rate thereby tends to increase British exports and decrease British imports. British claims on foreigners then tend to exceed foreign claims on Great Britain. The difference may be paid for by gold shipments to Great Britain, by a transfer to Britishers of sterling balances held by foreigners in London, or by a transfer of balances in other countries to British ownership. A transfer of foreign-held sterling balances to Britishers is equivalent to a reduction in the short-term debts of Great Britain; a transfer of bank balances in other countries to Britishers gives Britain greater assets abroad and means, in effect, that there has been a short-term capital export by Great Britain.

A rise in the pound sterling rate — when a dollar, for example, costs less in British currency than before — will have effects precisely the opposite of those just described.

If, in the absence of direct controls or tariff increases, the value of the pound sterling in terms of other currencies is such as to equalize receipts from and payments to foreigners without requiring transfers of gold or short-term balances between Great Britain and other countries, then the exchange rate of the pound against other currencies can be said to be in equilibrium. Such a rate is therefore termed the "equilibrium rate."[3]

Actual Rate Fluctuates

Defined in this sense, the equilibrium rate actually seldom exists, since some outflow or inflow of gold or some transfer of ownership of short-term balances between countries is always taking place. The actual rate of exchange therefore always deviates somewhat from the equilibrium rate. But so long as the actual rate fluctuates about the equilibrium rate, causing a movement of gold and short-term balances first in one direction and then in another, the deviation is not alarming. It would be unnecessary as well as impossible to try to keep the actual rate always at the equilibrium level. Only if the actual rate deviates for a considerable period from the equilibrium rate, therefore, can one say that the currency of the country is "overvalued" or "undervalued." Overvaluation of a country's currency in the foreign exchange market then causes, by definition, a *sustained* outflow of gold and/or accumulation of balances in that country by foreigners;[4] undervaluation of a country's currency causes a *sustained* inflow of gold and/or an accumulation of short-term balances abroad.[5] In either of these cases, a

3. This statement needs to be modified in two respects: First, if gold is one form of international currency, a country may continually add a certain amount of the current world output of gold to its reserves. This influx of international currency, which is required to keep the international liquidity of a country on the same relative level, is compatible with the existence of an "equilibrium" rate of exchange. Second, in the text it is implicitly assumed that short-term balances move between countries only because of disequilibrium in the balance of payments. Such short-term capital movements may be called "equilibrating" movements. But short-term capital movements may also occur as the result of political uncertainty or the fear of exchange depreciation. Such capital movements, in contrast to the first type, do not result from but *cause* a disequilibrium in the balance of payments.

If a country has a sustained inflow of short-term balances of the equilibrating type, the actual exchange rate is, in our terminology, above the equilibrium rate, and a devaluation of the currency may be required. The willingness of foreigners to hold more balances in a country whose balance of payments is in disequilibrium tends to check, temporarily, the depreciation of its currency. If, on the other hand, foreigners, for political reasons, or because they fear depreciation of their own currency, transfer funds to another country, their action tends to *raise* the external value of the currency of the receiving country instead of merely checking its fall. This does not mean, however, that the external value of the currency of the receiving country should be appreciated. This would be unwise in view of the temporary nature of such inflows of flight capital. It follows that inflows or outflows of "hot" money must be disregarded in deciding whether the actual external value of a country's currency reflects its equilibrium value.

4. Or a reduction of balances held by that country abroad.
5. Or a reduction of the balances held in that country by foreigners.

country is — in the language of the Bretton Woods Fund Agreement — in a state of "fundamental disequilibrium" with respect to its balance of payments.[6]

If gold flows out and foreigners acquire short-term balances in a country, the ratio of the country's reserves to its sight liabilities declines. The authorities must take action when the ratio approaches what they consider, on the basis of experience, is a safe minimum. The problem is analogous to that of a bank that experiences a drain on its cash reserves and/or an increase in its sight liabilities (demand deposits). When the ratio of cash to sight liabilities nears what the bank considers the minimum required to keep liquid, the bank must take measures to stop the cash drain and/or to check the increase in its sight liabilities.

Maintaining Equilibrium

Appropriate action for the monetary authorities, if the actual rate is persistently above the equilibrium rate, can be along only one of two lines. The balance of payments can be forced into equilibrium at

6. The term "fundamental disequilibrium in the balance of payments" used in the Bretton Woods Fund Agreement has revived the discussion of the meaning of the equilibrium rate of exchange. (See Ragnar Nurkse, *Conditions of International Monetary Equilibrium*, International Finance Section, Princeton University, Princeton, 1945, pp. 1 ff.; Gottfried Haberler, "Currency Depreciation and the International Monetary Fund," *Review of Economic Statistics*, November 1944, pp. 178–81; Alvin H. Hansen, "A Brief Note on 'Fundamental Disequilibrium,'" *ibid.*, pp. 182–84.) One of the points at issue is whether one should talk of an "equilibrium rate" at all, as long as there is unemployment in a country. The pound sterling was, in the opinion of most experts, overvalued in the years 1925–1931. Yet the balance of payments over the whole period was roughly in equilibrium. This equilibrium in the balance of payments at the old gold parity of the pound sterling was achieved only at the cost of reduced employment and depression in certain industries. Nurkse concludes, therefore, that the criterion of full employment should be included in the definition of the equilibrium rate of exchange. The linking of the concept of the equilibrium rate of exchange with full employment raises difficulties of its own, however. First, the concept of full employment is not theoretically clear. Second, in a situation of world-wide unemployment, since not all the currencies of the world can be overvalued simultaneously, the currency of a country could be called overvalued only if the level of unemployment in the country was relatively greater than in other countries, a fact not easy to establish and probably even more difficult to induce other countries to accept. For this and other reasons, the definition of an equilibrium rate used in the text leaves aside entirely the employment problem. The level of the equilibrium rate (not its definition) is, of course, dependent on the level of employment. In the case of Great Britain between 1925 and 1931, for instance, the equilibrium rate in a situation of full employment would have been represented by a lower value in the pound sterling than actually prevailed. It follows that harmony between the actual rate of exchange and the equilibrium rate (in our terminology) is compatible with an unsatisfactory state of the domestic economy.

the prevailing rate by internal deflation — that is, by reducing imports and increasing exports through the fall in home incomes and prices. Alternatively, the actual rate may be lowered; this lower rate tends to cut imports and raise exports even though domestic money costs, prices and incomes remain unchanged. (See p. 131 and Chapter 5, pp. 105–07.) When exchange rates were fixed as under the gold standard, the first course had to be adopted, that is, imports were checked and exports raised by deflating domestic incomes and prices. Under the Fund plan the choice can be the other way about: the country's foreign exchange rate can be lowered, thus cheapening domestic products for foreigners and making foreign products more expensive for domestic consumers, but avoiding deflationary pressure on home prices and incomes.

When the actual rate is below the equilibrium rate, the international liquidity position of the country tends to improve. If the two rates are to be brought together, the improved liquidity position requires either a rise in domestic prices and incomes through an appropriate monetary policy, or an appreciation of the value of the currency. Usually, however, a country is less willing to raise the value of its currency when its liquidity increases than to lower the value when its liquidity decreases.

Purchasing-Power-Parity Theory

Can we go beyond the statement that a country's rate of exchange reflects the equilibrium rate, so long as neither gold nor short-term balances move into or out of the country? The so-called purchasing-power-parity theory of the equilibrium rate of exchange holds that the equilibrium rate of exchange between two countries is the rate that reflects the relative purchasing power of the two currency units, each in its own country. If, on the average, for example, one pound sterling buys as much in England as four dollars buy in the United States, the equilibrium exchange rate between the two currencies is one pound sterling for four dollars. This is the absolute form of the theory because it defines the equilibrium rate between any two currencies at any given time. But the purchasing-power-parity theory can also be used to relate changes in prices to a changing equilibrium rate of exchange. This is the comparative form of the theory. As applied to the dollar-sterling relationship it asserts (in Professor Pigou's formulation) that

. . . if we start from a position of equilibrium, and conditions alter, the consequent *change* in the norm of exchange will be proportionate to the *change* in the ratio between sterling and dollar prices.[7]

More concretely, if, for example, the price level in England rises by, say, 70 per cent and in the United States by only 40 per cent in any interval, the new equilibrium rate of exchange between the dollar and the sterling is reached if the value of the dollar, in terms of the sterling, rises in the ratio 170 to 140, i.e., 21.4 per cent. So long as the appreciation of the dollar is less than 21.4 per cent, so the argument runs, the United States continues as a cheap market for British buyers (importers) and as an unprofitable market for British sellers (exporters); hence the demand for dollars to pay for British imports will exceed the supply of dollars from British exports. This inequality will continue until the exchange rate raises the dollar to its equilibrium value in terms of the pound sterling.

Flaws in the Theory

The purchasing-power-parity theory thus has an absolute and a comparative formulation. Critical discussion of the theory during the past twenty years has shown that many factors other than the relative movement of price levels influence the demand for a country's exports and a country's demand for imports. Examples of such other factors are spontaneous shifts in the demand by one country for the products of the other; shifts in demand resulting from tariff changes; and a drastic change in a country's debtor-creditor position.

The purchasing-power-parity theory, then, in its comparative version, assumes that these other factors remain sufficiently constant to be disregarded. But in fact, they never are constant; consequently, calculations of the purchasing-power parity can never yield a completely accurate equilibrium rate of exchange. This does not mean, however, that purchasing-power-parity calculations are useless. General changes in prices in different countries relative to each other are important. When the changes are extensive, they are undoubtedly the *most* important single factor in influencing imports and exports and therefore in determining the equilibrium exchange rate. Calculation of the purchasing-power parity between two currencies, therefore, can at least

7. A. C. Pigou, "The Foreign Exchanges," *Quarterly Journal of Economics*, 1922, p. 64.

enable us to discover the range within which the equilibrium rate of exchange is likely to lie. In any case, no other method gives concrete results.[8]

Calculation of Purchasing-Power Parity

Theoretically, the base period against which the movement of relative price levels and changes in exchange rates are measured should be one in which the actual exchange rate reflects the equilibrium rate. In practice, this condition cannot be fully met, so that purchasing-power-parity calculations are necessarily subject to further error.

Special difficulties arise if the problem is to calculate the purchasing-power parity during or immediately after a war. These difficulties are the result of temporarily dislocated production and of price control and rationing. Purchasing-power parity calculated from controlled prices obviously cannot reveal what the equilibrium rate of exchange would be if the controls were removed. If Great Britain were to abolish price control and rationing as well as foreign exchange controls, the effect would be a rise in domestic prices and a heavy demand for imports. Almost certainly the pound sterling would sharply depreciate. The exchange rate that would bring Great Britain's balance of payments into equilibrium under such circumstances would certainly be much lower in terms of other currencies than the rate corresponding to the purchasing-power parity calculated from controlled prices. Later, when British industry had converted to peacetime production and built up exports, domestic prices would fall and the pound sterling would rise again. By retaining controls, Great Britain can avoid an extravagant fall in the exchange value of the pound. The equilibrium

8. Any attempt to calculate purchasing-power parities must first settle on the price index to be used. None of the existing price indexes is altogether satisfactory for the purpose. The cost of living index is too heavily weighted with the prices of commodities and services (such as house rents) that never enter into international trade. Thus the cost of living index may rise more in one country than in another without appreciable influence on exports and imports and therefore on foreign exchange rates. The wholesale price indexes, on the other hand, are often heavily weighted with the prices of internationally traded goods. They are thus likely ". . . to understate any existing over- or undervaluation of the currency, because internationally traded goods adjust themselves quickly between different countries." (Gottfried Haberler, "The Choice of Exchange Rates After the War," *American Economic Review,* June 1945, pp. 311–12.) This disadvantage of wholesale indexes for determining purchasing-power parities is currently less serious when there is no world market but only separate national markets. Of the available alternatives, the wholesale price index, although open to objections, appears the most useful for determining which currencies are at present overvalued and which undervalued.

rate after reconversion would probably be nearer the rate calculated from the purchasing-power parity before reconversion than the rate that would establish itself during reconversion.

Accordingly, purchasing-power-parity calculations based on, say, early 1946 prices cannot reveal correct equilibrium rates of exchange. In adjusting the external values of their currencies, most countries must rely largely on the trial and error method. If, however, very large discrepancies between the relative movements of national price levels during the war are found together with exchange rates that have remained fixed or changed little, an overvaluation or undervaluation of the currencies concerned is clearly indicated. Comparison of the relative movements of price levels will at least show what direction the revision of exchange rates must take. The exact extent of the adjustment will have to be determined largely by trial and error. In order to determine in general which currencies are overvalued and which undervalued, the price level changes in various countries between 1939 and 1945 may be compared with the simultaneous changes in the exchange value of the currencies of these countries.

PRICE LEVELS AND EXCHANGE RATES

Currency Inflation Countries

The countries of the world can be roughly grouped at present according to the degree of inflation experienced. Extreme cases of inflation, for example, are China, Hungary and Greece.

Inflation in Hungary (as this is written) has reached astronomical heights. There are no "official" exchange rates or reliable indexes of internal prices. But conditions are undoubtedly disastrous.

According to the London *Economist*,[9] the Chairman of the Hongkong and Shanghai Banking Corporation stated that the index for wholesale prices of domestic commodities in Chungking in March 1945 was more than 1,200 times its 1937 level. According to the same source, the official exchange rate for the Chinese dollar in March 1945 was three English pence. A 50 per cent discount was conceded on this rate for certain foreign remittances, giving a rate of 160 Chinese dollars to the pound or about 40 Chinese dollars to the American dollar (as against 3.37 in 1937 and 13.43 in June 1939).

9. June 23, 1945, p. 861.

The official foreign exchange market under these circumstances had little meaning. As has been said:

. . . Only a nominal amount of business passes through it. The real market is the outside market, where U.S. dollar notes and gold changes hands at widely varying but huge premiums over the nominal official parity. In consequence, the Hongkong and Shanghai Bank, which at Chungking is an "approved" bank for exchange control and consequently must deal at official rates, has been virtually debarred from any exchange business.[10]

Clearly, the Chinese dollar, which by mid-1945 had officially depreciated only to about one third its value in June 1939 — while prices on the average had risen more than a thousand times — is vastly overvalued at the official rate. Here there could be no argument.

In Greece, by November 1944, inflation had pushed the note circulation to 2.5 quintillion drachmas. At that point, a currency reform established one new drachma as equal to 50 billion old drachmas. The same reform decree set the sterling rate at 600 dr. (the rate for computing the pay of English troops is 500 dr.) and the rate for the gold pound at 2,400 dr.[11] Yet the Greek government was unable to stop the inflation. Not long after the November 1944 currency reform, the government was forced to raise its quotations for the gold pound; and in the unofficial markets, the quotations for the gold pound have been ten times as high as the official quotations. By June 1945 the government was forced to carry out a new devaluation of the drachma, fixing it at 2,000 dr. to the paper pound and 4,000 dr. to the gold pound.[12] As the quotations for the gold pound in the unofficial market are several times as high as the official rate for the gold pound, the official gold price obviously overvalues the drachma. Moreover, the Greek government still continued to finance its budget deficit by printing more money. Further revaluations appear to be unavoidable.

More Moderate Examples

Not only China and Greece have overvalued currencies. Currency inflation in the postwar interval is all too common, even though in other countries the degree of inflation is not of these astronomical proportions. France and the middle eastern countries are examples of more moderate inflation. By the middle of 1945, controlled prices in France

10. *Ibid.*, p. 361.
11. *Ibid.*, June 2, 1945, p. 742.
12. *Ibid.*, June 9, 1945, p. 780.

were two and a half times the 1939 level; and in the highly developed black market, prices were frequently several times higher. Wages rose over the same period by about 230 per cent, whereas in Great Britain they rose only 50 per cent.[13] The then official exchange rate, however, was two American cents for a French franc as against 2.65 cents in June 1939, representing a depreciation of only 23 per cent. Even though it is impossible to gauge the true equilibrium rate of the French franc, the franc was clearly overvalued in the middle of 1945. This overvaluation was partially recognized by the French government when it depreciated the franc in December 1945 from 2 cents to .84 cents for one franc.

Other clear cases of overvaluation are found in the Middle East and India. Wholesale prices in the spring of 1945, compared with the first half of 1939, were three times as high in India, more than four and a half times as high in Iran (here the cost of living index was almost eight times as high), and more than three times as high in Egypt. These increases compared with a rise in wholesale prices of only about 40 per cent in the United States and 80 per cent in England. Nevertheless, the exchange rate between the pound sterling and the Indian rupee, and the pound sterling and the Egyptian pound remained unchanged; the adjustment that took place between the Iranian rial and the pound sterling or the dollar does not recognize the relative price movements in the respective countries. The adjustments of the Indian rupee and the Egyptian pound vis-à-vis the dollar merely reflect the adjustment between the pound sterling and the dollar.

Borderline Cases

In such countries as Great Britain, the British Dominions, Belgium, the Scandinavian countries and some South American countries, the course of price movements relative to exchange rates makes it uncertain in many cases whether their currencies are overvalued or undervalued in terms of the American dollar. The cost of living index in some of these countries has risen less, in others more, than the cost of living index in the United States, but the differences do not justify any firm conclusions. Discrepancies between their corresponding wholesale price indexes are, in general, considerably larger, as shown in Table 23.

13. *Ibid.*, August 18, 1945, p. 237.

TABLE 23

EXCHANGE RATES AND PRICE LEVELS OF SELECTED COUNTRIES,
1939 AND MIDDLE OF 1945

(*Indexes: First Half of 1939 = 100*)

Country	Exchange Rates (*Official*) (*Value of Country's Currency Unit in U.S. Cents*)		*Wholesale Price Index in June 1945*	*Cost of Living Index in June 1945*
	June 1939	*June 1945*		
(*In Cents*)				
United States	—	—	139[a]	130[a]
Great Britain	468.2	403.5	175[b]	133[b]
Union of South Africa	463.3	398.0	159	133
Australia	373.1	322.8	140	123
New Zealand	374.6	324.4	150	101[c]
Canada	99.77	90.91	141	120
Egypt	480.2	413.8	323	283
India	34.92	30.12	300[d]	238
Iran	5.82	3.077	477	792[e]
Argentina				
Official exchange rate	31.22	29.77⎞	212	134
Free-exchange rate	23.15	24.88⎠		
Chile				
Official exchange rate	5.17	5.16⎤		
Free-exchange rate	2.98	3.23⎬	218	234
Export rate	4.00	4.00⎦		
Mexico	19.75	20.58	200	210
Belgium	3.40	2.28	f	f
Denmark	20.90	21.01	194	159
Norway	23.52	20.16	183	156
Sweden	24.11	23.84	180	143
France	2.65	2.00	250[g]	f
Italy	5.26	1.00[h]	f	f
Germany	40.10	10.00[h]	i	i
Japan	27.28	6.66[h]	j	j

Source: Monthly Bulletin of Statistics, League of Nations, Geneva, September 1945, pp. 301–05, and later issues; and *Statistical Year-Book of the League of Nations, 1941–42,* League of Nations, Geneva, 1942.II.A.8, pp. 188 ff.

a. Bureau of Labor Statistics index.

b. Board of Trade index.

c. New wartime index on the basis December 1942 = 100; old index at that date (on the basis of the first half of 1939 = 100) was 112.

d. April 1945.

Wholesale price indexes suggest that the pound sterling may be overvalued. The currencies of Argentina, Chile and Mexico may also be overvalued.[14] Because of the different conclusions suggested by the wholesale price and cost of living indexes respectively, and in view of the wide margin of error inevitably attaching to any purchasing-power-parity calculation, the question of overvaluation or undervaluation of their currencies in terms of the dollar cannot be decided for countries like Great Britain, Argentina, Chile and Mexico. Present exchange rates may reflect purchasing-power parity as calculated on the basis of rationing and controlled prices. But if price control and rationing were dropped and exchange markets put on a supply-demand basis, many currencies would change in relation to the dollar. In this sense these currencies are overvalued. In the longer run, when domestic production and export capacity have been restored, present exchange rates may not be out of line. But whether the present exchange rates between these countries and the United States will even approximately reflect equilibrium rates over the longer term cannot possibly be determined now.

The Defeated Nations

A final group of countries consists of the former Axis countries. For these, no official exchange rates are quoted except for computing the pay of the occupying forces. Economic disorganization and confusion are so acute in Germany and Japan, however, that it is futile to compare price levels and exchange rates. The same applies to southeastern European countries.

The facts as briefly reviewed show clearly that many postwar exchange rates in 1946 were definitely out of line with the reality of the price situation; that in many countries the question of whether their

14. This is true for Mexico even on the basis of the cost of living index.

Footnotes to Table 23 (*Contd.*)
    e. October 1944.
    f. Not available.
    g. December 1944. Provisional index number of regulated wholesale prices, published by the "Statistique Générale de France."
    h. For purposes of computing pay of occupying troops.
    i. Last wholesale index (November 1944) was 111; last cost of living index (December 1944), 112.
    j. Last wholesale index (October 1944) was 165; last cost of living index (November 1944), 161.

currencies were overvalued or undervalued cannot be decided; and that for former enemy countries it makes no sense even to pose the question. As most national price levels are not likely to remain unchanged, whatever exchange rates may have appeared "reasonable" in 1946 may well be absurd in 1947.

ADJUSTMENTS OF EXCHANGE RATES

Where currencies are clearly overvalued, the question arises whether any attempt should be made to adjust the exchange rates *during* the transition period while foreign exchange control or import licensing still prevails. The nature of the problem can best be seen by examining the French case before the devaluation of the franc in December 1945. If, as is highly probable, the devaluation left the franc still overvalued, the analysis is no less useful.

Effects of Overvaluation

The advantage of an overvalued currency consists in the more favorable terms of trade obtainable. A country with an overvalued currency can obtain a given volume of imports in exchange for a smaller volume of exports than if its currency were not overvalued. This was not an important factor for France in 1945 because the bulk of its imports was financed either by its own dollar balances, by American loans or by the credit the British government put at its disposal in the payments agreement between them concluded early in 1945. Although France gave the same amount of credit to Great Britain in this agreement, it was France that made use of the British credit, not Great Britain of the French credit. The movement of commodities was almost exclusively from Great Britain to France.

The overvaluation of the French franc, however, was partly responsible for the slow revival of French export trade. Some French commodities, such as perfumes, undoubtedly could be exported even at the exchange rate of two American cents for one franc. Others, such as iron ore, the French government had to subsidize in order to make their export profitable.

The danger of the overvaluation of the French franc was, and still is, that it hinders the development of export industries during the reconstruction period. These are essential if France is ever to return to a free-exchange market. To be sure, as long as the French price and wage structure is still changing rapidly, any exchange rate that may be set is likely to be unstable. Several successive adjustments may have to be made.

France is only one example among many available. All countries that have to develop their export capacity to finance their imports have an interest in keeping the external values of their currencies in line with relative price movements. Overvaluation retards the development of export industries. The retention of foreign exchange control or import licensing, therefore, does not eliminate the necessity for harmonizing price levels at home and abroad through exchange rate adjustments. If price levels in the other countries do not all move in step, adjustments may sometimes be required in the country's exchange rates vis-à-vis only one or a few, but not all, other countries. For instance, a rise in the exchange rate between the pound sterling and the Indian and Egyptian currencies may be required, whereas the exchange rate between the pound sterling and the dollar may be quite satisfactory.

Adjustments Cannot Be Permanent

The structure of exchange rates connecting the various currencies cannot be settled once and for all. Even if, at the start of the operations of the International Monetary Fund, all existing exchange rates were thoroughly overhauled, the new structure would be unlikely to endure.[15] More than one adjustment of the exchange rate will probably be necessary because the national price levels are not likely to move parallel to one another. In some countries, such as China, and in many European countries, Hungary for instance, inflation is proceeding at a rapid though not identical rate. In the United States and Great Britain the inflation potential is considerable, owing to the pressure from wage increases, to the spending of accumulated consumer balances and (in the United States) to the spending of dollar balances by foreign countries. The degree of inflation to be expected in the United States

15. According to the Bretton Woods Fund Agreement, the initial determination of par value is based on the rates prevailing sixty days before the entry into force of the agreement (except for those countries whose territory was occupied by the enemy). However, the member can notify the Fund or the Fund can notify the member that it regards this par value as unsatisfactory. The Fund and member shall then agree upon a suitable par value for the currency.

and Great Britain, however, is much less than in some European countries.

Inflationary vs. Deflationary Tendencies

There is another group of countries in which deflationary tendencies could easily develop. The wartime inflation in some of the countries holding large sterling balances was intimately connected with their accumulation. In India, Egypt and Iran the governments financed local military expenditures with additional currency created for the purpose, against the asset of newly acquired sterling balances in London. In so far as these sterling balances are liquidated, the opposite process may take place. If the governments sell the balances to private importers against national currency, local currency will be withdrawn from circulation unless the government decides to spend a corresponding amount at home, or unless additional private borrowing occurs.

In short, parallel movements of national price levels are not immediately in prospect. Rather, the outlook is definitely for inflation proceeding at different rates in different countries. The International Monetary Fund will operate in circumstances very much like those of the first six years after World War I, when inflation swept most European countries, and it will probably be obliged to adjust the world's exchange rate structure more than once. An orderly adjustment will probably be facilitated by the Fund's existence.[16]

THE INTERNATIONAL MONETARY FUND

We have identified the post-transition period with the time when a large part of the world is again engaged in multilateral trade, and free-exchange markets have been re-established. No one knows when that will be. The fact, however, that the Bretton Woods Fund Agreement aims, in principle, at multilateralism and free-exchange markets

16. Because of the danger of inflation the International Monetary Fund may start its voyage in a rough sea. It may begin its operations in a state of "fundamental disequilibrium." The Fund aims, in principle, at stable exchange rates. It cannot fulfill this task so long as inflation rages in the member countries. It is unfortunate that this particular aim of stable exchange rates has been so much stressed in public discussions of the Bretton Woods scheme. If the Fund, as is likely, has to adjust exchange rates frequently, it runs some risk of being discredited in the public eye before it can really fulfill its main function, that is, to provide a satisfactory international monetary mechanism for "normal" conditions, conditions expected to prevail when the unhappy inheritance from the war has been largely liquidated.

requires that the plan be discussed on the assumption that these will some day again be the rule.

POSSIBLE SOLUTIONS OF THE MONETARY PROBLEM

In the interwar period three main methods were used to achieve equilibrium in the balance of payments: changes in domestic prices and incomes (under the gold standard); foreign exchange control; and adjustments of exchange rates. The last method was very effectively used by Great Britain in the 1930's. Great Britain, as keeper of the international currency reserves for a bloc of countries tied to the pound sterling, regulated the value of the pound sterling vis-à-vis non-bloc countries with the aid of a stabilization fund, and managed successfully to insulate its economy against shocks originating from short-term capital transfers from or to Great Britain.

The strong opposition of many countries to the gold standard precluded its early reintroduction after World War II. Most countries were unwilling to subject their domestic monetary policy to control by an automatic mechanism that might bring about deflation and domestic unemployment whenever a negative balance of payments led to a substantial loss of gold. Nor could foreign exchange control be regarded as a desirable system. If all countries used foreign exchange control, the result would almost inevitably be bilateral trade arrangements between pairs of countries. International trade would no longer flow in the channels indicated by comparative advantage. Big countries, in so far as they are important markets for small countries, would be able to turn the terms of trade in their favor, and political power would become a dominant factor in international trade, as was the case with Germany in the 1930's.

While the gold standard and foreign exchange control, therefore, could not seriously be considered as possible long-run, permanent international monetary systems after World War II, an extension of the British system was definitely within the realm of possibility. The United States and Great Britain, each as the financial center of a number of "satellite" countries, could have regulated the dollar-sterling exchange rates by close cooperation between their respective stabilization funds. The two most important trading countries would then have been responsible for regulating the exchange rate between the two currencies that dominate world trade. This type of arrangement, usually referred to as the "key currency approach," was advocated by Professor John H. Williams.[17] It is now unnecessary to discuss the merits and demerits of the "key currency approach." The Bretton Woods Conference actually adopted an alternative plan, which in principle gave no priority of position to currencies of particular countries. Within the framework of the Bretton Woods plan close cooperation may well develop in practice between the United States and Great Britain; many countries may voluntarily decide to tie their currencies either to the dollar or to the pound sterling. An arrangement of this kind would almost certainly facilitate the administration of the Fund.

The Bretton Woods Fund Agreement clearly reveals that its draftsmen were guided by the experience of the monetary confusion of the 1930's. Their aim was to avoid such difficulties as the post-1929 flights of capital, competitive currency depreciation, exchange control and bilateral agreements.

Hybrid System

The agreement is, in fact, a compromise among the various monetary systems that existed during the interwar period. More nearly than anything else it envisages a world similar to that of the 1930's, and it attempts to solve the problems of international monetary relations by retaining some feature of almost every monetary system then in effect. The Bretton Woods Fund Agreement favors stable foreign exchange rates without, however, excluding the possibility of devaluation; it favors a multilateral trading and clearing system without entirely excluding foreign exchange control; it retains gold as part of the international currency supply without giving gold the role it had under the gold standard. It is a hybrid system.

THE ROLE OF GOLD IN THE FUND

Although the reintroduction of the gold standard was out of the question, there seemed to be little sense in casting out gold altogether. Gold is a convenient medium for settling international accounts, and the interests of the United States as owner of a huge gold stock, and of South Africa and other gold-producing countries, are opposed to

17. *Post-War Monetary Plans and Other Essays*, Knopf, New York, 1944, Pt. I.

the complete demonetization of gold. It therefore still plays a role in the Bretton Woods scheme.

The quotas of the member countries must be paid partly in gold. Gold serves as the common denominator for calculating the par value of the currency of each member (Article IV, Section 1) ; and gold is retained as an international medium of exchange for settling international transactions (Article IV, Section 4b). The international currency at the disposal of any country thus is equal to that country's quota in the Fund, plus its own gold stock, plus such foreign balances as it holds outside the Fund in countries whose currencies are freely convertible into other currencies and are customarily accepted in the settlement of international accounts. The total quantity of international currency will therefore exceed the amount existing before the war by the increase in the world's monetary gold stock since 1939 (minus whatever amount is actually paid on quota subscription to the Fund), and if all countries join, by the $8.8 billion of quotas in the Fund. In addition, foreign short-term balances in the United States, which can also be used for international payments, have increased by $4.4 billion since 1939. The total increase in all three forms must initially amount to nearly $17 billion. (See Table 21, p. 111.)

ADJUSTMENT THROUGH EXCHANGE RATE CHANGES

Although the Fund plan retains gold as a medium of international payments, inflows and outflows of gold are no longer to govern domestic monetary policy. The new mechanism for adjusting balances of payments relies on currency devaluations and foreign exchange control instead of deflation and inflation of income and price levels.

The Problem of "Fundamental Disequilibrium"

Under the Bretton Woods plan each member country is free to pursue any domestic monetary policy it may desire. If the domestic policy brings about a "fundamental disequilibrium" in the balance of payments, the member may propose a change in the par value of its currency. The term "fundamental disequilibrium" is not defined in the agreement and may be expected to lead to lively controversies. As already defined (pp. 132–33), a "fundamental disequilibrium" exists for any country when it is experiencing a sustained outflow of gold, a sustained decline in balances owned abroad or a sustained accumulation of balances by foreigners. If the Fund is in operation, such an accumulation of balances by foreigners would be replaced by an accumulation of the country's currency in the Fund. Such an accumulation amounts to a credit given by the Fund to the country with the negative balance of payments, inasmuch as the Fund provides the country with foreign currencies by accepting in exchange additional balances in that particular country. (Actually, the country whose currencies in the Fund decrease provides the credit to the country with the negative balance of payments.)

Because the accumulation of a country's currency in the Fund signifies a short-term capital movement *into* that country, the Bretton Woods scheme quite logically requires that the country should pay interest on its balances in the Fund, if they exceed a certain limit or increase too rapidly. (Article V, Section 8.)

A country in "fundamental disequilibrium" has the unrestricted right to devalue its currency on its own initiative within the limit of 10 per cent of its initial par value, and to devalue with the concurrence of the Fund beyond this 10 per cent limit. (Article IV, Section 5c.) The Fund shall concur when it is satisfied that the devaluation is necessary to correct a fundamental disequilibrium, no matter whether the disequilibrium originated outside the country or resulted from the economic policy of that country itself.[18] Much depends, therefore, on the interpretation the Fund gives to the term "fundamental disequilibrium."[19]

In the event of a sustained drain on a country's currency in the Fund,

18. The Fund "shall not object to a proposed change because of the domestic social or political policies of the member proposing the change." (Article IV, Section 5f.)

19. An example may serve to show the appropriateness of our earlier definition of the term "fundamental disequilibrium." (See text, pp. 132–33.) Let us imagine a country in a situation similar to that of Great Britain in the period 1925–1930. Britain's balance of payments was roughly in equilibrium; yet the alleged overvaluation of the pound has often been held responsible for a high level of domestic unemployment. If the concept of "fundamental disequilibrium" is linked with the employment situation, as some writers have suggested, a country in a situation like that of Great Britain in the late 1920's would have the right to propose, and the Fund could not object to, a devaluation of its currency. This means that a country in which unemployment exists would be allowed to devalue for the purpose of increasing its exports; a "beggar-my-neighbor" policy would be sanctioned in this case by the Bretton Woods Fund Agreement. If our definition of a "fundamental disequilibrium" is accepted, however, this possibility is excluded; the country could propose such a devaluation only if it was following an expansionist monetary policy at home in order to overcome unemployment, and if this policy had led to a negative balance of payments and thus to a sustained gold outflow and/or to an accumulation of the country's currency in the Fund.

Foreign Exchange Rates   149

which is the reverse of the situation just discussed, an appreciation of
the country's currency would be logical. Although there is nothing in
the Bretton Woods Fund Agreement to prevent a country from proposing, and the Fund from accepting, such a change, proposals for
the appreciation of a country's currency are not likely, since such action tends to reduce exports. The agreement proposes to deal with
these situations in a different way: the Fund may declare the currency of the country concerned "scarce"; that is, it may propose foreign exchange control against a country whose currency tends to disappear from the Fund. The burden of adjusting balances of payments is
thus borne partly by the countries with the negative balances, and
partly by the country whose currency is declared scarce.

ADJUSTMENT THROUGH FOREIGN EXCHANGE CONTROL

Probably because one of the main reasons for disturbances in the
balances of payments during the 1930's was the flight of capital from
country to country, the Fund plan permits members to control capital
transactions. A member is not permitted, as a rule, to use the Fund's
resources to meet a large outflow of capital, and the Fund may request
a member to exercise control of capital transactions to prevent such
use of the Fund's resources. (Article VI.)

If, despite all the provisions in the Bretton Woods Fund Agreement
for dealing with disequilibrium in the balance of payments, a country's
currency in the Fund should be nearly exhausted, the Fund may, as
was pointed out above, declare this currency "scarce." The Fund will
then apportion the scarce currency "with due regard to the relative
needs of members, the general international economic situation and
any other pertinent considerations." (Article VII, Section 3a.) And
members of the Fund are, after consultation with the Fund, entitled
to introduce foreign exchange control for the scarce currency.

Implications of Control of Capital Movements

The scarce-currency provision and the provisions relating to the
control of capital movements may have far-reaching implications.
How capital movements can be controlled without simultaneously
controlling transactions on current account is far from obvious. If
foreign exchange control is to be exercised for capital movements, the
control of the sale and purchase of foreign exchange must be central-

ized. Each applicant for foreign exchange will be obliged to state the purpose for which he requires it. Also, exporters will have to declare the proceeds from their exports and offer them for sale to the central authority. If traders are not under such obligations, either they may leave the export proceeds abroad — thus in effect making a capital export on their own account — or, if they need domestic funds currently, they may sell the proceeds against domestic currency to others who wish to make a capital export. In order to prevent capital exports, therefore, all foreign exchange will have to be offered to, and bought from, a central authority. Experience with foreign exchange control in the 1930's has shown, however, that the rule requiring all recipients of foreign exchange to sell it to an official agency is not easily enforced, especially without a licensing system for exports. Unless the government imposes some system that will provide it with complete information about visible and invisible exports, it cannot prevent capital exports. Control of capital movements thus probably requires complete registration of all transactions involving foreign exchange. Once such a system of registration is established there is a temptation to use it for other purposes than the control of capital movements — for example, to control the import of commodities.

In times of strain on the balance of payments, this temptation may become quite irresistible. In short, the control of capital movements may easily lead to the control of current transactions as well.

Other Consequences of Foreign Exchange Control

Nowadays, capital movements are partly motivated by political considerations. The greater the political instability within and between countries, the greater is the desire to transfer funds to what are considered the safest havens. But short-term capital movements are also influenced by expectations about the future course of exchange rates. And here the Bretton Woods Fund plan provides a stimulus of its own. Under the plan, devaluation is recognized as the normal and accepted method of dealing with a sustained drain on a country's reserves of international currency. Potential speculators may now expect devaluation to follow such a foreign drain with greater certainty than in the past. Accordingly, if a country's currency is accumulating in the Fund, it will be taken as a sign that the country is likely soon to propose a devaluation. Speculators will then have an incentive to purchase

foreign currency, and exporters will prefer to leave their export proceeds abroad until the devaluation has actually taken place. Because
of the possibility of politically and speculatively motivated short-term
capital movements, their control was naturally made an integral part
of the new plan. Yet, necessary as the control may be within the plan,
it may have unfortunate consequences not originally intended.

A further consequence of the foreign exchange control provision,
and of the devaluation provisions of the Bretton Woods plan, is that
they may diminish the incentive or willingness of private investors to
make long-term investments abroad. The twin dangers that the repatriation of their capital may become impossible if the debtor country introduces foreign exchange control or that, where the loan is
contracted in the debtor's currency, losses on foreign investments will
be incurred if the currency of the debtor country is devalued together
make private long-term investment in foreign countries less appealing. (Conceivably, of course, worse conditions might prevail in the
absence of the Fund.) The bulk of long-term foreign lending may have
to be either direct government lending or private lending with a government guarantee. Government loans, or even private loans with a
government guarantee, are always in some measure acts of state and
never wholly free of political considerations. National policy and
foreign lending may therefore become more closely linked under the
Bretton Woods arrangements than they have been in the past. (These
matters are considered at greater length in Chapter 9.)

CONDITIONS FOR SUCCESSFUL OPERATION

Any international monetary system can work satisfactorily only if
the international accounts of the participating countries are approximately in equilibrium. The purpose of a formalized international
monetary mechanism can be only to help a country overcome temporary deficits in its balance of payments. No country can expect subsidies over a long period from the other countries in the system. Unless
reasonable equilibrium in international accounts is established and
maintained, the "escape" provisions of the Bretton Woods plan (devaluation, scarce-currency provisions) will have to be evoked too
frequently, with the result that the whole plan may fail to limit fluctuations in exchange rates and will be permanently discredited.

We have already stressed that one should expect neither stable exchange rates nor free-exchange markets in the immediate future. The Fund cannot hope to attain its main objective in the transition period. Its ability to achieve its purposes in the more distant future will depend mainly on two conditions.

Ensuring an Adequate Supply of Dollars

First, the United States, after making the foreign loans that are envisaged for the near future, must allow for an import surplus large enough to prevent a chronic shortage of dollars.[20] American imports are largely dependent on the general state of domestic economic activity. Thus the dollar supply in the exchange market is heavily contingent upon the future trend of national income in the United States. It depends, also, on American commercial policy. Obstacles to the import of commodities should as far as possible be removed. And, as the United States is unlikely to reduce its tariff unilaterally, the Bretton Woods Fund Agreement needs to be supplemented by an international conference and agreement on tariff reductions, the removal of quotas, etc. Such a conference of the United Nations, at which it is proposed to work out a trade charter, is indeed planned for 1947.

Preventing Circumvention of Fund Provisions

Other reasons reinforce the need for a trade charter. There are many ways in which a country, complying with the provisions of the Fund Agreement, can formally avoid foreign exchange control for current transactions but yet retain its essence. For instance, instead of regulating the allotments of foreign exchange to imports, a country can license imports. In this way it can achieve the same result as it would have achieved by foreign exchange control. If the purpose of the agreement is not to be defeated, the trade charter of the United Nations should make it virtually impossible for the member nations to circumvent its provisions on foreign exchange control by these or other methods.

Avoiding Depression

Second, it is improbable that the Fund can survive a major world depression like that after 1929. Under the pressure of a severe depres-

20. The Department of Commerce has shown in *The United States in the World Economy* (Bureau of Foreign and Domestic Commerce, 1943) that much of the interwar period was characterized by a shortage of dollars. See also text, Chapter 9.

sion, countries are apt to set aside all considerations of international cooperation and to adopt a wholly self-regarding attitude, as was clearly evident in the early 1930's. The Fund plan does not provide any sanctions that would enable the Fund to prevent a member from withdrawing from the Fund, if that member considered it was in its national interest to do so. The United States as the paramount economic power in the world, and the largest market for the exports of many foreign countries, perhaps carries the major responsibility for avoiding another world-wide depression. If the United States succeeds, through appropriate "full-employment" policies, in avoiding a great domestic depression, the chances that the Bretton Woods plan will function satisfactorily will be greatly enhanced.

Rules of Conduct and Behavior

Finally, how successful any compromise such as the Bretton Woods plan can ever be in practice depends largely on the men in charge, and on the whole spirit pervading the organization. The Fund plan is as yet only in the preliminary stage. After a few years of actual operation, rules of conduct will probably develop that cannot at present be foreseen. Certain practices may well evolve into a code of "proper" behavior. The functioning of the plan will, moreover, differ according to whether the United States and Great Britain do or do not cooperate closely, and whether the small countries do or do not follow their lead. Actual practice may be quite different from anything one can at present infer from the documents.

Chapter 7

CONTEMPORARY INTERNATIONAL LENDING

THE BRETTON WOODS Agreements are intended to create conditions for a revival of world trade. The Fund Agreement allows the member countries to control short-term capital movements that might disrupt foreign exchange rates and thus hamper international transactions. The Bretton Woods Agreements also provide for an "International Bank for Reconstruction and Development," to promote beneficial international investment. The Bank and the Fund are to work in harmony.

In the immediate future the demand for foreign capital will come from countries whose productive capacity has suffered from the war; such countries require imports before they can pay for them with current exports. In the longer run, the industrialization of low-income areas will be the main purpose of international investment. As the United States will be the main source of loan funds, the problem of international lending is of special importance to the American economy.

Present-day theories of international investment differ substantially from what was nearly universal only two decades ago. The emphasis is now much more on the probable effect on employment of both short-term capital movements and long-term lending — a projection of depression experience into postwar thinking. To be sure, prospective borrowing and lending countries do not see the employment problem in relation to foreign investment from quite the same point of view. But the responsibility for employment and national income that governments now bear makes it certain that foreign investment will come more and more under their direct jurisdiction. Unlike, say, twenty years ago, foreign investment must now be integrated with national economic policy as a whole. But governments in their foreign relations cannot completely separate economic and foreign policy. The two intertwine. Consequently, foreign investment in the years ahead is likely to be more tinged with political considerations because it bears upon home employment, and because it involves relations with other countries.[1]

This chapter examines the problem of foreign investment from the point of view of prospective lenders, while Chapter 8 approaches the problem from the borrowers' side. Chapter 9 considers these together, with particular reference to the problems confronting the United States.

THE PATTERN OF INTERNATIONAL DEBT: 1938–1945

Net creditor countries have been few, net debtors many. On long-term account, Great Britain has been the largest international creditor since the Industrial Revolution. Since the French Revolution, it has been the chief banker for international commerce. (Cf. Chapter 2.) Although France, Germany and the Netherlands were important creditors in 1914, their long-term investments combined were not so large as Great Britain's when World War I began, and France and Germany emerged from World War I with their investments greatly depleted. During World War I, Great Britain suffered some reduction of its creditor status and the United States shifted from a debtor to a creditor position. Yet, despite heavy foreign investment by the United States during the 1920's, Great Britain in 1929 was still the largest long-term creditor.

Between 1938 and 1944 there appears to have been a disappearance of long-term international investments of about $24 billion, a tremendous sum. Much of this was a "buying back" by debtor countries of securities held by creditors abroad in 1938. The virtual disappearance of Germany and France from the list of long-term creditor countries is indicative of their economic decline.

The distribution among the principal creditors of long-term international investment in millions of current dollars, according to the best estimates available, is shown in Table 24. These are par- or face-

1. National governments in the past have sometimes tried to influence foreign investment. Prior to 1914 the French foreign office tried to influence the direction of French investments abroad, and partly succeeded, notably in the case of Russia. (Cf. Eugene Staley, *War and the Private Investor,* Doubleday, New York, 1935.) Similarly, American foreign investments during the 1920's required formal assertion by the State Department that proposed loans were "unobjectionable" on political grounds. But there is a difference between trying to fix the direction of foreign investment — investment that would occur in any case — or stating that a particular loan raises no objections, and between a policy that openly links foreign lending with national economic policy and foreign policy as a whole.

TABLE 24

LONG-TERM INTERNATIONAL INVESTMENTS, 1914–1944

(*In Millions*)

Country	1914	1929	1938	1944
World total	$41,600+	$47,500	$52,828	$28,468
United States	2,500	14,700	11,491	11,400
Great Britain	19,500	18,200	22,910	13,968[a]
France	8,600	3,500	3,859	1,600
Germany	6,700	1,100	676	[b]
Netherlands	2,000	2,300	4,818	1,500
Switzerland	1,300	2,000	1,610	[b]
Other countries	1,000	5,700	7,464	[b]
World trade in current dollars	$40,598[c]	$68,619	$46,500	—

Source: For 1914 and 1929, Eugene Staley, *War and the Private Investor*, Doubleday, New York, 1935, App. A; for 1938, Cleona Lewis, *Debtor and Creditor Countries: 1938, 1944*, The Brookings Institution, Washington, 1945, App.; for 1944, *ibid.*, Chap. 2. The American portfolio investments have been given a value of $2.5 billion *par value* instead of $1.7 billion *market value* reported in *ibid.*, p. 25, so that they are comparable with the earlier years. British investment holdings have been converted to dollars at $5 in 1938 and at $4 in 1944 to the pound. The British figure, moreover, is probably too large. (Cf. text, Chapter 5, pp. 108–09; also Arthur I. Bloomfield, *The British Balance of Payments Problem*, International Finance Section, Princeton University, Princeton, 1945, p. 8.) The figures for France and the Netherlands are exceedingly rough but are probably not overestimates.

a. The reduction of $9 billion in the dollar value of 1944 British holdings is partly the result of using a dollar conversion rate of $4 in 1944 as against $5 in 1938. The British White Paper (*Statistical Material Presented During the Washington Negotiations*, Cmd. 6707, 1945) states that the value of British holdings at the end of the war cannot be properly estimated. See text, Chapter 5, p. 108.

b. Not available.

c. 1913.

value figures for portfolio investments (shares, bonds, notes, etc.) and actual commitments, in so far as these can be ascertained, for direct investments.[2]

2. *The United States in the World Economy*, Department of Commerce, 1943, p. 101. The terms "portfolio investments" and "direct investments" approximately designate whether the initiative has come from the borrower or from the lender (investor). In the case of economically less developed countries, portfolio investments are likely to be government obligations. The distinguishing feature of direct investments is that they represent the results of American (or British, Dutch, Canadian, etc.) efforts to develop business opportunities outside the country. This may be done through a foreign subsidiary

TABLE 25

LONG-TERM POSITION OF THE PRINCIPAL DEBTOR COUNTRIES, 1938

(*In Billions*)

Debtor Country	Foreign Obligations			Foreign Investments
	Direct	Portfolio	Total	
Canada	$2.5	$4.1	$6.6	$1.9
Australia	.7	2.2	3.7[a]	.3
Argentina	2.6	.6	3.2	.04
India	1.3	1.5	2.8	—
Germany	.9	1.8	2.7	.7
China	1.8	.8	2.6	.8
Netherlands East Indies	1.7	.7	2.4	—
Brazil	.7	1.3	2.0	—
Mexico	.9	.9	1.8	.02
South Africa and Rhodesia	.8	.6	1.4	—
Chile	.9	.4	1.3	.02

Source: Cleona Lewis, *Debtor and Creditor Countries: 1938, 1944,* The Brookings Institution, Washington, 1945, p. 12.

a. The character of the remaining $800 million of Australian obligations has not been determined.

No comparable compilation for debtor countries appears to be available for 1914 and 1929. For 1938, however, Cleona Lewis has carefully compiled figures for the principal debtor countries on long-term account.[3] Canada was the largest debtor, with a total of $6.6 billion in gross foreign obligations in 1938. The figures thereafter scale down from $3.7 billion for Australia to $1.3 billion for Chile. The eleven leading debtor countries represented together $30.5 billion, or

corporation, through direct ownership of assets abroad (mines, plants, distribution facilities, etc.) or through merely an influential minority interest in a foreign enterprise. The choice of means depends on a variety of legal and tax considerations that need not be dealt with here. Direct investments have been defined (for the United States for example) as ". . . all foreign enterprises controlled by American corporations or individuals or in the management of which Americans have an important voice." (*Ibid.*) The figures in the table, therefore, are neither market values nor the capitalized earning power of investment commitments, with the exception of the French figure of $8.6 billion in 1914, which was capitalized from earnings estimates undertaken by Eugene Staley. Especially for 1914 and 1929, the figures given are imperfect but still, perhaps, the most reliable data available.

3. *Debtor and Creditor Countries: 1938, 1944,* The Brookings Institution, Washington, 1945.

55 per cent of an estimated world total of $55 billion in foreign in-
debtedness.[4] (See Table 25.)

Not only did the long-term international investment holdings of
Great Britain, France and, to a lesser extent, the United States decrease
during World War II, but, as pointed out in Chapter 4, World War II
also brought about an enormous increase in short-term indebtedness.
And, more important, the chief long-term creditors became the chief
short-term debtors.

According to an estimate by the Bank for International Settlements,
gross international short-term indebtedness shrank from approximately
70 billion Swiss francs in 1930 to 32 billion Swiss francs by the end of
1933. This is an American dollar equivalent of $13.6 billion and $7.9
billion respectively.[5] Apparently, no comparable global figures exist
for later years. For 1938, however, the gross short-term indebtedness
of the United States and Great Britain can be estimated at about $5.7
billion.[6]

The contrast between this prewar total gross dollar and sterling

4. Table 24 shows total world indebtedness at $52.8 billion when computed from the
side of the creditors. It is not possible to reconcile these figures except through omissions
on the one side or possible double counting on the other. Cf. *ibid.*

5. *Fourth Annual Report,* Bank for International Settlements, Basle, 1934, p. 27. The
conversions to dollars have been made at average annual rates of exchange ruling during
1930 and 1933 between the U.S. dollar and the Swiss franc. These rates were taken from
the *Statistical Abstract of the United States, 1936,* Bureau of the Census.

6. This figure of $5.7 billion is arrived at as follows: Total short-term liabilities to
foreigners of American banks at the end of 1938 are reported in the *Federal Reserve
Bulletin* at $1,996 million, or just short of $2 billion. The short-term balances to the
account of foreigners in London are stated to have been $3.7 billion in 1938 according
to the British White Paper (*Statistical Material Presented During the Washington Negotiations,* Cmd. 6707, 1945).

It is of interest to note the estimates of the *net* short-term debtor position of the United
States at selected dates. These are shown below:

*International Short-Term Debts and Assets of the United States**

(In Billions)

Year	Debts	Assets	Net Position
1919	$ .8	$ .5	$– .3
1930	2.7	2.0	– .7
1933	.5	1.1	.6
1939	3.3	.6	–2.7
1944 (September 30)	6.1	.5	–5.6

* 1919–1939 from *The United States in the World Economy,* p. 123; 1944 from Robert L. Sammons, "International Investment Position of the United States," *Foreign Commerce Weekly,* January 27, 1945, pp. 5 ff.

short-term indebtedness of $5.7 billion and the estimated $22.4 billion early in 1946 is indeed striking.[7]

Two important points therefore emerge.

First, although on long-term account gross the United States and Great Britain are the only two important creditor nations, each accumulated substantial short-term obligations to foreigners during World War II. British short-term obligations at £4 billion probably exceed the value of Britain's long-term investment holdings.[8] As already indicated, the United States at the end of September 1944 was also a net debtor nation. Thus, the two principal prewar creditor nations, the United States and Great Britain, were probably no longer net creditors at the end of World War II. Each of their accounts in the international ledger showed debit balances.

Second, the world total of long-term claims and obligations has been reduced by about $24 billion (see Table 24) while short-term claims have risen to $22.4 billion (an increase of $16.7 billion). This is a complete reversal of prewar relationships between long-term and short-term claims. In a world at peace such a complete reversal would only occur slowly over many decades. And national export capacities and import needs would gradually adapt to the changing debt structure. Six war years are certainly not time enough for patterns of domestic production to adjust to this completely changed pattern of international obligations. As this volume has frequently emphasized, the financial side and the real resources side of the international economy must function in reasonable harmony. But no structure of real resources is sufficiently flexible to adapt at once to the abrupt changes

7. The $22.4 billion estimate is obtained as follows: At the end of 1945 sterling short-term balances are reported at £4 billion. As of February 28, 1946, the total short-term dollar obligations of American banks to foreigners is stated to be $6.4 billion. Converting the pounds sterling at $4 produces a total of $22.4 billion at the end of February 1946 in combined dollar and sterling short-term balances. If we assume that, on the average, commodity prices were roughly 40 per cent higher at the end of 1945 than at the end of 1938, then, compared with the 1938 figure of $5.7 billion, the 1945 short-term balances in "real terms" stood at $16.0 billion, or nearly three times as large. But it is dollars and pounds that the United States and Great Britain must pay to their creditors, so that the $22.4 billion cannot be disregarded and the $16.0 billion figure substituted instead in the calculations.

We must remember that these are short-term liabilities only. For the United States there were long-term liabilities as well. See text, Table 20.

8. The British holdings of long-term investments at the end of the war are said not to be capable of accurate valuation. See British White Paper, Cmd. 6707 or text, Table 24 and Chapter 5, p. 108.

in international claims and obligations that occurred between 1939 and 1945.

One further point: A very large proportion of the large foreign short-term debts accumulated by both Great Britain and the United States during the war have been to the account of national governments. They are not private balances. They are in the hands of national governments and central banks. The long-term foreign investment holdings of the United States and Great Britain, on the other hand, are, for the most part, privately owned. Hence, there is the unique state of affairs that private citizens hold the claims against foreigners, while foreign governments hold the claims against the American and British economies.

WHY LEND ABROAD: THE CREDITOR VIEWPOINT

Existing international debtor-creditor obligations on long-term account are the residue of the only type of international investment operation that had acceptance during the 19th century and, perhaps, even down to 1929. This was investment on private capitalistic lines and was consistent with the assumptions, beliefs and ideology on which economic activity then rested.

But today the air is filled with new voices that, although they discuss international investment in much the same words and phrases, give new meanings and connotations to the old phraseology and ideas. In part, this is a consequence of the changes World War II wrought in world affairs. In a more fundamental sense, however, the shift in outlook, the reorientation of purposes, and the whole range of ancillary considerations that follows from them, have deeper explanations. The newer views on foreign investment are traceable to two principal sources: first, to the disappearance of that common ideology in political and economic affairs that served as a basis of international intercourse at least down to 1914; and second, to the responsibility that governments now shoulder for positive economic policy. It is particularly important to bear these changes constantly in mind in present-day discussions of international investment.

LIBERAL LAISSEZ FAIRE

Before the Great Depression the question "Why foreign investment?" would have sounded strange to American or British investors.

It was then axiomatic to most people that foreign investment, like any other, was undertaken because of the expected yield. Private persons endeavored to direct their investment funds into those undertakings in those countries that promised the highest yield. Foreign investment presented no special problem of motive.[9]

The private profit viewpoint in foreign investment has by no means disappeared. But it is no longer universal. The view that foreign investment provided merely one avenue along which the private pursuit of gain naturally moved was part and parcel of the general belief in the beneficence and efficacy of free private enterprise. It belonged with liberalism in the 19th century sense. It betokened a firm belief in private property and free contract; it was harmonious with the conviction that national governments should leave economic affairs to a system of markets and prices in which individuals sought their own private gain. In contrast with more recent views, there was an implicit denial that national governments, as such, had any responsibility for national income and employment. The denial was implicit rather than explicit because it was widely accepted that these matters would take care of themselves if left to the price and market system.

The broad social benefits of foreign investment motivated by the lure of private gain consisted in widening the area over which specialization and trade could function effectively. If division of labor in the national economy increased national output and welfare, then, so the formal argument ran, a world-wide division of labor would also augment national incomes. The development of natural resources abroad through foreign investment, motivated, to be sure, by private profits, would mean cheaper sources of supply whose benefits competition would pass on to consumers in the form of lower prices or in a greater variety of goods available. If the return from foreign investment was greater than from home investment, it was clear that people as a whole would gain. Foreign investment was the logical counterpart to international division of labor.[10] It was only a segment of the more basic

9. At least it requires no further elaboration at the formal level of analysis. A proper description of the historical process of 19th century foreign investment would have to include speculation and a spirit of adventure as playing a considerable, if unmeasurable, role.

10. From the perspective of the middle of the 20th century, it is quite remarkable the degree to which the theory of international trade and finance is an *English* theory. That is to say, the problems treated, the cases envisaged, and the manner of their presentation,

problem of relative costs and prices and the allocation of scarce labor
and capital between alternative uses in a manner to maximize the well-
being of consumers.

These earlier views on foreign investment, which were attacked
even in the 1920's, lost much of their vigor after 1929. On the one hand,
private investors found foreign commitments less attractive than a few
years earlier; defaults, repudiations and confiscations became distress-
ingly common as many borrowing countries suffered exchange difficulties or shifted their social and economic outlook farther to the left.
On the other hand, governments found there was an acute difference
between a steady flow of long-term capital in search of more attractive
yields and erratic capital movements inspired by fear. The more defaults and repudiations there were, the more insistently private holders
of capital sought safe havens for their funds.

FLIGHT CAPITAL VS. THE GENERAL WELFARE

The virtual cessation of fresh foreign lending on private long-term
account after 1929, and the rush to liquidate previous long- and short-
term commitments abroad, precipitated governments into what previously had been largely a private affair — at least on the lenders' side
— between lenders and borrowers in different countries. Here, as in
so many other instances after 1929, events maneuvered governments
into a position of economic control and responsibility for which they
had no inherited taste.

Troublemaking Capital Movements

A sudden outflow or inflow of capital that is large relative to the
volume of other transactions — principally commodity and service
transactions — will seriously disturb the exchange rate and upset domestic economic activity. Not all capital movements, however, are
bound to cause trouble. A small capital movement can be absorbed
quickly without disturbance. And even a large capital movement will
not cause difficulty if it proceeds slowly and steadily. But a rapid,

---

have their nearest real counterpart in a small island engaged in active trade with the
rest of the world from which it draws food and raw materials in return for manufactured
goods and as a return on previous investments abroad. The more complex problems of
trade between highly industrialized countries making highly similar products in which
nonprice competition is characteristic were hardly touched upon until quite recent times.
So also the problem of international investment for countries that do not fit the English
conditions was scarcely considered by the earlier writers.

abrupt movement, large relative to the volume of other transactions bearing upon the country's exchange rate in the short period, inevitably causes trouble. For example, a country whose commodity and service exports and imports normally tend to offset one another at, say, around 100 per month at prevailing rates of exchange would be seriously embarrassed by a sudden inflow or outflow of short-term funds of 25 to 50 per month. The resulting exchange disturbance, or gold flow, would probably produce serious repercussions in the domestic economy.[11] Such difficulties, in historical fact, were the prime reason for the introduction of exchange control and stabilization funds.

Movements in the rate of exchange during disturbed periods are, of course, not necessarily single, isolated events of short duration. If an unregulated currency begins to depreciate because of a heavy outward flow of funds, it may set in motion a cumulative movement which is self-accelerating. Speculators, expecting the rate to fall, sell the currency and thereby bring about, if their operations are sufficiently large, the very fall that was expected. And conversely with appreciation. In these circumstances a country's currency may fluctuate wildly under pressure of exchange dealings not directly connected at all with imports or exports. Devaluations may be caused similarly. For example:

Sweden . . . was forced off the gold standard, only eight days after the United Kingdom, not by any current disequilibrium in the balance of payments but by a sudden outward transfer of funds by both foreigners and nationals who realized that Sweden's exports depended largely on the British market and that therefore the krona might sooner or later have to follow the pound. The flight of capital from France, which started soon after the devaluation of the dollar and grew especially after that of the belga, was largely prompted by the prospect of devaluation, a prospect which materialized after a long delay.[12]

Effects on Employment and Income

The significance of exchange rate fluctuations (or gold flows) induced by large short-term capital movements lies in their effect on

11. It must not be supposed that only "foreigners" will endeavor to withdraw capital from the country if, for any reason, the country seems an unattractive place to hold assets. The country's nationals may desire to transfer their wealth holdings abroad and so cause a "capital flight" even where no prior foreign borrowing has occurred.

12. *International Currency Experience*, League of Nations, Geneva, 1944.II.A.4, p. 123. Also, in discussion of the pound sterling after September 1931, we read, "The depreciation of the pound at that time was determined largely by the outflow of foreign funds and that outflow itself was largely determined at any given moment by the prospect of further depreciation." *Ibid.*, p. 118.

domestic employment and national income. A sudden rise in the ex-change rate for a country's currency makes all exports more expensive, so that foreigners tend to buy less. On the other hand, imports are encouraged by the higher exchange rate. An inflow of gold makes for higher internal incomes and prices and similarly stimulates imports. In either case, greater imports adversely affect domestic employment unless offset by other factors.[13] An outflow of short-term funds, including gold, tends to lower exchange rates and so tends to stimulate employment in the export industries through making their products cheaper to foreign buyers.[14]

Under gold-standard conditions, the outflow of gold should theoretically deflate incomes and prices in the country losing gold — an internal deflation. This may not be altogether easy to carry through under modern conditions. In any case, employment is likely to slump while prices are drifting to lower levels.

13. Imported goods tend to be cheaper to domestic buyers with the higher exchange rate, and in so far as exported goods are made from imported raw materials, this tends to offset the depressing effect on employment. But in the usual case, raw material cost is small relative to total cost, so that the net effect is adverse for employment. And the now cheaper imports will be substituted for home-produced goods to some extent with a similar adverse effect on home employment.

14. Actually, as many readers will recognize, the above is a simplified version of a highly complicated process that would require a whole book to expound in detail. One or two comments designed to avoid any serious misconceptions will have to suffice here.

In the first place, it is not certain that a devaluation of the currency will always increase exports and diminish imports, so as to improve the balance of payments. If exports encounter a foreign demand that is likely to be inelastic with respect to price, the foreign exchange made available through exports may actually diminish. Similarly, a highly inelastic demand for imports may mean that the rise in their price will require more foreign exchange to pay for them. The combination of these two circumstances is possible, although highly unlikely. But even in this case, unless the foreign demand for exports is completely inelastic, employment in the export industries will rise as a result of devaluation. It should always be kept in mind, however, that most countries do not have a single list of commodities that are exported or imported; rather, what is imported and what exported depends on relative prices at home and abroad and changes in their relationships. This assumes an absence of control through quota arrangements.

A *depreciating* rate of exchange may not increase exports if it is believed that the fall still has some distance to go. This is a special case of the familiar proposition in economics that a lowering of price will not increase sales if it is expected that *still lower* prices will shortly prevail. Hence, depreciating exchange rates may have an adverse effect on exports while the depreciation is in progress. Similarly, a falling exchange rate may cause anticipatory buying abroad for import into the home country. See *International Currency Experience* for details.

The elimination of these complications from the discussion in the text above does not affect our main contention that short-term flight capital and speculative capital movements are likely to be unfavorable for home employment.

Governmental Controls Adopted

Violent gold movements or drastic changes in exchange rates, which heavy unchecked capital movements can engender, require a corresponding flexibility throughout the national economy. Prices must be plastic and resources for production highly adaptable. In the early 1930's, most countries found that, despite drastic measures, prices of commodities as well as of factors of production were not sufficiently plastic nor were productive resources sufficiently mobile to accommodate the capital movements that harried the foreign exchange markets. For example, in June 1931 the Bruening government in Germany issued emergency decrees to meet the flight of capital from the country by inducing a severe internal deflation. According to Brown:

The main features of these [decrees] were further salary cuts for government officials, reductions in war pensions, reduction in departmental estimates, more indirect taxation, and a "crisis tax" on wages and incomes. Further, state and communal budgets were also reduced, principally by salary cuts, and reforms in the unemployment insurance system designed to reduce its cost were undertaken. These drastic deflationary measures provoked a political crisis. . . . The severity of the crisis may be judged from the fact that there were times during June when absolutely no market for reichsmarks existed in Switzerland.[15]

Yet, even with drastic measures, German prices and productive resources were not sufficiently malleable to adapt to capital withdrawals without producing widespread unemployment. The German experience was only a more acute version of similar occurrences throughout central Europe and other regions.

When national governments, already worried by domestic unemployment, realized that the flight of capital — either foreign-owned or home-owned — from the country could make for further unemployment if they instituted deflation as a remedy, it is not surprising that they chose instead to restrict the capital movements directly. In view of all the circumstances of the time — rising unemployment, shrinking export markets, a deflation that had already gone some distance and a general tone of fear and distrust — the choice actually made by most countries is not, in retrospect, surprising. For, as Professor Ellis has written:

15. William Adams Brown, *The International Gold Standard Reinterpreted, 1914–1934*, National Bureau of Economic Research, New York, 1940, Vol. II, pp. 1041–42.

Capital withdrawals from a national economy present an exact parallel with depositors' runs upon banks; if the phenomenon is sufficiently severe, the same remedy has to be applied, namely, a closing of the wicket.[16]

Freedom of the individual to dispose of his property as he saw fit had to give way to controls believed to be for the collective good. Capital movements in the early 1930's thus came under the watchful eye of governments, from which scrutiny, with few exceptions, they have not since been withdrawn.

GOVERNMENT FOREIGN LENDING

The conclusion of World War II left only three major world powers, each with a special economic philosophy and point of view peculiarly its own. Grouped around each of these countries are a number of smaller countries that, for a variety of reasons, find their national welfare more intimately tied to one of the three than to either of the other two. In these circumstances, a consensus on all phases of international economic affairs is not to be expected at once, if ever. Conference and attempts at compromise are the order of the day.

One nearly inevitable consequence of this three-power world is the strong tendency for international economic affairs to become inextricably intertwined with foreign policy. For Russia such a marriage of politics and economics in foreign affairs implies no break with past practice. But for Great Britain, and especially for the United States, the deviation from established custom is more marked. Consequently, lending abroad may now have to be reckoned in a larger ledger than most Americans have been accustomed to use in computing the returns from foreign investment. When the unit for which costs and benefits of foreign lending are computed is the nation as a whole, in all its varied aspects and relationships, something more than the sum lent and the interest received may properly be taken into account.[17] When foreign lending becomes an instrumentality of foreign policy as a whole, its usefulness cannot be judged exclusively by reckoning the costs and returns in the account books of private finance. Foreign lend-

16. Howard S. Ellis, *Exchange Control in Central Europe,* Harvard University Press, Cambridge (Mass.), 1941, p. 8.

17. The United States government, acting for the people of the United States as a whole, may have shown great wisdom in constructing a huge airfield in Newfoundland during the recent war, even though such an investment would be unprofitable from the private point of view.

ing on government account may be an appropriate instrument of American foreign policy in the contemporary world.

The prospect of foreign investment by governments is also enhanced by the responsibility that the British, American and many other democratic governments have now assumed for a positive economic policy in support of domestic employment and acceptable living standards. Such an acknowledged responsibility may, for some countries (in particular the United States, it is often now argued), suggest the wisdom of government lending abroad to support home employment, even where private investment abroad would not occur and where no considerations of foreign policy are involved.

Relation to Foreign Policy

A national government does not direct its affairs with the object of showing a money profit in the commercial sense. The "costs" it incurs and the "benefits" it obtains for its citizens are very real even though not wholly reducible to a money balance. Yet, costs and benefits can be appraised notwithstanding the impossibility of reducing them in all cases to pecuniary terms. Any national policy based on considered judgment (rather than emotionalism or pure chance) implies a prior weighing of the prospective costs and benefits to the whole nation.[18] Considerations such as these, which cannot be judged in money terms, promise to weigh heavily in foreign lending by the United States government.

Economic reconstruction offers a prime example of possible benefits from American foreign lending beyond the principal sums advanced and the interest return promised. Rapid and orderly reconstruction of European and Asiatic countries that have been physically devastated or had their economies seriously disrupted by the war would greatly benefit the people of the United States. Foreign lending would hasten reconstruction. Hence, having in mind the possible alternative courses of events if loans are not forthcoming from the United States, foreign

18. History, of course, contains many examples of policies invoked more in anger and revenge than in response to considered judgment. Similarly, a chance combination of circumstances may be responsible for a policy emerging in a form that is indefensible from any rational point of view. The so-called Morgenthau plan for the pastoralization of the German economy would be considered by some an example of the first, and the Hawley-Smoot tariff of 1930, which was generally regarded as a bad measure even by those who voted for it, might be cited as an instance of the second.

lending for reconstruction purposes could be urged as an undertaking in America's best interests. The benefits to the United States might include an avoidance of internal readjustments that would otherwise be necessary, a resumption of world trade at an earlier date, an increased friendliness to the United States in the countries concerned, prevention of disease and epidemics, and various similar considerations.

The British loan of $3.75 billion was partly motivated by nonpecuniary factors. Presumably the United States, the major country professing a firm belief in the virtues of competition and free enterprise, has an interest in seeing free foreign exchange markets replace exchange control, in having discriminatory trade restrictions disappear and, in general, in restoring a multilateral world trade at fixed exchange rates along free-enterprise lines. Great Britain probably cannot return to any such system without American assistance, in view of its import needs and its short-term sterling debts. Consequently, if the United States desires an early return to multilateral trade, it is a defensible American policy to make a large loan to Great Britain as a means of removing the formidable obstacles that now bar Britain from resuming multilateral trade. Similarly, it could be argued, other countries will not abandon prohibitive tariffs, exchange restrictions, quota arrangements, bilateral clearings, etc., unless they see in the offing ample supplies of foreign exchange, especially American dollars. An American loan could provide the desired foreign exchange and so contribute to the broad objective that American policy is seeking to foster in world trade. If one agrees that America's best interests will be served by a revival of multilateral trade at stable exchange rates and the progressive removal of trade barriers, then it is clearly arguable that American foreign lending, perhaps on a very large scale, is one means of removing the obstacles that now stand in the way.

The possibilities of using foreign lending to help attain broad national objectives are, of course, limited by the need other countries have for American dollars and by the alternatives available to them. In Great Britain, for example, a group of economists at Oxford argued vigorously that multilateral trade offered Great Britain far smaller attractions than the alternative policy of deliberate exploitation of its postwar trading opportunities.[19] Some other countries, such as France

19. See T. Balogh, "The International Aspects of Full Employment," in *The Economics of Full Employment*, Institute of Statistics, Oxford University, Blackwell & Mott,

and the Netherlands, already possess substantial dollar balances, so that the attractions of American loans may not loom so large in view of the concessions that they might be expected to make in return. Economic reconstruction for some countries is possible without foreign borrowing, and for them the persuasive power of American loans would be less.

These considerations inherent in proposals to link American foreign lending with foreign policy are often present nowadays when people discuss foreign lending by the United States. It is no longer, in the minds of many, a simple matter of foreign investment on private account. However, these newer points of view are many times entirely overlooked by those who insist on examining all proposals for lending abroad by the American government from the strictly private, pecuniary point of view. As the *New York Herald Tribune* recently editorialized on "Economic Statesmanship" in relation to approval of the British loan:

> This is not said as a personal reflection upon the Senator. It is advanced as an illustration of that perilous attitude which, in reducing all major questions of international financial policy to a greedy huckster's concept of a dollars-and-cents accounting, threatens to lose us a rational world in order to gain a few bookkeeping entries of no consequence in themselves.[20]

The inherently different basis of reckoning and the absence of frankness by the exponents on each side are provocative of great confusion and even, at times, of distrust between the disputants.[21]

Oxford, 1945; also, by the same author, "The Foreign Balance and Full Employment," *Bulletin of the Oxford Institute of Statistics,* Vol. V, Supplement No. 5.

20. February 1, 1946.

21. A further word on this point seems necessary to avoid possible misinterpretation. Government officials, in their public discussions of foreign lending by the American government, have not gone as far as they might to emphasize that nonpecuniary considerations are well to the fore in formulating a loan policy. They are wont to leave the impression that government lending is operating according to the same criteria, albeit on a larger scale, as lending on private account. The consequence is that, *on the assumption that the same criteria are being used,* persons outside the government are apt to assess the displayed judgment of the government officials at a fairly low figure. This is unfortunate in the extreme, because in point of fact it seems reasonably certain that the same criteria are not being invoked. Some further difficulty arises from the fact that government officials find it necessary to use the words "loan" or "investment" in discussing their operations when they would admit that a more accurate description would give more emphasis to the possibility of default by the borrowing country, a possibility which the lending negotiators are well aware of in all their dealings. And furthermore, even granted the contingency of default, it could be demonstrated that the "loan" was not inappropriate from the point of view of the American national interest. Nevertheless, the use of this eu-

The Economic Case

The arguments advanced for government lending abroad that rest on more narrowly economic considerations have taken a variety of forms. Professor Hansen's recent statement that "The conference [of the ILO] gave to the world a telling slogan which will not soon be forgotten: 'Poverty anywhere constitutes a danger to prosperity everywhere' "[22] is surely open to dispute. Responsible persons, however, have urged foreign lending by the United States for many purposes: to expand American exports; to raise living standards in low-income areas and so contribute to world peace; to reduce the ups and downs of business cycles in the United States and so, because of America's preponderance in world trade, in the world as a whole; to offset the large savings at high income levels in the American economy; and for other purposes. A detailed analysis of all the arguments advanced from time to time is neither possible nor profitable. Some of these have already been translated into operating policies by federal agencies such as the Export-Import Bank.[23]

Foreign Investment to Raise National Income

One basic line of reasoning, however, runs through nearly all such arguments for foreign lending. This reasoning relates investment abroad to employment and national income in the lending country. In so far as the arguments for foreign lending go beyond loose generalities or laudable hopes, they have their principal economic foundations in this relation between foreign lending and home employment.

The emphasis on foreign investment as a means of sustaining national income and employment in highly industrialized countries springs from the fear that such economies are always threatened by

---

phemistic language does not contribute to mutual understanding and confidence between persons within and without the government.

22. Alvin H. Hansen, *America's Role in the World Economy*, Norton, New York, 1945, p. 125.

23. For instance, concerning the Export-Import Bank we read that "The Bank promotes foreign trade . . . by financing exports in connection with development projects and programs in foreign countries. Loans of the latter type have a further indirect effect upon United States foreign trade; for they assist in building up the economies and raising the levels of income of foreign countries, which thereby become better markets for American products and better suppliers of imports to this country. Thus, the Export-Import Bank is guided in its lending policies by the demonstrated fact that the best trading partners of the United States are countries which have reached the highest state of economic development." "New Policy Statement by Export-Import Bank" (official announcement by the Bank), *Foreign Commerce Weekly*, September 29, 1945, p. 4.

underemployment because of a failure to maintain aggregate investment and consumption outlays. At high levels of national income, savings tend to be large. If these savings are not offset by equally large investment expenditures, then national income will fall. This is the accepted doctrine.[24] There should be no misunderstanding as to *why* foreign investment is believed to be helpful in promoting or sustaining home employment.

Foreign lending is favorable to employment and national income in the lending country to the extent that it increases aggregate domestic spending beyond what it would be without foreign loans: the virtue of the foreign investment is precisely in the net contribution it makes to aggregate spending. Were the foreign loans to be held in unspent balances in the lending country, income and employment in the lending country would be unaffected. A subsidy to exports, a government program to purchase domestic goods and give them away to persons outside the country, a bounty to foreign buyers of domestic exportable goods—any or all of these would have the same immediate effect on domestic employment as investment abroad.[25] Foreign investment, then, stimulates home employment in the degree to which it increases aggregate spending in the lending country beyond what it would otherwise be.

Foreign investment is also favorable to home employment, it is sometimes said, because it tends to increase the export balance or diminish the import surplus. This is merely an alternative, but occasionally more useful, formulation of the arguments just presented. A rise in the export surplus or a decline in the import surplus means that increased spending has gone for goods produced within the economy. Any process that leads to a net increase in aggregate outlay for goods and services is favorable for employment.[26]

24. We are not here concerned with expounding the details of Keynesian analysis of the relationship between investment, consumption, income and employment. But it may be mentioned in passing that the problem can also be attacked by measures aimed at increasing consumption at the expense of saving. Most persons who argue for foreign investment to aid domestic employment would also argue for measures to increase consumption as well. They would insist, probably, that both are necessary but that neither alone, given the prevailing viewpoints and political considerations, is likely to be adequate to sustain national income at full-employment levels.

25. We are not implying, of course, that all these devices are equally acceptable on other grounds.

26. It is not suggested that contemporary pleas for large-scale foreign investment are usually couched in such a bald form as we have just used. Our purpose here is to state

Foreign Investment Has No Special Virtue

We have consistently spoken of a *net* increase in aggregate outlay as occasioned by foreign lending. The adjective is important. If the foreign investment merely replaced home investment or home consumption, there would be no net contribution to employment from foreign investment. The gain in employment might follow a somewhat different sequence or have a different reaction time. But, in an over-all view, foreign investment has no special virtues — probably even some weaknesses — over home investment as a sustainer of domestic national income.

This argument has recently been urged in various forms — though along with other considerations — in support of foreign lending by the United States in the postwar period. For example, a recent pamphlet by the National Planning Association reads:

> With relatively unchanged income distribution and savings patterns, current savings by individuals and corporations at full employment in or about 1950 would probably amount to about $25–30 billion annually. If a national fiscal policy similar to that prevailing just prior to the war is restored, it is unlikely that more than $20 billion of this amount could be absorbed in domestic private investment to maintain and moderately improve the national plant. This would leave a savings investment deficit of $5–10 billion. Compensatory government expenditure to maintain full employment, given this situation, would require either that the equal sums be borrowed, with a resultant budgetary deficit, or that idle funds be taxed away. These expedients, of course, are stringently limited by political considerations. Government loans to finance exports have less political vulnerability, while private foreign investment is scarcely questionable on this basis.

---

the essentials of the analysis, not to make a case for or against foreign lending in a particular historical situation.

The effect of an export surplus on domestic employment and income will largely be determined by the kinds of goods and services for which the borrowed funds are spent. The possible variations here are enormous. In late 1945 and early 1946, some of the lending by the American Export-Import Bank was being used to finance equipment purchases and purchases of American cotton from the Commodity Credit Corporation. Now, purchases of cotton or wheat held as surplus by a government agency would have a minimum effect on domestic employment. In general the disinvestment of excess inventories (from either foreign or domestic investment) will have an exceedingly small effect on home employment, if any. The purchase of railroad rolling stock, on the other hand, would probably have a fairly high "multiplier" effect on employment and income. The number of possible patterns that might emerge from spending a given dollar sum made available through foreign lending is legion, and not much can be said about the problem in general terms. One of the authors has further discussed this problem elsewhere: Norman S. Buchanan, *International Investment and Domestic Welfare*, Holt, New York, 1945, pp. 143 ff.

It is, therefore, sound national policy to strive for the maximum stimulus to private foreign investment (supplemented when necessary by public capital export) as well as maximum private domestic investment. We refer, of course, only to sound and productive foreign investment.[27]

And a report by a special House Committee of Congress says of foreign loans:

> For the United States, they provide an investment outlet for excess savings and thus help to keep at a high level the domestic output and employment offered by our free enterprise system.[28]

Other expressions of the same general argument are commonly heard.

All such arguments for foreign investment draw their force from the expected contribution to net domestic spending. The analysis can easily be extended to the case of anticyclical timing or the transition from war to peace. The basic point in all such programs is their net contribution to total money expenditures.[29]

THE AMERICAN EXPORT-IMPORT BANK

The chief source of international loans, apart from governments themselves and the International Bank for Reconstruction and Development, is at present the American Export-Import Bank. By the Export-Import Bank Act of 1945, the Bank was made a permanent independent agency of the government. Its purpose is to aid "in the financing and facilitating of exports and imports and the exchange of commodities between the United States or any of its territories or in-

---

27. *America's New Opportunities in World Trade,* Planning Pamphlets, Nos. 37–38, Washington, 1944, pp. 50–51 (notes omitted).

28. *The Post-War Foreign Economic Policy of the United States,* House Special Committee on Post-War Foreign Economic Policy of the United States, H. Rept. 541, 79th Cong., 1st sess., 1945, p. 19.

29. All such arguments are equally applicable to any country in which there is danger of unemployment through excessive saving not matched by new investment. In discussion relating to the immediate postwar period and the decades to follow, the argument is almost without exception applied only to the United States. The reasons appear to be the following: It is felt that other industrial countries — Great Britain, Germany, France, Italy, etc. — will have adequate investment outlets at home. They will not need foreign investment as a vent for savings. Also present (by implication mainly) is the consideration that the costs of reconstruction and industrial development on the scale and at the rate envisioned are so great that other countries could not contribute more than a very small portion of the total international lending required. Their total savings are too small. When the discussion is of foreign lending running to scores of billions of dollars, there is only one possible source of supply. But as a proposition in economics, foreign lending to support domestic employment is applicable to any economy where investment tends to flag relative to savings.

sular possessions and any foreign country or the agencies or nationals thereof."[30] The Bank's capital of $1 billion is subscribed by the United States. The Bank can borrow two and a half times that sum from the Secretary of the Treasury, so that the total funds available for foreign lending are at present $3.5 billion. This sum represents the maximum of loans and guarantees that the Bank can have outstanding at any time. The Bank may not compete with private lenders; where foreign governments or individuals can tap private funds, the Bank must refrain from lending.

As a rule, the Bank lends for specific purposes only, and finances only "purchases of materials and equipment produced or manufactured in the United States and the technical services of American firms and individuals as distinguished from outlays for materials and labor in the borrowing country or purchases in third countries."[31] Thus, if the Bank grants a country a line of credit for reconstruction purposes (e.g., the loan to France of $550 million at the end of 1945), the borrower must specify the type of commodities — such as transportation equipment, machinery, raw materials, or whatever — it wants to buy in the United States, and must use the whole credit for purchases in this country. At the end of 1945, the total commitments outstanding were $1.6 billion, so that the lending capacity remaining at that time amounted to $1.9 billion.[32]

The National Advisory Council on International Monetary and Financial Problems has recommended that the lending power of the Export-Import Bank be increased by $1.25 billion.[33] The committee made this recommendation on the basis of estimated urgent foreign needs amounting to $3.25 billion in the period January 1946 through June 1947, deducting therefrom the unused lending capacity of the Export-Import Bank of about $2 billion. The committee confined itself to only the most urgent needs in prospect and stated that

30. "New Policy Statement by Export-Import Bank," p. 4.
31. *Ibid.*, p. 5.
32. "The Foreign Loan Policy of the United States," *Federal Reserve Bulletin*, March 1946, p. 230.
33. The Council was established by Congress as part of the Bretton Woods Agreement Act. It consists of the Secretaries of the Treasury, State, Commerce, the Chairman of the Board of Governors of the Federal Reserve System and the Chairman of the Board of Directors of the Export-Import Bank. The Council is intended to coordinate the American lending and credit programs and to integrate American policies with the operations of the International Bank.

among the factors taken into consideration in making loans of this character are: (1) the urgency of the need of the borrower; (2) the borrower's own resources; (3) the possibility of obtaining the loan from other sources: private capital markets and other governments; (4) the ability of the borrower to make effective use of the funds; (5) the capacity of the borrower to repay; and (6) the impact of the loan on our domestic economy.[34]

These are obviously statements in the most general terms; how they will be applied to specific loan applications is not now discernible.

THE INTERNATIONAL BANK

The International Bank for Reconstruction and Development was formally established in the last days of 1945. The total subscription allotments amount to $9,100 million, of which $3,175 million is to be subscribed by the United States and $1,300 million by the United Kingdom. Russia's allotment was set at $1,200 million. The authorized capital stock is $10 billion and can be increased when the Bank deems it advisable. (Article II, Section 2.) But not all forty-four governments that were eligible to sign the agreement before December 31, 1945 actually did so. The nonsigning countries were Russia, Australia, New Zealand, Venezuela, Haiti, El Salvador, Nicaragua, Panama and Liberia; Colombia signed the Fund Agreement but not the Bank. The total amount subscribed by the spring of 1946, therefore, amounted to only $7.67 billion.

The subscription of each member is divided into three parts: 2 per cent is to be paid in gold; 18 per cent is subject to call, and if called, is to be paid in the currency of the member, but the currency can be loaned only with the approval of the member country;[35] the remaining 80 per cent, subject to call, must be paid at the option of the member either in gold or United States dollars or in the currency "required to discharge the obligations of the Bank for the purpose of which the call is made." (Article II, Sections 5 and 7.)

The Bank's *own* loan fund, according to the agreement, is in reality 20 per cent of the subscriptions — that is, as of spring 1946, $1.534 billion. The remaining 80 per cent of the subscriptions is subject to call, but only to meet obligations of the Bank incurred as a result of its "di-

34. "The Foreign Loan Policy of the United States," p. 228.
35. This provision enables a country with a precarious balance-of-payments position to prevent the additional pressure on its balance of payments that would result from the spending of its currency by the borrower.

rect loans out of funds raised in the market of a member or otherwise borrowed by the bank" [Article IV, Section 1 (a) (ii)] or to meet guarantees it has given. In other words, 80 per cent of the subscriptions will presumably not be called by the Bank unless it suffers losses. Thus it must be clearly understood that the bulk of the Bank's loans will be from funds it has itself borrowed in private capital markets. It is anticipated that much of the Bank's own borrowing will be in the United States.[36]

The Bank may make, participate in or guarantee loans to governments, to subdivisions of governments or to private enterprises. Loans other than those to governments must be guaranteed by the government, the central bank or some comparable agency of the member country in whose territory the project that is to be financed by the loans is located. As a rule, the International Bank, just as the Export-Import Bank, shall make only specific-purpose loans, but the borrower, unlike the borrower of Export-Import Bank loans, is free to spend the funds in any country. [Article III, Section 4 (i) and (vii) and Section 5 (a).] The main purpose of the International Bank is to assist in the reconstruction and development of the territories of its members.

THE FUTURE OF FOREIGN LENDING

Long-term investments already on the books came into existence at a time when the private pursuit of gain from foreign investment was highly respectable and the political and social environment was more homogenous. Furthermore, the patterns of international trade and of the international distribution of claims and obligations harmonized with one another tolerably well, at least until 1930. But the Great Depression and World War II brought such profound changes in the international debt structure, in the international distribution of needs and resources, and above all in the accepted future role of the state in economic matters, as to make unlikely any early return to the kind of international lending and borrowing that created the existing structure of long-term international investment. International lending will probably be resumed, perhaps on a greater scale than has ever prevailed before. But much of it will be international lending of a type that would have appeared unnecessary and indefensible two decades ago.

36. Cf. *Federal Reserve Bulletin,* April 1946, p. 368.

Private Investment Opportunities Limited

Present prospects are not bright for any great upsurge of private foreign investment. The United States, Canada, Sweden and Switzerland, and perhaps to a minor extent Great Britain after a time, are almost the only countries from which any large private investment abroad might conceivably flow in the foreseeable future. Moreover, the number of countries to which this investment might flow, where the political and social outlook is favorable to private undertakings, and where the record of political stability inspires confidence for new ventures, is few indeed. For example, corporations and individuals in the United States seeking profitable investment outlets abroad are not likely to be attracted to countries that, officially and explicitly, proclaim their preference for a type of economic organization in which private investment for profit receives, at best, a subsidiary role or a sullen tolerance. To be sure, the outlook may change. In some countries, parts of western Europe for example, the issue of the basic type of economic organization to be established still seems to be undecided. But there are not many countries where private enterprise from abroad is likely to be welcomed and left fairly free of burdensome restrictions.

Government Lending Will Increase

Hence, in so far as foreign lending occurs at all, government lending is likely to assume the major burden as compared with private lending; one way and another, it may conceivably run to quite large figures. But as we have emphasized, foreign lending will probably be actuated by mixed motives in which political, social and broad economic considerations relating to national income at home will all figure. A complex state of affairs will condition each decision to make or not to make a loan. Moreover, the reasons publicly alleged in justification of a particular loan will often not be the primary reasons that forced the decision. Nonetheless, the prospect unfolds that foreign lending on government account by the United States may run to large sums.

Chapter 8

WHY BORROW ABROAD: THE DEBTOR'S VIEW

TYPES OF FOREIGN BORROWING

INTERNATIONAL INVESTMENT is a two-sided affair. But the point of view that prompts action in the lending country may not coincide with that prevailing in the borrowing country. Nevertheless, some common purpose and understanding must exist between them if mutually beneficial international investment is to occur.

A country may be either passive or active in its foreign borrowing, even though the term "borrowing" suggests that the initiative comes from those needing funds. National governments, provinces or states, and business groups organized for private profit, have often in the past solicited loans from abroad. But in foreign investment the initiative has also frequently been taken by lenders, by foreign capitalists or their bankers who saw profitable business opportunities abroad and undertook to exploit them. In such cases, neither the citizens nor the government of the borrowing country sought loans from abroad. The lenders took the active role. However, customary usage would term both types of transactions "foreign borrowing." The phrase "debtor country" designates a nation's net status on international capital account rather than whether its receipt of foreign capital was active or passive. Its status at any particular time was the result of a host of individual transactions past and present, and seldom the result of a conscious national plan.

Intergovernmental borrowings were not the principal type of international capital movement prior to 1939.[1] Governments are everywhere assuming a greater role in economic affairs: many governments now plan industrialization and economic development schemes to be directed and financed by the state. In so far as these entail foreign borrowing, the government is the logical solicitor. Moreover, the Inter-

---

1. National governments have certainly frequently borrowed in the world's capital markets. But the lenders have usually been private individuals or bankers in the lending country, not national governments.

national Bank for Reconstruction and Development and the American Export-Import Bank contemplate loans chiefly to national governments or loans guaranteed by governments. The fact that their interest rates will as a rule be lower than those obtainable elsewhere encourages borrowing by national governments. On the whole, therefore, the prospect is for more intergovernmental borrowings and more government guarantees in future international long-term lending.[2]

Purposes of Foreign Borrowing

The purposes or motives likely to prompt future foreign borrowing fall into three broad categories.

First are reconstruction and adjustment loans. Either because of widespread war damage, as in France, Belgium, the Netherlands or Russia, or because of drastic shifts in the country's international financial position, as in the case of Great Britain, current import requirements far exceed currrent export capacities. A loan can finance the import surplus and thus speed reconstruction or ease the adjustment to a changed financial position. Loans of this type provide a breathing space to countries with special postwar problems: their basic purpose is to hasten reconstruction and allow a higher standard of living than would otherwise be possible or, as in the case of Great Britain, to permit a more gradual adaptation of export capacities and import needs to existing financial claims and obligations. Later, adjustment loans for purposes of currency stabilization may be negotiated, as after World War I. Greece has already solicited the United States for such a loan. Reconstruction and adjustment loans raise their own special problems. But in view of the analysis already made in Chapters 5 and 6, we shall not consider them further.

A second type of postwar foreign borrowing will undoubtedly consist of private commitments motivated by profit opportunities. Here "direct" investment will probably be more common than portfolio investments. Some American corporations are reported to have plans already for direct investments in plants and other facilities abroad. But, as previously pointed out (p. 177), not many countries today have a political and social climate hospitable to foreign, profit-seeking pri-

2. If, as we have already argued (pp. 167 ff.), foreign lending becomes more and more an integral part of foreign policy as a whole in the creditor countries, this is a further reason why the borrowers must also be national governments.

vate capital. The British Dominions, the United Kingdom, some western European countries and some Latin-American countries are at present the principal areas where profit-seeking foreign capital is at all welcome. And many of these do not need capital from abroad.

The third, and from the long-term point of view perhaps most important, type of foreign borrowing likely to occur in the years to come is borrowing for the industrialization and economic development of low-income areas. Such projects are much discussed today. They are of special importance to the United States as the largest potential lender for the external financing of planned industrialization.

THE URGE TO INDUSTRIALIZE

Economic development of the newer countries during the 19th and early 20th centuries was based essentially on the exploitation of profit opportunities in food and raw materials. A wide variety of products — wheat, coffee, tea, sugar, vegetable oils, mutton, beef, wool, cotton, rubber, tin, copper, tungsten, nitrates, petroleum, etc. — were developed over the years in different countries, and these were exchanged for the processed goods and manufactures of the older industrialized countries.[3] Unfortunately, in the late 1920's, agricultural protectionism — especially in Europe, but also in the United States — somewhat reduced the foreign markets of the food- and raw-material-producing countries. As the world depression gathered headway after 1929, rising unemployment and falling incomes in the industrial countries checked this mutually profitable exchange far more seriously. Food and raw material prices fell drastically, while production went on unchecked or even increased. At the same time, prices of manufactured goods from the industrial countries fell much less, with the result that food and raw material producers suffered worse terms of trade on such commerce as remained.[4]

3. The stage of development of the economies from which these foods and raw materials came was, however, far from identical. By 1929, for example, Australia and Canada had achieved considerable industrialization while the Malay States and the Netherlands Indies remained almost exclusively agricultural. The United States, although an important exporter of raw materials, was already highly industrialized by 1900.
4. ". . . the Canadian terms of trade thus deteriorated by about 20 per cent from the 'twenties to the 'thirties, although they improved again after 1935. This movement was . . . very unevenly spread over the various groups of exports. It was most pronounced in agricultural, vegetable, and animal products, and in wood, wood products, and paper, three groups of decisive importance for Canada's exports; and in fibres, textiles, and

Depression Stimulates Self-Sufficiency

The specific response to these unfavorable developments was not identical in all the newer countries. But the persistence of the depression with its hardships and suffering forced the raw-material-producing countries, as everywhere else, to reappraise their economic positions. National economic policy, and even to some extent colonial policy, increasingly emphasized economic stability and diversified production. Monoculture was discouraged. Diversification, self-sufficiency, "balanced production," industrialization and "stability" increasingly became the keynotes of policy in the economically newer countries. The 19th century views on international specialization and exchange seemed inapplicable to the crisis of the early 1930's. Moreover, autarchic economic policies in the older industrialized countries, with which the raw material countries had carried on a profitable commerce before 1930, only encouraged the drift toward industrialization and self-sufficiency in the "backward" areas.[5]

War Adds More Impetus

The decade between the end of the depression, about 1936, and the termination of World War II gave fresh impetus to programs for industrializing the newer countries. The depression-born urge to industrialize was subsequently nourished into strength by a variety of factors.

First in importance perhaps was the fact that the war itself seemed to demonstrate that centralized government control of production was both more efficient and more feasible administratively than had been believed. On the one hand, whole new industries were conjured into being by governments in the older industrial countries, and aggregate

---

textile products, a group of very small significance." E. Munzer, "Exports and National Income in Canada," *Canadian Journal of Economics and Political Science,* February 1945, p. 41.

5. Autarchy as an economic policy for Germany was, from one point of view, only the ultimate extension of attitudes and value judgments that were prevalent in nearly all countries during the depression. The first major move by the United States Congress to combat the depression, for example, was to enact the Hawley-Smoot tariff in 1930, which raised rates to the highest level in history. If the industrial countries insisted on excluding imports of food and raw materials (as well as manufactures), then the newer countries whose economies were organized for the export of these goods would have to develop home industry willy-nilly. In other words, the change that evolved in economic policy toward foreign trade in the industrial countries during the depression forced the newer countries to industrialize and to be more self-sufficient.

output increased astoundingly despite wartime difficulties. On the other hand, the war apparently settled the dispute as to whether Russia had or had not succeeded in industrializing her economy in a few short years. Both achievements seemed to emphasize the possibilities of deliberately planned industrialization.[6]

Second, the urge to industrialize was stimulated because many manufactured goods were unobtainable from abroad during the war. This was particularly annoying to the nonindustrialized raw material countries because, in contrast to the depression years, they now had adequate foreign exchange. But the conversion to war-goods production in the industrial countries caused many manufactures to disappear or become scarce while lack of cargo space and the fear that exported goods might assist the enemy reduced other normal exports to a mere trickle. Furthermore, some goods were destroyed in transit by enemy action. The result was that home industry and sources of raw materials and foods were greatly stimulated. The fact that these now exist will still further encourage economic development and industrialization as a deliberate policy.[7] A recent book about Latin America's future put it this way:

> But, while there is a long history in the various Latin-American nations of government attempts to foster industry, it is the Second World War which has really given an impetus to the development. An already-established desire in these countries for industrialization, which had existed over a considerable period before the war, added to the shortage of formerly imported goods, led to a marked pressure for industrial development.
>
> This evolution consists in general of three main divisions: the first is the establishment of an extremely limited capital goods industry; the second is the growth of mostly small manufacturing plants, largely in the consumer goods field, which has developed from the wartime difficulties of importing these goods from abroad; the third is the processing of local raw materials for ex-

6. An additional factor here was the fact that the immediate prewar years, and the war itself, showed that synthetic products and the use of nonsteam power had greater possibilities than had earlier been believed. The argument in the past had usually been that a shortage of coal and essential raw materials was a nearly insuperable barrier to industrialization. But the war seemed to show that there were many ways around such difficulties at less than prohibitive cost.

7. During the war some countries were cut off from foreign sources of supply and so tried to develop home agriculture. For some raw-material-producing and agricultural countries, this meant a greater diversification of agriculture with the object of being self-sufficient in food at least. Here again the prospects for elimination of such diversification are not bright even conceding that costs are perhaps somewhat higher.

port. The development of power and improved transportation facilities —
road, rail and air — is an important part of the picture.[8]

A similar course of events may be expected in many other countries.

Political and Cultural Factors

A third group of factors reinforcing the urge, sometimes determination, to industrialize and to develop the low-income areas now devoted mainly to agriculture consists of certain intangible but powerful
influences. The idealized aims of the United Nations, for example,
with evocative slogans such as "freedom from want," have exerted
influence.[9] Nationalist feeling and nationalist pride were probably intensified by the war. Economic development and industrialization programs have their political and cultural aspects, too.

In China, the Netherlands Indies, French Indo-China, Egypt and
India, the conviction seems to be widespread that the controlling "foreign" powers have in the past deliberately retarded economic development for selfish reasons. Thus, current proposals for industrialization
have a strong political and cultural drive. And it would be foolish to
pretend that such motives are of secondary importance. The following
quotation concerning the Chilean economy is of interest:

> We must become the first industrial country of South America . . . [This]
> principle points the true path of our future destiny. A country without its own
> industries is destined to end up as a colony of countries more industrialized
> than herself. It is manufacturing industry that gives the tone of progress. To
> possess natural riches, whether agricultural or mineral, amounts to nothing if
> the country cannot or does not know how to transform them. The mere wealth
> of materials without an industrious and intelligent population is rather a
> danger than an advantage. A people which is not capable of producing its own
> machinery, motors, tools and armaments, has no right to call itself inde-
> pendent.[10]

This language may be regarded as harmless exuberance or as an expression of deep-seated desires. In any case, whatever the fact in this

8. George Soule, David Efron and Norman T. Ness, *Latin America in the Future
World*, Rinehart, New York, 1945, pp. 259–60.
9. Where, as in World War II, government propaganda is carried on through all the
available media, such ideas take hold sometimes very quickly, albeit not always in quite
the form that the high policy makers had intended.
10. O. Alvarez Andrews in *El Mercurio* (Valparaiso), May 14, 1942, as quoted by
P. T. Ellsworth in *Chile: An Economy in Transition*, Macmillan, New York, 1945, p. 132.

particular instance, there can be little doubt that in Latin America, the Near East, India, and other parts of the Orient, nationalism and the insistence on "independence" cannot be disregarded in any realistic discussion of contemporary industrialization and economic development schemes. Nationalism certainly imparts a fervor that might otherwise be absent. Indeed, one of the prime difficulties in bringing these programs to fruition will be to prevent nationalistic enthusiasm from triumphing over economic reason.

Contemporary plans for raising national incomes and per capita consumption in underdeveloped areas through industrialization and other capital investments thus represent a complex mixture. Political, social, cultural and economic factors intricately combine and interweave to form programs that are far from single-purposed.

REAL INCOMES IN RELATION TO INDUSTRIALIZATION

If one surveys the earth's peoples with respect to industrialization and welfare, three important facts stand forth. First, manufacturing production — that is, production other than agriculture, extractive industries, trade and services — is distributed among the nations in a highly uneven manner. Second, the per capita consumption of manufactured goods shows an enormous difference between the wealthier industrialized countries and the poorer agricultural countries. Third, there is a marked inverse correlation between the proportion of the working population engaged in agriculture and the per capita level of real incomes. These broad generalizations, however, are subject to many additional considerations.

World Distribution of Manufacturing

Although manufacturing production has been becoming increasingly diffused throughout the world since 1870, it is still highly concentrated in a few countries. In 1870, the United Kingdom with 31.8 per cent, the United States with 23.3 per cent, and Germany with 13.2 per cent, together accounted for 68.3 per cent of the world's manufacturing production.[11] Although an index of world manufacturing production (1925–1929 = 100) rose from 14.4 in 1870 to 135.0 in 1938, these

11. *Industrialization and Foreign Trade,* League of Nations, Geneva, 1945.II.A.10, p. 13. The subsequent discussion of industrialization problems has drawn much from this excellent study by Dr. Folke Hilgerdt.

TABLE 26

PERCENTAGE DISTRIBUTION OF THE WORLD'S MANUFACTURING
PRODUCTION, 1870–1938

Country	1870	1881–1885	1896–1900	1906–1910	1913	1913[a]	1926–1929	1936–1938
World	100.0	100.0	100.0	100.0	100.0	100.0	100.0	100.0
United States	23.3	28.6	30.1	35.3	35.8	35.8	42.2	32.2
Germany	13.2	13.9	16.6	15.9	15.7	14.3	11.6	10.7
United Kingdom	31.8	26.6	19.5	14.7	14.0	14.1	9.4 .	9.2
France	10.3	8.6	7.1	6.4	6.4	7.0	6.6	4.5
Russia	3.7	3.4	5.0	5.0	5.5	4.4[b]	4.3[b]	18.5[b]
Italy	2.4	2.4	2.7	3.1	2.7	2.7	3.3	2.7
Belgium	2.9	2.5	2.2	2.0	2.1	2.1	1.9	1.3
Canada	1.0	1.3	1.4	2.0	2.3	2.3	2.4	2.0
Sweden	0.4	0.6	1.1	1.1	1.0	1.0	1.0	1.3
Finland	—	0.1	0.3	0.3	0.3	0.3	0.4	0.5
Japan	11.0	12.0	0.6	1.0	1.2	1.2	2.5	3.5
India			1.1	1.2	1.1	1.1	1.2	1.4
Others			12.3	12.0	11.9	13.7	13.2	12.2

Source: Industrialization and Foreign Trade, League of Nations, Geneva, 1945.II.A.10, p. 13.

a. The second line for 1913 represents the distribution according to the frontiers established after the 1914–1918 war.

b. U.S.S.R.

same three countries in 1938 still accounted for more than 50 per cent of the world's manufacturing production.[12] In other words, even though countries other than the United States, Great Britain and Germany increased their manufacturing output tremendously between 1870 and the late 1930's, they still could not claim, with the exception of Russia, any large fraction of the world's total. If figures were available for 1946, probably the United States could claim an even larger share of the world total than in 1939. The changes in the proportion of the world's total manufacturing production since 1870 are presented for the principal countries in Table 26. The virtual nonexistence of manufacturing over huge areas, often containing dense populations, is apparent at a glance.

12. *Ibid.,* pp. 138–40.

Uneven Consumption of Goods

The mere fact that a particular region produces no manufactured goods is economically of little moment, if it acquires manufactures by trade and exchange with the rest of the world. Iowa is less engaged in manufacturing than Ohio, but its production and trade afford its residents a high real income nonetheless. If a similar state of affairs prevailed in the world as a whole, the industrialization problem would not loom so large as it does.

The statistical evidence, incomplete though it is, shows clearly, however, that the national variations in per capita consumption of manufactured goods are enormous.[13] Dr. Hilgerdt's study estimates that as of 1926-1929 the per capita supply (production plus imports minus exports) of finished factory products other than foodstuffs was $254 for the United States; less than half this amount in the United Kingdom and Germany, $112 and $111 respectively; about $28 in Japan; $22 in Russia; and only $3 in China and India, which together accounted for about 40 per cent of the world's population.[14] (See Table 28.)

Colin Clark's well-known estimates of national income per head

13. In a measure the figures for the wealthy industrial countries somewhat exaggerate the *consumption* of manufactured goods, since the output figures here include capital goods as well as consumption goods. That is to say, some considerable output of capital goods was necessary annually to continue the flow of finished consumers' goods in manufactured form; some gross investment was for maintenance of existing productive resources and did not flow into consumption. There seems to be no way of eliminating this exaggeration. But the figures are crude at best and perhaps no great harm results.

14. As an example, in southeastern Europe, an area for which some elaborate plans have recently been put forward, variations were reported in the per capita consumption of certain standard articles in 1937 as follows:

Country	Cotton Goods (Kilos)	Paper (Kilos)	Soap (Fat Content in Kilos)	Sugar (Kilos)
Western Europe	8	30	6	32
Yugoslavia	2.0	3.5	0.7	5.4
Bulgaria	2.8	*	*	4.5
Romania	2.2	2.8	0.7	6.7
Greece	2.9	2.9	2.0	10.0
Poland	2.3	5.1	1.5	12.5
Hungary	2.4	10.0	*	12.7
Czechoslovakia	4.2	13.9	2.5	22.4
Austria	5.1	14.8	*	19.5

* Not available.

These data are adapted from PEP (Political and Economic Planning), *Economic Development in S.E. Europe,* London, 1945, p. 40. For the United States in 1937, the calculated consumption of sugar was 87.5 pounds per capita, or roughly 39.6 kilograms. *Statistical Abstract of the United States, 1943,* Bureau of the Census, p. 683.

TABLE 27

AVERAGE REAL INCOME PER HEAD OF EMPLOYED POPULATION IN
SELECTED COUNTRIES, 1925–1934

Country	Amount	Country	Amount
United States	$1,381	Czechoslovakia	$455
Canada	1,337	Greece	397
New Zealand	1,202	Finland	380
Great Britain	1,069	Hungary	359
Switzerland	1,018	Japan	353
Australia	980	Poland	352
Netherlands	855	Latvia	345
Eire	707	Italy	343
France	684	Estonia	341
Denmark	680	Yugoslavia	330
Sweden	653	U.S.S.R.	320
Germany	646	South Africa	276
Belgium	600	Bulgaria	259
Norway	539	Romania	243
Austria	511	Lithuania	207

Source: Colin Clark, *The Conditions of Economic Progress,* Macmillan, London, 1940, p. 41. Calculations in "international units," which have been defined as "the amount of goods and services which one dollar would purchase in the U.S.A. over the average of the period 1925–1934." *Ibid.,* pp. 39–41.

in various countries as of about 1925–1934 show similar wide deviations for consumption as a whole (not with exclusive reference to the consumption of manufactured goods). As contrasted with an average income *per employed person* in the United States and Canada of $1,381 and $1,337 respectively, he reports $352 for Poland, $259 for Bulgaria, $243 for Romania, $207 for Lithuania and an estimated low for China of $100–$120.[15] These figures are shown in Table 27.

15. Colin Clark, *The Conditions of Economic Progress,* Macmillan, London, 1940, pp. 41–42. It should be emphasized that these figures are subject to a considerable margin of error, in view of the scanty statistical data available for some countries. It may be questioned on the basis of observation whether France was indeed above Denmark and Germany and all these below Eire. The reader should not overlook the fact that, even within a high-income country such as the United States, there are enormous variations among the several states. For 1929, the figures per head of the *total* population show a variation from $1,208 in New York to $286 in Mississippi and $258 in South Carolina, with a national average set at $699. (Cf. Maurice Leven, Harold G. Moulton and Clark Warburton, *America's Capacity to Consume,* The Brookings Institution, Washington, 1934, p. 174.) In other countries the range of variation among different parts of the country would presumably be similarly great.

TABLE 28

ROUGH ESTIMATE OF THE SUPPLY OF FINISHED FACTORY PRODUCTS OTHER
THAN FOODSTUFFS, 1926–1929 ANNUAL AVERAGES

Country or Group	Population	Production (Gross Value)	Net Imports (+) or Exports (−)	Supply[a]
	(*In Millions*)			
World	1,960	$ 38	—	$ 38
United States	120	262	$− 8	254
United Kingdom	45.5	154	−42	112
Germany	64.5	134	−23	111
France	40.5	121	−25	96
Four British Dominions[b]	25	120	+44	164
Six minor industrial countries[c]	47	115	−15	100
Italy	40.5	62	− 2	60
Eight developed but not highly industrialized countries[d]	35	46	+34	80
Japan	62	31	− 3	28
U.S.S.R.	149	21	+ 1	22
Rest of the world except China and India	541	7	+ 6	13
China and India	790	2	+ 1	3

Source: Industrialization and Foreign Trade, League of Nations, Geneva, 1945.II.A.10, p. 22.

a. Total of production plus net imports or minus net exports.
b. Australia, Canada, New Zealand, Union of South Africa.
c. Austria, Belgium, Czechoslovakia, Netherlands, Sweden, Switzerland.
d. Argentina, British Malaya, Chile, Cuba, Denmark, Finland, Ireland, Norway. (Certain of these countries are industrially undeveloped but have an advanced economy of the colonial type.)
Note: The countries are arranged in order of production per head of population.

Thus, countries that are not important producers of manufactured goods are not, apart from certain important exceptions, large consumers of manufactured goods, as shown in Table 28.[16]

16. The exceptions are, of course, the British Dominions and the six minor industrial countries in Table 28.

Agriculture and Income

It is a striking fact that a fairly close relationship exists between low per capita incomes and a large percentage of the population engaged in agriculture. Countries standing low in the income scale — China, India, the Netherlands Indies, southeastern Europe, certain Latin-American countries — usually have 50 per cent or more of their population engaged in agriculture. Even New Zealand, Canada and Denmark, which are often thought of as predominantly agricultural countries, had only 28 per cent, 31 per cent and 36 per cent, respectively, of their gainfully employed populations in agriculture. But greater industrialization is not only a matter of a higher percentage of the working population engaged in manufacturing. As Dr. Hilgerdt has well stressed:

. . . the industrialization process does not simply result in the absorption by industry of part of the agricultural population. The chief fact brought out is that, as the share of population engaged in industry increases, so does that in all the other big occupational groups except agriculture. In particular, the population engaged in commerce and transport increases along with that in manufacturing.[17]

Hence, a country proposing to raise per capita incomes through industrialization must anticipate that as manufacturing grows, transport, commerce and administration will tend to absorb workers in about equal proportions. Table 29 shows the specific percentage distribution of employed population for a number of countries. It should be compared with Table 27 relating to per capita incomes.

We have already noted that countries with a high proportion of the employed population engaged in agriculture usually have relatively low per capita incomes. Equally noteworthy, however, is the fact that as the proportion of the population engaged in agriculture increases (and income decreases), the yield from agriculture per unit of arable land area also declines fairly steadily. In other words, countries having most of their population in agriculture tend also relatively to have the lowest yields per acre.

Table 30 ranges some of the countries shown in Table 29 in order of increasing proportion of the employed population in agriculture and shows in the adjoining columns their recorded yields in wheat, rye,

17. *Industrialization and Foreign Trade*, p. 28.

TABLE 29

PERCENTAGE DISTRIBUTION OF THE GAINFULLY OCCUPIED POPULATION, SELECTED YEARS

Country	Year	Agriculture, Fishing (1)	Mining (2)	Manufacturing, Handicraft (3)	Commerce, Transport (4)	Administration, Domestic Service, etc. (5)
Typical industrial countries						
United Kingdom	1930	7	5	32	23	33
Belgium	1930	17	6	42	21	14
Netherlands	1930	21	2	36	23	18
Switzerland	1930	21	–	45	19	15
United States	1930	22	2	30	27	19
Czechoslovakia	1930	28	2	40	14	16
Germany	1933	29	4	36	19	12
Austria	1934	32	1	33	16	18
Sweden	1930	36	1	31	18	14
France	1931	36	2	32	17	13
Italy	1936	48	1	28	13	10
Japan	1930	50	1	19	20	10
Other industrial countries						
Australia	1933	20	2	30	24	24
New Zealand	1936	28	–	24	26	22
Argentina	1930	30[a]	b	b	b	b
Canada	1931	31	2	25	23	19
Norway	1930	35	1	26	22	16
Denmark	1930	36	–	28	18	18
South Africa						
White population	1936	26	4	23	30	17
Others	1921	75	6	5	2	12
Less industrialized countries						
Chile	1930	38	6	22	16	18
Uruguay	1930	44[a]	b	b	b	b
Ireland	1936	48	–	15	13	24
Cuba	1919	49	–	20	16	15
Portugal	1930	51	1	18	9	21
Palestine	1931	51	1	15	15	18
Hungary	1930	54	1	23	10	12
Greece	1928	54	–	16	12	18

TABLE 29 (Contd.)

Country	Year	Agriculture, Fishing (1)	Mining (2)	Manufacturing, Handicraft (3)	Commerce, Transport (4)	Administration, Domestic Service, etc. (5)
Spain	1920	56	2	19	8	15
British Malaya	1930	56a	b	b	b	b
Finland	1930	64	–	14	7	15
Poland	1931	65	1	16	8	10
Estonia	1934	66	–	15	7	12
Latvia	1935	67	–	15	8	10
U.S.S.R.	1930	67a	b	b	b	b
Countries lagging in industrial development						
Egypt	1927	67	–	11	12	10
Mexico	1930	68	1	13	7	11
French Indo-China	1930	71a	b	b	b	b
Indiac	1931	72	–	11	7	10
Thailand	1930	72a	b	b	b	b
Colombia	1930	72a	b	b	b	b
Venezuela	1930	72a	b	b	b	b
China	1930	70–75a	b	b	b	b
Netherlands Indies	1930	73a	b	b	b	b
Peru	1930	74a	b	b	b	b
Brazil	1930	75a	b	b	b	b
Philippines	1930	76a	b	b	b	b
Iran	1930	76a	b	b	b	b
Romania	1930	78	–	7	5	10
Yugoslavia	1931	79	–	11	4	6
Lithuania	1923	80	–	6	3	11
Bulgaria	1934	80	–	8	4	8
Turkey	1935	82	–	8	4	6

Source: Industrialization and Foreign Trade, League of Nations, Geneva, 1945.II.A.10, pp. 26–27.

a. Share of total population dependent on agriculture around 1930. Figures supplied by the Office of Population Research, Princeton University.

b. Not available.

c. Men only.

Note: Within each group, the countries are arranged in order of the percentage in col. 1. The comparability of the figures is impaired by differences in statistical methods.

barley and potatoes. The yields tend to decline fairly steadily as we move down the table, with the exception of Australia, Argentina, the United States and Canada, which show a more precipitous decline in all four crops. Even Bulgaria, next to the bottom of the list with 80 per cent of its population in agriculture, had higher yields than these four countries in all except potatoes. The extensive type of farming operations carried on in the United States, Australia, Canada and Argentina give these countries a position apart.[18] But aside from these countries, the most thoroughly agricultural countries likewise seem to have the lowest yields per unit of area, as Table 30 shows. Possible explanations are agricultural overpopulation, poor quality of land, primitive methods of cultivation, or some combination of the three.

INFERENCES FOR FUTURE POLICY

Much of the world's population exists at a frightfully low standard of living. The evidence in the preceding pages certainly suggests that higher income levels are statistically associated with a decreasing proportion of the working population in agriculture. From this fact, the conclusion is often drawn that higher real incomes in the low-income areas depend on industrial development. Yet statistical correlation does not demonstrate causal relationship.

Industrialization alone is not necessarily an open-sesame to higher real incomes the world over. For although high-per-capita-income countries are usually industrialized, the high productivity per capita that affords them high incomes cannot logically be traced altogether to industrialization. In most instances, the industrialization is itself to be explained by a combination of rich natural resources, an energetic and skilled people, a topography and climate favorable to production, and not least in importance, usually a low population density. In other words, conditions were relatively favorable for a high-per-capita productivity with or without industrialization, and thus for a high-per-capita standard of living.

Without these basic factors, neither industrialization nor a high standard of living would have eventuated. That this is the more probable causal relationship, rather than one moving directly from indus-

18. In order to avoid any misunderstanding we should perhaps emphasize that relative costs cannot be inferred from average yields. Canadian or Argentine wheat is low-cost wheat in the world market despite low yields.

TABLE 30

<small>PROPORTION OF GAINFULLY EMPLOYED POPULATION IN AGRICULTURE AND
AGRICULTURAL YIELDS, 1927–1931 AVERAGE</small>

Country	Per Cent of Population in Agriculture	Yields			
		Wheat	Rye	Barley	Potatoes
		(In Hundreds of Kilos Per Hectare)			
United Kingdom	7	21.9	—	20.6	163.0
Belgium	17	25.4	23.6	27.0	207.0
United States	22	9.9	7.8	12.2	76.8
Czechoslovakia	28	16.9	16.0	18.0	133.9
Germany	29	20.5	16.4	19.7	148.7
Austria	32	15.6	13.4	15.8	141.0
Sweden	36	20.1	15.5	18.1	113.2
Japan	50	16.9	—	19.2	95.1
Australia	20	7.3	9.0	9.7	60.0
Argentina	30	8.2	3.6	6.4	63.3
Canada	31	11.4	9.2	12.3	92.7
Denmark	36	27.8	16.2	27.9	141.3
Poland	65	12.7	11.1	12.3	114.2
Estonia	66	11.1	11.7	10.0	110.9
Latvia	67	11.8	9.8	9.0	99.6
Romania	78	10.1	10.0	9.8	99.8
Yugoslavia	79	11.7	8.3	9.2	52.6
Lithuania	80	12.5	10.9	10.6	108.8
Bulgaria	80	11.6	10.4	13.2	37.8
Turkey	82	8.2	9.4	9.7	26.7

Sources: Population percentages from Table 29; yield figures from *Statistisches Jahrbuch für das deutsche Reich, 1934,* Internationale Uebersichten, Statistisches Reichsamt, pp. 38–41.

trialization to better standards of living, seems to be emphasized by the very marked differences in incomes within the high-income countries themselves. One would not usually argue that in the United States the low incomes in certain states are, in any fundamental sense, chargeable to the absence of industrialization, nor, what is even more important, that more industrialization would guarantee higher per capita incomes. It would be more reasonable to point to the poor natural resources, natural land barriers, deficiencies in skill, energy and attitude in the population, and the like, as causes of low incomes. Consequently, reasoning that more industrialization yields higher living standards may provide a tenuous base for economic development plans in some areas unless, perchance, the more fundamental favorable factors are also present. The danger of such faulty reasoning is especially great where "industrialization" is used in the narrow sense of simply creating more factories or industrial plants.

PROBLEMS OF DELIBERATE INDUSTRIALIZATION

No one could reasonably quarrel about the desirability of improving the miserable lot of half the world's population. But well-intentioned schemes that disregard the inescapable realities of the problem will inevitably end in disillusion and despair. Good works consist of more than benevolent intentions.

One might assume that future industrialization and economic development in low-income areas would follow a pattern similar to that traced by countries already industrialized. In the 19th and early 20th centuries, Japan, the British Dominions, Sweden, Switzerland and most of western Europe evolved from agrarian to industrial economies with rising standards of living. Partial industrialization was achieved by the Japanese in Manchuria after 1933. And on a smaller scale, with a number of special features, the economic development of Palestine has taken place. Careful study of these instances of industrialization and economic development should, one might suppose, provide the basis for a reasonable forecast of the probable course of industrial development in the existing low-income areas. Such studies would undoubtedly be illuminating; and they would forewarn against errors that might otherwise be committed in some industrialization programs.

But there are important differences between such industrialization as has already occurred and that now being planned. The regions that industrialized in the 19th century — western Europe, the United States, and to some extent the British Dominions — did so in accord with free-enterprise principles in areas rich in natural resources relative to their populations. As emphasized in Chapter 2, a common ideology and set of values prevailed and there was a century of nearly unbroken peace. Contemporary China, India and southeastern Europe are something else again. The recent partial industrialization of the U.S.S.R. is also unique in several respects. Apart from the fact that Russia has rich natural resources and virtually no population problem, the Russian industrialization program was spurred to a frenzied pace by an overriding fear of possible foreign aggression, and was administered throughout with a ruthlessness that might not invite repetition.[19] The Manchurian development, although never carried through to completion, also has its own special features. In other words, some circumspection is appropriate in applying what has occurred in Russia, the United States or other already industrialized areas to a program and forecast on industrialization for China, India, the Netherlands Indies, southeastern Europe or other poverty-stricken areas.

A proper study of these differences and the outlook for improved living standards in particular regions would require painstaking analysis. Nevertheless, a few general comments are made necessary by the international investment problem as a whole.[20]

19. The Russian case is also unique in that the program was carried through by a huge program of forced capital accumulation with almost no foreign borrowing beyond some medium-term commercial credits. Japanese industrialization did not entail much foreign borrowing either.

20. The literature on industrialization and economic development is increasing rapidly. As a general survey, Eugene Staley's *World Economic Development* (International Labor Office, Montreal, 1944) is a useful introduction to the subject. General in character, but with a different emphasis, is Dr. Hilgerdt's League of Nations study, *Industrialization and Foreign Trade*. Two useful articles by P. N. Rosenstein-Rodan are "Problems of Industrialization of Eastern and Southeastern Europe," *Economic Journal*, June–September 1943, and "The International Development of Economically Backward Areas," *International Affairs*, April 1944. Also to be mentioned is H. Frankel, "The Industrialization of Agricultural Countries," *Economic Journal*, June–September 1943. Besides these are a host of quasi-popular articles and numerous books devoted to special areas, e.g., PEP, *Economic Development in S.E. Europe*, and Soule *et al., op. cit.*

As used in current discussion, the term "economic development" is broader than industrialization. Projects such as the TVA or the Columbia River Development figure prominently in current discussions of what might be done through economic development. Worker-training schemes, swamp drainage, or even population control programs, would be included along with highway construction and harbor developments. An interesting recent discussion of the economic development of low-income areas (*International Development Loans*, National Planning Association, Planning Pamphlets, No. 15, Washington, 1942) distinguishes four general types of undertakings: (1) *basic undertakings* such as roads, irrigation, large hydroelectric power developments, etc.; (2) *reconstruction and conservation*, including, beyond the repair of war damage, reconstruction of cities, slum removal, prevention of soil erosion, flood control, etc.; (3) *exploitation* — "projects which provide new, additional, improved, or cheaper commodities in a country for export to foreign markets" — these are expected to be undertaken mainly by private enterprise on the basis of investment opportunities created by types (1) and (2) above; (4) *diversification*, which is defined (p. 20) as ". . . steps to diversify national economic activity, for the purpose of distributing employment eggs into several baskets,

THE COMPLEX CHARACTER OF INDUSTRIALIZATION

A country's attainment of industrial status can be variously defined according to emphasis and point of view. Certainly it involves an increase in the real capital resources available per head of population.[21] Alternatively, it is an increase in the proportion of industrial production to total national income, or perhaps better, a decrease in the proportion of agricultural production to national income.[22] A different emphasis would stress the gradual widening of the sphere of the "money economy." Again, from a sociological point of view, urbanization might be considered the important development. Industrialization is a many-sided process and no simple definition is entirely satisfactory.[23]

---

of resisting the downward tendency in the bargaining position of the producer of food-stuffs and raw materials against countries exporting manufactured products, and of increasing national economic power." This fourth group includes agricultural diversification, introduction of light industry and even of heavy industry.

Some interesting discussions of these problems are to be found also in H. D. Fong, *The Post-War Industrialization of China,* Planning Pamphlets, Nos. 12 and 13, National Planning Association, Washington, 1942.

The literature is growing rapidly, however, and no attempt at a complete reference list is made here.

21. For instance: ". . . an increase in the amount of capital equipment and productivity per employed person and variety of goods" (H. Frankel, "The Industrialization of Agricultural Countries," *Economic Journal,* June–September 1943, p. 191) ; "The movement of machinery and capital towards labor, instead of moving labor towards capital, is the process of industrialization, which, together with agrarian improvement, is the most important aspect of the economic development of the depressed areas" (P. N. Rosenstein-Rodan, "The International Development of Economically Backward Areas," *International Affairs,* April 1944, p. 161). Here the author emphasizes this solution because he sees no prospect of solving the problem of low-income areas by means of migration to high-income areas. Notice, however, that if the emphasis is simply on real capital resources per head of population, then the increased capital investment could theoretically occur in the primary industries. In fact, in some countries this might well be the most promising means of increasing consumption. The limits of productive capital investment in primary industries are perhaps lower than in manufacturing.

22. Colin Clark and others would use this designation and classify production into primary, secondary and tertiary. As industrialization proceeded, Clark would use as a measure the increasing proportions of the working population in secondary and tertiary production. In *Conditions of Economic Progress* (p. 182) he writes concerning the classification: "For convenience in international comparisons production may be defined as primary, secondary and tertiary. Under the former we include agricultural and pastoral production, fishing, forestry and hunting. Mining is more properly included with secondary production, covering manufacture, building construction and public works, gas and electricity supply. Tertiary production is defined by difference as consisting of all other economic activities, the principal of which are distribution, transport, public administration, domestic service and all other activities producing a non-material output."

23. Perhaps Hilgerdt's description is as useful as any: ". . . the industrialization process is not confined to the establishment of a manufacturing industry but involves a change in the whole economic structure of the country concerned. This change may be briefly

Capital Accumulation

Economists traditionally have classified productive factors into land, labor and capital.[24] With a given population and land area, an increase in total output can come about only through an increase in the total capital available for productive purposes and/or through an improved utilization of existing land, labor and equipment. If population and land area are given, greater output is possible only by achieving more capital per head, or by using all the factors of production more efficiently through improved technology.[25] In any given region, of course, both methods would probably be employed.

Capital accumulation for increased output in low-income areas is a two-sided process. On the one hand, the population as a whole must consume less than the whole annual product. On the other hand, savings must be directed into productive capital formation. Even in some very poor countries, savings are not negligible in the aggregate, but they are either hoarded or directed into unproductive capital formation. In the Balkans, for example, hoarding of currency notes is said to involve perhaps as much as 25 per cent of total circulation. Gold coins and foreign currency are also hoarded.[26] Similar hoarding habits have also prevailed for centuries in the Orient. Hoarding means that what is saved is not made available for industrial equipment or for agricultural improvements. Real capital accumulation — in the sense that the whole annual output is not currently consumed each year — has not been entirely lacking even in the very-low-income

---

characterized as implying an extended division of labour complemented by a system of distribution and exchange of goods functioning in a developed 'money economy.'" *Industrialization and Foreign Trade*, p. 30.

24. This is a crude tripartite classification, which naturally has often been extended. Recently Professor J. J. Spengler has suggested that "The complex of productive factors used jointly with labor may be divided roughly into five categories: (1) land, measured in terms of area and viewed as a situs for habitation and for agricultural and other productive activities; (2) nondepletable natural resources whose supply is essentially fixed; (3) depletable and nonreplaceable natural resources; (4) natural resources which are replaceable and whose supply is augmentable; and (5) equipment — i.e., machinery, buildings, etc." ("Population and Per Capita Income," *Annals of the American Academy of Political and Social Science*, January 1945, p. 183.) The virtues of such a classification for economic development schemes are obvious.

25. Improved technology may depend either on inventions, e.g., the development of new industrial processes, new species or breeds, etc., or on the application in the low-income area of techniques and processes that are already being used elsewhere. In most poverty areas economic development would consist to a high degree of borrowing from abroad long-familiar processes and techniques.

26. PEP, *Economic Development in S.E. Europe*, pp. 114–15.

areas. Yet there has been little resultant gain in productive efficiency, because the capital accumulation has taken the form of religious monuments, ancestral veneration, elaborate places of worship, and the like. Instead of acquiring more railroads, the population has rejoiced in finer temples. Such practices are apparently deeply rooted in the social, religious and moral values of the civilization — in the very tough cultural complex. They are not likely to be elbowed aside with a guarantee of bank deposits and the lure of 6 per cent.

Transportation, communication and marketing facilities are perhaps the most productive forms that real capital formation can initially assume in the low-income areas. Historically, the impetus here has usually come from external trade. The frequently enormous spread between the low prices in the interior and the much higher prices in world markets has stimulated the construction of railways, telegraphs, storage warehouses and similar facilities. Improvements of this kind tend to eliminate the "village economy" as the market widens in area and variety.[27] Without transport, local production can supply only local needs: industrialization has no scope for development. Even local agriculture and the exploitation of local natural resources is restricted or precluded altogether; the country remains economically primitive; incomes remain at a subsistence level.

Although improved communications may be initially stimulated by foreign trade opportunities, the growth of towns and markets tends to force capital accumulation for domestic industry and commerce. More people are eventually employed in supplying the needs of the urban areas for food, clothing, services, etc. The initial impulse may have come from export markets made possible by improved transportation. But local needs require some local industry. Aggregate output and per capita incomes tend to increase.

Thus, transport and communication facilities are perhaps the most important type of real capital formation for a country intent on industrialization and improved living standards. Beyond this conclusion, few valid generalizations are possible, because the types of industry that can be most productively developed in any region through capital investment will depend largely on the natural resources and the apti-

27. Cf. "Particularly in the tropics, railways and other means of communication have been essential for the establishment of order and of social and humanitarian reform, and upon them depends the ability to supply foodstuffs when famine threatens owing to failure of crops in some area. Everywhere they have played an important part in economic progress." *Industrialization and Foreign Trade*, p. 31.

tudes of the people. Textile production, at least of the cheaper varieties, seems to be feasible nearly everywhere. Leather handicrafts and simple food and raw material processing are also developed rather easily.

Although transportation is indispensable to greater industrialization and better living, transportation is also to a high degree "capital-intensive." That is, railways, roads, river developments and airports require a heavy capital investment in relation to their annual income. They therefore place a heavy drain on the limited annual savings of low-income countries. For many low-income countries this initial major barrier has never been surmounted: local savings and local ingenuity were insufficient to develop transport and communications, and foreign investment was not obtained — with the result that the country remained undeveloped.[28] Whether these obstacles can be surmounted in the future with the help of the International Bank for Reconstruction and Development, the Export-Import Bank, or some other agency, remains to be seen. Certainly the difficulty is real.[29]

Labor Training and Labor Mobility

Increased industrialization in low-income areas multiplies the need for skilled workers. The need is not alone for artisans and machine tenders. Supervisory personnel, technicians and managers are equally indispensable. If industrialization proceeds slowly over several generations, no serious difficulties will usually arise, because labor supply can keep pace with the slowly increasing demand. But a forced-draft industrialization, such as many countries apparently contemplate, will encounter genuine checks to output from mounting shortages of skilled labor. An agricultural population cannot acquire proficiency in industrial techniques overnight. In a measure, the process is organic and

28. An added difficulty is that a railroad is usually useless unless it covers some distance. One cannot build a railroad for just a mile or two. It must extend between two points of some economic importance or potentiality, and these are usually more than a few miles apart. Hence any useful railroad construction will typically require a large capital outlay. Piecemeal construction is valueless.

29. Railway developments have not been highly profitable undertakings for foreign capital in the past. Much of the American railway system that was initially financed by foreign lenders went through bankruptcy and reorganization in which the foreign bondholders were wiped out. The Latin-American railways have had a similar history. Railway development is perhaps the prime example of capital investment that is beneficial to the country as a whole but only rarely yields much net return to the private investors who finance it. Certainly the United States or Canada or Argentina gained from foreign borrowing to construct the railways. Probably Great Britain also gained. But the individual British investors who helped to finance such developments probably ended up, as a group, on the loss side of the ledger.

must evolve gradually despite the best efforts. In the U.S.S.R., skilled-labor shortages were a perennial limitation to output despite strenuous training programs. In 1929 more than 40 per cent of those holding posts requiring technical training were reported to be without such training.[30]

A proper labor-training program — including literacy, technical skills, managerial abilities, engineering, etc. — represents a long-term investment by the state for better incomes. An extensive program of this type is very important to any scheme for rapid industrialization.

A developing industrial society, in its initial and later stages alike, must maintain fluidity of its working population. Internal migrations from one area to another and from one occupation to another must be reasonably free. Industrial societies are societies in which the relative importance of different industries and different regions in the structure of production changes over the years.

Many low-income areas for which industrialization programs have been proposed, however, are characterized by social and religious institutions that strongly inhibit labor mobility. The key position of the family in Moslem countries, for example, tends to preclude migrations except by whole family groups.[31] The caste system in India similarly bars geographic and occupational migrations. Occidentals are apt to overlook such obstacles to effective industrialization in the Orient, because western society is now largely free from such barriers.[32] But in the Orient, as Professor Notestein has emphasized:

30. Alexander Baykov, *The Development of the Soviet Economic System,* Economic and Social Studies No. 5, National Institute of Economic and Social Research, Cambridge University Press, Cambridge (England), 1946, pp. 161, 217. The universities in the U.S.S.R. are said to have trained 170,000 specialists during the first five-year plan and 369,000 during the second five-year plan. In the same intervals the technical schools trained 291,000 and 623,000 respectively. Since at the end of the first five years (1932) there were some 22 million workers and employees in industry, the half million (461,-000) specialists and technical school graduates trained *during* the first five-year plan were less than 3 per cent of those employed in industry. This is a tiny fraction for a country that prior to 1928 was chiefly agricultural. *Ibid.,* p. 353.

31. Cf. "Many children, particularly many sons, afford something of an old-age security policy. It will be easier to live in comfort if many are contributing. Because of this attitude, perhaps, it is difficult to persuade Egyptians to migrate. The elders do not want the young to leave home. In consequence, such migration as there is, is largely by families as units." W. Wendell Cleland, "A Population Plan for Egypt," in *Demographic Studies of Selected Areas of Rapid Growth,* Milbank Memorial Fund, New York, 1944, p. 132.

32. "Many Indians would like to see India an independent nation, but not at the expense of their religion. Many would like to see India a wealthier nation, but not at the expense of their own relative wealth. Many would like to see India an educated nation, but not if it includes the lower castes. . . . Many would like to enjoy the privilege of

High evaluations are placed on the perpetuation of the family, clan or other group, but low evaluations on the individual and his welfare. These values are deeply imbedded and rigidly enforced by social sanctions. Even under the impact of a rapidly shifting environment, they change only gradually.[33]

Land tenure systems, impossible tax arrangements and "otherworldly" religious tenets similarly operate to restrict the kind of occupational mobility industrial development requires. These are important and complicated subjects that can only be mentioned here in passing. But they suggest that industrialization is an organic process, and in many ways a psychological process, amounting to much more than providing warehouses or factory buildings.

MALTHUS REINCARNATE: THE POPULATION PROBLEM

Among the low-income agricultural areas for which industrialization and economic development programs have been proposed, a surprising number face the "population problem" in acute form. Specifically, Egypt, India, China, Korea, Formosa, Java, large sections of the Caribbean area, much of the Philippines and parts of the Balkans face the threat of having gains in total output largely swallowed up by increases in numbers.[34]

Between 1921 and 1941 India's population increased by 83 million,[35] or in other words, an increase in absolute numbers greater than all Germany in 1939 and equal to 62 per cent of the total population of the United States. But India has not had an outstandingly large *rate* of increase compared with other areas. The Egyptian population, at 16.6 million in 1939, is reported to have doubled, without immigration, since 1882.[36] India, with an annual growth rate of 1.21 per cent between 1921 and 1941, lagged far behind the Netherlands Indies

climbing socially, but not by the extension of that privilege to persons beneath themselves." Kingsley Davis, "Demographic Fact and Policy in India," in *ibid.*, p. 52.

33. Frank W. Notestein, "Problems of Policy in Relation to Areas of Heavy Population Pressure," in *ibid.*, pp. 145–46.

34. Cf. Notestein, *loc. cit.* Professor J. J. Spengler has written: "The population of the world falls, Thompson finds, into three groups: I, comprising 21 per cent, has natality and mortality under control; II, comprising 21 per cent, is bringing natality and mortality under control; III, comprising 58 per cent, has neither mortality nor natality under 'reasonably secure control.' In 1925–34, C. Clark's studies suggest, group I received about 58 per cent of the world's income; II, about 24 per cent; III, something like 18 per cent." *Op. cit.*, p. 191.

35. Davis, *loc. cit.*, p. 39.

36. Clyde V. Kiser, "The Demographic Position of Egypt," in *Demographic Studies of Selected Areas of Rapid Growth*, p. 99.

rate of 2.08 between 1920 and 1930 (the population in 1930 was already 60.7 million), and the 2.20 rate in the Philippines between 1918 and 1939, where the population in 1939 was estimated at 16 million.[37] Professor Notestein suggests that of a probable total world population of 3.3 billion people in the year 2000, perhaps 2 billion will be in Asia.[38]

The primary reason for population growth in low-income areas, where such growth has taken place, has been the decline in mortality rates. The birth rates are already high. Greater output from improved facilities, modern sanitation, contagious-disease control and better organization operate chiefly to reduce mortality rather than to increase birth rates. As those who are born survive for a longer interval, more persons survive through the economically and biologically "productive" years, with the result that the initial population growth arising from improved mortality rates tends to be cumulative for a time. This tendency becomes stronger, moreover, if, as frequently occurs, the improvement in mortality rates is most marked at the lower-age groups of infancy and childhood. Demographers can show, for any country for which the pertinent data are available, at what level the population will reach an "equilibrium."[39]

An appreciable and enduring improvement in living standards in the already densely populated areas — India, Java, Formosa, Korea, China, Egypt and the Caribbean — is dependent on a rise in total production accompanied by a decline in birth rates. But in most of these areas — despite some industrialization, public health measures, and urbanization — birth rates have held close to the biological maximum. Local cultures have not, so far, changed appreciably nor admitted newer beliefs that would cut the birth rate. As Professor Kingsley Davis has written, after having just pointed out the various steps successfully taken in India to reduce famine and epidemic:

But the gain has not depended on a great change in the texture of Indian life, and hence does not have any such change to rely on in the future. The local

37. Notestein, *loc. cit.*, p. 142.

38. "Population — The Long View," in *Food for the World,* Theodore W. Schultz (ed.), University of Chicago Press, Chicago, 1945, p. 57.

39. Cf., for example, John Lindberg, "Food Supply under a Program of Freedom from Want," *Social Research*, May 1945, pp. 189–95, and Frank W. Notestein *et al., The Future Population of Europe and the Soviet Union,* League of Nations, Geneva, 1944.II.A.2.

village still remains about as unsanitary as ever, the public apathy to health measures about as complete as ever, and the poverty almost as abject as ever. . . .

To the extent that additional control of mortality is achieved without altering the fundamental conditions of Indian life, and without therefore greatly affecting fertility, the gap between births and deaths will continue to widen and the population growth to accelerate. This will tend to create an unstable demographic situation, because if the external and somewhat artificial support of the reduced mortality should be withdrawn, there will be a larger population to be affected by a suddenly increased death rate.[40]

These sentences would apply with equal force to American efforts in Puerto Rico.

The very fact that mortality rates have indeed declined in the low-income areas during the past half century is itself evidence of somewhat improved average standards of living. For few would deny that an improvement in life expectancy is a net accretion to welfare. But the failure of birth rates to diminish has meant that the gain in per capita living standards has been far below what it might have been without the population growth and much less than proportionate to the rise in total output.

Whether for most of these regions a full-scale industrialization and economic development program — something far more ambitious than has ever been attempted in the past — would give a sufficiently sudden lift to per capita output for it to maintain itself through inducing a decline in birth rates, no one can say with certainty. The possibility unquestionably exists. The western European countries achieved it. The Japanese case seems to be still an open question.[41] The prospects in southeastern Europe and Latin America are perhaps more promising than in Asia. But not a large proportion of the low-income groups in the world as a whole is in these regions.

Until the problems of population and culture of the low-income areas are faced squarely in all their complexities, much of the other

40. *Loc. cit.,* pp. 47–48.
41. Cf. "The dynamics of fertility decline in Japan during the three-quarters of a century since the opening to the West offer little basis for optimism with reference to the possibilities of an early cessation to population growth in the overcrowded regions of Asia. It is true that fertility declined in Japan, but in 1935 fertility even in the large cities was very high in relation to that in the West. Fertility in rural areas and the small towns has declined only slightly except as the increasing age of marriage and the decreasing prevalence of informal marriages has decreased the fertility of younger women." Irene B. Taeuber and Edwin G. Beal, "The Dynamics of Population in Japan," in *Demographic Studies of Selected Areas of Rapid Growth,* p. 34.

discussion of improved living by means of industrialization and economic development seems somewhat beside the point.

CONCLUSIONS

The purpose of the foregoing analysis is not to suggest that "nothing can be done" for the low-income areas. Rather the intent has been to stress that industrialization for higher incomes and economic development are complicated undertakings involving much more than the generous provision of loan capital from the wealthier countries. With the exception of Russia, which is a unique case from more than one point of view, industrial development in the past has been attained slowly over four or five decades. An interval of several generations allows the process to assume an organic integration in its several parts, which is not so easily achieved when the program calls for moving ahead rapidly under forced draft. Yet, especially in the low-income areas where there is already a population problem, a quick forward advance seems to be the most promising approach toward higher real incomes. A more gradual assault on poverty income levels is likely to be repulsed by the sheer weight of multiplying humanity.

One would like to bask in the warm comfort of easy assurances that some writers have imparted to the whole problem by making it appear that everything will be easy if only capital is forthcoming from the richer countries. Although foreign assistance can play a role, it is not a universal passport to higher income levels.

THE CONTRIBUTION OF FOREIGN CAPITAL

Purely general discussions often leave the impression that because greater industrial and agricultural output in low-income countries depends partly on having more capital, the problem can be solved only by capital imports from abroad. The wealthier countries — so runs the argument — must provide the capital for the poorer countries if their incomes are to be bettered. Yet the actual process cannot be handled so easily. Foreign borrowing can assist or speed industrialization in low-income areas. But it is not all-important and in some instances might be dispensed with altogether.

REAL CAPITAL FORMATION

According to one careful estimate, the 8.5 million wage earners in American manufacturing industry in 1937 worked with $21.2 billion of capital assets other than land, or an average of $2,474 per wage earner.[42] In the same year, the total population of the continental United States was estimated at 128.8 million persons. The investment in capital assets other than land in manufacturing in the United States was therefore $164 per head. Now, to add to the present capital investment in manufacturing in India an amount of $20 per head (assuming no growth in population occurred in the process) would require $8 billion. A capital increment of this amount would obviously leave India still far behind the United States in capital equipment in manufacturing. Furthermore, without similar investments in transportation, warehouses, distribution facilities,[43] etc., the added investment in manufacturing would be of limited usefulness. The sheer magnitude of the capital sums required indicates that only a small part of the total investment necessary for industrialization can come from abroad under any reasonable assumptions.

A more important reason why only a small part of the total investment can come *directly* from abroad is indicated by the nature of the real capital needed. Any industrialized country has a large proportion of its total productive capital in the form of buildings, railway roadbeds, highways, harbor developments, dams, canals, sewage systems, river developments, and the like, which manifestly cannot be "imported" in any direct sense. They must be fabricated on the spot by local labor using local materials. Except for the rails and crossties, a railway line from the seacoast to the interior in an underdeveloped country cannot be imported; it must be constructed locally. Any assistance from abroad must necessarily be indirect in projects of this sort. Yet a very large proportion of the capital goods needed for industrialization is precisely of this type.[44]

IMPORT NEEDS, THE BALANCE OF PAYMENTS, AND
FOREIGN BORROWING

The comprehensive industrialization of an underdeveloped country will create special import needs and balance-of-payments difficulties,

42. Solomon Fabricant, *Employment in Manufacturing, 1899–1939*, National Bureau of Economic Research, New York, 1942, p. 257.
43. In 1937 the investment in steam railroads in the United States is reported (*Statistical Abstract of the United States, 1943*, p. 457) at $25.6 billion, or something less than $200 per head of population. This figure is probably an overstatement but is sufficient for illustrative purposes.
44. For a fuller discussion of the problems of this section, see Norman S. Buchanan, *International Investment and Domestic Welfare*, Holt, New York, 1945, especially Chaps. 2, 5, 6.

thereby creating a need for foreign loans unless unusual precautions are taken. There are three main reasons for this.

First, the actual process of industrialization requires that more machinery and supplies be imported than before. In the early stages, construction machinery and building supplies may be the chief items needed. Later, perhaps textile machinery, electrical machinery, railroad rolling stock and industrial raw materials will predominate. All in all, industrialization is usually impossible without increased imports of various products unobtainable in the home market. Imports will thus be directly stimulated by the industrialization process.

Second, as industrialization involves a large increase in total domestic investment outlays, it will generate an increased demand for imports simply because aggregate money income will rise. The new developments cannot proceed without investment expenditures; investment expenditures inevitably increase money incomes; and unless there are restrictions, part of the larger money incomes will be spent by the recipients for foreign-made goods. Goods formerly imported, such as simple manufactures, will be imported in greater volume and new items will enter the list. Hence, there will be an induced rise in imports if steps are not taken to prevent it. Effective countermeasures would be higher income taxes, import prohibitions or higher duties, and perhaps also increased excise taxes on domestic and foreign "luxury" goods.[45]

Third, industrialization also operates to reduce exports below their former level, at least in its earlier stages. More domestically produced raw materials, including foods, will be consumed at home rather than sent abroad. Labor will be drawn away from some of the former export industries to work on the newer projects that are the essence of the

45. In some areas higher income taxes may not be possible for the masses of the people because the economy is not sufficiently developed to allow personal income taxes to be used. Income taxes presuppose a fairly high development of the techniques of record keeping. In this case, sales taxes or turnover taxes would presumably have to be used despite their inequities in burden. Higher import duties simply prevent people from spending their now higher incomes on foreign-made goods by making them more expensive. But it is also desirable to prevent economic resources at home from being drawn into the production of luxury goods because this means that fewer resources are available for pushing the industrialization program. Hence, heavy excise taxes on luxury goods may be necessary to prevent their manufacture and consumption. A system of priorities for labor and materials, with luxury goods getting a very low rating, would be an alternative control technique. But only passing reference to these administrative problems is appropriate here.

industrialization process. One cannot be altogether certain in these matters, but exports would probably tend to decline in any program of rapid industrialization.

But the combination of falling exports and rising imports automatically makes for shortage of foreign exchange, which the industrializing country must overcome. Exchange control is one possibility: the government can simply ration scarce foreign exchange among the many claimants. From an international point of view, exchange control is not a happy solution. (See Chapter 6.) A foreign loan, or a stream of foreign loans, is an alternative, and in most instances a superior, solution. The industrialization process itself thus tends to create a scarcity of foreign exchange, but foreign borrowing can overcome the shortage.

HOW MUCH FOREIGN BORROWING?

A moment's reflection will indicate that the amount of foreign borrowing for a particular industrialization program is not any precisely definable sum that can be set down in advance. It will depend, first, on the possibilities for increasing exports and checking imports in the industrializing country, and thus providing the needed foreign exchange without recourse to foreign borrowing. Wide differences among countries, in this respect, will unquestionably prevail. In some cases, the industrialization process will lead to extensive development of export industries. But this will not be possible at once, so that, for a time, foreign borrowing will be nearly unavoidable. In other cases, emphasis may fall strongly on avoiding imports altogether: even machinery that can be obtained from abroad more cheaply may not be imported; instead, orders may be placed at home in order to develop a machinery industry within the country. Confronted by such widely varying possibilities, one can scarcely be definite about the amount of "necessary" foreign borrowing.

The amount of foreign borrowing needed to assist industrialization will depend secondly on how drastically the country is willing to cut current consumption in order to accelerate capital formation and on how rapidly the country is determined to carry through its plans. In general, the greater the restriction of current consumption, the less the need for foreign borrowing. And the greater the speed required by the program, the greater the need for foreign borrowing. The need for foreign borrowing is thus linked directly to the amount of current consumption and the rapidity of industrialization.

If the country is willing to reduce consumption from current output to very low levels so that capital formation can proceed apace, then foreign borrowing may even be avoided altogether. The U.S.S.R. industrialized virtually without foreign loans except for some medium-term commercial credits. But this entailed holding output of consumers' goods at exceedingly low levels, and even exporting grain to pay for needed imports despite the fact that some people were starving at home. This will be precisely the difficulty in some low-income areas today, where the level of consumption is so exceedingly low that any reduction will force starvation, or at least great hardship, on many millions of people. Yet without an increase in domestic savings not much real capital formation can occur. More equalitarian distribution of income would lessen the danger of starvation but would probably diminish capital accumulation too. The formation of productive capital inevitably means cutting consumption or diverting resources from nonproductive capital formation. But there is a limit to deprivation, and foreign borrowing may lighten the burden by allowing consumption to be maintained at a satisfactory level through greater imports while productive capital formation proceeds.

Clearly, the pace set for attaining an industrial status will lessen or aggravate the reductions in consumption required. A five-year or ten-year program will require more outside assistance per year to supplement domestic consumption than one extending over a quarter century.[46] A very poor country that endeavored to industrialize at a very rapid rate would have to borrow enormous sums abroad or allow many of its people to die of starvation.

Thus there is no simple answer to the question of how much foreign borrowing is "necessary" to assist in the industrialization of economically backward areas. External factors determine the technical possibilities, but the ability, and above all the willingness, of people to put themselves on short rations determines the practical answer.

---

46. We use the phrase "to supplement domestic consumption" to cover all three difficulties (discussed on pp. 205 ff.) tending to create a shortage of foreign exchange. Necessary imports can be paid for out of current exports by cutting home consumption; avoiding induced imports has an identical effect in cutting home consumption. If exports, instead of being allowed to fall as industrialization proceeds, are in fact maintained, this means a reduction in domestic consumption too. Foreign borrowing, therefore, is an alternative to a reduction in home consumption.

AMERICA AS THE PRINCIPAL LENDER

The International Bank for Reconstruction and Development is now the only international lending agency intended to finance industrial development in low-income areas. But in the early postwar years, at least part of its resources will be used for reconstruction. The American Export-Import Bank will probably assist in economic development in certain areas. This means that direct lending by the International Bank, private loans guaranteed by the Bank, and Export-Import Bank loans are the major lending sources to which industrializing countries can turn. These agencies, in turn, will draw their funds in large measure from the American economy. The United States therefore has a large stake in the whole program of industrialization of low-income areas.

Two further comments are appropriate. First, American investors — both private and governmental — must have a thorough understanding of the problems of forced-draft industrialization and a sophisticated view of the difficulties to be surmounted. This involves a good deal more than a well-intentioned desire to make people in low-income areas "better off." If the United States is to perform its creditor role effectively there must be full recognition that this is a much larger role than any country has ever before essayed in long-term international lending. It calls for some intense study of the structure of the problems involved, a deep understanding of their setting, and considerable insight into the nature of the peoples and areas concerned.

In the second place, the effects of industrialization abroad on the American economy, domestically and internationally, need to be thoroughly explored in regard to both the interval of capital outflow and the later return flow of interest and amortization receipts. These influences need to be analyzed in two different respects: first, as regards the financial structure, where the focus is on American money incomes, prices, exchange rates, interest rates, etc.; second, in respect to the flow of real output in the United States, where the focus is on the structure of production, the types of exports and imports, and in general on the flexibility of real resource utilization in the American economy. Much of this will be highly speculative and only a long analysis can be expected to reveal even the main avenues of change. But the importance of such an analysis can scarcely be overstressed.

Chapter 9

CAPITAL EXPORT, TRADE AND AMERICAN POLICY

INTERNATIONAL INVESTMENT affects the volume and direction of international trade, in the obvious sense that both would be different had the investment not occurred. But trade flows cannot be analyzed so that the specific effects of investment operations can be identified in terms of particular goods and services. What can be demonstrated and what is highly pertinent, however, is the over-all effect of international investment operations on the flow of trade and on the balance of payments of lending and borrowing countries. Some of these effects are fairly immediate and direct; others are more delayed and circuitous. Together, they comprise an intricate series of cause and effect relationships of great practical importance.

Foreign investment, broadly considered, is variously a problem in the balance of payments, in exports and imports, and in the ever-changing pattern of world trade as a whole. Consequently, foreign investment policy inevitably becomes intertwined with foreign exchange policy, with commercial policy and with international economic relations in general.

THE FLOW OF CAPITAL AND TRADE

The complexities of foreign investment in relation to trade and the balance of payments are perhaps most easily understood by starting with simple cases free of distracting complications. The exposition can then be applied to a particular country without difficulty.

EFFECTS OF FOREIGN INVESTMENT ON TRADE

If the United States government makes a loan to the British government, or if an American corporation purchases an assembly plant in England, the immediate effect in either case is an increase in the sum of American dollars at the disposal of the British people.[1] The kinds

1. The dollars made available to the British in this example may be dollars previously held by Americans, so that their potential expenditures are correspondingly reduced, or the dollars may be newly created out of the banking system.

of goods and services for which these dollars are spent determine the direct effect of the foreign lending on the American economy. For it must not be forgotten that American dollars are ultimately spendable only for American commodities and services. Either the British government or British citizens will spend the dollars for American goods and services, or the dollars will be exchanged for some other currency — say, Egyptian pounds, in which case the Egyptians will spend them for American goods and services. Regardless of how many intermediate transfers there may be, American foreign lending increases the number of dollars in the hands of non-Americans. And these added dollars can be spent, if they are spent at all, only for American goods and services.[2]

These few facts show clearly that the initial effect of American foreign lending is to increase American exports relative to American imports: America will tend to have an "export surplus." In the case of the borrowing country, the loan from the United States will tend to increase its imports relative to its exports: it will tend to have an "import surplus."

A loan, in the strict sense, involves an interest charge and a repayment schedule. The borrower expects to pay, and the lender expects to receive, a flow of interest payments and a flow of payments on principal account. The effect of these payments on exports and imports must in all respects be the reverse of the effects of the original loan. The creditor country has an inflow of interest and principal payments from abroad, which will allow it to import more than it otherwise could: repayment tends to give the lender an import surplus and the debtor an export surplus.

If the effect of an outburst of American foreign lending is to increase the dollars in the hands of foreigners and thus increase American exports, and if the effect of the service charges on these loans as interest and principal payments is simply the reverse — that is, to cause the former borrowers to export more in order to obtain dollars — then the effects on export trade of any *constant* stream of fresh lending will sooner or later be overcome by the return stream of service charges. How rapidly the inflow from service charges overtakes the outflow from fresh lending depends on the volume of new lending and the interest and amortization schedule. Any number of patterns is con-

2. Clearly, gold is here treated as a commodity and not regarded as over and apart from other commodities.

ceivable. The principle, however, remains the same: new lending increases the dollars in the hands of foreigners and so tends to increase American exports; interest and amortization charges paid on earlier loans tend to increase American imports.[3] The two work in opposite directions: for given sums there is a definable relationship between them.

How rapidly the income from previous investments will overtake the gross outflow from fresh investment commitments depends on the terms of the loan contract. It is a simple problem of arithmetic, in which the required data are the rate of interest at which the loans are made and the amortization schedule assigning the terms of repayment. Whenever the inflow of payments from earlier lending equals the outflow arising from new lending, the net effect on the trade *balance* in the lending country is neutral. In order to gain some notion of the sums involved, and because in the United States foreign lending as a means of increasing exports and home employment has been much discussed (pp. 170 ff.), it is interesting to examine some recent calculations relating rates of new lending to income receipts.

Randall Hinshaw has posed the problem by asking, "How much new lending per annum at various rates of interest is necessary to maintain an export surplus of $1 billion per annum?" His formulation, in other words, simply asks how much lending is necessary each year to support an export surplus of $1 billion a year *greater than would otherwise occur*.[4] In the first year, obviously, $1 billion of exports would result from $1 billion of new lending, if all the funds lent are spent for export goods that year. If we take a 2 per cent rate of interest and set the amortization rate at zero throughout the calculations, $2 billion must be lent in the thirty-fifth year to produce an export surplus of $1 billion. At a 5 per cent rate, $2.08 billion must be lent in the fifteenth year to give the same result. And at a 7 per cent rate, almost $2 billion

3. We must emphasize that for both the fresh lending and the service charges in the above paragraph and elsewhere, when we speak of an "increase in exports" or "an increase in imports" we mean always *relative to* "imports" or "exports" as the case may be. Absolute increases or decreases are not important for the purpose immediately in hand, but only relative changes.

4. An export surplus could arise without any formal lending program, e.g., through the granting of short-term credits or because of the liquidation of previously held balances in the hands of foreigners not arising from any earlier borrowing. Mr. Hinshaw's interest lies in an *increment* of the export balance by $1 billion. Cf. his article, "Foreign Investment and American Employment," *American Economic Review, Supplement*, May 1946, pp. 661–71.

must be lent as early as the tenth year. The general rule, naturally, is that the lower the rate of interest on the original loan, the more slowly the necessary sum of additional lending rises, and that for any rate of interest, the longer the time interval, the larger the amount that must be lent to maintain the export surplus at $1 billion. These calculations are presented in Table 31. It should be emphasized that the calculations in Table 31 assume no in-payments for amortization.

TABLE 31

ANNUAL AMOUNT OF NET LENDING REQUIRED AT VARIOUS INTEREST RATES
TO MAINTAIN AN ANNUAL EXPORT SURPLUS OF $1 BILLION

(In Billions)

Year	2%	3%	4%	5%	6%	7%	8%
5th	$1.10	$1.16	$1.22	$ 1.28	$ 1.34	$ 1.40	$ 1.47
10th	1.22	1.34	1.48	1.63	1.79	1.97	2.16
15th	1.35	1.56	1.80	2.08	2.40	2.76	3.17
20th	1.49	1.81	2.19	2.65	3.21	3.87	4.66
25th	1.64	2.09	2.67	3.39	4.29	5.43	6.85
30th	1.81	2.43	3.24	4.32	5.74	7.61	10.06
35th	2.00	2.81	3.95	5.52	7.69	10.68	14.79
40th	2.21	3.26	4.80	7.04	10.29	14.97	21.72
45th	2.44	3.78	5.84	8.99	13.76	21.00	31.92
50th	2.69	4.38	7.11	11.47	18.42	29.46	46.90

Source: Randall Hinshaw, "Foreign Investment and American Employment," *American Economic Review, Supplement,* May 1946, p. 666.

The probabilities are that nearly all foreign lending contracts will contain amortization clauses for the repayment of the principal. These may take many forms. The British loan already discussed (pp. 122 ff.) calls for no amortization payments in the early years; but this is only one type of schedule among many possible.

Amortization obviously increases the annual inflow of payments from earlier lending, and therefore, following the line of analysis used above, greatly increases the volume of fresh lending required to maintain an export surplus of $1 billion. Assuming twenty-year loans with equal annual payments (interest and amortization combined), an amount of $2.44 billion must be lent in the fifteenth year at a 2 per cent rate to maintain a $1 billion export surplus, as against $2 billion in the thirty-fifth year without amortization. At a 5 per cent rate, the amount is $2.16 billion in the tenth year. At a 3 per cent rate, a rate at which the Export-Import Bank has negotiated many of its loans, $1.92 billion is needed in the tenth year. Table 32 shows the effects of including amortization charges at various rates of interest on the volume of lending necessary to maintain an export surplus of $1 billion a year.

TABLE 32

ANNUAL AMOUNT OF TWENTY-YEAR LOANS REQUIRED AT VARIOUS
INTEREST RATES TO MAINTAIN AN ANNUAL EXPORT SURPLUS
OF $1 BILLION[a]

(*In Billions*)

Year	2%	3%	4%	5%	6%
5th	$1.35	$1.38	$1.43	$1.47	$1.52
10th	1.81	1.92	2.03	2.16	2.31
15th	2.44	2.65	2.90	3.18	3.50
20th	3.28	3.67	4.14	4.68	5.32
25th	4.41	5.08	5.90	6.88	8.09

Source: Randall Hinshaw, "Foreign Investment and American Employment," *American Economic Review, Supplement,* May 1946, p. 667.

a. It is assumed in this table that the sum of interest plus amortization on each loan is paid in equal installments.

Any lending program designed to keep a constant export surplus must thus push larger and larger sums into borrowers' hands as the years pass. The higher the interest rate and the shorter the amortization period of the individual loans, the more rapidly does the volume of required new lending expand. These are the crucial variables.

No foreign-lending policy of the United States is likely to aim at supporting a constant export surplus. Or to put it another way, no American foreign-lending policy that contemplates an ever-expanding volume of fresh loans is politically possible or economically realistic. But this means that any feasible American foreign loan program must reckon with the day when income and amortization payments will exceed new lending abroad.[5] The ultimate consequence of a foreign-lend-

5. For an interesting and detailed analysis of the effect of foreign lending on the American balance of payments under assumptions that appear to be not altogether im-

ing program, therefore, is an import, not an export, surplus in so far as the loan contracts are fulfilled. Any other expectation means that the loans are disguised gifts, that they are made under such terms and conditions that default is inevitable, or that their terms are so loosely drawn that in effect they do not require repayment.

AMERICAN LOANS IN RELATION TO IMPORTS

In the predictable future, there appears to be no serious question of the ability of the United States to make loans available to foreign countries for economic reconstruction and industrialization. The funds could be made available. The exports could be shipped. And, within limits, the goods exported because of the loans would not seriously impair American consumption nor appreciably raise American prices.

The crucial problem is the willingness and ability of the American economy to absorb imports for debt service and amortization. Sooner or later, these will inevitably overtake the volume of new lending so that a negative trade balance becomes a condition, or rather the essence, of drawing income from earlier commitments abroad. Apart from outright gifts or gifts disguised as loans for political purposes, the income from foreign investments is their rational justification on a pecuniary basis. The capacity to draw the income is therefore fundamental to the whole venture.

This is a problem that the American economy faced once before. Between 1920 and 1930 the United States made a boisterous debut in the field of foreign investment. But difficulties arose similar to those that may again plague the American economy if a new investment program is carried out.

Lending in the 1920's

At the beginning of 1920, the United States is reported to have held $2,576 million (par value) in portfolio foreign investments and $3,880 million in direct foreign investments, or a total of $6,456 mil-

---

plausible, see Hal B. Lary, "The Domestic Effects of Foreign Investment," *American Economic Review, Supplement,* May 1946, pp. 672–86. Dr. Lary assumes (p. 672) a "gross outflow of American capital aggregating $50,000,000,000 over the next 20 years. This volume of investment would not proceed at an even annual rate but would be concentrated in the early part of the period — $20,000,000,000 in the first 5 years and the remaining $30,000,000,000 spread, at a gradually declining rate, over the following 15 years. Thereafter we may assume that investment levels off to a regular annual flow of $1,000-000,000."

lion. By 1930 this total had risen to $15,172 million, and by 1940 declined again to $9,790 million.[6]

Between 1920 and 1940, chiefly in the years 1923–1930, the United States is estimated to have invested $11.7 billion abroad. Direct investments accounted for $3.2 billion and portfolio securities for $8.5 billion. The outflow was far from even from year to year. The big years for new capital issues were 1927 and 1928, with more than $1 billion in each year; 1928 and 1929 were the peak years for direct investments. More than $600 million was committed in 1929 alone. After 1930, both new portfolio and new direct investments declined to nominal amounts; there was even a net inflow of direct investments from abroad in some years. (See Chart 6.)

What of the remittances to the United States from abroad arising from these investments? Income from portfolio investments and direct investments combined totaled $12.36 billion between 1920 and 1940. Receipts from amortization and net resales of securities were $4.9 billion.[7] Thus, interest, dividends, amortization payments and resales together amounted to $17.37 billion.[8] Chart 6 portrays these relationships graphically for the twenty-one-year period. At $17.37 billion, the inflow of payments received between 1920 and 1940 was not far short of new lending of $11.7 billion during the same years plus the $6.45 billion estimated value of American foreign investment holdings at the beginning of 1920. Granted such a rough equivalence, one

6. The complete breakdown (all figures exclusive of any "war debts") at the three dates is as follows:

Value of United States Long-Term Investments Abroad (In Millions) *

End of Year	Total	Portfolio†	Direct
1919	$ 6,456	$2,576	$3,880
1930	15,172	7,205	7,967
1940	9,790	2,790	7,000

* "Foreign Investment Experience of the United States, 1920–1940," Bureau of Foreign and Domestic Commerce, March 19, 1945, p. 1 (mimeographed). Unless otherwise indicated, the statistical data that immediately follow are from this source.
† Par values in 1919 and 1930, market values in 1940.

7. Net resales of securities occur when American holders of foreign securities sell these to foreigners. Americans buy them originally but do not hold them until maturity.

8. Computed from data appearing in "Foreign Investment Experience of the United States, 1920–1940." Income from direct investments was typically the largest item of the three. It amounted to 62 per cent of the total income from all investments over the twenty-one-year period. It was even 40 per cent of combined income and amortization receipts. But direct investments were only 28 per cent of total new investments over the same interval. Clearly, they were the more profitable commitments by a wide margin.

Chart 6. Income and Amortization Receipts From United States Long-Term Foreign Investments in Relation to Gross Capital Outflow, 1920–1940

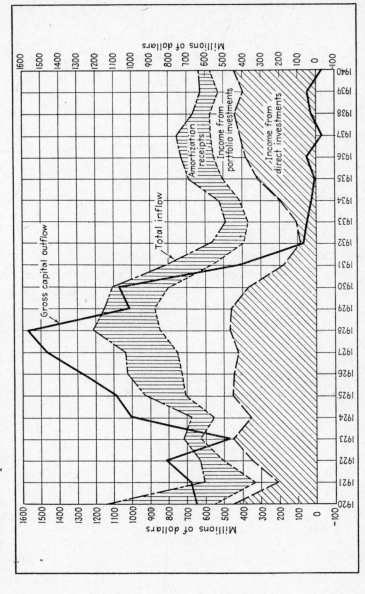

Source: "Foreign Investment Experience of the United States, 1920–1940," Bureau of Foreign and Domestic Commerce, March 19, 1945 (mimeographed).

Note: A minus sign indicates a net inflow of American direct-investment capital from abroad, data on this class of investments being available only on a net basis.

217

recently suggested line of reasoning would set the "net" return from foreign lending by the United States at the value of foreign investment holdings remaining at the end of 1940, or $9.7 billion. Calculated in this manner, the United States as a whole "got back" between 1920 and 1940 an amount equal to the whole of its original commitments in foreign investments, and "gained" whatever value attached to the foreign investments still held at the end of 1940.[9]

Nonetheless, America's experience with foreign lending in the 1920's was far from satisfactory, and certainly provides no proper blueprint for future policy. As the Department of Commerce aptly stated:

> Unfortunately, two cardinal mistakes were made: (1) There was, far too frequently, an extremely poor choice of investment risks, reflecting both the absence of any official policy and the abuse and mismanagement of the capital market by inexperienced and unscrupulous investment houses temporarily attracted by opportunities for abnormal profits; (2) largely as a result, the outflow of American capital behaved in an erratic fashion, rising to a peak in the first half of 1928 and falling sharply thereafter.[10]

The purposes for which loans were made were often ill advised, and from an international point of view, the outflow of capital was too uneven and too uncertain to provide an enduring basis for international trade and finance.

Some Lessons From the 1920's

An export of capital from America means that American exports are more easily available to the world at large. Dollars are relatively more plentiful. Over a decade other countries can adapt themselves —

---

9. See *ibid.*, pp. 1–2. The argument is also quoted, apparently with approval, by the House Special Committee on Post-War Economic Policy and Planning in *The Post-War Foreign Economic Policy of the United States*, H.Rept. 541, 79th Cong., 1st sess., 1945, pp. 20–21.

Perhaps the most serious criticism to be made of this line of reasoning is that it assumes that the time distribution of the receipts is of no consequence. At *any* interest rate, total receipts from an investment commitment will eventually exceed the original commitment, *if the time period is long enough*. But surely this is no criterion of the worthwhileness of the venture. Even with a high loss ratio, aggregate interest receipts will overtake original commitments eventually. By the same mode of reasoning one could show that the interurban railways in the United States — a notoriously unsuccessful industry by the usual criteria — were worth while because some few of them have paid and continue to pay returns and these may ultimately exceed total commitments in interurban railways. The then value of the outstanding securities would be the "net return" from interurban railway investments.

10. *The United States in the World Economy*, Bureau of Foreign and Domestic Commerce, 1943, p. 19.

their structure of trade, their balance of payments, their commercial policies — to this capital outflow. But the world economy probably cannot adjust overnight to a sudden termination of American capital export and accommodate itself instead to an American economy that sucks capital from abroad. The reversal of flow may not unduly disturb the American economy, because it is so large. But for most other countries it sets the storm signals flying. The disturbed conditions abroad are then reflected in the American economy through a resulting decline in exports. Hence, perhaps the first lesson to be drawn from American foreign lending in the 1920's lies in the extreme dangers to the rest of the world of such an uneven and erratic American capital flow.

The second lesson from American capital export in the 1920's is that foreign lending on a large scale is inconsistent with a commercial policy that severely restricts imports. As already explained, a stream of foreign lending sooner or later will produce a balance-of-payments position that can be settled only by an import surplus on the part of the creditor country. In the 1920's, because of the yield rates and amortization schedules, only a slight decline in the rate of new lending was necessary to create a negative balance of payments for the United States on long-term capital account. Yet the slackening of new lending after 1929 was accompanied, not by a cut in import restrictions, which might have eased the problems of debt service for debtor countries, but by raising import duties in the Hawley-Smoot Tariff Act. The result was that the default ratio increased and by its very increase put a damper on fresh lending.

Finally, the record of the 1930's suggests most emphatically that perhaps the prime determinant of the solvency of American loans abroad is the level of national income and employment in the American domestic economy. American imports are such a high proportion of total world trade that a prosperous America means large American imports, thus providing dollar exchange from which debt service can be met. An unstable American economy is likely to produce a high default ratio for even a well-conceived and well-integrated American foreign-lending program.

No Real Policy

The three foregoing propositions reduce virtually to the generalization that American foreign investment in the 1920's conformed to no discernible policy, but was rather merely one consequence among many of domestic economic conditions and domestic economic policies. To a much higher degree than in most countries, domestic affairs held the center of the stage and dominated action. Foreign investment, and even commercial policy, slipped into the performance as well as they could in minor supporting roles. When foreign investment became unattractive compared with investment at home, American investors stopped lending abroad. But from the point of view of the rest of the world, this was highly unsatisfactory because of the sheer bulk of the American economy in the world scene: small changes from the point of view of the American economy are often large changes from the point of view of other countries. A decision by American investors to invest an additional $1 billion at home instead of abroad may not be serious in its effects on the American economy; but it may leave smaller economies stranded with no ready substitute for the previous outflow of American capital. The Hawley-Smoot tariff in 1930 could not have been expected to arrest the American slump after 1929; yet the tariff and the slump together meant a serious loss of markets for producers all over the world, and consequently an increasing inability to meet debt service on American investments abroad. Thus, as Hal B. Lary recently wrote:

Under the combined influence of the fall in business activity and in prices, the imposition of the tariff of 1930, and the cessation of new foreign investment, the total amount of dollars paid out by the United States to foreign countries fell from $7,400,000,000 in 1929 to only $2,400,000,000 in 1932. At the same time foreign countries had contractual debt-service payments of some $900,000,000 due to the United States each year. Under such circumstances it was inevitable that many of these obligations should be defaulted. By comparison with the magnitude of these strains, all other explanations of the relatively unsatisfactory outcome of the past foreign lending experience of the United States must be of distinctly secondary significance.[11]

In fact, the United States had no "policy" on foreign investment between the two wars. In the 1920's, when capital was flowing abroad, there was a benign faith in the efficacy of free enterprise and the private pursuit of gain. In the 1930's, government policy was dominated by domestic economic conditions with scant reference to the effects, for example, of higher tariffs and currency devaluation on the international position of a creditor country. By the time the Hull Trade Agree-

11. *Op. cit.,* p. 683.

ments program got under way, most of the damage had been done. Private investors in America had little zest for new foreign investments. Foreign countries were loath to rely upon a spigot that could so suddenly be turned off.

A CAPITAL EXPORT POLICY FOR THE UNITED STATES

Current policy can never be wholly formulated from past experience because the contemporary scene never altogether conforms to the past. Mere scrupulous care to shun old mistakes will often mean that new realities are disregarded.

APPLYING THE LESSONS OF THE PAST

The authors of *The United States in the World Economy* conclude that

. . . the unfortunate results experienced on the part of this country's foreign investments should serve not to stifle initiative in this field but rather to point the way to sounder policies and practices. The fundamental requirement is that investment programs be formulated on a comprehensive and long-range basis and executed at a reasonably regular rate and in a manner that will both strengthen the economic and social structure of the borrowing country and provide reasonable returns and adequate safeguards to the investor.[12]

Both points — sounder loans and a steadier rate of lending — we have already discussed. Yet at least one of these — steadying the rate of foreign lending — seems likely to be no less difficult in the future than in the past.

On the first recommendation — sounder loans — probably a greater realization exists today than twenty years ago that the purposes for which loans are made are crucial to borrower and lender alike. A foreign loan must directly or indirectly improve the ability of the borrowing country to make net exports available, or debt service cannot be met.[13] But industrialization programs, presumably one of the major occasions for American lending abroad, will probably not encounter

12. P. 19.
13. A greater flexibility in debt-service provisions appears to be appropriate. Fixed interest payments and fixed amortization quotas have perhaps been too common in the past, in view of the attendant risks and uncertainties. The distinction between maintaining debt service in the currency of the borrowing country and debt service in American dollars needs to be drawn here, however. The former can be fairly rigid in comparison with the latter, which necessitates acquiring foreign exchange under what may be difficult circumstances.

this difficulty provided that industrialization is not organized on autarchical principles[14] and that foreign borrowing is only a small part of total capital investment.[15]

No one questions the desirability of a steady, rather than an erratic, flow of American capital abroad. Yet the means by which steadiness in foreign lending is to be achieved is not obvious. As Joan Robinson, writing from England, recently remarked:

. . . no mechanism has yet been suggested which can prevent lending from being erratic in modern conditions, except long-term international planning, which has many obstacles to overcome both in American ideals of individualism and in the nationalism of prospective borrowers.[16]

Even though new American lending abroad promises to be much more on government account than in the past — because of its closer link with American foreign policy as a whole and because of the apathy of American private investors toward foreign investments — this does not of itself assure a steady rate of lending. Certainly the government can conceivably take a longer view than private investors, and it is also clearly free of some of the fears and uncertainties that beset the private capitalist. However, government agencies get their funds from Congress, and Congress is sensitive to the electorate.[17] Congress will be continually reappraising government lending abroad. A steady stream of foreign lending is not automatically assured because it flows under government auspices.

Furthermore, the huge sums now often proposed make the risks to the rest of the world all the greater. At $3–4 billion gross new lending abroad yearly, the amounts are three to four times those actually committed even in the boom years of the 1920's. Large erratic capital movements on government account will be no less disturbing to the world economy than those on private account.

14. That is, provided that the aim of the industrialization program is not to withdraw as completely as possible from trade relations with other countries.

15. In the preceding chapter (pp. 207 ff.) we have sought to show why only a small fraction of the necessary capital for industrialization can come from abroad in any case. Perhaps the present policy of the Export-Import Bank in limiting loans usually to the amount of indispensable purchases from abroad — machinery, technicians' services, raw materials, etc. — comes close to a satisfactory working rule here. But the lenders must watch the investment program in the industrializing country *as a whole* for its effect on imports and exports and hence on the ability to maintain debt service.

16. *Economic Journal,* December 1945, p. 406.

17. Offhand, one would not assume that the electorate in the United States was likely to take a "longer view" in economic matters than private capitalists.

The Problem of Imports

The key problem in American foreign investment policy, however, is the problem of imports. An import balance is the ultimate expectancy of foreign lending. An import surplus or widespread defaults must result from investment abroad unless new loans proceed at an ever-increasing volume. The volume of American imports depends, as we have shown, on the level of prosperity in the United States and of tariff duties on imports. On the whole, a domestic slump in the United States has not usually merely caused a direct decline in imports but has evoked as well a fresh campaign for higher barriers against "disastrous" foreign competition. Is a more enlightened policy assured for the future?[18]

Those who now urge large-scale American investment abroad seem to believe that the absorption of adequate imports, even without tariff changes, will present no serious problem. They point out, first, that the United States is consuming its nonreplaceable raw materials at such a rapid rate that increased imports are indispensable. Furthermore, they argue, the secular growth of American national income, with few cyclical "lapses from full employment," will cause American imports of goods and services to rise substantially as a matter of course. Any worry about imports as the sequel to foreign lending is unnecessary; the problem, it is argued, solves itself. This point of view was recently expressed as follows:

. . . the relationship [between exports and imports] may be profoundly altered during the next several decades. As our industry expands and as the population becomes increasingly concentrated in secondary and tertiary production, United States requirements of imported goods, particularly primary commodities, will become increasingly indispensable. The war has demonstrated what vast quantities of raw materials are required to feed American industry at full production, and at the same time has made serious inroads on the country's natural resources . . . the evolution of the United States during the present century may not be unlike that of the United Kingdom during the 19th century.[19]

In other words, such broad underlying developments may be sufficient by themselves to draw enough imports from the rest of the world to

18. A policy that allowed the imports problem to be solved for the United States merely by gold imports seems to the authors no solution at all.

19. Lary, *op. cit.,* p. 681.

maintain debt service even on large foreign investments. This is certainly a possible solution and it would indeed be a happy one.

In a price economy, however, imports resulting from prior lending would flow into the American market according to the difference between the supply price of home producers and the laid-down cost at the port of entry from abroad. Imports would compete, directly or indirectly, with domestic production. In the absence of imports, domestic suppliers would get a relatively higher price for their output. Traditional American practice among producer groups in these matters is not to suffer quietly but to get busy politically.[20] How effective their pleas will be is anyone's guess. The point to be stressed, however, is that the general welfare and the maintenance of debt service on the earlier foreign lending require that Congress turn a deaf ear to such demands for higher duties. Investment policy ultimately becomes a question of commercial policy.

To conclude: America's experience with foreign lending shows clearly that a steadier rate of lending would be desirable for all concerned, and that if loans are not to be defaulted, imports must be permitted even though some domestic producers will suffer as a result. Yet private investors will continue to seek their own gain, and democratic governments must be responsive to their voters, so one does not readily see how the requisite steady rate of foreign lending can be definitely assured in the future. With a totalitarian government, it is altogether another story. The problem of the import surplus as the inevitable sequel to foreign investment seems likely to persist. One cannot be too sure in these matters. But a blithe confidence that because these particular weaknesses in previous American lending are now obvious they need never rise again, seems quite insufficient.

RATIONALE OF CAPITAL EXPORTS

What kinds of benefits might conceivably accrue to the United States from capital export; what are the worthy objectives that can be attained or approximated? The answer seems to be threefold: First, capital export might simply be profitable in pecuniary terms. Second, it might improve national income by raising and maintaining domestic

20. Cf., for example, the statements of various industry groups on the renewal of the Trade Agreements Act in *Hearings on H.R. 3240,* "1945 Extension of the Reciprocal Trade Agreements Act," Committee on Finance, U.S. Senate, 79th Cong., 1st sess., 1945. The view that imports do not injure *any* home producer is of course patently false. The argument for international specialization and trade does not contend this. It does contend

employment at a high level. Third, capital export might encourage the kind of economic and political world that the United States would like to see prevail.

The Profit Motive

The export of capital in anticipation of pecuniary returns has motivated most peacetime capital exports even though the anticipations were not always realized. Individuals or business enterprises took the initiative and reaped the gains or losses accordingly. And so long as the United States espouses an economic system based on principles of free private enterprise it presumably would encourage such commitments.

The contemporary world is so oriented, however, that future capital exports motivated by prospective yield need not be wholly restricted to individuals.

In the past the size of privately financed undertakings has necessarily been limited.[21] Larger, though still "profitable" undertakings, such as the deliberate industrialization of a whole region, may well be possible if governments are willing to play the role of financier and entrepreneur.[22] How extensively the United States might wish to finance such undertakings *on the assumption that the returns are reasonably well assured,* no one can now say. The important point is that these investments or loans are made because of the yield to be obtained and not because of political and social sympathies.[23] Within these limits, however, perhaps the American government may find a large number

---

that the benefits to consumers outweigh the injuries to protected producers, who have to shift to other lines of production or accept lower profits than if the duties were maintained. H. L. Coe, representing the Bicycle Institute of America, was quite correct to insist (*ibid.,* pp. 415 ff.) that imported British bicycles made American manufacturers less prosperous than they might otherwise be. But the argument for accepting imports does not stop at producers' interests alone.

21. Another difficulty is the problem of restricting the benefits to those who finance the project. Where the benefits, for example, are generally diffused throughout a whole region, as in a flood control scheme, only a public authority can be the entrepreneur.

22. Our earlier discussion in Chapter 8 of the problems of industrialization and their relation to foreign borrowing should be kept in mind here. For a discussion strongly emphasizing the virtues of the government as entrepreneur in such projects, see Eduard Heimann, "Developmental Schemes, Planning and Full Employment: The Economic Theory of the TVA," *International Post-War Problems,* January 1946, pp. 1–18.

23. As will be clear from the discussion below, even profitable investments on government account are unlikely where the political and social arrangements in the borrowing country are not such as the United States, as a political entity, would wish to encourage. Our point here is that investments of the type discussed above would be motivated by yield and not by the favorable or improving political and social climate in the borrowing country. An unfavorable climate would preclude an otherwise attractive loan; but a favorable climate would not evidence an attractive yield.

of suitable projects. The first and most obvious justification for capital export, therefore, is foreign investment to secure an attractive yield.[24]

Relation to Home Employment

The influence of capital export on home employment has already been explored. The contribution of foreign lending to home employment consists, as we have seen, in the increase in aggregate spending in the American economy that it brings about: as such it ranks with other measures designed to increase expenditures for consumption goods or capital goods. New investment abroad, furthermore, must steadily increase at a fairly rapid rate, on any reasonable assumptions as to interest and amortization, in order to maintain any given export surplus. How important these considerations may be in formulating a capital export policy for America clearly depends on the relative magnitudes involved — on the relation between employment arising from exports and total employment and on the relation between foreign investment and total investment.

The significant fact is that for no recent period have exports accounted for more than a small fraction of total employment. A Department of Commerce study reports that:

A comparison of the estimates of persons engaged in producing for export with total employment in the United States reveals that, in 1929, 6.6 per cent of the total employed persons were engaged in producing for export. By 1933 this figure had fallen to 6 per cent and in 1935 to 4.7. In 1937 the figure rose to 5.1 per cent.[25]

But as total employment includes a number of industries for which no assignment to exports could be made — for example, construction, public utilities, service trades, etc. — a more reasonable comparison is perhaps between total employment in agriculture, manufactures, mining and transportation and the numbers engaged in production for export in these industries. Even on this basis, the percentages are low:

24. How high the yield would have to be in order to be "attractive" cannot well be specified in general terms. Certainly a government investment abroad that promised a yield less than the going rate on the American public debt would not be attractive in the sense used here. Beyond that, the risks involved would have to be computed and allowed for in the terms of the loan.

25. "An Estimate of the Number of Persons Engaged in the Production, Distribution and Servicing of Goods for Export," Bureau of Foreign and Domestic Commerce, January 10, 1939, p. 3 (mimeographed).

12.4 per cent in 1929, 11.1 per cent in 1933, 8.9 per cent in 1935 and 9.6 per cent in 1937.[26]

A more recent study by the Bureau of Labor Statistics concludes that in 1939, $3.3 billion of exports accounted, directly or indirectly, for the employment of 960,000 persons, which was 3.2 per cent of all *non-agricultural* employment.[27] *On the assumption that approximately the same proportions would hold for increases in exports,* one could say that an additional $1 billion of exports in 1939, induced by foreign investment of an equal amount, would have increased nonagricultural employment in the United States by 287,000 persons, or by less than one per cent of total nonagricultural employment. Clearly, a large volume of foreign investment would have been necessary in 1939 to affect nonagricultural employment appreciably.[28]

We have already stressed that an export surplus of $1 billion as a consequence of foreign lending requires an ever-expanding volume of new loans each year if the surplus is to be maintained. (Cf. Table 32.) Twenty-year loans at 4 per cent would necessitate $2.03 billion of additional loans by the tenth year. To obtain the employment stimulus resulting from $1 billion increased exports requires a rapidly rising rate of new foreign lending. This automatically raises a difficulty: the greater the investment abroad, the higher becomes the proportion of foreign investment to total American investment. At $4 billion a year, foreign investment might be 13 to 16 per cent of aggregate gross investment ($25–30 billion) at levels approximating full employment. Domestic needs probably set an upper limit beyond which the rate of

26. *Ibid.* An exceedingly large amount of the total employment traceable to exports was in agriculture, especially in cotton, in which home production was heavily subsidized, particularly after 1933.

27. See Jerome Cornfield, "Employment Resulting from United States Exports, 1939," *Monthly Labor Review,* May 1945, pp. 37–38. See also, however, W. W. Leontief, "Exports, Imports, Domestic Output, and Employment," *Quarterly Journal of Economics,* February 1946, pp. 171–93, for an elaborate calculation of the employment effects of exports in the United States for 1939. Using an income-expenditure approach, Leontief gets a figure for "export-dependent employment" in the American economy in 1939 of 10.1 per cent. This figure is *not* comparable with that of Cornfield above; but the details of Leontief's methods and results cannot be described here.

28. One could argue that $1 billion of foreign lending would increase American exports by more than $1 billion because of certain "multiplier" effects. For example, it could be argued that the additional exports directly occasioned by the lending would mean higher incomes in the United States and that as these were spent, a portion would be spent on imported goods; but the increased dollar balances in the hands of foreigners would in turn be spent for American goods, and so American exports would be greater. Analyzed in this way, a variety of indirect effects might be brought into the picture.

foreign investment could not easily rise. Under competitive conditions, home investment would tend to become increasingly attractive to investors, and thus the amount invested abroad would decline. If the government were the lending agent, it would not be able to expand its foreign lending indefinitely without creating shortages in the home market. Hence, the export stimulus would in time disappear altogether.

If the foregoing analysis is correct, it follows that foreign lending is a poor device with which to support full employment. A large volume of foreign investment would be needed to make any serious difference in the level of home employment; and it would have to increase steadily in order to maintain its effectiveness. A rational policy of capital export for the United States would not attach great importance to its domestic employment effects. High levels of national income must be achieved primarily by other means.

Nonpecuniary Motives

The nonpecuniary reasons for transferring dollars to foreigners could be many and various. Even in less troubled times foreign countries have received dollar remittances as gifts from their emigrants to the United States, in the form of support to foreign missions, as donations by various foundations, and the like. More recently, the United States has contributed large sums to UNRRA for relief and rehabilitation. All these make dollars available to other countries; they are not prompted by yield considerations nor by the urge to improve home employment. From an economic point of view, however, these are identical with foreign loans except that there is no return flow of interest and amortization payment. They are, in a sense, a capital export — a capital export for nonpecuniary reasons.

Capital export for nonpecuniary reasons, however, need not be restricted wholly to contributions born of charity. As a large and important nation, the United States, like other countries, has certain interests. These interests result in certain policies for which capital export may be a useful instrument. More specifically, the United States presumably will be better off for example, if economic reconstruction and rehabilitation proceed smoothly and rapidly. If capital exports assist in this process, then, within limits, the price is worth paying without regard to the possibility of ultimate repayment. In fact an outright gift, plainly labeled as such, may be the best solution in certain instances.

As another example, one may point to the Bretton Woods Agreements and the proposals for the international conference on world trade and employment to be held in 1947.[29] In a broad view, the Fund, the Bank and the trade conference proposals are all of a piece. They all look forward to a world with multilateral trade, fairly stable exchange rates, international capital movements and a commercial policy in all countries that minimizes restrictions on international trade. Presumably this is the kind of world American policy makers regard as most in harmony with American ideals and interests. Yet, as matters now stand, many countries do not see their way clear to put into effect at once the kind of policies that might allow such a world to come into being. American capital exports may be one way of clearing the obstacles in the way. As such, their justification turns on their effectiveness as means to that end and not on any nice calculations of percentage yields or foreign trade "multipliers."

Capital exports, prompted by such motives, clearly raise problems of the greatest importance and difficulty. The problems are real, and no great imagination is required to conceive of circumstances and conditions in which capital exports from the United States might assist in their solution.[30]

While granting the legitimacy of capital exports for such purposes, wise practice would differentiate them clearly from foreign investments in which the primary purpose is more narrowly pecuniary. This is not to say that some capital exports of a political nature might not take the form of a loan agreement whose terms are actually fulfilled. But such capital exports might also occur when ultimate repayment was highly problematical. Loans of the other kind, by contrast, would not be made at all unless the yield prospects were in themselves attractive.

29. *Proposals for Expansion of World Trade and Employment,* Publication 2411, Department of State, 1945.

30. Occasionally an economist speaks bluntly in public on these matters. For example: "We are, in fact, committed to the defense of Western Europe against all comers. It can only be to our advantage to make our political commitment open and mutually binding. Even leaving the political advantages aside, from an economic point of view it is obvious that we can well afford to make major commitments for the defense of the British Empire, provided we attain economic entry into the Empire on equal terms and, provided future Anglo-American economic relations are based on genuine partnership.

"Conversely, it is a vital concern of ours that the problems of England and our Western European Allies should not be solved along isolationist lines. The creation of a new, enlarged sterling area, thoroughly cartelized, and cemented with political understandings, is inimical to American interests." Imre de Vegh, "Peace Aims, Capital Requirements, and International Lending," *American Economic Review,* May 1945, pp. 259–60.

A Final Word

Throughout the preceding discussion, the phrase "capital export policy" instead of "foreign investment policy" has been used consistently. This was deliberate. There is much evidence to confirm the belief that "foreign investment policy" is too narrow a concept to cover all the cases in which the United States might find its own best interests served by making dollars available to other countries. The words "investment" or "lending" still carry the connotation of anticipated yield and anticipated repayment of principal.[31] Only part of the term "capital export" falls in this category. What is needed, therefore, is a "capital export policy," not merely a "foreign investment" or a "foreign-lending" policy.

The conclusion to which our analysis leads is that capital export as foreign investment and capital export for essentially broad economic, social and political purposes in harmony with American interests are the two main purposes to be considered in formulating policy. Beneficial effects on domestic employment should more properly be considered secondary, providing added purpose but not of sufficient importance to commend capital export on their own account.[32] Capital export for nonpecuniary reasons will presumably play its greatest role in the immediate postwar years. But in a reasonably stable world, free of the threat of war and revolution, such capital exports would presumably dwindle and ultimately vanish altogether. Capital export would then become synonymous with capital investment abroad on either private or government account. Indeed, such capital movements would be the only type in harmony with the kind of international economic order to which contemporary American policy seems to point.

31. Cf. also the discussion in Chapter 7 (pp. 168 ff.) on this point. Part of the difficulty has its roots in the use of the term "investment" in recent Keynesian economics. Here the word means expenditures for, or the value of the output of, nonconsumption goods. As such it has no necessary relationship to the commitment of funds by private individuals or governments in the anticipation of a satisfactory rate of return on cost.

32. The employment effects of capital export are, of course, independent of the motives prompting the decision. Home employment gains as much direct stimulus from a gift as from a sound investment. If one can assume full employment, then an investment will augment real incomes through the return flow of goods and services as interest receipts and amortization. These will add more to real income in the United States — if full employment prevails — than equivalent investment at home, provided the yield is higher. If unemployment is the bogey, then a gift is superior in both the short and long run because there is no return flow of imports to wear down home employment.

Chapter 10

COMMERCIAL POLICY: LESSONS FROM EXPERIENCE

THE CRUCIAL problem of international economic reconstruction is to devise a new institutional framework for the beneficial exploitation of the world's productive resources that will permit the products they yield to flow easily across national boundaries from areas of abundance to areas of relative scarcity. As shown in Chapters 5 and 6, this presupposes adequate arrangements for exchanging currencies, because, in the first instance, all international purchases and sales are money transactions. Further, if the world's productive resources are to be effectively developed, the best available techniques must be applied to potentially productive resources in various segments of the globe. And this requires productive international investment. (See Chapters 7–9.)

Surely the ultimate purpose of the Bretton Woods proposals and international investment is to increase the international flow of goods and services. National governments, it is therefore assumed, will not check this flow by directly restricting imports from other countries. What use is an elaborate machinery for handling foreign exchange and international investment, if national governments are determined to minimize trade and service transactions with other countries? New institutional arrangements for turning resources to better use, however, imply some consensus on the principles of commercial policy — that is, the control of exports and imports.

THE DEVELOPMENT OF COMMERCIAL POLICY

World War I and the Great Depression produced a conspicuous change in both the methods and goals of commercial policy. Commercial policy became more and more conditioned by the general economic climate of the time and the newer forms of economic organization. Balance-of-payments difficulties and unemployment tended to foster policies of severe restrictionism, while in centrally planned economies foreign trade became either an outright government monopoly or was stringently regulated through foreign exchange control or import licenses.

Before World War I, commercial policy meant tariff policy. And tariff policy represented almost the whole of a nation's international economic policy. Adherence to the gold standard precluded such devices as currency devaluation or foreign exchange control. There were almost no legal restrictions on international capital movements. The goals and instruments of commercial policy were simple compared with those that later developed. The instruments consisted almost exclusively of the tariff and the long-term commercial treaty. Moreover, commercial treaties usually embodied the "most-favored-nation" clause, which provided equal treatment for foreign exports regardless of their countries of origin. The purposes of tariffs were usually limited to the raising of revenue, or to protecting certain branches of industry or agriculture from foreign competition. Governments either believed such protection was "in the national interest" or they yielded to pressure groups. The aims were as simple as the tools.

The Interwar Period

All this changed in the interwar period. During the first world war and the years immediately following, import quotas and foreign exchange control made their appearance for the first time on an extensive scale. But governments then regarded such quantitative controls as temporary, to be abandoned as soon as circumstances permitted. All international conferences dealing with problems of commercial policy, from the Brussels Conference of 1920 to the World Economic Conference of 1927 in Geneva, condemned such restrictions. Quantitative restrictions had for the most part disappeared by the end of the 1920's. The Great Depression after 1929, however, revived all the old forms of trade restrictions and spawned many new ones besides. It also induced many countries to change the external value of their currencies for much the same reasons.

The desire to "protect" certain industries or certain branches of agriculture was not lacking in the new wave of protectionism during the depression. Such was undoubtedly the original motive in most countries for introducing quotas or for raising tariffs. As time passed, however, this motive merged with the intensifying desire to protect the balance of payments and to combat domestic unemployment.

Many countries experienced balance-of-payments difficulties as the depression deepened. The reasons were various. Some countries — especially agricultural and raw-material-producing countries — experienced a catastrophic fall in the value of their total exports. Prices of primary products slumped and the world market took less. Their balance-of-payments position was necessarily weakened as a result. But their balance-of-payments position was still further weakened by the cessation of the inflow of long-term capital from abroad — with which they had habitually financed part of their import surpluses.

Out of a total of nearly ten milliards of dollars of new foreign securities issued during 1924–28 on the four chief capital markets of the world (the United States, the United Kingdom, the Netherlands and Sweden) over half was issued on behalf of agricultural countries outside Europe. This flow of capital ceased in 1929.[1]

Great Britain and Germany saw their balance of payments disrupted by sudden withdrawals of foreign capital. The gold bloc countries — France, Belgium, Holland and Switzerland — had special difficulties of their own. These arose, initially, because the maintenance of the old gold parity of their currencies in the face of devaluation by other countries impaired their competitive position in the world market; and, later, because the anticipated devaluation of their currencies, as in the case of France, led to capital flight. In the struggle to restore equilibrium in the balance of payments, measures ranged from the introduction or raising of tariffs, as in Great Britain, to the imposition of quotas and import licensing, and from currency devaluation to exchange control.

The 1930's

Disturbances in the balance of payments were not the sole reason for the resurgence of restrictionism in the early 1930's. A compelling reason was the desire to bolster domestic production and employment. By curtailing imports and trying to bolster exports, it was thought that home employment could perhaps be increased. Either of these two objectives — of protecting the balance of payments or of maintaining domestic employment — could be pursued singly. Thus a country that had no balance-of-payments difficulties could nevertheless raise its tariff, as the United States did in 1930, or devalue its

1. Frederic Benham, "The Muddle of the Thirties," *Political Science Quarterly*, December 1944, p. 536. This article was also published in *Economica*, February 1945, pp. 1–9.

currency, in order to increase employment in industries producing for the domestic market, and when the currency was devalued, in industries producing for export. A country may also take restrictive measures solely for the purpose of righting the balance of payments, as in the case where its exports decline because of conditions abroad. Such measures are likely to affect employment even though their primary object is to improve the balance of payments.[2]

The two objectives of combating unemployment and adjusting the balance of payments, however, are often complementary. If one country follows an expansionist monetary policy in isolation in order to reduce unemployment, its balance of payments will usually become negative, because the increase in domestic incomes leads to increased imports and also, in most circumstances, to decreased exports. The country may then resort to restrictive measures that allow it to follow an expansionist policy without having to cope with disequilibrium in its balance of payments.

The events of the early 1930's, however, show that once a few countries resort to devaluation, quotas or foreign exchange control, others retaliate. The process is cumulative. For example:

It will still be remembered, for instance, how France, in the course of the 1929–1932 depression, introduced an elaborate system of quotas and licenses. The restrictions imposed on the import of coal led the Dutch, German, and Polish exporters of coal to the markets in Belgium which, thereupon, introduced also a quota system for coal imports. This together with a license tax of 10–15 frs. per ton brought down British coal exports to Belgium from over 4 million tons in 1929 to 1½ million tons in 1933 (and to 760,000 tons in 1939) while those to France declined between 1929 and 1933 from 13 million tons to 8½ million tons. The depreciation of sterling caused partly by U.K.'s falling exports had catastrophic effects on the Belgian industry, and detrimentally affected France as well.[3]

Any country embarking on a policy of domestic expansion to reduce unemployment would be able to avoid complications in its balance of payments only if other countries followed suit, so that domestic incomes in the different countries moved more or less in step. In such circum-

2. Home employment need not necessarily improve, however. A raw-material-producing country whose export market collapses may have to restrict the imports of finished goods, but because the latter are not produced domestically, no increase of employment will result.

3. S. Moos, "The Foreign Trade of West-European Countries," *Bulletin of the Oxford Institute of Statistics,* January 13, 1945, p. 10.

stances none could seriously fear a deficit in its balance of payments greater than could be met out of its reserves of gold or foreign balances.[4]

Three Major Lessons

From the experience of the 1930's certain lessons can be drawn.

First, commercial policy must now be considered as an integral part of general economic policy, particularly that part relating to employment and monetary policy.

Second, only if most countries succeed in returning to a system of world trade and foreign lending in which major disturbances of balances of payments due to abrupt shifts in commodity and capital flow are avoided can the world hope to get rid of the more pernicious types of interference with foreign trade such as foreign exchange control, quotas and import licensing.

Third — and this is closely connected with the previous point — unless major depressions are avoided, governments will probably be unable to refrain from these types of interference with foreign trade. The *Proposals for Expansion of World Trade and Employment* submitted by the Department of State in November 1945, as a basis for discussion of an international trade conference to be convoked in 1947, rightly stress that a successful employment policy is essential for a relaxation of trade controls and expansion of world trade:

> The attainment of approximately full employment by the major industrial and trading nations, and its maintenance on a reasonably assured basis, are essential to the expansion of international trade on which the full prosperity of these and other nations depends; to the full realization of the objectives of all liberal international agreements in such fields as commercial policy, commodity problems, restrictive business practices, monetary stabilization and investment; and, therefore, to the preservation of world peace and security.[5]

A grave, even burdensome, responsibility devolves upon the United States in this respect. The importance of the United States as a market for world exports and as a potential lender renders the success or failure of its employment policy crucial for the rest of the world. Less restric-

4. It must be further assumed that no capital flight for political reasons takes place and that none of the countries follows a totalitarian economic policy of directing the whole economic system from above, since such direction invariably involves control over imports and exports.

5. Publication 2411, p. 9.

tionism in the outside world requires that the United States succeed in maintaining a high level of employment at home.

ECONOMIC EFFECTS OF TRADE RESTRICTIONISM

To analyze in detail all the various types of restrictionism and their effects on the economy of the country using them, as well as on its own trading partners, would require a large volume.[6] But how they serve their purpose and what their economic effects are can be indicated in very general terms. Since restrictions can fulfill three major functions — maintenance of employment, protection of the balance of payments and assistance to special groups of domestic producers — the discussion must center around the question of how effectively, and at what cost, they perform these functions.[7]

MAINTENANCE OF EMPLOYMENT

As already explained, combating unemployment and protecting the balance of payments are in practice often interrelated, because a successful employment policy in a single country frequently causes a disequilibrium in its balance of payments. But, first, what happens when a country whose balance of payments is in equilibrium makes direct use of restrictionist methods in an effort to increase employment, without simultaneously embarking on a program of domestic monetary expansion?

Any or all of the four principal methods of restriction — currency devaluation, quotas, tariffs, foreign exchange control — can be used to stimulate home employment. Currency devaluation is undoubtedly the most effective, because it not only reduces imports but also increases exports. Its effectiveness is not permanent, but it is more than transitory because costs and prices are not completely plastic. The other methods, unless they are combined with export subsidies, directly affect

6. For interesting accounts of some of the complexities of modern trade controls, see Henry J. Tasca, *World Trading Systems,* International Institute of Intellectual Cooperation, Paris, 1939, and Margaret S. Gordon, *Barriers to World Trade,* Macmillan, New York, 1941.

7. In order not to overload the discussion, we shall not analyze separately the effects of so-called "indirect" methods of protectionism, such as sanitary restrictions on the importation of animals, meat and plants, the arbitrary assessment of the value of imports in the case of ad valorem duties, and others. The effects are not different from those of other forms of protectionism. Thus, sanitary restrictions are similar in effect to those of quotas (the quota may, of course, be zero), and higher valuations of imports amount to an increase in the tariff level.

imports only. However, tariffs, quotas, etc., by raising the domestic prices of imported commodities that are fabricated into exports, tend to reduce exports.[8] All four methods of restriction tend to "export unemployment," for they all reduce the exports of other countries to the countries adopting restrictions. Currency devaluation, and the other methods also — if combined with export subsidies — weaken the competitive position of other countries both at home and abroad.

Although such methods may appear to benefit the country that applies them, they are, internationally, undesirable methods of combating unemployment. The only exception would be where it can be shown that in the other countries conditions are such that a negative balance of trade would not damage home employment.[9]

Any international trade charter binding all countries to certain "rules of the game" in commercial policy would have to outlaw these practices. It is therefore gratifying to find in the State Department's *Proposals for Expansion of World Trade and Employment* the suggestion that "No nation will seek to maintain employment through measures which are likely to create unemployment in other countries."[10] One may hope that this precept will be more honored in the future than it was on the road to World War II.

PROTECTION OF THE BALANCE OF PAYMENTS

A country's balance of payments can be disrupted by forces originating abroad or at home. The collapse of export markets or the withdrawal of short-term funds is often beyond a country's control. But a domestic monetary expansion, on the other hand, is a consequence of a voluntary decision. Disequilibrium resulting from internal causes may be more profitably analyzed here, partly because the Bretton Woods plan anticipates the control of capital movements, and partly because many of the effects of disequilibrium from internal causes and from external causes are analytically much the same.

8. Currency devaluation also raises the prices of imported commodities in terms of domestic currency, but the effect on exports of this rise is, as a rule, more than counterbalanced by the decline in the prices of domestically produced commodities in terms of foreign currencies.
9. The most complete and sophisticated discussion of the whole variety of techniques for improving and maintaining home employment via foreign trade is perhaps T. Balogh, "The International Aspects of Full Employment," in *The Economics of Full Employment*, Institute of Statistics, Oxford University, Blackwell & Mott, Oxford, 1945.
10. P. 9.

Restrictionism is less injurious to other countries if it is combined with domestic monetary expansion than if it is used without an expansionist monetary policy. For if a country is expanding its national income, by imposing restrictions it may merely be trying to prevent an increase in imports upsetting to its balance of payments. Hence there need be no actual decline induced in the exports of other countries. The usual objection, that countries applying restrictionist methods are following a beggar-my-neighbor policy and are "exporting unemployment," is therefore not applicable.

Foreign Exchange Control

For the purpose of protecting the balance of payments, the most effective method is undoubtedly foreign exchange control. By forbidding transfers on capital account, and holding imports of goods and services down to whatever level is permitted by the supply of foreign exchange, a country can automatically keep its balance of payments in equilibrium.

Foreign exchange control has drawbacks, however, for the country imposing it, and even greater drawbacks for the world as a whole. In many ways it is the most objectionable method of trade interference. It not only entails costs and inconvenience for the traders who must conform with foreign-exchange-control regulations; it is also costly to the government and banks, which require staffs of thousands of people to work out and enforce the regulations. For example:

> Since its inception in the crisis of July, 1931, in Germany "modern" money had required three general control laws, upwards of 50 separate decrees of amendment and adaptation, and something in the neighborhood of 500 administrative rulings, to say nothing of clearing, compensation, and payment agreements with partner countries.[11]

But far more important than the direct costs, both for the exchange control country and for the world as a whole, is the diversion of foreign trade into channels different from those that would result from the operation of comparative-cost differentials. The total benefits derived from international trade are thus much reduced.

Three main reasons account for the "unnatural" diversion of foreign trade under a system of foreign exchange control.

11. Howard S. Ellis, *Exchange Control in Central Europe,* Harvard University Press, Cambridge (Mass.), 1941, p. 166.

First, an importer can buy only from those countries that are willing to accept the currency at his disposal, and an exporter can sell only to countries that permit their importers to purchase the exporter's currency. Second, the exchange control country, being constantly short of foreign exchange of nonclearing countries, generally attempts to conclude bilateral clearing agreements with other exchange control countries, so that imports can be bartered for exports. Such agreements tend to reduce the share of free-exchange countries in its total trade in favor of other exchange control countries. Third, there is a tendency to equalize exports with imports bilaterally[12] with other foreign-exchange-control countries, and the same tendency prevails in trade with all the free-exchange countries taken together.[13]

Quotas

Quotas were also used, particularly by the so-called gold bloc countries, in the early 1930's in order to protect the balance of payments.[14] They are less effective for this purpose than foreign exchange control, since they do not automatically restrict imports to what can be financed by the foreign exchange received from exports. Even if every imported commodity were subjected to a quota, the supply of foreign exchange might still fall short of the amount required to finance the fixed quotas of imports. Moreover, the quota system does nothing to solve the problem of capital transfers. In practice, no country has yet extended the quota system to all imported commodities: some imports are usually

12. Temporarily, of course, one exchange control country may accumulate balances in another exchange control country as did some of the southeastern European countries in Germany. But in the long run the country that owns such balances has to accept goods if it wants to get anything at all.

13. Foreign exchange control is an almost inexhaustible subject. Only a few of the many objections that can be raised against the system have been indicated in the text. The effects of foreign exchange control on the terms of trade, the practice of subsidizing exports that foreign-exchange-control countries are forced to adopt if they want to export at all, and the various ingenious methods used for this purpose, the problem of economic and political penetration of the weaker foreign-exchange-control countries by a stronger one — these and a host of other problems would have to be discussed in a thorough analysis of foreign-exchange-control practices. For details refer to Ellis, *op. cit.*, and Jacob Viner, *Trade Relations Between Free-Market and Controlled Economies,* League of Nations, Geneva, 1943.II.A.4.

14. The scope of the quota and licenses system in prewar years can be gauged from the following figures, which give the approximate percentage of the total value of imports subject to this type of restriction in 1937: France 58 per cent, Switzerland 52 per cent, Norway 12 per cent, United Kingdom 8 per cent. *Quantitative Trade Controls: Their Causes and Nature,* League of Nations, Geneva, 1943.II.A.5, p. 19.

left free to respond to an increased demand resulting from expansion of incomes in the domestic economy. A country that relies on the quota system to protect its balance of payments still needs an ample supply of international currency to finance a possible deficit. Otherwise it may be forced to lower existing quotas still further and to extend quotas to new commodities.

Quotas, like foreign exchange control, necessarily discriminate among foreign producers. Even if quotas, or foreign exchange allocations, are based on some supposedly representative period and are distributed among countries according to their import shares in the base period, they still discriminate. For such a procedure freezes the status quo; new producers in foreign countries, even though they may be more efficient, cannot possibly get into the market. Differences in costs of production cease to be the decisive factor determining the sources of imports. Thus, quotas, though less effective than foreign exchange control, nevertheless have many of the same objectionable features.[15]

Tariffs

Tariffs are clearly the least satisfactory method of protecting the balance of payments. The tariff cannot usually be rapidly adapted to changing circumstances.[16] Problems such as a disequilibrium in the bal-

---

15. *Import licensing* need not be considered as a separate system of control. In order to make a quota system effective, and yet avoid hopeless confusion as to when and from what countries imports under quota may be brought in, import licensing is indispensable. In other words, a quota system almost inevitably requires a system of import licensing. Conceivably, a country could have import licensing without formally announced quotas. In this case, the quota is adaptable to the changing mood or disposition of the import-licensing authorities. A general system of import licensing can achieve many of the results of foreign exchange control.

16. In the United States the President has the right to increase or reduce duties by 50 per cent of those existing on January 1, 1945. But such changes in duties can be accomplished only by negotiating trade agreements with foreign countries. They cannot, therefore, be imposed quickly and on a broad front, as would be required if the tariff weapon were to be used to protect the balance of payments (an emergency not likely to arise in the case of the United States).

In Great Britain, an Import Duties Advisory Committee was established by the Import Duties Act of 1932 with the power (within certain limits) to recommend to the Treasury changes in duties or imposition of new duties — recommendations that the Treasury then could (and in most cases did) carry out by Treasury Orders. An Order imposing a custom duty had to be approved by the House within twenty-eight days, but other Orders continued in force unless the House resolved that they should be annulled. See *Trade Regulations and Commercial Policy of the United Kingdom*, by the Research Staff of the National Institute of Economic and Social Research, Cambridge University Press, Cambridge (England), 1943, Chap. 4.

ance of payments require weapons that can be quickly taken up and quickly laid aside. A tariff once introduced will, as a rule, persist beyond the temporary difficulties, and the country will find itself surrounded permanently by a protective wall initially intended only to help overcome a temporary difficulty. Tariffs are less flexible than quotas, exchange controls and import licensing, which can be quickly adapted to changing conditions at home and abroad.

Currency Devaluation

Currency devaluation is less certainly effective than foreign exchange control in protecting the balance of payments, largely because it does not prevent flight of capital. Indeed, it may even induce speculators who anticipate the devaluation to engage in short-term capital transfers. To make currency devaluation effective it must be combined with the control of capital movements, as suggested in the Bretton Woods Agreements. Currency devaluation is undoubtedly a less objectionable method of protecting the balance of payments than either exchange control or quotas. Unlike foreign exchange control or quotas, currency devaluation is nondiscriminatory as among foreign countries unless deliberately selective through multiple exchange rates. It does not interfere with the price mechanism; and it permits cost differentials to remain the decisive factor determining sources of supply.

Currency devaluation thus stands out as perhaps the least harmful, relatively, of all four methods for protecting the balance of payments. It interferes much less with the course of international trade as dictated by cost differentials than foreign exchange control or quotas, and if combined with the control of short-term capital movements, it is hardly less effective than foreign exchange control. It is decidedly more effective than quotas or tariffs.

PROTECTION OF DOMESTIC PRODUCERS

Currency devaluation, unless combined with multiple exchange rates, does not differentiate among different categories of domestic producers.[17] Consequently, it is useless if the purpose is to protect selected groups of domestic producers. Tariffs, quotas, exchange con-

17. This does not mean that the prices of imported commodities all rise by the same percentage. The degree of the price rise depends on the elasticity of demand of domestic consumers, and on the elasticity of supply of domestic as well as foreign producers.

trol and import licensing, on the other hand, can all be applied effectively toward this end.[18] Of these four, tariffs are probably the least objectionable. The tariff leaves the price mechanism intact; every importer is free to purchase commodities in the cheapest market with due allowance for duty levies. The tariff has the further advantage over quotas and foreign exchange control in that it can protect selected groups of domestic producers without discriminating among foreign suppliers.

Because the tariff does not interfere with the price mechanism and because it can be handled in a nondiscriminatory way, it is therefore a less harmful method of protecting special groups of domestic producers than either quotas or foreign exchange control.

RELATION TO THE FORM OF ECONOMIC ORGANIZATION

In some countries, government supervision and control of foreign trade are based on entirely different premises from those underlying the preceding discussion. Foreign trade controls, as they exist today, are not always born of a desire to protect domestic producers, employment or the balance of payments. Countries with centrally planned economies cannot dispense with them, because imports and exports, like everything else, must be planned in conjunction with domestic production. Countries with a centralized, over-all economic control trade either through an outright state monopoly or through a comprehensive system of foreign exchange control and import licensing. The type of foreign trade controls found indispensable by the United States and Great Britain in operating their war economies is unavoidable in centrally planned economies in peace and war alike. If foreign trade is not controlled by the price system, control by a planning authority is inescapable. Consequently in such countries it is idle to suppose that government controls of foreign trade will disappear. As long as these centrally planned economies continue, one must expect complete government control of their international economic relations. It would

18. It is often stated that quotas, because they allow only a fixed amount of imports, are a more effective method of protecting particular industries or branches of agriculture. In principle, this statement is wrong. Theoretically, it is always possible to reduce the imports of a commodity to any amount that may be desired by imposing an appropriately high tariff. If imports are to be kept at the given level, tariffs would, of course, have to be frequently adjusted, since supply and demand conditions for commodities are always changing.

be naive to expect anything else. And full government control means either state monopoly or complete exchange control with import-export control. Just how far and by what means trade can develop between unplanned economies, such as that of the United States, and centrally planned economies, such as that of Russia, remains one of the major unsolved problems of the postwar world.

SUMMARY

To sum up, any one of the four methods of protectionism — currency devaluation, tariffs, quotas with import licensing, foreign exchange control — can be used to restore equilibrium in the balance of payments, to combat unemployment and, excepting currency devaluation, to protect designated groups of domestic producers. Though foreign exchange control may be abolished, the same results, with varying degrees of success, may be achieved by using any one of the other forms of protectionism. No great step toward freeing world trade will have been made if, for example, foreign exchange control is formally abolished but import licensing is used to the same ends.

All four methods of restrictionism can be used in a manner that increases unemployment in other countries. Only when the restrictions are accompanied by domestic economic expansion is the damage to other countries kept to a minimum.

If the problem is to combat domestic unemployment while keeping the balance of payments in equilibrium, the appropriate method is currency devaluation in combination, if necessary, with control over capital movements.

If the problem is to protect specific groups of domestic producers, the tariff is the least harmful way of doing it.

Tariffs, then, are the least objectionable instruments to protect special groups of producers; and currency devaluation, in combination with the control of capital movements, to protect the balance of payments. Nevertheless, even these methods should not be applied if they involve an "export of unemployment."

Countries with centrally planned and controlled economies are a case apart. Their foreign trade is based on different premises. They cannot, by their very nature, dispense with comprehensive controls.

The foregoing analysis is in general conformity with the provisions of the Bretton Woods Agreements and with the State Department's

Proposals for Expansion of World Trade and Employment. But both Bretton Woods and the *Proposals* presuppose a world economy free from disastrous slumps. Only if the participant countries succeed in avoiding severe depressions can they be expected to adhere to the "rules of the game" laid down in the Bretton Woods Agreements and in the proposed "International Trade Charter" envisaged as the outcome of the International Trade Conference in 1947.

THE RECIPROCAL TRADE AGREEMENTS PROGRAM

The United States after 1934 tried to stem the rising tide of protectionism and discriminatory trade practices. The Reciprocal Trade Agreements Act was originally passed in June 1934, and was afterward renewed several times. The latest renewal, in 1945, gave the President increased authority to reduce tariffs by concluding reciprocal trade agreements with other countries. Previously he had the authority to reduce or raise tariffs by not more than 50 per cent of the level prevailing in June 1934 when the original act was passed; these rates were virtually the Hawley-Smoot rates. He may now raise or lower them by 50 per cent of the level existing on January 1, 1945. For many items, the rates in January 1945 were below the Hawley-Smoot level owing to reductions achieved in earlier trade agreements. Under the authority of the original act and the renewals preceding the one of 1945, the United States had concluded a total of twenty-seven nondiscriminatory trade agreements.

Effects on Trade

How effective the American trade agreements program has been in increasing the volume of American trade is not easily ascertained. Statistics purporting to show that the agreements have led to a considerable expansion of American trade with trade-agreement countries are often cited in evidence. By the end of 1939, eighteen agreeements were still in force. According to figures published by the Bureau of Foreign and Domestic Commerce, the two-year average of total exports to trade-agreement countries increased between 1934–1935 and 1938–1939 by 62.8 per cent, whereas exports to nonagreement countries increased by only 31.7 per cent.[19] The corresponding figures for imports are 21.6 per cent and 12.5 per cent respectively.

19. *Hearings on H.R. 3240,* "1945 Extension on the Reciprocal Trade Agreements

Such figures, however, are inconclusive. They do not show whether the agreements led to an expansion of total American trade or only to a shift in its direction. In other words, did American trade with agreement countries gain at the expense of trade with nonagreement countries?

Other Influences at Work

Again, the lowering of tariffs in foreign countries through trade agreements is only one of many factors exerting an influence on the volume of American exports. Changes in national income abroad also affect the demand for American exports. With an upswing in business in a foreign country, its imports from the United States tend to rise — trade agreements or no trade agreements — if dollars are available. The influence of general business conditions, both in the United States and abroad, would therefore have to be eliminated before any conclusive statement could be made about the effect of trade agreements on foreign trade. Still another factor to be taken into account is the extent of trade restrictions imposed by nonagreement countries. Thus, the volume of trade with nonagreement countries may have lagged behind the volume of trade with agreement countries, not because of an "abnormal" expansion of American trade with trade-agreement countries, but because new restrictions elsewhere caused a less than "normal" expansion of trade with nonagreement countries. Foreign exchange control by many European countries, especially by Germany, was undoubtedly largely responsible for the relatively small increase in American trade with nonagreement countries during the period considered.[20]

Act," Committee on Finance, U.S. Senate, 79th Cong., 1st sess., 1945, p. 17. The figures exclude trade with Newfoundland, and non-self-governing British colonies, Turkey and Venezuela, the latter two on the ground that as the agreements with these two countries had only just been concluded in 1939, they had been in effect for too short a time to justify inclusion for the purposes of comparison.

20. The elimination of Germany alone from the group of nonagreement countries, for instance, would substantially raise the percentage increase of American exports to and imports from the remaining nonagreement countries. The rise in American imports from this group between 1934–1935 and 1938–1939 would then amount to 15.5 per cent instead of 12.5 per cent; the rise in exports, to 37.7 per cent instead of 31.7 per cent. As the figures include 1939, they are in any case influenced by the outbreak of war, which shut off many of the nonagreement countries from trade relations with the United States.

That the statistics of the Bureau of Foreign and Domestic Commerce do not prove what they are supposed to prove can easily be shown by reference to particular countries. As the agreements with Venezuela and Turkey came into effect only in December and

Tariff Level Lower

Whatever its effects to date on the foreign trade of the United States, the trade agreements program has undoubtedly lowered the general tariff level. Mr. W. L. Clayton testified in 1945 that in respect to 42 per cent of dutiable imports by value, duties have been reduced by the full 50 per cent authorized by the original act; and that in respect to 21 per cent of dutiable imports, reductions have been made in varying lesser percentages. When the act was renewed in 1945, the Hawley-Smoot tariff was still in force for 37 per cent of dutiable imports.[21]

These figures might seem to contradict the consistent contention of government representatives testifying before congressional committees that the trade agreements brought no serious harm to any domestic producers. But this contradiction may be more apparent than real. The period between 1934 and 1937 was one of business revival. Tariff reductions in periods of business revival are less bothersome to domestic producers than reductions in any other phase of the business cycle. A tariff reduction, if business conditions are improving, may lead to a greater share of imports in the total supply of a commodity without forcing a reduction in domestic supply. Trade agreements, evidently, are best concluded in periods when domestic trade is rising, or is at least brisk. The substantial reduction of the tariff through trade agreements would not have been politically possible had business conditions not been on an upswing at the time.

Escape Clauses

The texts of the agreements amply testify to the preoccupation of the government with their effects on domestic producers. The agreements often circumscribe the concessions by reclassification of dutiable items and they usually contain escape clauses that may be invoked in case unexpectedly large imports threaten the market of domestic producers. An escape clause in the Mexican agreement, for instance, pro-

---

May 1939, they cannot have affected American trade with these two countries in the years before 1939. They may therefore be treated as nonagreement countries during the period 1934–1939. (The Bureau excludes them both from the category of trade-agreement countries and from the category of nonagreement countries.) Exports to Venezuela rose between 1934–1935 and 1938–1939 by 221 per cent and exports to Turkey by 200 per cent, as against an average rise of exports to agreement countries by only 62.8 per cent.

21. *Hearings on H.R. 3240*, p. 8.

vides that if as a result of the agreement any commodity is imported in such volume as seriously to harm domestic producers, the President can impose quantitative restrictions, or even go so far as to cancel the concessions.[22] This particular clause was unique; but similar, though perhaps less sweeping, escape clauses are attached to other trade agreements. Thus Article XII of the reciprocal trade agreement with Uruguay, signed in July 1942, reads:

> If the Government of either country should consider that any circumstance, or any measure adopted by the other Government, even though it does not conflict with the terms of this Agreement, has the effect of nullifying or impairing any object of the Agreement or of prejudicing an industry or the commerce of that country, such other Government shall give sympathetic consideration to such representations or proposals as may be made with a view to effecting a mutually satisfactory adjustment of the matter. If no agreement is reached with respect to such representations or proposals, the Government making them shall be free to suspend or terminate this Agreement in whole or in part on thirty days' written notice.[23]

The House Ways and Means Committee in its report on the bill for the extension of the trade agreement in 1945 emphasizes the desirability of such clauses in future trade agreements:

> Pursuant to the wise authority conferred by the original act not only to proclaim changes in duties but also impose "additional import restrictions," concessions have been circumscribed whenever necessary, by reclassifications, changes in form of duties, tariff quotas, and absolute quotas. It is the intent of the law and also that of the committee, that these same protective measures shall be used in connection with future agreements whenever circumstances require them.[24]

Boldness Essential

Such a hesitant attitude on the part of the United States is not an encouraging sign. If there is to be effective reduction of world trade barriers, the leadership of the United States is required. Cautious hedging on the part of the country in the strongest economic position will not inspire confidence. Only a bold example can persuade other nations to follow American leadership. It is possible that the United

22. *Ibid.,* p. 20.
23. *Reciprocal Trade Agreement and Supplemental Exchanges of Notes Between the United States of America and Uruguay,* Executive Agreement Series 276, Publication 1880, Department of State, 1943, pp. 13–14.
24. *Hearings on H.R. 3240,* p. 8.

States may succeed in bringing about a general reduction of trade barriers by using its economic strength as a bargaining weapon. But such methods arouse resentment and are successful only so long as foreign countries are in dire need of help. The wholehearted cooperation of foreign nations can be achieved, if at all, only if the United States shows an unhesitating willingness to reduce its own tariff.[25]

25. In 1945 the State Department published *Proposals for Expansion of World Trade and Employment* (Publication 2411) for consideration by an International Conference on Trade and Employment. It is to these *Proposals* that this chapter and, particularly, the following one occasionally refer. While this book was in press, the United States government published, in September 1946, a new document, *Suggested Charter for an International Trade Organization* (of the United Nations). This *Suggested Charter* was adopted as the basis for its deliberations by the Preparatory Committee of the International Conference on Trade and Employment, which held a meeting in London between October 15 and November 26, 1946. The result of this meeting was a new document, *Preliminary Copy of Redraft of a Charter for an International Trade Organization,* distributed in mimeographed form by the State Department and later printed by the National Foreign Trade Council. The Preparatory Committee is to hold a second meeting, in April 1947, in Geneva, to be followed by an International Trade and Employment Conference in the fall of 1947. The Charter that will emerge from this conference is to be submitted to the Congress of the United States and the governments of other countries, and if all goes well, the International Trade Organization might come into existence in 1948.

In the appendix the reader will find reproduced the original American *Proposals for Expansion of World Trade and Employment.* This document is included in its entirety because it is discussed at various points in this and the succeeding chapter. These original proposals have been modified several times.

Such examination of the redrafts of the original American proposals as has been possible while this volume is in press shows quite clearly that the new version, on the whole, is more generous than the original in granting exceptions to the use of quantitative trade restrictions and discriminatory trade practices.

The first *Report of the Preparatory Committee of the United Nations Conference on Trade and Employment* (United Nations Publications Number E/PC/T/33) contains all the documents, subsequent to the original American proposals, agreed upon up to the end of 1946.

Unfortunately their very late appearance, as well as their excessive length, precludes the inclusion of these reports and documents in the present volume.

Chapter 11

FUTURE COMMERCIAL POLICY

DURING WORLD WAR II almost all governments controlled foreign trade, in varying degrees, by means of foreign exchange control, import and export licensing, bilateral agreements and outright prohibitions. If world trade is to expand once again, existing restrictions must be sharply reduced. What are the prospects for achieving a return to multilateral trade, an abolition of the more obnoxious types of trade restrictions and a lowering of the tariff barriers that remain?

CONFLICTING INTERESTS

Nations have always conducted their commercial policy to suit their real or imagined national interests. Despite the lip service many governments have paid to the ideal of promoting world trade, they have in practice all too often flouted this ideal. Unemployment, a negative balance of payments, military preparedness and the influence of pressure groups have all, at various times and places, led governments to deviate from professed ideals. National policies often contradict one another. It is obviously impossible, for instance, for all nations through restrictive measures to achieve an export surplus simultaneously. If all try to achieve this end by protectionist devices, the net result must inevitably be a reduction in international trade. What appears to be a "reasonable" policy from the point of view of one nation often becomes absurd, even in the narrow sense of achieving the intended effect, if policies of other nations are taken into account.

If postwar commercial policy is not to deteriorate into strife between nations as in the 1930's, the trading countries must adhere to certain standards of behavior. The common ideology of the 19th century once provided such standards. As in many other spheres, these standards of collective behavior broke down in the 1930's and the disintegration was accelerated by World War II. The State Department's *Proposals for Expansion of World Trade and Employment*,[1] which are intended to serve as a basis for an international trade conference

1. Publication 2411, 1945. (Reproduced in Appendix 3.)

in 1947, represent an attempt to re-establish, by agreement among the United Nations, such "rules of the game." Whether an agreement can effectively replace the unquestioned standards of conduct to which governments formerly adhered as a matter of course, remains to be seen.

GREAT BRITAIN

A survey of British public opinion at the end of 1945, as expressed in newspapers, weekly magazines and parliamentary debates, shows clearly not only that the American loan to Great Britain was accepted with certain qualms, but also that the State Department's proposals for an international trade charter were viewed with some apprehension.[2]

The British government has published the statistical material submitted by its delegates to the American government during the loan negotiations.[3] The British government concluded from this statistical material that Great Britain must raise the volume of its exports by 75 per cent over 1938 if its international accounts were to be balanced in the future. (See pp. 117–18.) In 1938 its exports were roughly 10 per cent of world exports. Consequently, to attain the required goal, Britain would have to increase its share in world exports from 10 to 17.5 per cent with a world volume as in 1938. If the volume of world exports in the future does not exceed the volume for 1938, the increase in Great Britain's share must take place at the expense of other nations' exports. If world trade increases above the 1938 figure, not all the increase in British exports need be at the expense of other countries. There is, however, little early prospect of a large increase in world trade. The argument, sometimes advanced, that Great Britain can increase its exports merely by replacing Germany and Japan in the export markets of the world, is false. For if Germany's and Japan's exports are small in the future, their imports will also be small. Great Britain's exports to these two countries will therefore fall below the prewar level and so will its exports to those third countries that, before the war, financed part of their imports from Great Britain by exports to Germany and Japan.

2. "Second Thoughts," *The Economist,* December 15, 1945, pp. 849 ff.; "The Trade Proposals," pp. 853 ff.; and "The Consequences," December 22, 1945, pp. 897 ff.
3. *Statistical Material Presented During the Washington Negotiations,* British White Paper, Cmd. 6707, 1945.

In addition to these difficulties, Great Britain cannot be expected to increase its exports of raw materials and agricultural products. The increase in exports must be wholly or mainly in manufactured commodities. Great Britain's export drive must therefore increase the export of manufactures by roughly 100 per cent in order to achieve an increase of 75 per cent in total exports.

Criticisms of United States Policy

It would be optimistic to suppose that Great Britain could reach this export goal even under highly favorable conditions. Consequently, the British have been somewhat critical of the State Department's *Proposals,* and to a lesser degree of the Fund Agreement. If both are accepted, some British critics have argued, Great Britain loses many of the weapons it could otherwise mobilize for its export drive. Under the Fund Agreement it can devalue its currency unilaterally by only 10 per cent. It cannot use its strongest weapon — its importance as a market for foreign countries — because bilateral agreements, being discriminatory in nature, are excluded under the State Department's *Proposals.* This means that Great Britain cannot increase its exports by "inducing" other countries to buy from it under the threat that otherwise they would be excluded from the British market. Furthermore, the critics emphasize, Empire preferences are to be greatly reduced and eventually eliminated under the *Proposals.* The *Proposals* would also prevent Great Britain from making bulk purchases — that is, from buying most of a country's exportable surplus of a commodity in return for purchases of British exports. Bulk purchases, according to the *Proposals,* are considered discriminatory. Finally, Britain would not be allowed to subsidize manufactures if such subsidies led to price differences between the home and foreign markets, since such subsidies are "in principle" outlawed three years after the adoption of the trade charter.[4]

In short, some British critics have urged, the State Department's trade proposals would hem Britain in just when it requires the utmost freedom to increase exports. Britain can still, of course, reduce its imports to help it reach an equilibrium in its balances of payments. But cutting imports would lower the British standard of living, and

---

4. An "escape clause" is attached to this provision, however.

would contradict the idea of an "expansion of world trade," that is, the whole purpose of the State Department *Proposals*.

The critics see little hope that Britain will succeed in increasing its exports by 75 per cent, if the Bretton Woods Fund Agreement and the proposed International Trade Charter are enforced. In their eyes the *Proposals* chiefly reflect American interests in world trade, for which British interests are to be sacrificed.

The Official View

The *official* British view on the loan and the trade proposals, on the other hand, has been consistently one of support and agreement. In a brilliant speech before the House of Lords, the late Lord Keynes endeavored to answer most of the criticisms referred to above. Undoubtedly, informed opinion in England is not all of one mind concerning the appropriate policies for Britain to pursue in its present difficulties. Many genuinely believe that a return to multilateral trade along the lines proposed by the United States is in the best interests of Great Britain and the rest of the world. Others are frankly more skeptical, but since the approval of the loan by the American Congress and British assurances to support the trade proposals at the forthcoming conference, these earlier differences of opinion are less significant.

THE UNITED STATES

The official American attitude toward postwar commercial policy is almost the reverse of that of the British critics described above. The United States favors multilateralism; nondiscriminatory trade practices; reduction of trade barriers, including its own; and free competition in the world market. These are the principles on which the State Department's proposals for a trade charter rest. To be sure, escape clauses in the trade charter qualify almost all statements of principle. This is perhaps inevitable in any document to which the governments of a number of nations have to agree and that must be submitted to national legislatures. Nonetheless, multilateralism, reduction of trade barriers, and competition are unquestionably the ideals on which the American trade proposals are based. The United States is championing a liberal trade philosophy, and thus is taking up the role that Britain played before World War I.

It would be pointless to deny, however, that a world-wide relaxation of trade restrictions and restoration of multilateral trade in the near future now serves the particular interest of the United States, just as it served British interests in earlier days. American industry is now in a strong competitive position in the world market. Because of curtailed productive capacity in many countries, there is no immediate prospect of large imports of manufactures to compete with American industry at home. And the widespread fear that domestic investment opportunities may diminish enhances the desirability of foreign lending and the resulting export surplus, to those responsible for framing economic policy. Foreign investment may help to sustain domestic employment. The real test for the American attitude toward trade policy will come only when interest and amortization payments on foreign investment cause the American trade balance to reverse itself. Large imports are invariably less appealing than new exports.

RUSSIA AND OTHER CONTROLLED ECONOMIES

Russia's commercial policy is inevitably entirely different from that of Great Britain or the United States. With a state monopoly of foreign trade, Russian imports and exports are part of its national economic plan. A "liberal" trade policy in the usual sense is out of the question. The American proposals for a trade charter stipulate with respect to complete state monopolies of foreign trade, that their purchases and sales "shall be influenced solely by commercial considerations, such as price, quality, marketability, transportation and terms of purchase or sale." In other words, Russian purchases and sales should be made on a nondiscriminatory basis. Moreover, state monopolies "should undertake to purchase annually from members . . . products valued at not less than an aggregate amount to be agreed upon." (Chapter III, Section E.) In practice, it will be easy for a state monopoly to influence the terms of its purchases by exploiting its strong position as a prospective large buyer; in so doing it can always claim to be living up to the agreement inasmuch as it buys where the commodity is cheapest or the terms of sale most advantageous. There are no sure means of ascertaining — certainly not from outside the country — whether the exports of a state monopoly are "subsidized" or not. In short, the usual concepts applicable to exports and imports in a private enterprise system are inapplicable to the foreign trade of a centrally planned economy.

As might be supposed, the recent Russian commercial treaties with

Romania, Hungary and Bulgaria bear little resemblance to commercial treaties familiar to western countries. They are instruments for achieving economic penetration of countries in Russia's sphere of influence.

The Russian-Romanian Agreement of May 8, 1945, for instance, provides for joint trading companies — the boards of which consist half of Russian members and half Romanian.[5] The Agreement provides for a joint banking institution in Bucharest. A joint oil concern is also to be formed, which all the Romanian oil companies must enter, and to which the Romanian government must cede half of its crude petroleum royalties and exclusive boring rights on Romanian soil. The Russians are to provide the oil equipment.[6] Another joint company is planned for the development of navigation: the Romanian government will cede to this company exclusive rights to use the harbors and harbor installations of the major Romanian ports. The agreements with Hungary and Bulgaria are similar, and agreements with other countries in the Russian sphere of influence may follow.

The "rules of the game" laid down in the American trade charter obviously do not, and cannot, apply to trade relations between Russia and the countries in Russia's sphere of influence if events pursue their present course.

Germany and Japan are also not likely, for some time at least, to follow the western pattern in their trade with other countries. Freedom of private enterprise no longer exists in these countries in any full sense. For some time to come, their exports and imports will probably be controlled by the occupying powers. The nature and quantities of their exports and imports will be the result of a compromise among the political and economic interests of the occupying powers, rather than the result, in the language of the *Proposals,* of "commercial considerations, such as price, quality, marketability, transportation and terms of purchase or sale."

5. An account of the Russian and Romanian trade agreement is given in *The Economist,* October 20, 1945, pp. 561 ff.

6. "It very soon turned out that the Soviet contribution would consist largely of oil-field equipment which they had taken over as war booty from the Germans — notwithstanding that much of this equipment had been acquired by the Germans during the course of the war from British, French, Belgian, and other western interests incapable of defending themselves at that time. It has been stated on good authority that 50,000 tons of oilfield equipment were removed from Roumania by the Russians during 1944 (and more have since been taken from the Unirea plant), and that of this some 87 per cent was British and Allied property." *Ibid.,* p. 561.

Germany, Japan, Russia and the countries now dominated by Russia took 20 per cent of world imports in 1938 and provided 22 per cent of world exports. These countries, formerly accounting for about a fifth of world trade, will live under different economic regimes from the rest of the world, and their trade relations with other countries will be dictated by different considerations.

OTHER COUNTRIES

Although other countries will presumably be attracted to a system of multilateral trade that allows them to buy imports where they are cheapest, their interests are not in all respects identical. Some of the Dominions may favor the retention of imperial preferences that favor their agricultural products in the British market. Some countries may favor bulk foreign purchases if thereby they can sell the whole of their exportable surplus of a commodity to one market — for example, the sale of mutton by New Zealand to Great Britain. Still others have state monopolies in certain commodities — for instance China, in tea, tungsten, bristles and some others. Finally, there are the many countries where industrialization made great progress during World War II that will be bent on protecting their new industries by high tariffs.[7]

7. By the beginning of 1946, the removal of special wartime controls over foreign trade had made considerable progress in the United States, Canada and South Africa. In the United States relatively few commodities were at that time still subject to export licenses, and only fourteen categories of industrial materials were still under governmental import control. Canada had also relaxed import and export controls and had abolished the 10 per cent war tax, which was imposed during the war on imports from non-Empire countries. South Africa had abolished import permits or certificates of essentiality for all goods from the United States that could be exported under general export licenses.

On the other hand, little progress toward relaxation of import restrictions had been made in the United Kingdom and some of the Dominions. Imports into New Zealand from countries outside the sterling area were even more severely restricted than during the war. Most South American countries had introduced additional import restrictions by supplementing their foreign exchange control by an import-licensing system; the purpose was to prevent the accumulated dollar balances from being used for the import of luxury items and goods that compete with certain war-developed domestic industries. Some Latin-American countries have increased their tariffs (e.g., Brazil on wool and woolen goods, Mexico on chemicals, iron and steel products and on many others).

The liberated European countries, at the beginning of 1946, still purchased their imports through official purchasing missions. Trade had not yet been restored to private hands. A network of bilateral agreements between pairs of countries formed the basis of trade among European countries. See the instructive survey in Henry Chalmers, "Current Trends in Foreign Trade Policies," *Foreign Commerce Weekly,* February 9, 16 and 23, 1946.

The trend is thus by no means wholly toward a relaxation of trade barriers. The desire to protect newly developed industries has already found expression in the actions of a number of Latin-American countries.

AN INTERNATIONAL TRADE CHARTER

We have already pointed out that the State Department's proposals for an international trade charter are an attempt to re-create a system of rules for the commercial policies of all countries.

What is needed is a broad and yet detailed agreement, among many nations, dealing at one time with many different sorts of governmental restrictions upon trade, reducing all of them at once on a balanced and equitable basis, and *stating rules and principles* within which the restrictions permitted to remain should be administered.[8]

OBSTACLES TO WORLD-WIDE TARIFF REDUCTIONS

If restrictions on trade are to be modified and rules for conducting commercial policy established, a concerted effort on the part of all nations is essential. Agreements between two nations alone, even if they embody the unconditional most-favored-nation clause, cannot replace a multinational agreement for the simultaneous reduction of trade restrictions. The most-favored-nation clause has lost its effectiveness largely through the adoption of discriminatory tariff classifications, and by the practice of reducing duties only on those commodities for which the treaty partner is the most important supplier.[9] The clause is virtually inapplicable where quotas and exchange control are used. Only multilateral negotiations can bring about a substantial reduction of trade barriers on a world-wide scale; but multilateral agreements are hard to obtain.

Failure of Past Efforts

The usual difficulties of reaching trade agreements between two nations are multiplied greatly if many nations must agree. The League of Nations attempted in vain to reduce trade barriers through multilateral agreements. The League first tried to bring about agreement among countries to fix maximum limits for the duties on each category of merchandise; but countries with high tariffs objected that they would lose the freedom to raise tariffs while countries with low tariffs would retain that freedom. The League then tried to obtain an agreement on an equal percentage reduction of duties; this was opposed

8. *Proposals for Expansion of World Trade and Employment*, p. 3 (italics added).
9. The most-favored-nation clause does not benefit other nations if the definition of the commodity is narrowed down to such an extent. See also the statement by the House Ways and Means Committee quoted on p. 247.

by countries with low tariffs on the grounds that it would penalize them in relation to countries with higher tariffs. The League then tried to reach an agreement on tariff reductions on certain groups of commodities beginning with semimanufactures; countries in the process of industrializing, whose main exports were still agricultural, objected to such a reduction and naturally pointed to the high tariffs on agricultural products in other countries that hampered *their* exports. The efforts of the League thus failed to produce any results.[10]

Future Prospects

Are future prospects brighter? In view of the conflict of national interests in commercial policy, a conflict far more acute than existed in the interwar period, it cannot seriously be argued that they are. The only new favorable factors are the willingness of the United States to take the lead in reducing trade barriers and the fact that since the passage of the Trade Agreements Act its tariff is no longer non-negotiable. The preponderant economic and political influence of the United States makes its present interest in tariff reductions of paramount importance. To what extent the United States will succeed in overcoming resistance to tariff reductions, which many countries will undoubtedly offer, cannot be forecast. The State Department's draft of an International Trade Charter reflects, in its many escape clauses, the difficulties the Department already anticipates. A few illustrations of such escape clauses are worth noting.

Qualifications of the Principle

A primary aim of the Charter — the reduction of tariffs — is qualified by the provision that "Commitments with regard to tariffs should permit countries to take temporary action to prevent sudden and widespread injury to the producers concerned. Undertakings for reducing tariffs should therefore contain an escape clause to cover such contingencies." (*Proposals,* Chapter III, Section B3.)

In fact, really effective reductions of tariffs are almost certain to cause injury to the producers directly concerned.

Quantitative trade restrictions such as quotas are, "in principle," to be eliminated. But exceptions are allowed for the transition period;

10. *Commercial Policy in the Post-War World,* League of Nations, Geneva, 1945.II. A.7, pp. 15 ff.

for intergovernmental commodity agreements; for agricultural products whenever quantitative trade restrictions are necessary either to enforce governmental measures designed to restrict production, or "to remove a temporary surplus of like domestic products by making such surpluses available to certain groups of domestic consumers free of charge or at prices below the current market level." Exceptions are also provided for a country that finds it necessary to protect its balance of payments, and for certain other contingencies.

Is much left of the "principle"?

Export subsidies that lead to a foreign price lower than the domestic price are "in principle" to be eliminated three years after the Trade Charter has come into force. But again the proposals admit exceptions: the three-year time limit can be extended under certain conditions, and products in surplus supply are exempt.

The proposals, as *The Economist* put it, "abound in qualifications, and they trim the basic postulates freely to fit present day facts. . . . It is extremely difficult to translate such a document, compact of ideals and reservations, into practical terms and intentions."[11] It is characteristic that *The Economist,* viewing the document from the British position, criticizes it because it "trims the basic postulates" to fit only those present-day facts impressive to American eyes, and because it protects American at the expense of British interests. Other countries may have similar objections. It remains to be seen in what form the trade charter will be accepted, and how it will function in a world no longer held together by common standards of conduct, a world in which international trade must be redirected into peacetime channels, and in which national interests as expressed in commercial policy are in serious conflict.

THE PRESENT OPPORTUNITY

Despite all this, the postwar interval offers an unusually felicitous opportunity for a general reduction of trade barriers for a number of reasons. The protectionist spirit is weakest when domestic employment is high. The United States, Great Britain and most other countries are unlikely soon to be faced with unemployment on a large scale. Heavy unemployment is probable only in countries with a serious shortage of raw materials and production facilities, but such unemployment cannot possibly be removed through high trade barriers. On

11. "The Trade Proposals," December 15, 1945, p. 853.

the contrary, such barriers would aggravate the difficulties of importing necessary goods. The urgent need of many countries for imports is, indeed, an additional reason why the transition period is especially propitious for reducing trade barriers.

Furthermore, reconversion offers a "unique opportunity . . . for choosing those lines of production that can stand on their own feet without heavy tariff protection or subsidies."[12] In order to draw industry into those lines, tariffs must be reduced *during the transition period.* Industry can then be induced to convert with freer trade as a consideration instead of *re*converting on the basis of protectionism. This consideration applies to all countries faced with a reconversion problem.

It may certainly be argued that the United States will be protected from foreign competition during the next few years even though tariffs are reduced. Some of its former competitors, such as Germany and Japan, will be out of the world market, and others, like Great Britain, must first rebuild their export capacity. Hence, one might urge that lower tariffs would not now affect the course of reconversion. This argument, however, does not apply to industries in which more distant returns necessarily enter into the profitability calculations of new investments. These industries may still be encouraged, by the reduction of tariffs, not to convert to lines of production likely to be exposed in the long run to cheaper foreign competition.

Despite their need of imports, Great Britain and the continental European countries will have to continue foreign exchange control or licensing systems for some time to come in order to protect their balance of payments. Safeguarding the balance of payments by these methods will necessarily protect domestic producers, even if tariffs are reduced. Again, however, the reduction in tariffs need not be ineffective, provided the governments make clear their intentions to abolish quantitative import controls in the not too distant future.

The increased authority granted to the President in 1945 enables the United States to take the lead in reducing tariffs by making tariff concessions in exchange for a reduction of trade barriers in other countries. It is planned by the State Department to

. . . undertake negotiations under the Trade Agreements Act with several other governments as soon as a mutually satisfactory basis can be found, the

---

12. Cordell Hull in *United States Department of State Bulletin,* May 20, 1944.

required notices published, the statutory public hearings held, and their results considered. These negotiations cannot practicably be conducted with all countries at the same time, but the effort should be to get forward with the work, commencing before the general Conference convenes and continuing until every friendly country has participated in the enterprise.[13]

Under this new authority the United States can offer substantial tariff reductions. How effectively the authority will be used depends partly on the concessions other nations are willing to offer, and partly on the resistance of domestic producers to American tariff reductions. If the authority is not effectively used, and if the International Trade Conference does not reach an international agreement on tariff reductions before reconversion is completed, a highly favorable combination of circumstances will have gone unexploited.

INTERGOVERNMENTAL COMMODITY AGREEMENTS: A SPECIAL PROBLEM

Exceptions are a danger to any rule. An international trade charter based on the principles of multilateral trade, reduction of trade barriers, nondiscrimination and competition may be shot through with so many exceptions that they become in practice more important than the principles. *Ad hoc* reasoning can always produce arguments for an exception, rather than the rule, in any particular case. In shipping, for example, where Great Britain has a clear advantage over the United States, it is easy to argue that military considerations justify American subsidies, even though subsidies, in principle, are outlawed in the American proposals. Similarly, the military importance of rubber may be held to necessitate protection of the synthetic rubber industry against competition from natural rubber, even though the general objective is the reduction of trade barriers.

Every country has special interests in certain commodities and services. Each will be tempted to apply the principle only where it has a comparative advantage and to claim exceptions for commodities in which it has a comparative disadvantage. The reasons for making an exception will always be made to sound persuasive. Without a determined willingness on all sides to make sacrifices, the principles of the Trade Charter will not govern trade policy and practice.

We cannot analyze all the special problems of commercial policy

13. *Proposals for Expansion of World Trade and Employment*, p. 4.

relating to all the various categories of commodities. One group of commodities, however, has given rise to a type of commercial policy likely to become of great future importance. Agricultural products and raw materials were the subject of intergovernmental commodity agreements even before 1939; attempts to conclude such agreements will undoubtedly be revived, and perhaps intensified, in the future. These agreements take a variety of forms: they may simply be buffer stock schemes; they may allot export quotas; or they may go a step further and fix production quotas by countries. If they establish export or production quotas they clearly break the rule of competition in international trade. Nevertheless, international commodity agreements are permitted under the State Department's *Proposals*.

Intergovernmental commodity agreements existed in the past for wheat, sugar, tea, coffee, beef, timber, tin and rubber,[14] and many more were proposed at one time or another. For example, agreements concerning dairy products, wine, cocoa and copper were under consideration during the London Economic Conference in 1933. The International Cotton Meeting held in Washington in 1939 authorized the establishment of an International Cotton Advisory Committee, but action was postponed by the outbreak of the war.

Protect Producers' Interests

Many products, moreover, were controlled before 1939 by the producers themselves with the sanction, but not the open participation, of governments — for example, lead, nickel, zinc, aluminum, mercury, potash, sulphur, petroleum, quinine, raw silk, raw steel and steel products.[15] However, only intergovernmental agreements will be considered here: The policy of the United States is not to favor private combinations, as is evident from the State Department's *Proposals*. In addition, intergovernmental commodity agreements are in the future likely to replace private combinations. Experience has shown that the

14. The text of these agreements can be found in *Intergovernmental Commodity Control Agreements*, International Labor Office, Montreal, 1943. A survey of the agreements is also given in J. D. Black and J. S. Tsou, "International Commodity Agreements," *Quarterly Journal of Economics*, August 1944, pp. 523 ff.

15. Cf. the study by George W. Stocking and Myron W. Watkins, *Cartels in Action*, Twentieth Century Fund, New York, 1946.

producers are, in any case, usually the dominant force behind inter-governmental agreements even if these agreements provide for the representation of consumers' interests. This is not astonishing, since the primary purpose of intergovernmental commodity agreements is to protect producers against the effects of falling prices for their products. No intergovernmental commodity agreement has yet been concluded because prices were too high for consumers. Past agreements clearly reflect the predominant influence of producers' interests. Thus the wheat agreement concluded in 1942 between four wheat-export countries — Argentina, Australia, Canada and the United States — and one wheat-importing country — Great Britain — states that the prices fixed "shall be such as will in the opinion of the Council, a) return reasonably remunerative prices to producers in the exporting countries, b) be fair to consumers in importing countries, c) be in reasonable relationship to prices of other commodities . . ."[16] This definition, though generally vague,[17] is definite as far as the producers' interests are concerned: The producers are promised profits. Producers will be more than willing to have intergovernmental agreements replace private agreements, if this silences public opposition to producers' combinations without entailing any loss of profits.

National Schemes Lead to International Control

Intergovernmental commodity agreements have usually followed efforts of single governments to protect particular domestic producers by raising prices and restricting production. Attempts by countries acting alone to keep up world prices are as a rule ineffective. For if one or a few producing countries raise prices, other producing countries often benefit from the resulting higher price without expense to themselves. For instance, the Stevenson rubber restriction scheme of 1922, which applied only to rubber producers in the British Empire, had to be repealed in 1928 largely because it led to an expansion of production outside the area of control, mainly by native planters in the Nether-

16. *Intergovernmental Commodity Control Agreements*, p. 17.
17. In this and in other agreements (as well as in many governmental statements on price policy) the term "fair" or "reasonable" price recurs more and more frequently. The moralist may see in the frequent use of such terms a proof of the irrepressible desire of men to apply moral standards to all human behavior. The cynic may see in it a hypocritical attempt by interested groups to cover up their private interests with the language of the moralist.

lands East Indies. In 1934 a new agreement was concluded, applying this time to 90 per cent of the world's rubber production. Similarly, the American policy of supporting the domestic cotton price led to an expansion of cotton production in other areas and to a decline in American exports. By 1938, the United States was supplying only 20 per cent of foreign consumption as compared with about 47 per cent in 1928.[18] Representatives of the cotton-producing countries agreed in September 1939 that ". . . the regulation of the world cotton supplies in relation to demand would help materially in improving the existing unbalanced conditions."[19] Only the outbreak of the war prevented further action toward an international cotton agreement.

Thus, national attempts to control the prices or the output of commodities have a strong tendency to lead to international control schemes.

WHY COMMODITY CONTROLS?

Agricultural and Mineral Production

Why have governments attempted, either singly or in concert with others, to control certain primary products while they have made no similar large-scale attempts to control manufactured commodities?

Obviously, agricultural production is subject to uncertainties of the weather that are absent in most manufactures. But this is not sufficient to explain the existence of commodity control schemes. For although weather does not affect mining, there are many control schemes for minerals. Moreover, weather conditions affected agriculture before 1914; but the pricing system so operated that in many commodities private traders stored part of the crop in good years and sold from stocks in bad years.

Nor do depressions necessarily affect agriculture or mining more than manufacturing. Capital goods industries usually suffer from depressions more than any other. Other reasons must therefore be sought to explain why certain types of primary products have been subjected to control schemes whereas manufactured products have not.

18. *The United States in the World Economy,* Economic Series No. 23, Bureau of Foreign and Domestic Commerce, 1943, p. 60. See also Stocking and Watkins, *op. cit.,* and *idem, Cartels or Competition?,* to be published in 1947 by the Twentieth Century Fund.
19. *Intergovernmental Commodity Control Agreements,* p. 132.

Standardized Products More Easily Controlled

Commodity control schemes work best if the product is standardized, as in the case of cotton, wheat or certain minerals. If, as in many manufacturing industries, the products are differentiated and subject to rapid obsolescence, a control scheme that fixes prices or regulates production encounters almost insurmountable administrative difficulties. International cartels in manufacturing therefore usually divide markets among producing countries without attempting to control prices.

Whenever there are relatively few producers, they can easily devise their own control schemes, as in the European iron and steel industry, in the potash industry, in the aluminum industry and many others. But where production is in the hands of thousands of independent producers, as in wheat, cotton and coffee, agreement among producers is practically out of the question. An active minority of the producers may, however, attempt to act through the government. Governments are usually willing, for a variety of reasons, to protect farmers and miners against the effects of a decline in the prices of their products. They may yield to well-organized pressure groups; they may believe that farming, for other than economic reasons, is a particularly desirable occupation or that military preparedness requires a prosperous domestic agriculture. In some countries, the production of one mineral or one agricultural crop is the largest single industry and the source of the principal export, as coffee for Brazil, rubber for British Malaya, sugar for Cuba, tin for Bolivia. If the export market of such an industry declines, the result is severe unemployment and pressure on the country's balance of payments. The government may then be driven to protect the industry by a national or international control scheme.

The Problem of Changes in Demand

In the last analysis, national and international control schemes probably rest on the fact that agricultural and mineral production adjust only very slowly to changes in demand.

For some agricultural products, such as rubber and coffee, the period of maturation is very long. It takes four or five years for coffee trees, and still longer for rubber trees, to reach the productive stage. Rubber and coffee producers who plant in response to high current prices may find that by the time the increased product is available, demand has slackened. And even if the demand has not declined, the greater output of the many producers may drive the price down so far as to reduce producers' total receipts. Even if the price of the product does not fall that far, it may decline enough to make a contraction of production desirable, and this is again a slow process. These peculiarities go far to explain why rubber and coffee producers, for example, favor national and international control schemes.

Even when the period of maturation is short, the supplies of agricultural products adapt themselves only slowly to cyclical and long-run changes in demand. Farmers are often said to react to a decline in price by producing more instead of less in an attempt to compensate by increasing the total amount sold. Even when production is reduced, because of the decline in price, it may not be reduced sufficiently to match decreased demand; moreover, uncontrollable weather factors may in part counteract the effect of acreage reduction initiated by a decline in demand.[20]

Long-Run Shifts in Demand

Much more serious, however, is the lack of adaptability of production to long-run shifts in demand. Professor T. W. Schultz has pointed out that the demand for agricultural products is now increasing at a slower rate than formerly, whereas the supply is increasing at an accelerated rate. There are two principal reasons why the rate of increase in demand is declining. On the one hand, the rate of population increase in the western world is slowing down. On the other hand, the income-elasticity of demand for agricultural products is small, so that an increase in national incomes per head tends to benefit agriculture less than other sectors of the economy. At the same time, the supply of agricultural products now tends to increase at a more rapid rate because of continual technological advances in agriculture. This increased output tends to encounter a demand having a low price-elasticity with adverse effects on producers' incomes. The surplus farm labor, created by the introduction of laborsaving devices in agriculture, must ultimately be absorbed outside of agriculture. Because this necessary absorption proceeds only slowly, agriculture shows a persistent tendency toward overproduction.

20. For a discussion of the possible types of reactions of supply to demand see Mordecai Ezekiel, "The Cobweb Theorem," *Quarterly Journal of Economics,* February 1938, pp. 255–80.

The major consequences point to a continuing chronic disequilibrium affecting agriculture, which arises primarily from the excess supply of labor that accumulates and burdens agriculture. The mechanism of relative prices has had severe shortcomings in transferring excess supplies of labor out of agriculture when we look at the experience of 1920–43.[21]

Special circumstances, as in wheat and cotton, have aggravated the difficulties for exporting countries. The production of substitutes for cotton, under the protection of high tariffs in some European countries, decreased the demand for cotton. Similarly, the protection European governments gave to agriculture after the first world war led to a decline in the demand for imported wheat, as shown in Table 33.[22]

TABLE 33

PERCENTAGE OF TOTAL WHEAT CONSUMPTION IMPORTED FROM ABROAD, 1909–1937

Country	1909–1914	1922–1927	1932–1937
Belgium	76.0	74.2	70.1
Czechoslovakia	a	34.0	2.2
Finland	a	86.1	56.3
France	13.4	16.9	3.1
Germany	[36.5]	35.0	4.5
Netherlands	a	82.6	59.1
Sweden	46.6	45.7	0.1
United Kingdom	[77.4]	78.5	77.2

Source: P. de Hevesy, *World Wheat Planning and Economic Planning in General*, Oxford University Press, Oxford, 1940, App. XVIII. Figures in brackets are estimates made in January 1939 by the Secretariat of the Wheat Advisory Committee, London.
a. Not available.

This "artificial" decline in the demand for wheat and cotton exports — in conjunction with the long-run tendency of agricultural production to exceed demand — was the main reason why exporting countries adopted control schemes for these products. If the difficulties could be

21. T. W. Schultz, "Food and Agriculture in a Developing Economy," in *Food for the World*, T. W. Schultz (ed.), University of Chicago Press, Chicago, 1945, p. 320.
22. The protection of wheat producers in the various importing countries presents a truly astonishing maze of different devices. A survey of the various measures adopted in the principal importing countries is given in P. de Hevesy's book, *World Wheat Planning and Economic Planning in General*, Oxford University Press, Oxford, 1940, App. XIV.

ascribed solely to protectionism, a relaxation of trade barriers for these products would solve the problem of surplus production. But as matters stand, the relaxation of trade barriers would not be sufficient. Surplus resources would have to shift from agriculture to counteract the long-run tendency to a chronic disequilibrium.

The production of minerals also adapts only slowly to changes in demand. The demand for minerals fluctuates with variations in the production of manufactures into which the minerals enter. The mining industry has heavy overhead costs. As a result, output declines only slightly as prices decline. If the losses lead to closing the mines altogether, some productive capacity needed for the next boom may be permanently destroyed. The existence of surplus capacity in the production of many minerals, which was largely a legacy from World War I, was a major reason for the adoption of control schemes in the interwar period.

Buffer Stock Schemes as the Remedy

Unstable markets for primary products resulting from slow adaptability of production to purely cyclical fluctuations in demand will obviously disappear as soon as a way is found of eliminating, or mitigating, industrial fluctuations. Commodity controls would then be unnecessary. But as long as cyclical fluctuations continue, buffer stock schemes (without production or export quotas) seem to be the appropriate remedy.[23] An intergovernmental buffer stock agency could establish a minimum price at which it is willing to buy any amount offered on the market, and a maximum price at which it is willing to sell any amount demanded, with the margin between the two prices serving to cover the costs of storage and of administering the scheme. The actual price — so long as the agency possesses stocks — could then fluctuate only between these two limits. Such a scheme would stabilize the price, and thus the production, of the commodity, within certain limits, over the period of the cycle. Such schemes would have the advantage, compared with those that fix export or production quotas, that they do not abolish competition. Moreover, they temper protectionist tendencies, for the incentive to protect producers against

23. They could also be used with advantage in cases where the length of the period of maturation (coffee, rubber) causes inadequate adaptation of production to price changes.

competition from abroad has always been strongest in depression, when imports are offered at very low prices.

The Delegation on Economic Depressions of the League of Nations has advocated such buffer stock schemes.[24] The United Nations Conference on Food and Agriculture, held in Hot Springs in 1943, did not propose a definite scheme but merely stated that:

> International commodity arrangements may play a useful part in the advancement of these ends but further study is necessary to establish the precise forms which these arrangements should take and whether and to what extent regulation of production may be needed.[25]

The Conference recommended that an international organization should be created to

> . . . study the feasibility and desirability of such arrangements with reference to individual commodities and, in appropriate cases, to initiate or review such arrangements to be entered into between governments. . . .[26]

It was indicated that such arrangements should include effective representation of consumers as well as producers; should seek to supply consumption needs from the most efficient source at prices "fair to both consumers and producers"; and should provide for an orderly disposal of surpluses and further maintenances of adequate reserves.[27] The delegates, however, could not agree on the precise form of such arrangements. One group favored buffer schemes but opposed schemes for restricting production; whereas a second group favored restrictions on output.

The Final Verdict

If the buffer stock schemes that have been described are to work satisfactorily, certain difficult conditions must be fulfilled. The most important of these follow.

Governments must abstain from subsidizing the export of the commodity concerned. For instance, if a buffer stock scheme exists for tin,

24. *Economic Stability in the Post-War World,* Report of the Delegation on Economic Depressions, Pt. II, League of Nations, Geneva, 1945.II.A.2, Chap. 19.
25. *Final Act and Section Reports,* United Nations Conference on Food and Agriculture, Section XXV, International Commodity Arrangements, Publication 1948, Department of State.
26. *Ibid.*
27. *Ibid.*

Bolivia cannot be allowed to subsidize its export, however great may be the temptation for Bolivia to increase its supply of foreign exchange by stimulating tin exports through subsidies. Otherwise Bolivia could load increased supplies of tin on the buffer stock agency. If the buying price set by the buffer stock agency does not determine the supply, in the long run the scheme must either break down or be replaced by an international scheme that fixes exports and/or production quotas.

The agency, furthermore, must be strong enough to resist the pressure of producers to set excessive prices. An abnormally high price would stimulate production, and the buffer stock agency would find that its stocks persistently accumulated. In that event, if the agency were unwilling to reduce the price in order to move the surplus stock, the scheme would give way to one employing export quotas, production quotas, or both.

The greatest obstacle to the successful management of buffer stock schemes lies in long-run tendencies in demand and supply. Although the scheme may have been launched with a price that could not be considered too high at the time, the same price may become too high if supply tends to exceed demand. This is a real danger with respect to agricultural commodities. The buffer stock agency must then be prepared to lower the price periodically in spite of strong producers' resistance. If stocks accumulate in boom periods, this is clear evidence that the purchase price set by the agency has become too high and should be lowered. If the resistance of producers prevents a price reduction, the alternative is again to proceed to a more elaborate scheme that restricts production.

Advantages Over Other Schemes

The management of buffer stocks is a difficult task, but if it can be satisfactorily accomplished they are a desirable form of international commodity agreement — much more desirable than schemes fixing export or production quotas. The main objection to quota arrangements is that they almost invariably tend to freeze the status quo. They are in practice restriction schemes, in the sense that they prevent producers from exporting (in the case of export quotas), or from producing (in the case of production quotas), more than a given amount. Theoretically quotas might be adjusted periodically, in accordance with the long-run tendencies of demand and supply. But as one group of delegates to the United Nations Conference on Food and Agriculture put it:

. . . in practice the bodies administering them had, in the past, too often shown an inherent tendency to keep production at a low level in order to insure high prices.[28]

Indeed, if the restriction scheme does not raise prices in the long run, one may well ask what purpose it can serve that could not be better served by a simple buffer stock scheme. If the purpose of an international commodity agreement is solely to eliminate price fluctuations not stemming from the long-run trend, a well-managed buffer stock scheme can serve that purpose with a much less cumbersome administrative machinery than a scheme that allocates production or export quotas.

As such schemes are necessarily restrictive they contravene one of the fundamental recommendations of the United Nations Conference:

There was unanimity on a point that has been stressed repeatedly throughout the Conference, namely that the world, after the war, should follow a bold policy of economic expansion instead of the timid regime of scarcity which characterized the 1930s.[29]

Restriction schemes have other disadvantages. They do nothing to eliminate high-cost producers; on the contrary, they tend to protect them.[30] They can be successful only if they are all-inclusive. If one country stays outside, it can increase its production, undersell the other countries, and thus increase its share in the world market (as was illustrated by the case of the Stevenson rubber scheme or the American cotton scheme). Even if all producing countries enter the agreement in the beginning, the incentive remains for any one of them to "contract out" afterward and to reap the benefits of the scheme at the expense of the countries that stay in.

For all these reasons the verdict must be that intergovernmental

28. *Final Act and Section Reports,* United Nations Conference on Food and Agriculture, p. 59.

29. *Ibid.*

30. The American trade proposals seem to assume (Chapter V, Section 3c) that intergovernmental commodity agreements are to be used as one means of bringing about a shift of manpower and capital out of the overexpanded industry. The "high-cost" producers are presumably those who should shift to alternative employments. The whole of the section of the American proposals relating to intergovernmental commodity agreements (Chapter V) is certainly intended to limit their use as much as possible.

buffer stock agencies are justified if they content themselves with eliminating "perverse" fluctuations of prices around the long-run trend, but that intergovernmental cartel arrangements should not be sanctioned.

Professor E. S. Mason has pointed out that the interests of the United States, from a purely national point of view, are in the main opposed to international commodity agreements that attempt to determine output and prices. American imports of raw materials and unprocessed foods in normal times vastly exceed American exports of these commodities.

Under the circumstances, it would seem extremely unwise for the United States to promote a system of international controls which are bound to increase the value of our imports more than they increase the value of our exports.[31]

In this instance, American interests fortunately coincide with the interests of the world at large.

31. E. S. Mason, "The Future of Commodity Agreements," in *Food for the World*, p. 245.

Chapter 12

THE SUMMING UP

THREE MAIN difficulties stand in the way of an early and lasting reconstruction of international trade and international investment.

First, people in different countries hold widely divergent views concerning the objectives of economic policy, as well as the most efficacious means of reaching identical ends. Nor do these differences rest altogether on economic considerations.

The whole range of special problems growing directly out of the war constitutes a second barrier. These are the "transition" problems in contrast to the longer-run problems of international reorganization.

Finally, there is that whole group of problems that arise from the necessity of harmonizing national domestic economic policies with international economic policies conducive to, and consistent with, a healthy growth of international trade and investment. More bluntly, the problem here is how to devise ways and means to maintain national full employment that are consistent with a multilateral trading system in which trade restrictions are at a minimum.

IDEOLOGICAL AND POLITICAL DISHARMONIES

Victory in World War II did not settle basic ideological issues. The victors are not yet agreed on the kind of world that is to be built on the ruins of war. Even the general objectives of the peace settlement are still far from clear. Until there is some consensus on the objectives, little progress is to be expected.[1]

This lack of a common ideology among the victors inevitably re-

1. "To begin with, international morality, although extolled *ad nauseam* in official pronouncements, has no accepted standards and conveys no precise meaning. What is regarded as 'moral' today may be branded as a gross 'immorality' tomorrow. Until recently the United States was the great exponent of neutrality, yet during the recent war neutrality was denounced by America's authoritative spokesmen as akin to treason, and great pressure was brought to bear on neutral countries to make them join the ranks of the Allies. What at any particular moment is considered 'moral' in Washington may appear in an entirely different light in London or Paris, to say nothing of Moscow, Berlin, Rome and Tokyo." Michael T. Florinsky, "The Soviet Union and International Agreements," *Political Science Quarterly*, March 1946, p. 88.

tards political and economic reconstruction. Successful peace treaties have usually proceeded from common ideals among the victors to the broad objectives to be sought in the peace settlement. To illustrate:

At the end of the Thirty Years' war in 1648, the Treaty of Muenster settled the Catholic-Protestant issue so that it was never reopened. In 1713 the Treaty of Utrecht settled the Spanish Succession with equal finality. In 1815 the Treaty of Vienna resulted in one hundred years of *Pax Britannica*. On each of these occasions there existed an essential identity of ideologies and broad consensus regarding the ultimate objective of policy among all participants.[2]

World War I was a victory for democratic ideals in all countries economically or politically to the fore at the time. This common ideology provided a basis for reconstruction. The free-enterprise system was not seriously questioned. Political democracy and economic liberalism were accepted as working ideals. To be sure, they did not long endure in some countries. And the peace of Versailles proved to be a much less successful settlement than, for instance, the Treaty of Vienna. But as long as democratic ideals reigned, the reconstruction of the world economy proceeded along common lines.

At the end of World War II, the world is divided into countries with omnipotent governments and countries with democratic governments on the western pattern. Germany, Italy and Japan have been defeated and their nondemocratic governments have disappeared. But the communist version of an omnipotent government not only still exists in Russia but has spread to some eastern European countries and parts of the Orient. It may extend itself still more widely in the future.

Differences Among Democratic Nations

Even the democratic countries display marked differences. Although Great Britain and the United States preserve representative government, guarantee the rights of individuals and permit freedom of expression, they differ substantially in their handling of economic affairs. The British Labor Government expects to nationalize heavy industry and transportation. In general, the British government directs and controls economic activity much more than the American government. The continental democracies adhere more closely to the British pattern of economic organization than to the American system that

2. Imre de Vegh, "International Aspects of England's Reconstruction," *Proceedings of the Academy of Political Science*, January 1946, p. 41.

still relies heavily on private enterprise within a price and market system.

Communist vs. Democratic Ideas

The deep cleavage between the communist states and the western democracies is illustrated by the now common practice of using the same words to mean quite different things. To communists, "freedom of the press," of which the western democracies are so proud, means "freedom" to sell one's opinion to a capitalistic publishing concern that decides what opinions can be voiced; freedom to choose one's job means freedom of the capitalists to exploit the workers who must sell their labor to the highest bidder. "Democracy" to the communist does not signify a parliamentary regime, but government by the Communist Party. And similarly with many other political and economic terms. The different meanings investing the same words in communist and democratic countries are symptomatic of the completely different scale of values current in each.

These ideological and political differences frame the setting within which the restoration of international trade must proceed. Their influence is pervasive, and all too often they poison the atmosphere with misunderstanding and distrust. If territorial Russia alone were involved, the reconstruction of international trade on liberal principles would not be seriously hampered. Russia's foreign trade has never been large — less than three quarters of Swiss trade throughout the interwar period — and it promises to remain small in the next decade. But in Russian satellite countries foreign trade will probably now be wholly government controlled, too. And presumably the military authorities will manage German and Japanese trade for some time to come. In other words, the postwar reconstruction of world trade on liberal principles means the world minus Russia, minus the Russian satellite countries, and probably minus Germany and Japan. These are important omissions.

Trend Toward Nationalization

The trend toward nationalization of industry in western Europe is a further complication. Nationalization of industry tends to put foreign trade increasingly in government hands. The national government becomes the sole exporter and the sole importer. But the rules governing trade relationships among free-enterprise economies are not necessarily suitable for trade among governments or among governments and individuals. The assumption of the Bretton Woods Agreements and the American international trade proposals that, in most countries, foreign trade after the transition period will revert largely to private hands may not be warranted. Faith and confidence in free enterprise are scarcely high in many parts of the world. Ideologically, politically and economically, the world today is certainly not an integrated and harmonious whole. Economically, Russia and the United States are obviously in sharpest contrast. Great Britain occupies a middle ground. In many countries the choice between alternatives hangs in the balance; the next few years will probably resolve the issue. And in making their choice, the concrete performances of the American free-enterprise system, the Russian communist system and the British experiment in socialism are likely to provide the most persuasive evidence from the economic point of view.

AREAS OF TRANSITORY DISHARMONY

Even if there were no political and ideological differences, and all the economically important countries were willing to join in a system of multilateral trade, multilateralism and free-exchange markets could not be restored immediately.

A multilateral trading system with free-exchange markets and stable exchange rates presupposes that a deficit in the balance of payments of any country does not exceed the gold and foreign balances at its disposal. This condition does not now exist. Many obstacles must be removed before a new stable pattern of international trade can emerge.

General Trends

Although nobody can now visualize the exact pattern of international trade five years or a decade hence, certain general trends can probably be anticipated with some confidence.

Great Britain will need larger exports of commodities and services than before World War II; the repayment of its short-term debts and service charges on the American loan will make its balance of payments on commodity and services account positive rather than negative. The United States, in contrast to prewar years, will be obliged to accept larger imports of goods and services than it exports, as soon as interest and amortization payments on its investments abroad exceed its current capital exports. If France and other continental European countries receive large loans in the immediate future, they, too, must increase exports of goods and services more than imports, in order to repay their debts. German and Japanese exports must approximately equal imports, provided no current reparations are levied. Countries in process of industrialization will be increasingly important markets for industrialized countries, and they will probably finance part of their imports by loans from the industrialized countries; their balance of payments on current account will therefore tend to be negative while industrialization proceeds.

The direction of the flow of international trade will change, too. The increase in Great Britain's exports will go largely to non-European countries; its European market is likely to decline in relative importance. The eastern European countries are not likely to supply agricultural products to the rest of Europe in exchange for manufactures to the same extent as before the war. Japan will not be as important a market for the United States nor as important a supplier of eastern Asiatic countries as before 1939. Throughout the world, exporters and importers will have to establish new contacts and build up new export and import organizations. The main financing of international trade may shift from London to New York. Such major adjustments take time even under favorable conditions.

Basic Conditions for Economic Stability

Before any such new and stable pattern of international trade can emerge, certain conditions must be fulfilled.

Many countries at present are unable to export, either because their productive capacity has been reduced by the war or because they have not yet fully converted to peacetime production.

The reconstruction of the export capacity of many countries requires first of all that the health of the people be restored. No country can develop productive capacity on 1,200 or less calories daily per person. But to rebuild export capacity also requires importation of raw materials and capital goods; and as these countries cannot pay for imports with exports, credits must finance imports for a time. The lending program of the United States and Canada is designed to take care of part of these import needs. It seems unlikely that countries with insufficient export capacity will abolish quantitative import controls and join in a system

of free foreign exchange markets before they have successfully negotiated this crucial phase of reconstruction.

In addition to this disparity between import needs and export capacity, there are three main obstacles to the free flow of international
trade and a return to free-exchange markets.

First, the war left a distribution of international financial claims
that, at least in the case of Great Britain, is out of harmony with the
export capacity of the debtor. Great Britain must first solve its debt
problem by canceling part of its short-term debts and funding the rest
before it can relax its quantitative import controls. Great Britain's
annual repayments must be set at a reasonably low figure if Britain's
exports are to finance its basic import needs as well as its debt service.

Second, foreign exchange rates and national price structures must be
reintegrated. If they are not so adjusted, countries with overvalued
currencies will lack incentive to develop necessary exports.

Third, the inflation now mounting in so many countries must be
arrested before these countries can remove their quantitative trade restrictions. They would be unwise to allow free-exchange markets so
long as inflation continues. Wild fluctuations in foreign exchange
rates would disturb their foreign trade. Speculation in foreign exchange would probably lead to undervaluation of their currencies.
Prices of imported commodities would rise disproportionately, and
this in turn would add to the inflation.

Five Requirements for Multilateral Trade

The conditions necessary for a return to multilateral trade and free-
exchange markets, then, are these:

First: Relief is the most immediate requirement, in order to restore
the most important productive factor: men.

Second: Capital imports into those countries whose productive apparatus has suffered most during the war are required in order to
achieve reconstruction.

Third: The British debt problem must be solved, by reducing the
annual payments for interest and amortization to manageable proportions.

Fourth: The existing structure of foreign exchange rates must be
adjusted; and it must stay in harmony with the relative movements of
national price levels.

Fifth: Inflation in the countries participating in international trade must be halted.

During the transition, the broad objectives of a reduction of trade restrictions, multilateralism, and free-exchange markets must be kept firmly in mind. Otherwise, the problems of the transition period may be solved by methods that preclude any return to multilateralism. Great Britain, for instance, could try to solve its export problem by retaining the dollar pool, intensifying its trade within the sterling area and concluding bilateral agreements with non-sterling-area countries. Other countries could also try to carry on trade by means of bilateral agreements. Strong forces driving in this direction are undoubtedly at work, and there is not too much time to check them. Fortunately, the authors of the Bretton Woods Agreements, the American proposals for an international trade charter[3] and the Anglo-American Loan Agreement clearly realized that the long-run goal of multilateralism must determine the methods by which the transition problems are to be solved.

LONG-RUN CONDITIONS FOR MULTILATERAL TRADE

The solution of the transition problems opens the way to a multilateral trading system, reduction of trade barriers, and free-exchange markets. Such a system presupposes that three requirements are fulfilled: (1) the members of the system must formulate and apply certain rules of conduct appropriate to multilateralism; (2) serious depressions must be avoided; and (3) political stability must be achieved.

THE "RULES OF THE GAME"

Satisfactory international economic relations demand certain standards of conduct in national economic policy. The rules cannot be static nor can they be borrowed from an earlier era, such as the 19th century. The absence of any accepted standards of conduct to which nations can freely adhere is perhaps now the most serious obstacle to a resumption of multilateral trade.

The standards inherited from the 19th century have been dissolving since 1931. The process began after World War I, but in the 1930's the standards disappeared almost completely. International economic

3. *Proposals for Expansion of World Trade and Employment,* Publication 2411, Department of State, 1945.

relations deteriorated into economic warfare long before World War II: currency warfare, quantitative trade restrictions, subsidies, foreign exchange control, calculated economic exploitation of weaker countries through bilateral trade agreements, were all too common. The results were ultimately disastrous, economically as well as politically.

To be effective, the new rules must be more than international agreements to refrain from certain obnoxious practices in economic policy. Nations must see the necessity for such standards of conduct and must willingly adhere to them, even when no formal agreements exist.

The 19th century rules will not answer the need now. Nations are no longer willing to yield sovereignty over domestic economic affairs, as under the gold standard, for the sake of a world trading system. Full employment and domestic economic welfare are well to the fore on the postwar agenda of all countries. The new standards of conduct for international trade must be framed accordingly.

"Full Employment" and International Trade

National governments have accepted responsibility for a positive economic policy; and the focus of this policy is national income and employment.[4] National economic policy will in the future aim at high and stable levels of employment.

This emphasis on home employment has far-reaching consequences for international trade and commercial policy. No government can control economic events in other parts of the world; but because each country is linked with the rest of the world through its foreign trade, foreign developments may easily interfere with a country's full-employment policy. Similarly, economic policies to promote full employment at home affect imports and exports and may upset a country's

---

4. The responsibility that modern governments now carry for economic welfare is essentially a responsibility to develop and apply positive policies with respect to national income — its aggregate size, its interpersonal distribution, its cyclical stability and its temporal security. These four aspects are not equally important in all countries. In the poorer countries, the aggregate size of income is likely to be more important than the other three aspects because *per capita* income is so low. So, for example, in Russia, all energy was funneled into a huge capital accumulation program to increase national output. The underindustrialized countries of the present day have similar plans. But in the United States, western Europe and the British Dominions, cyclical instability, inequalities in income distribution and security for particular income receivers are likely to bother the policy makers more than achieving a secular growth of national income. Of course, from the Physiocrats through Adam Smith, Alexander Hamilton, and others, the political economists have paid major attention to augmenting national income as an aggregate — "making the country wealthy."

balance-of-payments position. In other words, foreign economic relations constrict a country's freedom to pursue a full-employment policy by any and all means available.[5]

Possible conflicts between national "full-employment" policies and policies to promote international trade make new rules indispensable. Domestic employment is likely to receive priority from most governments whenever a conflict arises. Consequently, in the event of threatened unemployment, the rules must promote the least harmful interferences with international trade.

The Bretton Woods Agreements and the American *Proposals for Expansion of World Trade and Employment* explicitly recognize that the new rules for international trade must leave governments free to follow an autonomous economic policy. Indeed, both attempt to guarantee a maximum of national autonomy in economic policy, and yet to preserve the essential features of multilateral trade and to abolish quantitative trade controls.

The Monetary Fund Agreement stipulates, in effect, that if a nation's full-employment policy conflicts with the maintenance of stable exchange rates, the stability of the exchange rates may be sacrificed. However, changes in the exchange rates cannot, in principle, be carried out unilaterally but must be agreed to by the other members of the Fund. An orderly procedure in which all Fund members participate is thereby substituted for the hasty, competitive, independent changes in exchange rates so common in the 1930's. Similarly, a country may control capital movements if they disturb the domestic economy. Foreign exchange control on current account is permissible for a "scarce" currency. The *Proposals* outlaw methods of commercial policy that tend to export unemployment. Many other provisions could be cited. But the important point is that both the Bretton Woods Agreements and the trade proposals attempt to prescribe standards of conduct that, while acknowledging the priority of national full-employment policies, still try to minimize their adverse effects on international trade. Restrictions on international trade are not outlawed, but they must conform to certain permissible types.

5. The events of the 1930's provide ample illustration. The "export of unemployment" from one country to another by currency devaluation or other methods of commercial policy, the domestic disturbances resulting from the outflow or inflow of flight capital, the balance-of-payments troubles arising from an expansionist monetary policy, are all familiar cases in point.

If all the nations participating in the Monetary Fund pursued similar policies to maintain home employment and were equally successful, many of the foregoing problems would not arise. But this is unlikely. There is need, therefore, for an international agency that coordinates national monetary policies in the different countries. Such coordinating functions are contemplated for the Economic and Social Council of the United Nations Organization.[6] The American *Proposals*, indeed, suggest that the Economic and Social Council is the proper body to deal with full-employment policies. A successful coordination of national full-employment policies would reduce the need for quantitative trade controls that might otherwise appear. The better the coordination, the less common and the less serious will be the conflicts between policies aiming at full employment and policies aiming at maximizing foreign trade. An expansion of multilateral world trade and sustained national full employment might then proceed hand in hand.

Income Security, Industrialization and Multilateral Trade

National economic policy has been increasingly concerned with the problem of "income security," especially in the industrialized wealthier countries, which have in the past accounted for the bulk of world trade. This is not precisely the same as the problem of full employment just discussed; it is not a matter of trying to iron out oscillations in the output of goods and services as a whole. Rather, the problem is to assure income recipients their incomes from present sources. This demand for income security may well prove to be a barrier to achieving vigorous international trade on a multilateral basis.

Various groups in modern industrial society sense the insecurity of their personal incomes derived from their particular specialties. Some wage earners may feel that technical improvements or cheap imports are a potential threat to their expensive skills. Manufacturers may feel that new developments in other industries or other countries may endanger sunk investments. Farmers may fear cheap food from abroad. And so, all through an economy characterized by specialization in production, each group is conscious of its own income insecurity. In democracies, the policy makers cannot wholly disregard the insistent

6. See Leroy D. Stinebower, *The Economic and Social Council*, Commission to Study the Organization of the Peace, New York, 1946.

demands of farmers, manufacturers, labor groups and others for protection against income insecurity. Consequently, policy reflects these pressures from particular groups in nearly all industrial countries.[7]

The nonindustrialized low-income countries, for which industrialization and plans of economic development are now in vogue, desire, above all else, a sharp increase in national output: cyclical income stability and income security for particular groups in such countries are of less concern than how to achieve and maintain a substantial increase in total output per head.[8] Forcing extensive changes in the patterns of output and occupations is, in one sense, the aim of the policy makers, as these changes are essential to industrialization.

In the already industrialized countries, on the other hand, the emphasis in economic policy is nearly the reverse. In the United States, the United Kingdom, the British Dominions and western European countries, the problem of economic policy is how to make effective use of existing productive resources, how to maintain a stable national income with a long-time upward trend, and yet not impose too much income insecurity on the specialized groups of which the economy is composed. The task of economic policy, in brief, is to get "full employment," but not at any cost. It must be achieved without unduly disturbing farmers, wage earners, manufacturers, traders, and producers generally, in their familiar occupations and without infringing on their traditional rights and freedoms with authoritarian methods.[9]

But industrialization for higher incomes in the poorer countries in-

7. Cf. Stuart Chase, *Democracy Under Pressure,* Twentieth Century Fund, New York, 1945.

8. These countries, too, want to have full employment in the sense that they do not wish to delay the industrialization process by allowing usable manpower and land to stand idle. But their problem of full employment is of a different character than that of the industrial countries.

9. This is not to say that the secular growth or possible decline of national income is of no concern at all, but merely that this concerns the policy makers in the high-income countries much less than in the low-income countries.

In promoting full employment, the state must be careful that its policies do not impinge upon other "values" to a degree that will generally be regarded as excessive. "Equality," in a variety of senses, may be one of the values that the people hold dear, and for which they will willingly forego some possible gain in their material welfare. Similarly with "freedom" or "liberty." Colonel Blimp with his rantings about "meddlers," for example, strikes a harmonious chord in many Americans and Englishmen even though he may be quite incomprehensible to people in some other countries. Policy makers must ever keep such considerations in mind, even though most people do not have precise, carefully formulated definitions of these ultimate values ready to hand for appraising economic policy. And one may point out parenthetically that these intangible, but nonetheless real, values are the chief reason why certain policies go unquestioned in some countries but are quite unthinkable in others.

creases the necessary adjustments in the patterns of employment and output in the older countries. At least, such adjustments will be more numerous if the industrialization process occurs within the framework of a trading system in which trade restrictions are reduced to a minimum. But greater changes in the composition of national output and in the allocation of the labor force and capital equipment among industries are not easily reconciled with the personal income security now so highly prized in the older industrial countries. In the United States, for example, personal income security for cotton textile operatives is not altogether compatible with encouraging imports of cotton goods from the industrializing countries so that they may buy more American machinery. Cotton textile operatives do not easily become machine producers.

Industrialization in the newer countries will force two kinds of structural adjustments on the older countries. Some export markets will dwindle because of industrialization abroad, causing declining incomes for producers and laborers in the industries concerned. As industrialization proceeds abroad, some home industries will meet increased competition from the newer countries either in the home market, in outside markets, or in both. British experience vis-à-vis Japan's industrialization is a case in point.

In short, countries whose citizens greatly prize personal income security will find that new industrialization forces domestic adjustments if the industrialization occurs within a multilateral trading system. And the quicker the pace of industrialization abroad and the slower the rate of population growth at home, the less easily will the structural changes be achieved.

If the low-income countries are determined to industrialize and the high-income countries are forced to provide a high degree of personal income security, then a reduction of trade barriers is neither easy to establish nor easy to maintain. Two tendencies are therefore likely to operate powerfully against multilateralism: the industrializing countries may industrialize in a way that minimizes participation in world trade; and the industrialized countries may avoid the necessary structural adjustments in favor of providing personal income security.

American Agricultural Policy as an Example

There is no better evidence of this tendency to avoid the structural adjustments implied by a world trading system than American agricultural policy during recent years. Broadly speaking, the tendency all the way through has been to use subsidies and tariffs to avoid contracting domestic production of agricultural commodities. The whole reasoning behind "support prices," "parity prices," etc., may be defended on the grounds of "doing something" for agriculture, and it may be motivated by the highest humanitarian impulses. But an American agricultural policy of this kind does not harmonize at all with the principles underlying the American trade proposals looking toward a world trading system designed to maximize real incomes by allowing commodities to be produced where costs are lowest and to be exported to the best markets.

Unfortunately, the American agricultural problem has been intensified by the war-necessitated expansion. (See Chapter 4, pp. 91 ff.)

Agricultural groups are highly organized in the United States and, in cooperation with the United States Department of Agriculture, will probably resist strongly a contraction in agricultural production in favor of cheaper imports from abroad. Yet a highly industrialized nation such as the United States probably does not have a marked comparative advantage in food production. Food exports will almost certainly decline once the temporary food crisis has passed, and food imports, in the absence of tariffs or prohibitions, could be expected to increase from areas with lower production costs. Unfortunately, from the point of view of a rational reorganization of world production and trade, the selfish interests of agricultural groups receive support from those who regard any dependence on foreign countries for food as a threat to national security. No one knows to what extent various types of agriculture would be forced to contract were tariff duties and subsidies in the United States abolished. It seems plausible, however, that only a small portion of domestic output would have to disappear in a good many instances: that is, that fringe of high-cost producers now kept in production by subsidies and tariffs. This possible conflict between American foreign economic policy and American agricultural policy may be extremely serious.

This problem is not incapable of solution, but it has not yet been faced squarely. The policy makers, though aware of the problem, tend to speak softly and tread lightly. Nevertheless, a multilateral trading system with a minimum of trade barriers is a system in which structural adjustments are unavoidable and, despite the hardships they may cause, are judged worth their cost. But as we have just tried to show, national economic policies directed toward greater world trade may prove to be seriously incompatible with other policies when discussions "in principle" are replaced by day-to-day practice.

This whole problem has a close kinship to the problem of technological progress in relation to income security. Every technical invention tends to produce either a cheaper product or a better product. But at the same time it often creates unemployment for specialized workers whose skills are displaced and makes obsolete the capital equipment formerly used. The persons directly concerned in the industry experiencing the technical advance are often injured. And they often try to protect themselves against such injury. So, for instance, the painters' union has rules about mechanical sprayers, the city building codes preserve obsolete construction practices, and so forth. But the essence of technical progress is that it allows a greater flow of goods and services from the available manpower, materials, land and machinery.

When imports are available at a cheaper price from abroad, this indicates that domestic productive resources can be better used in other directions. Thus, the world stock of productive resources will be used more effectively. Structural changes are called for. But there is no denying that such changes impose hardship on particular groups: their incomes are affected adversely by the cheap imports; their investments may be rendered valueless. But the country as a whole, and the world as a whole, can gain only from using its inheritance of productive resources to produce more and better goods and services for mankind.[10]

Adjustments to World Trade Changes

In the highly industrialized countries, national policy cannot altogether avoid protecting special groups against unfavorable adjustments forced by events taking place abroad. But such protection can be minimized and assistance confined to ways that minimize hindrances to world trade.

The tariff should be the chief instrument of protection. It is the least

10. This topic has been examined at length by Allan G. B. Fisher in *The Clash of Progress and Security,* Macmillan, London, 1935, and in *Economic Progress and Social Security,* Macmillan, London, 1945.

harmful device because — unless absolutely prohibitive — it leaves the price mechanism intact. Quotas, import licensing and foreign exchange control, on the other hand, impinge on or render ineffective the price mechanism. The American *Proposals for Expansion of World Trade and Employment* are sound on this point, for in principle they outlaw quotas, import licensing and foreign exchange control, even though they permit such devices in special circumstances.

Protection of injured groups should not take the form mainly of reducing imports. Governments might instead directly assist those adversely affected by foreign competition. Assistance to the injured could just as well facilitate the necessary rearrangements in production as hamper these adjustments. This implies measures primarily to increase the mobility of labor: easing costs of transfer to other industries; providing efficient employment exchanges; assisting new workers to avoid shrinking industries; and above all, perhaps, providing retraining facilities and a better general education for all. As one writer recently stated:

> Mental discipline, wide experience and a good stock of knowledge enable men and women rapidly to adapt themselves to new requirements. A good education forms eager learners: confident of acquiring a new craft even at a later age.[11]

Some modifications in the tax system and in unemployment insurance practices would also encourage greater mobility of resources. Incomes might be temporarily guaranteed while a shift in occupation was in progress. If a protective tariff were introduced, it would properly carry a proviso for its own reduction and ultimate abolition at predetermined dates. All along the line, assistance to those adversely affected by imports would emphasize that protection and government assistance were only temporary and that the aim of policy was to promote, not check, adjustment. Such efforts as these would permit world trade to grow without entailing unnecessary hardship.

Partial unemployment resulting from new products and new sources of supply in world trade is obviously much less troublesome if total employment remains high. For alternative employments are then plentiful. In the United States during World War II, for example, a high

11. Michael Polanyi, *Full Employment and Free Trade,* Cambridge University Press, Cambridge (England), 1945, p. 95.

aggregate demand enabled a multiplicity of occupational readjustments to take place without much trouble.[12] When alternative employments are scarce, on the other hand, the cry for protection from foreign competition is loudest.

If national governments, as a matter of principle, always intervened in the direction of achieving the most effective use of the world's productive resources within a world trading system, and accordingly tried to improve mobility and flexibility in their own countries, the outlook for international trade would be considerably improved.

STABILITY OF THE WORLD ECONOMY

Under a system of international trade, booms or depressions tend to spread from one country to another. To maintain national incomes at a high level, therefore, will require coordinated international action. National action alone will not suffice.

In a serious depression, nations are apt to jettison international cooperation. The new standards of conduct embodied in the Monetary Fund and the trade proposals would probably not survive another world depression. Countries would again resort to currency warfare, exchange control, import quotas, etc., as they did in the 1930's. Consequently, the proposed future organization of world trade depends to a marked degree on avoiding a major world depression.

Crucial Role of the United States

The first requirement for avoiding a world depression is an intelligent national policy in all countries with respect to the business cycle.[13] Here the greatest responsibility lies with the United States. Because of its importance as a market for other nations and as a source of investment capital, a stable American economy would be a major contribution to international stability. Furthermore, in a world that fearfully identifies a free-enterprise economic system with instability, it behooves the United States, as the chief proponent of such a system, to demon-

12. These adjustments were on a tremendous scale, both from an occupational and a geographical point of view. As a result of the priorities system, a host of people who formerly were engaged in the distribution of consumers' durable goods had nothing to sell. They turned to new tasks. People migrated from the interior to the seacoast shipyards in large numbers.

13. The reader is referred to the excellent study on methods of business cycle control by the League of Nations: *Economic Stability in the Post-War World,* Report of the Delegation on Economic Depressions, Pt. II, Geneva, 1945.II.A.2.

strate that free enterprise and full employment are not incompatible. If the United States can avoid wide cyclical swings in national income, world trade can probably develop to the great mutual benefit of all countries; but if not, the outlook is poor indeed.

National Measures Not Enough

Measures on a national level for controlling the business cycle are, however, not sufficient. As the League of Nations Delegation on Economic Depressions expressed it:

> It is of the greatest importance that governments should not be handicapped in the application of contra-cyclical policies by the difficulty of obtaining agreement by other countries regarding the application of essential parallel policies. It is no less important that governments should not pursue policies in isolation regardless of their influence on other countries and thus render the successful pursuit of common and effective policies impossible.[14]

The Delegation therefore made five recommendations to this end:[15] adoption of "more liberal and dynamic commercial and economic policies" — this is the fundamental idea of the American proposals for an international trade charter; the creation of an "international mechanism for the orderly conduct of foreign exchange operations" — such an institution has been created by the Bretton Woods Agreements; "the creation of an international institution which will stimulate and encourage the international movement of capital for productive purposes" — the role assigned to the International Bank for Reconstruction and Development agreed upon at Bretton Woods; and "international action for the solution of the problems of primary production."[16]

As its fifth recommendation, the Delegation suggested the creation of a body to coordinate national economic policies and so minimize disruptions in the balance of payments arising from unequal rates of economic expansion in the various countries. To this end the United Nations Organization has created the Economic and Social Council, which is to coordinate the policy of the independent special agencies, such as the Monetary Fund, the International Bank, the International Trade

14. *Economic Stability in the Post-War World*, p. 278.
15. *Ibid.*, p. 280.
16. This requires buffer stock schemes to minimize cyclical price and output fluctuations in primary products. Countries whose exports consist primarily of such primary products would thus gain greater stability in their balance of payments.

Organization, etc. The Council, through the Fund and the Bank, could carry out a contracyclical policy directly should the proposed coordination not entirely succeed. The Bank, for instance, could promote foreign lending by those countries in which business was slackening. The Fund could lessen the strain on those countries whose balances of payments usually turn negative in a slump. The Fund might therefore operate as a powerful contracyclical agency in the international scene.[17]

POLITICAL STABILITY

International economic relations cannot be separated nowadays from international political relations. An enduring expansion of world trade requires stable political conditions. Conflicting national ideologies adversely affect international trade, because they entail the use of different methods for dealing with international trade. Government trading, state monopolies and foreign exchange control will probably not disappear so long as totalitarian governments remain. But these technical devices are less important than the fact that free multilateral trade is not likely to flourish when nations are fearful and suspicious of one another.

Fear of War

The fear of war interferes with the development of international trade in many ways. Under such circumstances, national economic policy is likely to be ever mindful of the possible effects of alternative policies on the nation's security and independence. In the international sphere, such considerations are of paramount importance in determining national economic policy. The problems of exports and imports, investment abroad and receipt of foreign capital at home, the presence or absence of certain industries — all assume a different coloration in a hostile, suspicious world. Each must be considered and given due weight, together with national income, in formulating economic policy.

National fears and apprehensions split nations into hostile camps:

17. But in order to do so, the Fund must guard against being short of the currency most in demand in a period of world-wide depression. It is possible, for instance, that the dollar currency may more or less disappear from the Fund during the transition period in which the rest of the world is in need of dollars. If this were to happen, the Fund could not provide the currency that is most likely to be in demand should a world-wide depression develop.

countries align themselves in groups that, though they may strive for a maximum trade among the members of the group, aim at self-sufficiency for the group as a whole. Strategic considerations are then apt to override economic considerations. Naturally, self-sufficiency on the part of groups of nations minimizes trade between the different groups. Multilateral trade on a global basis becomes impossible.

Political and Economic Problems Merge

The problem of the future of international trade thus merges with the international political problem. The two are today inseparable.

It is the task of the United Nations Organization to create a world in which international political disputes may be settled by discussion and compromise rather than by war. The success of the new international economic organizations such as the International Bank and the Monetary Fund presupposes the political success of the United Nations. Here the future welfare of mankind now rests.

REPORT OF THE COMMITTEE

Chapter 13

REPORT OF THE COMMITTEE ON FOREIGN
ECONOMIC RELATIONS

THIS IS a report on American foreign economic policy. It is made by a Committee appointed by the Trustees of the Twentieth Century Fund. The Committee's assignment was (1) to study and review the findings of an extensive investigation of our foreign economic relations made by a special research staff appointed by the Fund and (2) to review the foreign economic policy of the United States in the light of those findings.

This report is an American product in the sense that it is directed toward international measures that we, the American people, are in a position to take, measures that will not, in fact, be taken by peoples anywhere if we do not pursue them. It is not concerned with specific details of policy formation, but rather with the general spirit and orientation of the policies this country should adopt. It is written neither from the viewpoint nor in the spirit of narrow, national, materialistic advantage; and in this sense it is not exclusively American. The policies we recommend can, we believe, be adopted to their own advantage by peoples everywhere.

RE-ESTABLISHMENT OF INTERNATIONAL TRADE ON A MULTILATERAL BASIS

Stated in very general terms, the foreign economic policy of the United States is dedicated to the expansion of international trade (a) through the elimination of bilateralism and discrimination, and (b) through the re-establishment of foreign trade on a multilateral basis. Our government has devoted itself assiduously for over a decade to the accomplishment of these objectives: before the war, in the initiation of its reciprocal trade agreements program; during the war, in the pledges that it received in the negotiation of lend-lease or mutual-aid agreements; and now, since the close of hostilities, in the formulation, in cooperation with Great Britain, of its proposals for an International Trade Charter and an International Trade Organization. An international conference to advance these agreed proposals is now imminent.

The Committee is wholeheartedly in accord with the objectives toward which our foreign policy is directed. It does not believe, however, that the present foreign economic program of our government is sufficiently realistic or broadly based to achieve them.

Within a multilateral trading system, all of the participating countries agree to minimize special arrangements, public or private, that discriminate among the members in their foreign economic relations. To achieve its full advantages, each participating member country should reduce its own barriers to foreign trade to the minimum compatible with a healthy internal economy and the necessities of defense.

Such a system provides a basis for the diffusion of well-being and the development of higher and more varied standards of consumption because it seeks to enable the peoples of each country to purchase raw materials, foodstuffs and manufactured products where they can be produced most efficiently and most cheaply. At the same time, by providing a very wide market, it stimulates in each country the most efficient industries. A flow of productive foreign investment from the more advanced countries to aid the development of more backward areas is an integral part of a multilateral system, which, if it is to succeed, must make provision for the repayment of this investment.

Special bilateral arrangements that foster the foreign commerce of some of the members to the exclusion of others, export subsidies, arbitrary quotas, barter deals and state trading, all fall outside the spirit and successful practice of multilateralism. In a multilateral system the volume, direction and composition of foreign trade are determined primarily by consumers and producers operating in competitive international markets instead of by official agreements negotiated between states.

In the judgment of the Committee, the re-establishment of an effective multilateral trading system is not merely a worthy end of foreign policy, it is a *sine qua non* for the achievement of that durable peace, blessed with prosperity under freedom, for which the American people have fought so strenuously. An effective multilateral system is basic to that peace because (1) it will permit us to maintain an economy in this country vitalized by initiative and freedom so long as we choose to do so; (2) it will transfer the conduct of most commercial bargains from official negotiations to the market, or subject them to the discipline of the market, and will thus reduce international friction over trade, and minimize opportunities for discrimination among nations and the exercise of economic coercion; and (3) it will foster the contribution that a greater volume of international trade can make to the development of progressively higher and more varied standards of consumption.

SCOPE OF A MULTILATERAL TRADING SYSTEM

Ideally, a multilateral trading system should be world-wide; all nations should enter wholeheartedly into a common and agreed system of nondiscriminatory trade. But universality is not essential. It *is* essential that (1) the area covered by multilateral trade be sufficiently large and varied to afford an adequate basis of populations, skills and resources for mutually beneficial exchange and to avoid the necessity for major economic readjustments, and (2) the nations and peoples that enter into the multilateral system do so wholeheartedly, resolved in view of the benefits it will confer, to accept its responsibilities.

A multilateral system should be open to all who desire to enter. The Committee feels, however, that the government has erred in its efforts to re-establish such a system by placing too great emphasis on universality. We must admit that the history and development of some countries has not led them in the direction of multilateralism.[1] At the present time, in fact, the various countries of the world can be classified into three broad groups.

On the one extreme are the countries like the United States whose internal economy, as a matter of choice, is organized to provide a maximum of freedom. Most of these countries, naturally, favor the re-establishment of a multilateral system of foreign trade.

At the other extreme are countries like the U.S.S.R. whose internal economy, as a matter of choice,[2] is organized on a centrally administered basis. While a multilateral system is in no sense inimical to the welfare of these countries, we must recognize in all fairness that

---

1. "I agree. The danger is that if such a country were permitted to participate, in the absence of agreement, it would manipulate the system to its own ends, thus completely destroying its multilateral character. I feel that the only chance of success would be by excluding such a country from the system," R. J. Watt.

2. "This is not the people's choice," R. J. Watt.

they are not naturally candidates for membership. Any desire on their part to enter such a system would be based more on reasons of prestige, or the pursuit of a cooperative foreign political policy, than on intrinsic economic benefits to be received. Without drastic changes in their internal economic and administrative arrangements, most of the commitments that they would be required to assume would have to be subject to major qualification or reservation.

Distinct from this group, there is a group of countries now emerging from the war the economies of which are now organized, not as a matter of choice but of necessity, along administered lines. Their aspiration is to return to an internal economic organization with much greater freedom. Among this group are countries falling on both sides of the current line of political tension. At the present moment no member of this group, irrespective of its general philosophy, is actually in a position to relax its agencies of centrally administered control, particularly in the area of foreign economic relations. All of these countries are potential candidates for membership in a multilateral system. Before those who desire to do so can participate effectively, however, political security must be re-established and their internal economy must be restored to the basis of a "going concern."[3]

It is the first and third groups of countries that constitute the natural potential membership for a successful, workable multilateral system. Fortunately these two groups cover the preponderant area and resources that are most interdependent economically. The overwhelming bulk of world trade before the war was conducted among the peoples of western Europe, of the British Commonwealth, of the Western Hemisphere, and of Japan, the Philippines and Indonesia. Within this area there is extensive specialization in production for international markets. These countries, consequently, have much at stake in the re-establishment of multilateral trade, for without it major

3. "Is it at all practical to include in any multilateral system countries whose economies are dominated by the U.S.S.R.? If they are included, and if, as suggested further on in the report, they are therefore assisted by the United States, should we not find ourselves merely helping the U.S.S.R. through these countries to use our assistance for its own ends, which are contrary to the multilateral system, and affording an opportunity to undermine the system? To be realistic, I feel that since the hope of restoring these countries 'to the basis of a going concern' within the foreseeable future is practically nonexistent, it should be considered outside the multilateral system for the purposes of this report. When this clear distinction is made, we can then discuss rehabilitation, etc., of the countries whose economies are 'organized to provide a maximum of freedom,' " R. J. Watt.

economic adaptations will be inevitable and the smaller states will be exposed to a considerable degree of economic pressure.

THE NEED FOR REHABILITATION

A first prerequisite for the re-establishment of a multilateral system is that the devastated and exhausted countries desiring to join be restored to a "going concern" basis. Internal inflation must be controlled, currencies must be stabilized, fiscal systems restored, transportation, wharf and power facilities repaired, and factories rebuilt and stocked with working capital. In most cases this rehabilitation will require some foreign aid, particularly aid from this country, at least to the extent of permission to buy necessary commodities that are in short supply. In the case of countries that lack the necessary foreign exchange, direct financial aid in the form of loans or grants is indicated.

That this need has been recognized by our government is demonstrated by the British, French and other loans. This aid has often been justified on the basis of our recent war association, and for this justification the Committee has sympathy. However, it wishes to emphasize most strongly at this point that, quite apart from moral or political considerations, rehabilitation aid, as distinct from relief, is basic to the reconstruction of a workable system of expanding multilateral foreign trade.

But internal rehabilitation and reconstruction must be carried through mainly by the countries themselves. Technical assistance, raw materials of foreign origin and machines can be imported with the aid of foreign exchange. But the bulk of capital equipment essential to reconstruction or increased production consists of roads, buildings, structures and other immovables that must be built by local labor, using mostly local resources. Foreign aid can at best provide only a small part of the total need. Provision for such aid, however, is crucial. It is the "seed money" that makes rehabilitation and reconstruction possible.

The Committee recommends that this country, in pursuit of its basic foreign economic policy, continue to make rehabilitation aid available to potential members of a multilateral trading system. The total amount, so vital to the achievement of peace, is infinitesimal in comparison with the costs of war. The main criteria for the amount and character of aid are three. First, the recipient country must desire to join a multilateral trading system, must be prepared to accept its responsibilities and must be in a position to do so. Second, the aid furnished must be adequate to do the job, i.e., it must be sufficient to strike a balance in its international payments. Third, it must be realistic. Foreign aid is rarely justified and serves little purpose where it is excessive or where it is wasted.

The Committee makes no general recommendation for or against rehabilitation aid to countries that are not candidates for a multilateral system. Its justification in most instances would be found primarily in moral or political, not economic, considerations.

The more quickly rehabilitation is carried through, the more quickly will the war-ravaged countries be restored to a self-sustaining basis without further need for relief. Much can be said, consequently, for the view that rehabilitation aid should take the form of grants rather than loans. For this reason, when it does take the form of loans, they should not be considered in the same category as ordinary commercial loans or investments. For example, the question whether aid should be extended or not cannot be judged solely on an analysis of "ability to repay." The economic considerations involved are much more complex. Financial aid of this character, furthermore, should be provided mainly from public resources. Private resources will help in many ways, but they cannot carry the main load.

Much can also be said for the view that responsibility for providing rehabilitation aid should be shared among all those United Nations in a position to contribute. This pattern has been followed in the case of the relief provided by UNRRA and underlay the recent policy decision in Washington to refer further applicants for foreign loans to the new International Bank for Reconstruction and Development. In the judgment of the Committee that decision was a mistake. The Committee does not question the desirability in general of sharing responsibility for rehabilitation aid, but in the concrete circumstances that we face, it deplores this use of the International Bank.

Specifically, the Committee is apprehensive lest the immediate task of rehabilitation unduly absorb the resources of the Bank and divert its attention from a much more important and fundamental responsibility. The success of a multilateral trading system, once achieved, will depend in large measure on the operation of the International Bank and of the International Monetary Fund. It should be their function to cope with the financial shocks, adaptations and adjustments inherent in a relatively free, dynamic world economy. It should be their task to help maintain international conditions favorable to a high and stable level of employment *after* rehabilitation is completed. It would be extremely shortsighted, in the judgment of the Committee, to permit the financial resources of these two crucially important institutions to become depleted during the current phase of rehabilitation.

The Committee believes that our government can best advance its foreign economic policy at this juncture by proceeding to finish the job of foreign rehabilitation promptly. It should do this in cooperation with other nations when possible, but alone if necessary. The additional financial aid that will be required is not unduly large. The greater part will come from this country in any case, whether the pattern is a pattern of shared responsibility or not. The Committee recommends accordingly that the resources of the Export-Import Bank be increased, that its charter be broadened, and that it be directed to assume primary responsibility for our remaining contribution to the job of rehabilitation.

THE NEED FOR POLITICAL SECURITY

In the case of many potential members of a multilateral trading system, the need for economic rehabilitation, though pressing, is only a temporary obstacle to the system's re-establishment. A more basic obstacle by far is the sense of political tension and insecurity that continues to pervade large areas of the world. So long as this continues, it will be impossible for many governments to relax their agencies of economic management enough to permit a multilateral system to function. For under conditions of political insecurity, either internal or external, accompanied as they are by the imminent fear of loss through war destruction, invasion or confiscation, the motivations that operate in a free economy do not lead to long-term productive investment designed to increase output and to raise the standards of living. On the contrary, they lead to an excessive desire for liquidity, to short-term and quickly reversible business decisions, to hoarding and to capital flight. A society haunted by these fears must of necessity maintain strict and meticulous control of the economic activities of its citizens, whatever its general economic philosophy.

The people of the United States have committed themselves to the achievement of a peace sufficiently durable to permit the various peoples of the world opportunity to choose freely the pattern and form of their internal economic organization. The success of the foreign economic policy of the United States is completely dependent on the achievement of that objective. The Committee desires that there be no doubt in the minds of the American people on this point. Multilateralism as the basis for international economic relationships is adapted neither to the conduct of war nor to active mobilization for war. It requires, in fact, as the first step in its achievement the demobilization of the agencies of economic warfare.

DEFICIENCIES IN OUR FOREIGN ECONOMIC PROGRAM

Once rehabilitation has been completed, and political tranquillity restored, the major obstacles to the creation of a multilateral trading system will have been removed. The Committee finds, however, that there are two fundamental ways in which our foreign economic program is incomplete — in which we would fail to meet basic requirements for the successful operation of a multilateral trading system *after* it has been established. The first is our failure to provide adequately for the international institutions that will be required to buttress economic stability at high levels of employment in the postwar world. The second is our failure to provide adequately for a sufficient increase in our imports to maintain the equilibrium in our balance of payments so necessary to our own continued prosperity as well as to that of the outside world.

In these two respects, also, has our foreign economic program failed to assess the basic considerations that have deterred potential foreign members of a multilateral system from a more active dedication to its achievement. These two deficiencies largely account for the skepticism with which our foreign economic program has been viewed abroad, even by its friends. To put the matter bluntly, they have created doubts of the quality of economic leadership that the country will provide in the postwar world for the multilateral trading system that it espouses. These attitudes of skepticism, hesitation and doubt are based on two especially bitter experiences.

The first came from the devastating repercussions of the Great Depression and of the depression of 1937 upon our foreign customers. There is a fear in many foreign quarters, amounting almost to a phobia, that this country with its highly dynamic economy will again follow the pattern of "boom and bust" and that societies that integrate their trade too closely with ours will be the major victims.

The second grew out of the attitude toward imports that has been traditional in the United States, an attitude that culminated in the enactment of the Smoot-Hawley high-tariff law at the very beginning of the Great Depression. Those who feel this deeply think that the United States, despite its promises to make effective use of the Reciprocal Trade Agreements Act, will not, in fact, reduce tariffs to the point where any large volume of additional imports is permitted to enter the United States. They maintain that economic expansion achieved with the aid of American investment funds will be unsound since repayment through the sale of goods in our markets will not be allowed, and that general bankruptcy followed by depression, rather than progressive expansion, will result.

As Americans we must admit the weight of these misgivings. The world situation today is far different from that in the long stretches of the past century when a dynamic and expanding volume of international trade on a multilateral basis resulted in such a phenomenal increase in standards of living. Then Great Britain, not the United States, was the predominant industrial economy of the world, and Britain rather than the United States was looked to as the most desired market and the final source of financial aid. It was Britain that was called upon to take leadership in the formulation of world economic policy. In its exercise of these responsibilities Britain was aided by the fact that its economy has always been less volatile than that of this country, less subject to wide and sudden swings of activity from prosperity to depression. In addition, Great Britain during that period adhered to the principles of free trade. The British market stood ready to absorb imports in quantity without important official barrier or hindrance, and in this way helped foreign debtors to repay their loans.

Now the responsibility for economic leadership has shifted to this country, for the American economy is far larger than that of any other potential member of a multilateral trading group. We must assume these responsibilities at a time when we are still shackled by our tradition of protectionism, and when we have much to learn of the interrelationships of foreign trade and investment. The foreboding with which the world now scans the direction of the American economy is not without justification. The American economy *is* volatile. We Americans are not confident of our ability to mitigate its range of fluctuation nor are we agreed on the detail or scope of the internal policies that would be necessary to do so.

These major defects in our foreign economic program must be repaired, these misgivings must be allayed, if we are to succeed in our determination to re-create an international economic environment favorable to expanding multilateral trade. Our present program remains inadequate and incomplete so long as it restricts its main emphasis to (a) rehabilitation, (b) the elimination of state trading and bilateral controls, and (c) commitments to abjure measures of internal expansion that exaggerate unemployment abroad. These are all vital parts of a workable economic program. But they are not enough. An adequate program must provide for a substantial increase in our imports. It must also provide agreed, workable techniques that will cushion the shock of another domestic depression and minimize its foreign repercussions. For the economic fabric abroad is still much too fragile to withstand the shock of another depression, such as that of 1937, without violent social and political reactions.

MAINTENANCE OF HIGH LEVELS OF EMPLOYMENT

The problem of mitigating the violence of our fluctuations and of their impact upon the world economy has already been partly met. Though much remains to be done, the contracyclical institutions of the American economy have been developed and expanded in many directions in recent years. For example, we can now count on an established and functioning system of unemployment insurance to temper, in some measure at least, the volatility of our economy. On the external side also, we have not been entirely idle. The newly created International Monetary Fund will constitute a powerful agency to assist in the re-establishment of equilibrium in the foreign exchanges, in the maintenance of that equilibrium during periods of financial strain and in helping to remove from the exchanges the devastating repercussions of capital flight.

The Monetary Fund, acting alone, however, will not be able to stem forces of contraction as powerful as those that operated in 1937 — to say nothing of those present in more serious depressions. To accomplish this result there are two additional measures that are essential in the judgment of the Committee. The first should counteract tendencies toward contraction in the flow of productive foreign investment funds, while the second should operate to cushion the shock of depression in the great world markets for primary products and raw materials. The Committee has prepared recommendations to meet each of these needs. In its judgment, the adoption of these recommendations would go far to minimize the international repercussions of depressions.

STABILITY OF FOREIGN INVESTMENT

In the judgment of the Committee the new International Bank for Reconstruction and Development can be operated to act as a powerful contracyclical instrument to stabilize the flow of foreign investment. For this important function no change would be required in its organization, resources or general orientation. It would be desirable, however, to amend its instructions.

It is the opinion of the Committee that our government failed to probe deeply enough in its diagnosis of the economic problems it would face when it approved the current instructions to the Bank. As now established, it is the mandate of the International Bank to finance both reconstruction and long-term development. But it has no specific mandate to schedule its huge financial operations in such a way as to counteract the high degree of volatility that normally characterizes the flow of foreign investment funds. Under these circumstances, the danger is acute that the Bank will operate to accentuate, rather than to mitigate, the current cycle of prosperity and depression. It may even become an accessory factor in a "boom and bust" development.[4]

Earlier in this report the Committee recommended *against* the current policy of referring applications for rehabilitation loans to the International Bank. Exactly the same considerations apply to loans for reconstruction if they are intended to finance the construction required to rebuild an economy into a "going concern." This is really rehabilitation. It is pressing. It cannot afford to wait. Any institution charged with financing this kind of reconstruction must act quickly and facilitate its most rapid progress.

Long-term development programs, on the other hand, *can* be under-

4. "The fact that the bank has no specific mandate is important. Directive policy-making should probably be lodged with the International Trade and Employment Agency, the Bank cooperating," R. J. Watt.

taken with more deliberation. They do not have to be pushed to completion at the earliest possible date. Considered from the point of view of the general welfare, it is highly desirable that they be scheduled at a tempo that will permit a quick speed-up when other supports of a high level of employment tend to give way. In the judgment of the Committee, the International Bank should concentrate its financing on projects that meet these long-term conditions, while other institutions such as the Export-Import Bank should concentrate on rehabilitation.

The instructions of the International Bank do not now specifically prohibit an interpretation of its mandate that would make the Bank an active international contracyclical force, as recommended by the Committee; but it is highly doubtful whether its officials could in practice reinterpret its mandate in this way without specific instruction. The officials will be enmeshed in concrete, dynamic programs. They will want to bring them into successful operation as soon as possible and will find it irksome, in any case, to consider these more basic economic considerations. Also, without a specific mandate, they will be exposed to vigorous public criticism and to pressure from the countries being financed — which will naturally want the most rapid possible completion of their developmental programs.

The chances are, consequently, that the Bank will tend to commit the huge resources under its influence and direction too rapidly, and that these resources may add to the inflationary factors already actively at work. It would be a calamity if the next depression should find the new Bank with its resources committed to programs in process of active execution, without power to initiate new activities and without opportunity to accelerate further those already under way.

To correct this situation the Committee recommends that (1) international reconstruction loans for projects that must be rushed to completion be treated in much the same manner as rehabilitation loans and grants, and that both types of transaction be financed as far as possible directly by agencies such as the Export-Import Bank without recourse to the International Bank for Reconstruction and Development;[5] (2) the International Bank concentrate primarily on the financ-

5. "This would mean that a large part of the financing would come from the United States, since we are the nation most able to provide credit. Such a program of loans and/or grants should be carefully considered in relation to our domestic economy. As stated elsewhere in the report, economic stability in the United States is essential to world recovery and to the maintenance of economic equilibrium. Overlarge foreign loans or

ing of longer-term international reconstruction and developmental programs; and (3) it provide, in the financing of each program, for a sharp acceleration in case of depression.

The Committee considers it urgent to amend the instructions of the Bank to provide for these changes. A progressive, dynamic world economy on a multilateral basis cannot be reconstructed without the resumption of productive foreign investment. Such investment, properly directed, provides constructive outlets for the savings of the more advanced countries, spreads the practice of their skills and techniques and raises the productivity and standards of consumption of the less developed countries. In the past, however, the ebb and flow of investment on foreign account has been highly unstable — more so even than investment on internal account. This instability has been either a primary cause, or a sharp accelerator, of fluctuations in employment. Following 1929, for example, there was a sudden and almost complete reversal in the flow of productive investment funds from this country, a reversal that accounts for much of the depth, universality, severity and duration of the Great Depression. The new Bank can be managed so as to counteract this tendency and so to contribute greatly to a steady flow of orders on investment account and to stability of employment in the heavy industries, both in this country and abroad. No government official or officer of the new International Bank for Reconstruction and Development should doubt that the Bank is called upon to operate as a stabilizing force in the postwar world.

BUFFER STOCKS

A balanced foreign economic program adequate to deal with international aspects of the problem of depression also requires a "buffer stock" policy.

At the onset of depression a sharp sudden drop in imports almost invariably occurs that acts powerfully, probably more powerfully than any other single factor, to spread the depression internationally and to exaggerate its impact so as to bring disaster to many countries. This

---

grants could have a serious inflationary effect here at home, could contribute to the forces that bring on economic collapse and depression. It is vital for the United States to keep its currency stable. We cannot do it if we undertake a large program of loans and grants. Also, could we have adequate assurance that the loans or grants made by this country would be wisely administered for purposes of rehabilitation by the recipient country?" R. J. Watt.

is particularly true when the depression originates in the United States, not merely because our foreign trade is so large a part of world trade, but also because our imports are mostly crude products and raw materials a fair supply of which is usually on hand. At the first sign of a downturn in business these stocks are drawn on to provide for the requirements of current output, and further imports cease for a considerable period in the expectation of lower prices.

The Committee recommends most urgently that the government formulate a program adequate to deal with this situation. Repercussions as direct and sharp as these will not be counteracted successfully by the financial operations of the Monetary Fund or of the International Bank. More direct measures are required.

The Committee does not regard the negotiation of international commodity agreements, accompanied by production controls and export quotas, as the most promising approach to this problem. It shares the misgivings of the research staff that such agreements, if successful, would tend to subsidize uneconomic, high-cost production. While the Committee has more sympathy for the proposal that a multilateral pact be negotiated in which each country would agree to maintain at least a minimum volume of imports during a period of depression,[6] it doubts whether such a pact could be successfully negotiated, and whether, if negotiated, the obligations undertaken could be carried out by the financially exposed countries under conditions of depression.

The Committee suggests, instead, that our public authorities promptly formulate specific plans for an international buffer stock agency designed to operate in the international markets for storable raw materials.[7] It agrees with the research staff that, in principle, such operations would come nearer to meeting the economic requirements of this problem than either commodity agreements or minimum import

6. "As regards maintaining imports in a depression, this suggestion is worthy of further exploration to find ways and means of implementing such a program. Participating countries could give private business information indicating the importance of maintaining imports and secure their cooperation in doing so, etc.," R. J. Watt.

7. "Such an agency is extremely difficult to administer. Its stockpiles overhang the market, creating doubt and hesitancy because buyers on the market never know when it is going to sell and bring the price down. Great pressure is exerted to prevent the sale of the large stockpiles accumulated. No one knows when a 'period of high activity' is actually at hand, and the tendency is to postpone sale and accumulate ever larger stockpiles. This happened in cotton in the United States. Since we have not even found ourselves capable of administering our own national stockpiles of this type, how could we be sure an international agency would be successfully administered?" R. J. Watt.

guarantees. Such an agency would be directed to accumulate stockpiles of storable raw materials during the period of depression and to dispose of these stockpiles when high activity returns. If the agency were properly set up and soundly administered, these operations would act directly to maintain stability of employment everywhere, not only by contributing to stability in the production, income and buying power of primary producers, but also by minimizing the inventory risks of fabricators and dealers. They would also cushion the shock abroad of a business reaction in this country without imposing great strain on the balance of payments. The establishment of such an agency, to operate on a business basis without subsidy, was first recommended by the Delegation on Economic Depressions of the League of Nations. The Committee endorses their recommendation in principle. It considers the suggestion of great importance and recommends that specific proposals for such an agency, capable of evaluation and criticism, be worked out.

A proposal in the same general area but with different economic implications is now being debated in the Food and Agricultural Organization. The Committee sympathizes with the objectives of the FAO plan for a World Food Board but does not consider that the proposal, as now stated, meets the economic requirements of the problem of instability. The operations provided by the FAO proposals would require current subsidy, direct or indirect, and would not mitigate instability in the case of many of the most important international raw materials.

EXPANSION OF IMPORTS

In 1940 the Trade Agreements Act of 1934 came up for renewal, and, after sharp opposition, was extended until 1943. In that year the Act was prolonged for two years, and, after further sharp opposition, it was once more renewed in 1945 with greatly strengthened provisions. During all this period the government has made only negligible use of the powers it has taken such pains to obtain. The reason, of course, was the war, which largely eliminated, for the time being, both the need and the desirability of tariff negotiations. The delay served, however, to lend credence abroad to the suspicion that the United States is not sincere in its desire to reduce its tariff barriers.

No single action on the part of the American government would more quickly dispel doubts of the sincerity of its desire to foster two-way trade and to re-establish a genuine multilateral trading world than a prompt and vigorous use of the powers it has received from Congress in the Trade Agreements legislation. No other action would do so much to convince thoughtful critics that the foreign investment program on which we are embarked can be soundly executed. Against the background of the long and sordid story of political logrolling in the tariff making of this country, this action more than any other would signalize the quality and responsibility of the economic leadership that the United States is willing to assume in the postwar world.

Considered from the broad point of view of the public welfare, there is no doubt of the benefits to the people of this country, and to their standards of consumption, that would result from a more liberal attitude toward imports. Considered in relation to our actual and prospective balance of payments — particularly as it will be affected by our lending program — an expansion of imports is clearly essential if we are ultimately to avoid heavy losses in our export markets and drastic curtailment of employment in our export industries or defaults in our foreign investments.

The meticulous research findings underlying this report are eloquent on these points. Trade is, and must be, mutual. It is, and must be, two-sided. Our customers must be permitted to pay us for what we are ready and anxious to sell. Payments such as we now receive, mainly in the form of raw material imports and the provision of services, such as to tourists, and to our nationals abroad, are adapted to meet the problem only in part. These relatively narrow and restricted channels of two-way trade can scarcely be expected to provide either a sound or a long-continuing base for a program of foreign trade and investment such as is now contemplated. Larger and more varied imports must somehow be encouraged.[8]

The Committee does not wish to imply that it will be an easy task for our public authorities to meet this challenge. Large segments of our industry, providing much employment, have developed behind barriers of high-tariff protection. They form a strong vested interest in the maintenance of the privileges that they now enjoy. It is natural

8. "I heartily agree on the importance of this suggestion. Careful consideration should, however, be given to the protection of labor standards in developing the program suggested," R. J. Watt.

that they should fear and oppose any change in those privileges and that they should make this opposition politically effective. Under certain conditions their opposition would be justified. The public interest would not be served by abrupt and violent changes in the level of tariff protection that had the effect of creating widespread unemployment, uncertainty or business losses.

But the expansion of imports that our country needs will buttress, not undermine, the general welfare and will raise, not lower, standards of consumption. The elaborate machinery under which reciprocal trade agreements are negotiated, with their provision for extensive hearings, was expressly designed to preclude the possibility of tariff reductions that would react unfavorably on our economy. The danger of the present procedure is not that it may result in overly drastic reductions in our barriers to trade that would react against the public interest, but rather the reverse. We may negotiate many reciprocal agreements with many countries and still find that we have failed to secure an equilibrium in our balance of payments. A substantial increase in our level of imports is a necessity if we are to maintain health in our internal economy.

We have rarely faced a time so appropriate for prompt and vigorous action to rectify this situation as during recent months. Our economy has been running at a very high level, fifty per cent or more above prewar; consumer demand has held at levels far in excess of anything that we have ever known, or of the capacity of our industry to provide; we are now reaching the limits of our labor force; further expansion in our internal output will be almost wholly dependent on increased productivity of labor, on greater efficiency in marketing and on technical improvements in our industrial plant and equipment; inflationary tendencies are broadly prevalent. These are conditions that indicate the need for imports. These are the circumstances that favor industrial adaptation. They create the most appropriate possible occasion for the long-overdue substantial revision in our tariff structure.

An increase of imports under present conditions would not be at the expense of domestic production. Instead, it would provide our consumers with goods that they urgently need, goods that would otherwise remain scarce. It would help, therefore, to counteract inflation and to hold down the rise in living costs. The present domestic market is sufficiently large to absorb a substantial volume of imports without detriment to a high and sustained level of operations — even in heavily protected industries. Under such conditions, vigorous action to modernize our tariff structure would not tend to contract current operations but rather to minimize further expansion of capacity in our less efficient industries. Our economy is broadly based. The expansion of capacity that it needs is not in areas where public subsidy or protection is required, but where it is most efficient. In a fundamental sense our protected industries, themselves, would benefit from a move that caused them, at this opportune moment, to diversify their production and to direct their plans for expansion toward new lines of output.

The Committee does not wish to imply that there will not be occasions when our domestic markets will appear unable to absorb the full internal output of protected industries. To do so would assume that this country has solved the problem of maintaining economic stability. The Committee does take the position that the maintenance of protection during the current phase of high consumer demand has increased inflationary pressures and has tended to stimulate further expansion of capacity in overprotected industries. By maintaining high tariffs we are not only missing an opportunity to stimulate expansion in more promising directions, but are also helping to create the type of situation in which reaction develops.

OVERSTIMULATION OF EXPORTS

There is a danger that our public authorities, both in the negotiation of reciprocal tariff reductions and more generally in their official activity at home and abroad, will be moved by too narrow a conception of our total export trade. They may harbor the misconception that a hard-driven bargain that opens the markets of a particular country to a particular American export will expand our exports in general and will contribute to employment, welfare and prosperity in this country. They may seek to buttress sick and inefficient American export industries whose continued existence requires subsidy.

Under the circumstances that prevail today such export promotion does not expand our exports in general nor contribute to the well-being of the American people, except in certain narrowly defined cases — as, for example, where an efficient American export industry faces contraction because of the undeserved loss of a former export market. Because of the shortage of dollars that has been generally characteristic of the foreign exchanges ever since the first world war, an expansion in the export possibilities of any one American product will not tend in most cases to expand for long the total volume of our exports. It will act rather to restrict the foreign market for other American products.

The products most typical of American industry, those in whose production we excel, enjoy a high degree of consumer acceptance throughout the world. Foreign customers have demonstrated repeatedly their willingness to buy them up to the full limit of their dollar resources. Many of our foreign markets, in fact, are habitually short of dollars because they have chosen to purchase American products beyond the limits of prudent financial management. Our huge gold hoards, accumulated now for a whole generation, are in part evidence of this practice.

It is the duty and responsibility of our official representatives both in Washington and abroad to secure fair treatment for all American exporters, to strive to eliminate practices that discriminate against them, to ferret out special arrangements by governments or by cartels that operate to their detriment. These activities are not only justified on the basis of fairness to our nationals, they are indispensable to the creation and maintenance of a sound system of multilateral trade. They do not, however, appreciably diminish the shortage of dollars abroad that has operated for nearly a generation to restrict the vigor and growth of our natural export industries. Such growth would be most surely promoted by an expansion of our imports.

TECHNICAL IMPROVEMENTS IN TARIFF PROCEDURE

The Committee suggests that our official representatives, both in Washington and abroad, be alert to this need and devote their ingenuity to the discovery of ways and means by which imports can be made available to increase the well-being of the American people. To this end the Committee makes two specific proposals.

(1) The administrative procedures of our customs officials, developed during an era when the erection of high and ever higher barriers to export trade dominated the policy of the country, are interwoven with impediments to the smooth and efficient development of an import business, particularly if that business is small. These procedures should be reviewed, and appropriate remedial action should be instituted.

(2) Our present tariff schedules do not serve merely to protect

established industries that are providing a considerable volume of current employment. A businessman wishing to import a commodity that is virtually noncompetitive with any established American manufacture, where no appreciable internal dislocation of labor would be involved, may find that this commodity falls technically in a schedule where a very high tariff is imposed. This situation, which may result from sheer inadvertence in the drawing of the tariff schedules, or from obsolescence in tariff classifications established under different conditions, operates to penalize enterprise both in this country and abroad. It can be remedied by legislation under which free entry would be given to any import that could be shown, as a matter of *fact,* to be essentially noncompetitive with an established American product.

The Committee requests that these suggestions be considered on their merits. It hopes that they will stimulate others to seek new ways and means to facilitate the adaptation of the American economy to the conditions that now confront it.

TARIFF REDUCTIONS

The over-all effects of such technical measures, however, should not be overrated. They are valuable, but they will in no sense suffice at this juncture to bring about a sufficient increase of imports to meet our economic requirements or to adapt our economy to its appropriate role in the postwar world. The Committee recommends that the Administration proceed immediately, under the powers conferred in the Reciprocal Trade Agreements Act, to secure a substantial modification in our tariff structure. Such action is necessary (a) to counteract inflation, (b) to dampen a further rise in living costs, (c) to increase the availability of consumers' goods to the American people, and (d) to foster, at this propitious moment, the adaptation of the American economy to the new conditions that will be basic to peace and prosperity in the postwar world.

SUMMARY

The Committee believes that two obstacles impede the re-establishment of a multilateral system of trade, and two deficiencies in our foreign economic program create doubts that a multilateral system, once established, would be successful.

The current obstacles will be removed when political security has been re-established and when rehabilitation in the war-exhausted countries has eliminated bottlenecks and restored working capital to the point where these countries are again on a self-sustaining basis and are able to trade in world markets as "going concerns." Once these objectives have been attained, it should not be too difficult to re-establish a broadly based system of multilateral trade that would include most of the countries whose industries are interdependent.

The Committee recommends that the United States continue to extend rehabilitation aid on an adequate but realistic basis to all countries that are potential members of such a multilateral trading system. It recommends, further, that the Export-Import Bank be given primary responsibility to complete the job and that its resources be correspondingly increased.

The two deficiencies in our foreign economic program that imperil the success of a multilateral trading system, after it has been re-established, are our failure to make adequate provision to cushion the repercussions abroad of economic instability and our failure to provide for a sufficient increase in our imports to maintain equilibrium in our balance of payments. To promote international conditions favorable to economic stability, the Committee recommends two measures: (1) that the International Bank for Reconstruction and Development be operated to counteract the volatility that normally characterizes foreign investment; and (2) that the Administration formulate concrete, workable plans for the creation of an international buffer stock agency to operate directly toward stability in the great world markets for raw materials and prime commodities. To eliminate the second deficiency will require a substantial expansion of imports. The present moment, when consumers' demand is in excess of production and inflationary tendencies prevail, is particularly opportune to move on this problem. The Committee recommends (a) appropriate technical changes in our tariff procedure, and (b) prompt and vigorous use of the powers conferred on the Administration by the Reciprocal Trade Agreements Act.

THE CHALLENGE TO AMERICA

It was stated at the beginning that this report is not written from a narrow American point of view. Its recommendations could be adopted to advantage by any nation that wishes to benefit from the vitality of freedom in its internal economy and to avoid the tensions of bilateral, discriminatory arrangements in foreign trade. The Committee has endeavored to visualize the full range of our foreign economic problems and to devise a broad and balanced program adequate to deal with them. Properly executed, this program, in the judgment of the Committee, would provide the essential minimum conditions for a dynamic, expanding world economy.[9]

In the environment contemplated by this report, the lowering of political barriers to trade would permit peoples everywhere to enjoy the rising standards of consumption made possible by international specialization in production. With the removal of political impediments now interposed to the international flow and repayment of productive investment, the backward and less developed areas of the world would be in a position to obtain more abundantly the industrial equipment of advanced countries, and to learn the skills, techniques and "know-how" involved in its use. That environment cannot be created by any one country acting alone. It will require common effort to establish its foundations within three major areas where they are now weak or nonexistent in order (1) to carry rehabilitation and reconstruction to the point where peoples will be able to drop present unilateral and bilateral foreign trade controls; (2) to restore a sense of political security so that peoples who desire to participate may choose to join a multilateral trading world; and (3) to minimize and mitigate the international repercussions of depression by the creation of new international economic agencies.

The Committee desires to emphasize, however, that these considerations, even though they require the concurrence of many countries, lack appeal unless they are espoused first by the United States. There is no policy advocated in this report that would have a chance of operating with success anywhere, in any area of appreciable size, without the wholehearted participation of the United States. Our economic potential is too large, our foreign economic interrelationships

---

9. "To carry out the constructive suggestions made in this report will require action on the part of a qualified agency. If the International Trade Organization proposed by the United States is based on realism and has representation on a practical basis from labor, industry and agriculture, there would be some hope that the suggestions could be carried out. If this sort of representation is absent, and if the International Trade Organization is left purely on the political perifery, then these suggestions represent merely wishful thinking," R. J. Watt.

are too pervasive, to permit a multilateral system to function effectively without us. The creation of such a system, if it is to be created, will require the cooperation and participation of many nations. But from the United States it will require more. We must assume, in addition, the initiative required to bring it into being.

Time is running short. There is hesitation in many nations committed to the principles of freedom but compelled to practice the reverse. They will not remain long in this position. They must soon decide the road they will take. It would be ironical indeed if we lost that final decision, not because we were uncertain with regard to our aims, but because we failed to devise the appropriate means, or pushed too vigorously a foreign economic program inadequate to their realization.

WINFIELD W. RIEFLER, *Chairman*

PERCY W. BIDWELL
KERMIT EBY
PAUL G. HOFFMAN

JOSEPH C. ROVENSKY
THEODORE W. SCHULTZ
ROBERT J. WATT

APPENDIXES

TABLE A

GROWTH OF POPULATION IN SELECTED COUNTRIES, 1800–1900

(In Thousands)

Country	1800	1810	1820	1830	1840	1850	1860	1870	1880	1890	1900
Austria-Hungary	24,300	25,500	27,000	29,750	31,363	32,504	34,790	37,495	39,159	42,859	47,143
France	26,900	28,200	30,000	31,900	33,400	34,907	35,741	36,765	37,512	38,343	38,962
Germany	24,500	25,500	27,200	30,420	32,785	35,397	37,747	40,818	45,234	49,428	56,367
Great Britain and Ireland	16,526	18,634	21,411	24,536	27,207	27,902	29,484	32,018	35,425	38,305	42,191
Italy	18,124	18,500	19,000	20,850	22,300	23,900	25,100	26,650	28,294	30,515	32,475
Netherlands	2,150	2,250	2,400	2,640	2,896	3,096	3,325	3,616	4,061	4,565	5,179
Russia	38,000	42,000	46,000	51,200	55,600	60,000	65,000	73,000	83,537	95,908	109,700
Sweden	2,347	2,378	2,585	2,888	3,139	3,483	3,860	4,169	4,566	4,785	5,136
United States	5,308	7,239	9,638	12,866	17,069	23,192	31,443	38,558	50,156	62,622	76,303
Total Europe	186,978	198,565	212,965	233,908	250,966	265,922	282,885	305,399	331,743	362,878	400,524
Occidental Europe	122,578	128,865	137,740	151,308	162,166	171,372	181,162	192,761	207,186	221,265	240,153
Northwest Europe	62,829	66,875	72,886	81,650	88,576	94,092	100,444	108,290	119,353	129,395	144,429
Southwest Europe	59,749	61,990	64,854	69,658	73,590	77,280	80,718	84,471	87,833	91,870	95,724
Oriental Europe	64,400	96,700	75,225	82,600	88,800	94,550	101,723	112,638	124,557	141,613	160,371

Source: Gustav Sundbärg, *Aperçus statistiques internationaux*, Norstedt, Stockholm, 1906, pp. 28–29, 32. Figures for the United States taken from *Statistical Abstract of the United States*, 1943, Bureau of the Census, p. 4.

TABLE B

COMPOSITION OF UNITED STATES FOREIGN TRADE, 1921–1938

(Dollar Figures in Millions)

Annual Averages

Period	Crude Materials		Crude Foodstuffs		Manufactured Foodstuffs		Semimanufactured Products		Finished Products	
	Amount	Per Cent of Total	Amount	Per Cent of Total	Amount	Per Cent of Total	Amount	Per Cent of Total	Amount	Per Cent of Total
EXPORTS										
1921–1925	$1,187	27.5	$420	9.7	$601	13.9	$537	12.4	$1,566	36.3
1926–1930	1,144	24.4	300	6.4	456	9.7	663	14.1	2,126	45.3
1931–1935	601	30.2	77	3.8	176	8.8	289	14.5	846	42.6
1936–1938	669	20.5	137	4.2	518	15.8	517	15.8	1,431	43.7
IMPORTS										
1921–1925	1,290	37.4	383	11.1	448	13.0	609	17.7	720	20.9
1926–1930	1,484	36.8	507	12.5	398	9.9	763	18.9	882	21.9
1931–1935	492	28.9	266	15.6	234	13.7	319	18.7	393	23.0
1936–1938	760	31.3	347	14.2	347	14.2	503	20.7	478	19.6

Source: Statistical Abstract of the United States, 1943, Bureau of the Census, pp. 524, 525.

TABLE C
United States Balance of International Payments, 1919–1939
(In Millions of Dollars)

Type of transactions	1919	1920	1921	1922	1923	1924	1925	1926	1927	1928	1929
1. Current transactions											
Merchandise trade											
Receipts	7,920	8,228	4,485	3,832	4,167	4,591	4,910	4,809	4,865	5,128	5,241
Payments	3,904	5,278	2,509	3,113	3,792	3,610	4,227	4,431	4,185	4,091	4,399
Balance	+4,016	+2,950	+1,976	+719	+375	+981	+683	+378	+680	+1,037	+842
Other current transactions											
Shipping and freight											
Receipts	1,109	1,119	394	286	302	315	318	370	360	372	390
Payments	818	848	334	341	332	361	391	415	417	460	509
Balance	+291	+271	+60	-55	-30	-46	-73	-45	-57	-88	-119
Travel expenditures											
Receipts	56	67	76	61	71	77	83	110	114	121	139
Payments	123	190	200	243	260	303	347	372	400	448	483
Balance	-67	-123	-124	-182	-189	-226	-264	-262	-286	-327	-344
Personal remittances											
Receipts	40	63	49	48	65	57	47	50	49	50	51
Payments	732	579	393	269	309	325	355	348	343	338	339
Balance	-692	-516	-344	-221	-244	-268	-308	-298	-294	-288	-288
Institutional contributions — net	-140	-118	-106	-93	-84	-71	-65	-63	-61	-58	-55
Interest and dividends											
Receipts	544	588	405	544	676	602	752	793	821	922	982
Payments	130	120	105	105	130	140	170	200	240	275	330
Balance	+414	+468	+300	+439	+546	+462	+582	+593	+581	+647	+652

Type of transactions	1930	1931	1932	1933	1934	1935	1936	1937	1938	1939
1. Current transactions										
Merchandise trade										
Receipts	3,843	2,424	1,611	1,675	2,133	2,283	2,456	3,349	3,094	3,157
Payments	3,061	2,091	1,323	1,450	1,655	2,047	2,423	3,084	1,960	2,318
Balance	+782	+333	+288	+225	+478	+236	+33	+265	+1,134	+859
Other current transactions										
Shipping and freight										
Receipts	325	247	171	108	133	139	158	236	267	303
Payments	477	366	255	154	196	206	247	366	303	367
Balance	-152	-119	-84	-46	-63	-67	-89	-130	-36	-64
Travel expenditures										
Receipts	129	94	65	66	81	101	117	135	130	135
Payments	463	341	259	199	218	245	297	348	303	290
Balance	-334	-247	-194	-133	-137	-144	-180	-213	-173	-155
Personal remittances										
Receipts	43	28	17	17	19	20	22	28	37	36
Payments	300	262	199	178	151	155	170	170	152	144
Balance	-257	-234	-182	-161	-132	-135	-148	-142	-115	-108
Institutional contributions — net	-49	-45	-35	-30	-30	-27	-28	-33	-38	-43
Interest and dividends										
Receipts	876	674	460	417	436	521	568	577	584	541
Payments	295	220	135	115	135	155	270	295	200	230
Balance	+581	+454	+325	+302	+301	+366	+298	+282	+384	+311

Type of transactions	1919	1920	1921	1922	1923	1924	1925	1926	1927	1928	1929
1. Current transactions (contd.)											
Government aid and settlements											
Receipts	1,212	214	98	175	255	203	187	201	227	229	234
Payments	2,844	286	86	48	21	31	19	22	14	31	63
Balance	−1,632	−72	+12	+127	+234	+172	+168	+179	+213	+198	+171
Other government items											
Receipts	9	9	11	15	22	24	24	25	27	28	27
Payments	772	140	82	69	66	71	73	77	73	81	89
Balance	−763	−131	−71	−54	−44	−47	−49	−52	−46	−53	−62
Silver											
Receipts	239	114	52	63	72	110	99	92	76	87	83
Payments	89	88	63	71	74	74	64	69	55	68	64
Balance	+150	+26	−11	−8	−2	+36	+35	+23	+21	+19	+19
Miscellaneous adjustments and services — net	−79	−68	−98	−30	−14	−18	—	+1	−30	−60	−30
Total of other current transactions											
Receipts	3,209	2,174	1,085	1,192	1,463	1,388	1,510	1,642	1,674	1,809	1,906
Payments	5,727	2,437	1,467	1,269	1,290	1,394	1,484	1,566	1,633	1,819	1,962
Balance	−2,518	−263	−382	−77	+173	−6	+26	+76	+41	−10	−56
Total of all current transactions											
Receipts	11,129	10,402	5,570	5,024	5,630	5,979	6,420	6,451	6,539	6,937	7,147
Payments	9,631	7,715	3,976	4,382	5,082	5,004	5,711	5,997	5,818	5,910	6,361
Balance	+1,498	+2,687	+1,594	+642	+548	+975	+709	+454	+721	+1,027	+786
2. Gold movements											
Net gold exports or imports	+291	−95	−667	−239	−294	−258	+134	−98	−6	+392	−175

1. Current transactions (contd.)

Government aid and setlements										
Receipts	256	121	99	20	2	1	1	1	4	2
Payments	41	36	9	5	1	1	1	49	21	18
Balance	+215	+85	+90	+15	+1	—	—	-48	-17	-16
Other government items										
Receipts	27	26	25	27	30	31	31	31	31	42
Payments	87	90	87	78	72	89	95	78	77	81
Balance	-60	-64	-62	-51	-42	-58	-64	-47	-46	-39
Silver										
Receipts	54	27	14	19	17	19	9	9	7	14
Payments	43	29	20	60	108	415	123	97	213	91
Balance	+11	-2	-6	-41	-91	-396	-114	-88	-206	-77
Miscellaneous adjustments and services — net	-2	+14	+19	+28	+56	+69	+74	+123	+80	+64
Total of other current transactions										
Receipts	1,710	1,231	870	702	774	901	980	1,140	1,140	1,137
Payments	1,757	1,389	999	819	911	1,293	1,231	1,436	1,307	1,264
Balance	-47	-158	-129	-117	-137	-392	-251	-296	-167	-127
Total of all current transactions										
Receipts	5,553	3,655	2,481	2,377	2,907	3,184	3,436	4,489	4,234	4,314
Payments	4,818	3,480	2,322	2,269	2,566	3,340	3,654	4,520	3,267	3,582
Balance	+735	+175	+159	+108	+341	-156	-218	-31	+967	+732

2. Gold movements

Net gold exports or imports	-280	-145	+447	+174	-1,134	-1,739	-1,116	-1,586	-1,973	-3,574

Type of transactions	*1919*	*1920*	*1921*	*1922*	*1923*	*1924*	*1925*	*1926*	*1927*	*1928*	*1929*
2. Gold movements (*contd.*)											
Net change in earmarked gold	−127	+145	−19	+4	−1	+42	−32	+26	+160	−120	+55
Net gold movement	+164	+50	−686	−235	−295	−216	+102	−72	+154	+272	−120
3. Capital transactions											
Long-term capital movements											
Net flow through change in United States assets abroad	−169	−554	−588	−822	−45	−700	−570	−821	−987	−1,310	−636
Net flow through change in foreign assets in United States	−215	−278	−4	+7				+95	−50	+463	+358
Balance on long-term capital movements	−384	−832	−592	−815	−45	−700	−570	−726	−1,037	−847	−278
Short-term capital movements											
Net flow through change in United States assets abroad	b	b	b	b	−82	−109	−46	−36	−349	−231	−200
Net flow through change in foreign assets in United States	b	b	b	b	+49	+228	−60	+455	+934	−117	+196
Balance on short-term capital movements	b	b	b	b	−33	+119	−106	+419	+585	−348	−4
Balance on all capital transactions	−384	−832	−592	−815	−78	−581	−676	−307	−452	−1,195	−282
Unexplained items	−1,278	−1,905	−316	+408	−175	−178	−135	−75	−423	−104	−384

In the "Net flow through change in foreign assets in United States" (long-term) row the figure +7 is shown with a brace covering 1922–1923 and the figure +95 with a brace covering 1925–1926.

2. Gold movements (contd.)

Net change in earmarked gold	+2	+321	-458	-1	-44	+19	-31	+315	+316	+556
Net gold movement	-278	+176	-11	+173	-1,178	-1,720	-1,147	-1,271	-1,657	-3,018
3. Capital transactions										
Long-term capital movements										
Net flow through change in United States assets abroad	-364	+128	+251	-48	+185	+116	+177	+276	+40	+113
Net flow through change in foreign assets in United States	+66	+66	-26	+165	-15	+320	+600	+245	+57	-86
Balance on long-term capital movements	-298	+194	+225	+77[a]	+200[a]	+436	+777	+521	+97	+27
Short-term capital movements										
Net flow through change in United States assets abroad	-191	+628	+227	+35	+96	+424	+55	+45	+27	+211
Net flow through change in foreign assets in United States	-288	-1,265	-673	-454	+126	+648	+376	+311	+317	+1,259
Balance on short-term capital movements	-479	-637	-446	-419	+222	+1,072	+431	+356	+344	+1,470
Balance on all capital transactions	-777	-443	-221	-342	+422	+1,508	+1,208	+877	+441	+1,497
Unexplained items	+320	+92	+73	+61	+415	+368	+157	+425	+249	+789

Source: Hal B. Lary and Associates, *The United States in the World Economy*, Economic Series No. 23, Bureau of Foreign and Domestic Commerce, 1943, App.

a. The net long-term capital transaction figure for 1933 includes −$40 million and that for 1934 includes +$30 million representing the net transfer of funds in security arbitrage operations. These transactions cannot be divided between domestic and foreign securities in these years.

b. Not available.

TABLE D

World Shipping Receipts, 1929 and 1937

Country	1929		1937		Estimated Active Tonnage in International Trade in 1937
	Amount	Per Cent of Total	Amount	Per Cent of Total	
	(In Millions)		(In Millions)		(Millions of Gross Tons)
Total	$2,741	100.0ᵃ	$2,800	100.0ᵃ	53.4
United Kingdom	1,020	37.2	1,038	37.1	17.0
United States	351	12.8	189	6.7	3.5
Germany	243	8.8	266	10.3	3.9
Netherlands	167	6.1	174	6.2	2.6
France	146	5.3	117	4.2	2.5
Norway	133	4.8	221	7.9	4.3
Japan	103	3.8	126	4.5	4.3
Rest of world	578	21.8	669	23.9	15.3

Source: John S. Smith, "World Income from Shipping," *Foreign Commerce Weekly,* April 29, 1944, p. 3.

a. Because of rounding, percentages do not add exactly to totals.

TABLE E

Shipping Receipts in Relation to National Income, 1937

Country	Income From Shipping as Per Cent of National Income
United States	.09
United Kingdom	1.3
Germany	.3
Netherlands	2.4
France	.5
Norway	11.2
Japan	.7

Source: John S. Smith, "World Income from Shipping," *Foreign Commerce Weekly,* April 29, 1944.

TABLE F

Exports and General Imports of the United States, Percentage Distribution by Continents, 1871–1938

Annual Averages

Period	Per Cent of Total Exports							Per Cent of Total Imports						
	North America		South America	Europe	Asia	Oceania	Africa	North America		South America	Europe	Asia	Oceania	Africa
	Northern	Southern						Northern	Southern					
1871–1880	5.7	5.8	3.6	81.1	1.4	0.9	0.5	5.8	17.1	12.4	53.0	10.5	0.8	0.6
1881–1890	5.3	5.8	4.0	80.2	2.5	1.8	0.5	5.9	14.1	11.4	55.5	10.5	2.0	0.6
1891–1900	6.2	6.2	3.4	78.1	3.1	1.9	1.0	4.8	13.3	14.0	51.6	12.7	2.6	1.0
1901–1910	9.4	7.7	3.6	70.2	5.4	1.9	1.4	5.7	13.3	12.1	51.3	15.3	1.0	1.2
1911–1920	13.1	7.7	5.3	63.6	7.1	2.0	1.2	10.2	16.0	15.4	43.5	21.4	1.6	2.1
1921–1930	15.8	9.3	8.1	49.6	11.7	3.4	1.9	11.7	13.2	12.8	31.6	29.2	1.5	2.2
1931–1938	15.3	8.8	8.6	43.3	16.8	2.9	4.0	14.5	10.2	13.3	28.9	30.3	1.4	1.8

Source: Statistical Abstract of the United States, 1943, Bureau of the Census.

TABLE G

THE TEN MOST IMPORTANT COUNTRIES IN UNITED STATES EXPORTS, 1921–1925 AND 1936–1938

Country	1921–1925 Average		Country	1936–1938 Average	
	Amount	Per Cent of Total		Amount	Per Cent of Total
	(In Millions)			(In Millions)	
Total United States exports	$4,310	100.0		$2,925	100.0
United Kingdom	939	21.8	United Kingdom	499	17.1
Canada	619	14.4	Japan	244	8.3
Germany	383	8.9	Canada	454	15.3
France	265	6.1	France	143	4.9
Japan	242	5.6	Germany	112	3.8
Italy	185	4.3	Mexico	83	2.8
Cuba	181	4.2	Netherlands	81	2.8
Mexico	146	3.4	Argentina	79	2.7
Argentina	117	2.7	Cuba	79	2.7
Belgium	111	2.6	Philippine Islands	77	2.6

Source: Statistical Abstract of the United States, 1943, Bureau of the Census.

TABLE H

THE TEN MOST IMPORTANT COUNTRIES IN UNITED STATES IMPORTS, 1921–1925 AND 1936–1938

Country	1921–1925 Average		Country	1936–1938 Average	
	Amount	Per Cent of Total		Amount	Per Cent of Total
	(In Millions)			(In Millions)	
Total United States imports	$3,450	100.0		$2,461	100.0
Canada	394	11.4	Canada	341	14.3
United Kingdom	356	10.3	British Malaya	174	7.1
Japan	335	9.7	United Kingdom	174	7.2
Cuba	300	8.7	Japan	168	6.8
British Malaya	153	4.4	Cuba	127	5.2
Brazil	152	4.4	Philippine Islands	107	4.3
France	148	4.3	Brazil	107	4.3
Mexico	147	4.3	Netherlands Indies	85	3.5
China	142	4.1	Argentina	82	3.3
Germany	132	3.8	Germany	79	3.2

Source: Statistical Abstract of the United States, 1943, Bureau of the Census.

TABLE I

GEOGRAPHICAL DISTRIBUTION OF BRITISH INVESTMENTS ABROAD, 1938

Country or Region	Per Cent of Total
Total	100.0
British Empire	50.4
Canada	11.7
Australia	11.6
India and Ceylon	12.4
Rest of Empire	14.7
Europe	7.5
United States	12.0
Latin America[a]	20.5
Rest of world	9.6

Source: Figures calculated from information in Cleona Lewis, *Debtor and Creditor Countries: 1938, 1944,* The Brookings Institution, Washington, 1945.

a. This includes Central and South America and Mexico.

TABLE J

TYPES OF BRITISH FOREIGN INVESTMENTS, 1929 AND 1938

Year	Total (In Millions)	Loans to Central and Local Governments Overseas		Industrial Investments					
		Amount (In Millions)	Per Cent of Total	Share Capital		Loan Capital		Industries Not Otherwise Accounted For	
				Amount (In Millions)	Per Cent of Total	Amount (In Millions)	Per Cent of Total	Amount (In Millions)	Per Cent of Total
1929	£3,738	£1,412	37.8	£1,238	33.1	£788	21.1	£300	8.0
1938	3,692	1,398	37.9	1,231	33.3	663	17.6	400	11.2

Source: The figures for 1929 are taken from R. M. Kindersley, "British Oversea Investments," *Economic Journal,* December 1939. The figures for 1929 are taken from the December 1938 issue of the same journal.

TABLE K

BRITISH INVESTMENTS ABROAD, SELECTED YEARS

(*In Millions*)

Year	Total Outstanding (Nominal Value)	Income From Overseas Investments	New Overseas Issues	Sums Repaid
1913	£3,715	a	£198	a
1929	3,738	£231	96	£ 48
1933	3,665	150	83	69
1934	3,714	159	63	42
1935	3,788	172	51	81
1936	3,764	184	61	107
1937	3,754	198	60	61
1938	3,692	185	29	39

Sources: Figures (except for 1913) are those of R. M. Kindersley, which, before World War II, were currently published in the *Economic Journal*. Figures for 1913 from *The Economist,* November 15, 1930, p. 896. Kindersley's figures given in the table include his estimate of "unquoted investments" not covered by his detailed inquiry.

a. Not available.

Appendix 1

BRETTON WOODS AGREEMENTS

ARTICLES OF AGREEMENT OF THE INTERNATIONAL MONETARY FUND

LIST OF ARTICLES AND SECTIONS

SCHEDULES

The Governments on whose behalf the present Agreement is signed agree as follows:

INTRODUCTORY ARTICLE

The International Monetary Fund is established and shall operate in accordance with the following provisions:

ARTICLE I

PURPOSES

The purposes of the International Monetary Fund are:

(i) To promote international monetary cooperation through a permanent institution which provides the machinery for consultation and collaboration on international monetary problems.

(ii) To facilitate the expansion and balanced growth of international trade, and to contribute thereby to the promotion and maintenance of high levels of employment and real income and to the development of the productive resources of all members as primary objectives of economic policy.

(iii) To promote exchange stability, to maintain orderly exchange arrangements among members, and to avoid competitive exchange depreciation.

(iv) To assist in the establishment of a multilateral system of payments in respect of current transactions between members and in the elimination of foreign exchange restrictions which hamper the growth of world trade.

(v) To give confidence to members by making the Fund's resources available to them under adequate safeguards, thus providing them with opportunity to correct maladjustments in their balance of payments without resorting to measures destructive of national or international prosperity.

(vi) In accordance with the above, to shorten the duration and lessen the degree of disequilibrium in the international balances of payments of members.

The Fund shall be guided in all its decisions by the purposes set forth in this Article.

ARTICLE II
MEMBERSHIP

Section 1. *Original members*

The original members of the Fund shall be those of the countries represented at the United Nations Monetary and Financial Conference whose governments accept membership before the date specified in Article XX, Section 2 (e).

Section 2. *Other members*

Membership shall be open to the governments of other countries at such times and in accordance with such terms as may be prescribed by the Fund.

ARTICLE III
QUOTAS AND SUBSCRIPTIONS

Section 1. *Quotas*

Each member shall be assigned a quota. The quotas of the members represented at the United Nations Monetary and Financial Conference which accept membership before the date specified in Article XX, Section 2 (e), shall be those set forth in Schedule A. The quotas of other members shall be determined by the Fund.

Section 2. *Adjustment of quotas*

The Fund shall at intervals of five years review, and if it deems it appropriate propose an adjustment of, the quotas of the members. It may also, if it thinks fit, consider at any other time the adjustment of any particular quota at the request of the member concerned. A four-fifths majority of the total voting power shall be required for any change in quotas and no quota shall be changed without the consent of the member concerned.

Section 3. *Subscriptions: time, place, and form of payment*

(a) The subscription of each member shall be equal to its quota and shall be paid in full to the Fund at the appropriate depository on or before the date when the member becomes eligible under Article XX, Section 4 (c) or (d), to buy currencies from the Fund.

(b) Each member shall pay in gold, as a minimum, the smaller of

(i) twenty-five percent of its quota; or
(ii) ten percent of its net official holdings of gold and United States dollars as at the date when the Fund notifies members under Article XX, Section 4 (a) that it will shortly be in a position to begin exchange transactions.

Each member shall furnish to the Fund the data necessary to determine its net official holdings of gold and United States dollars.

(c) Each member shall pay the balance of its quota in its own currency.

(d) If the net official holdings of gold and United States dollars of any member as at the date referred to in (b) (ii) above are not ascertainable because its territories have been occupied by the enemy, the Fund shall fix an appropriate alternative date for determining such holdings. If such date is later than that on which the country becomes eligible under Article XX, Section 4 (c) or (d), to buy currencies from the Fund, the Fund and the member shall agree on a provisional gold payment to be made under (b) above, and the balance of the member's subscription shall be paid in the member's currency, subject to appropriate adjustment between the member and the Fund when the net official holdings have been ascertained.

Section 4. *Payments when quotas are changed*

(a) Each member which consents to an increase in its quota shall, within thirty days after the date of its consent, pay to the Fund twenty-five percent of the increase in gold and the balance in its own currency. If, however, on the date when the member consents to an increase, its monetary reserves are less than its new quota, the Fund may reduce the proportion of the increase to be paid in gold.

(b) If a member consents to a reduction in its quota, the Fund shall, within thirty days after the date of the consent, pay to the member an amount equal to the reduction. The payment shall be made in the member's currency and in such amount of gold as may be necessary to prevent reducing the Fund's holdings of the currency below seventy-five percent of the new quota.

Section 5. *Substitution of securities for currency*

The Fund shall accept from any member in place of any part of the member's currency which in the judgment of the Fund is not needed for its operations, notes or similar obligations issued by the member or the depository designated by the member under Article XIII, Section 2, which shall be non-negotiable, non-interest bearing and payable at their par value on demand by crediting the account of the Fund in the designated depository. This Section shall apply not only to currency subscribed by members but also to any currency otherwise due to, or acquired by, the Fund.

ARTICLE IV

PAR VALUES OF CURRENCIES

Section 1. *Expression of par values*

(a) The par value of the currency of each member shall be expressed in terms of gold as a common denominator or in terms of the United States dollar of the weight and fineness in effect on July 1, 1944.

(b) All computations relating to currencies of members for the purpose of applying the provisions of this Agreement shall be on the basis of their par values.

Section 2. *Gold purchases based on par values*

The Fund shall prescribe a margin above and below par value for transactions in gold by members, and no member shall buy gold at a price above par value plus the prescribed margin, or sell gold at a price below par value minus the prescribed margin.

Section 3. *Foreign exchange dealings based on parity*

The maximum and the minimum rates for exchange transactions between the currencies of members taking place within their territories shall not differ from parity

(i) in the case of spot exchange transactions, by more than one percent; and

(ii) in the case of other exchange transactions, by a margin which exceeds the margin for spot exchange transactions by more than the Fund considers reasonable.

Section 4. *Obligations regarding exchange stability*

(a) Each member undertakes to collaborate with the Fund to promote exchange stability, to maintain orderly exchange arrangements with other members, and to avoid competitive exchange alterations.

(b) Each member undertakes, through appropriate measures consistent with this Agreement, to permit within its territories exchange transactions between its currency and the currencies of other members only within the limits prescribed under Section 3 of this Article. A member whose monetary authorities, for the settlement of international transactions, in fact freely buy and sell gold within the limits prescribed by the Fund under Section 2 of this Article shall be deemed to be fulfilling this undertaking.

Section 5. *Changes in par values*

(a) A member shall not propose a change in the par value of its currency except to correct a fundamental disequilibrium.

(b) A change in the par value of a member's currency may be made only on the proposal of the member and only after consultation with the Fund.

(c) When a change is proposed, the Fund shall first take into account the changes, if any, which have already taken place in the initial par value of the member's currency as determined under Article XX, Section 4. If the proposed change, together with all previous changes, whether increases or decreases,

> (i) does not exceed ten percent of the initial par value, the Fund shall raise no objection,
>
> (ii) does not exceed a further ten percent of the initial par value, the Fund may either concur or object, but shall declare its attitude within seventy-two hours if the member so requests,
>
> (iii) is not within (i) or (ii) above, the Fund may either concur or object, but shall be entitled to a longer period in which to declare its attitude.

(d) Uniform changes in par values made under Section 7 of this Article shall not be taken into account in determining whether a proposed change falls within (i), (ii), or (iii) of (c) above.

(e) A member may change the par value of its currency without the concurrence of the Fund if the change does not affect the international transactions of members of the Fund.

(f) The Fund shall concur in a proposed change which is within the terms of (c) (ii) or (c) (iii) above if it is satisfied that the change is necessary to correct a fundamental disequilibrium. In particular, provided it is so satisfied, it shall not object to a proposed change because of the domestic social or political policies of the member proposing the change.

Section 6. *Effect of unauthorized changes*

If a member changes the par value of its currency despite the objection of the Fund, in cases where the Fund is entitled to object, the member shall be ineligible to use the resources of the Fund unless the Fund otherwise determines; and if, after the expiration of a reasonable period, the difference between the member and the Fund continues, the matter shall be subject to the provisions of Article XV, Section 2 (b).

Section 7. *Uniform changes in par values*

Notwithstanding the provisions of Section 5 (b) of this Article, the Fund by a majority of the total voting power may make uniform proportionate changes in the par values of the currencies of all members, provided each such change is approved by every member which has ten percent or more of the total of the quotas. The par value of a member's currency shall, however, not be changed under this provision if, within seventy-two hours of the Fund's action, the member informs the Fund that it does not wish the par value of its currency to be changed by such action.

Section 8. *Maintenance of gold value of the Fund's assets*

(a) The gold value of the Fund's assets shall be maintained notwithstanding changes in the par or foreign exchange value of the currency of any member.

(b) Whenever (i) the par value of a member's currency is reduced, or (ii) the foreign exchange value of a member's currency has, in the opinion of the Fund, depreciated to a significant extent within that member's territories, the member shall pay to the Fund within a reasonable time an amount of its own currency equal to the reduction in the gold value of its currency held by the Fund.

(c) Whenever the par value of a member's currency is increased, the Fund shall return to such member within a reasonable time an amount in its currency equal to the increase in the gold value of its currency held by the Fund.

(d) The provisions of this Section shall apply to a uniform proportionate change in the par values of the currencies of all members, unless at the time when such a change is proposed the Fund decides otherwise.

Section 9. *Separate currencies within a member's territories*

A member proposing a change in the par value of its currency shall be deemed, unless it declares otherwise, to be proposing a corresponding change in the par value of the separate currencies of all territories in respect of which it has accepted this Agreement under Article XX, Section 2 (g). It shall, however, be open to a member to declare that its proposal relates either to the metropolitan currency alone, or only to one or more specified separate currencies, or to the metropolitan currency and one or more specified separate currencies.

ARTICLE V
TRANSACTIONS WITH THE FUND
Section 1. *Agencies dealing with the Fund*

Each member shall deal with the Fund only through its Treasury, central bank, stabilization fund or other similar fiscal agency and the Fund shall deal only with or through the same agencies.

Section 2. *Limitation of Fund's operations*

Except as otherwise provided in this Agreement, operations on the account of the Fund shall be limited to transactions for the purpose of supplying a member, on the initiative of such member, with the currency of another member in exchange for gold or for the currency of the member desiring to make the purchase.

Section 3. *Conditions governing use of the Fund's resources*

(a) A member shall be entitled to buy the currency of another member from the Fund in exchange for its own currency subject to the following conditions:

(i) The member desiring to purchase the currency represents that it is presently needed for making in that currency payments which are consistent with the provisions of this Agreement;

(ii) The Fund has not given notice under Article VII, Section 3, that its holdings of the currency desired have become scarce;

(iii) The proposed purchase would not cause the Fund's holdings of the purchasing member's currency to increase by more than twenty-five percent of its quota during the period of twelve months ending on the date of the purchase nor to exceed two hundred percent of its quota, but the twenty-five percent limitation shall apply only to the extent that the Fund's holdings of the member's currency have been brought above seventy-five percent of its quota if they had been below that amount;

(iv) The Fund has not previously declared under Section 5 of this Article, Article IV, Section 6, Article VI, Section 1, or Article XV, Section 2 (a), that the member desiring to purchase is ineligible to use the resources of the Fund.

(b) A member shall not be entitled without the permission of the Fund to use the Fund's resources to acquire currency to hold against forward exchange transactions.

Section 4. *Waiver of conditions*

The Fund may in its discretion, and on terms which safeguard its interests, waive any of the conditions prescribed in Section 3 (a) of this Article, especially in the case of members with a record of avoiding large or continuous use of the Fund's resources. In making a waiver it shall take into consideration periodic or exceptional requirements of the member requesting the waiver. The Fund shall also take into consideration a member's willingness to pledge as collateral security gold, silver, securities, or other acceptable assets having a value sufficient in the opinion of the Fund to protect its interests and may require as a condition of waiver the pledge of such collateral security.

Section 5. *Ineligibility to use the Fund's resources*

Whenever the Fund is of the opinion that any member is using the resources of the Fund in a manner contrary to the purposes of the Fund, it shall present to the member a report setting forth the views of the Fund and prescribing a suitable time for reply. After presenting such a report to a member, the Fund may limit the use of its resources by the member. If no reply to the report is received from the member within the prescribed time, or if the reply received is unsatisfactory, the Fund may continue to limit the member's use of the Fund's resources or may, after giving reasonable notice to the member, declare it ineligible to use the resources of the Fund.

Section 6. *Purchases of currencies from the Fund for gold*

(a) Any member desiring to obtain, directly or indirectly, the currency of another member for gold shall, provided that it can do so with equal advantage, acquire it by the sale of gold to the Fund.

(b) Nothing in this Section shall be deemed to preclude any member from selling in any market gold newly produced from mines located within its territories.

Section 7. *Repurchase by a member of its currency held by the Fund*

(a) A member may repurchase from the Fund and the Fund shall sell for gold any part of the Fund's holdings of its currency in excess of its quota.

(b) At the end of each financial year of the Fund, a member shall repurchase from the Fund with gold or convertible currencies, as determined in accordance with Schedule B, part of the Fund's holdings of its currency under the following conditions:

(i) Each member shall use in repurchases of its own currency from the Fund an amount of its monetary reserves equal in value to one-half of any increase that has occurred during the year in the Fund's holdings of its currency plus one-half of any increase, or minus one-half of any decrease, that has occurred during the year in the member's monetary reserves. This rule shall not apply when a member's monetary reserves have decreased during the year by more than the Fund's holdings of its currency have increased.

(ii) If after the repurchase described in (i) above (if required) has been made, a member's holdings of another member's currency (or of gold acquired from that member) are found to have increased by reason of transactions in terms of that currency with other members or persons in their territories, the member whose holdings of such currency (or gold) have thus increased shall use the increase to repurchase its own currency from the Fund.

(c) None of the adjustments described in (b) above shall be carried to a point at which

(i) the member's monetary reserves are below its quota, or

(ii) the Fund's holdings of its currency are below seventy-five percent of its quota, or

(iii) the Fund's holdings of any currency required to be used are above seventy-five percent of the quota of the member concerned.

Section 8. *Charges*

(a) Any member buying the currency of another member from the Fund in exchange for its own currency shall pay a service charge uniform for all members of three-fourths percent in addition to the parity price. The Fund in its discretion may increase this service charge to not more than one percent or reduce it to not less than one-half percent.

(b) The Fund may levy a reasonable handling charge on any member buying gold from the Fund or selling gold to the Fund.

(c) The Fund shall levy charges uniform for all members which shall be payable by any member on the average daily balances of its currency held by the Fund in excess of its quota. These charges shall be at the following rates:

(i) *On amounts not more than twenty-five percent in excess of the quota:* no charge for the first three months; one-half percent per annum for the next nine months; and thereafter an increase in the charge of one-half percent for each subsequent year.

(ii) *On amounts more than twenty-five percent and not more than fifty percent in excess of the quota:* an additional one-half percent for the first year; and an additional one-half percent for each subsequent year.

(iii) *On each additional bracket of twenty-five percent in excess of the quota:* an additional one-half percent for the first year; and an additional one-half percent for each subsequent year.

(d) Whenever the Fund's holdings of a member's currency are such that the charge applicable to any bracket for any period has reached the rate of four percent per annum, the Fund and the member shall consider means by which the Fund's holdings of the currency can be reduced. Thereafter, the charges shall rise in accordance with the provisions of (c) above until they reach five percent and failing agreement, the Fund may then impose such charges as it deems appropriate.

(e) The rates referred to in (c) and (d) above may be changed by a three-fourths majority of the total voting power.

(f) All charges shall be paid in gold. If, however, the member's monetary reserves are less than one-half of its quota, it shall pay in gold only that proportion of the charges due which such reserves bear to one-half of its quota, and shall pay the balance in its own currency.

ARTICLE VI
CAPITAL TRANSFERS

Section 1. *Use of the Fund's resources for capital transfers*

(a) A member may not make net use of the Fund's resources to meet a large or sustained outflow of capital, and the Fund may request a member to exercise controls to prevent such use of the resources of the Fund. If, after receiving such a request, a member fails to exercise appropriate controls, the Fund may declare the member ineligible to use the resources of the Fund.

(b) Nothing in this Section shall be deemed

(i) to prevent the use of the resources of the Fund for capital transactions of reasonable amount required for the expansion of exports or in the ordinary course of trade, banking or other business, or

(ii) to affect capital movements which are met out of a member's own resources of gold and foreign exchange, but members undertake that such capital movements will be in accordance with the purposes of the Fund.

Section 2. *Special provisions for capital transfers*

If the Fund's holdings of the currency of a member have remained below seventy-five percent of its quota for an immediately preceding period of not less than six months, such member, if it has not been declared ineligible to use the resources of the Fund under Section 1 of this Article, Article IV, Section 6, Article V, Section 5, or Article XV, Section 2 (a), shall be entitled, notwithstanding the provisions of Section 1 (a) of this Article, to buy the currency of another member from the Fund with its own currency for any purpose, including capital transfers. Purchases for capital transfers under this Section shall not, however, be permitted if they have the effect of raising the Fund's holdings of the currency of the member desiring to purchase above seventy-five percent of its quota, or of reducing the Fund's holdings of the currency desired below seventy-five percent of the quota of the member whose currency is desired.

Section 3. *Controls of capital transfers*

Members may exercise such controls as are necessary to regulate international capital movements, but no member may exercise these controls in a manner which will restrict payments for current transactions or which will unduly delay transfers of funds in settlement of commitments, except as provided in Article VII, Section 3 (b), and in Article XIV, Section 2.

ARTICLE VII

SCARCE CURRENCIES

Section 1. *General scarcity of currency*

If the Fund finds that a general scarcity of a particular currency is developing, the Fund may so inform members and may issue a report setting forth the causes of the scarcity and containing recommendations designed to bring it to an end. A representative of the member whose currency is involved shall participate in the preparation of the report.

Section 2. *Measures to replenish the Fund's holdings of scarce currencies*

The Fund may, if it deems such action appropriate to replenish its holdings of any member's currency, take either or both of the following steps:

(i) Propose to the member that, on terms and conditions agreed between the Fund and the member, the latter lend its currency to the Fund or that, with the approval of the member, the Fund borrow such currency from some other source either within or outside the territories of the member, but no member shall be under any obligation to make such loans to the Fund or to approve the borrowing of its currency by the Fund from any other source.

(ii) Require the member to sell its currency to the Fund for gold.

Section 3. *Scarcity of the Fund's holdings*

(a) If it becomes evident to the Fund that the demand for a member's currency seriously threatens the Fund's ability to supply that currency, the Fund, whether or not it has issued a report under Section 1 of this Article, shall formally declare such currency scarce and shall thenceforth apportion its existing and accruing supply of the scarce currency with due regard to the relative needs of members, the general international economic situation and any other pertinent considerations. The Fund shall also issue a report concerning its action.

(b) A formal declaration under (a) above shall operate as an authorization to any member, after consultation with the Fund, temporarily to impose limitations on the freedom of exchange operations in the scarce currency. Subject to the provisions of Article IV, Sections 3 and 4, the member shall have complete jurisdiction in determining the nature of such limitations, but they shall be no more restrictive than is necessary to limit the demand for the scarce currency to the supply held by, or accruing to, the member in question; and they shall be relaxed and removed as rapidly as conditions permit.

(c) The authorization under (b) above shall expire whenever the Fund formally declares the currency in question to be no longer scarce.

Section 4. *Administration of restrictions*

Any member imposing restrictions in respect of the currency of any other member pursuant to the provisions of Section 3 (b) of this Article shall give sympathetic consideration to any representations by the other member regarding the administration of such restrictions.

Section 5. *Effect of other international agreements on restrictions*

Members agree not to invoke the obligations of any engagements entered into with other members prior to this Agreement in such a manner as will prevent the operation of the provisions of this Article.

ARTICLE VIII
GENERAL OBLIGATIONS OF MEMBERS

Section 1. *Introduction*

In addition to the obligations assumed under other articles of this Agreement, each member undertakes the obligations set out in this Article.

Section 2. *Avoidance of restrictions on current payments*

(a) Subject to the provisions of Article VII, Section 3 (b), and Article XIV, Section 2, no member shall, without the approval of the Fund, impose restrictions on the making of payments and transfers for current international transactions.

(b) Exchange contracts which involve the currency of any member and which are contrary to the exchange control regulations of that member maintained or imposed consistently with this Agreement shall be unenforceable in the territories of any member. In addition, members may, by mutual accord, co-operate in measures for the purpose of making the exchange control regulations of either member more effective, provided that such measures and regulations are consistent with this Agreement.

Section 3. *Avoidance of discriminatory currency practices*

No member shall engage in, or permit any of its fiscal agencies referred to in Article V, Section 1, to engage in, any discriminatory currency arrangements or multiple currency practices except as authorized under this Agreement or approved by the Fund. If such arrangements and practices are engaged in at the date when this Agreement enters into force the member concerned shall consult with the Fund as to their progressive removal unless they are maintained or imposed under Article XIV, Section 2, in which case the provisions of Section 4 of that Article shall apply.

Section 4. *Convertibility of foreign held balances*

(a) Each member shall buy balances of its currency held by another member if the latter, in requesting the purchase, represents

(i) that the balances to be bought have been recently acquired as a result of current transactions; or

(ii) that their conversion is needed for making payments for current transactions.

The buying member shall have the option to pay either in the currency of the member making the request or in gold.

(b) The obligation in (a) above shall not apply

(i) when the convertibility of the balances has been restricted consistently with Section 2 of this Article, or Article VI, Section 3; or

(ii) when the balances have accumulated as a result of transactions effected before the removal by a member of restrictions maintained or imposed under Article XIV, Section 2; or

(iii) when the balances have been acquired contrary to the exchange regulations of the member which is asked to buy them; or

(iv) when the currency of the member requesting the purchase has been declared scarce under Article VII, Section 3 (a) ; or

(v) when the member requested to make the purchase is for any reason not entitled to buy currencies of other members from the Fund for its own currency.

Section 5. *Furnishing of information*

(a) The Fund may require members to furnish it with such information as it deems necessary for its operations, including, as the minimum necessary for the effective discharge of the Fund's duties, national data on the following matters:

(i) Official holdings at home and abroad, of (1) gold, (2) foreign exchange.

(ii) Holdings at home and abroad by banking and financial agencies, other than official agencies, of (1) gold, (2) foreign exchange.

(iii) Production of gold.

(iv) Gold exports and imports according to countries of destination and origin.

(v) Total exports and imports of merchandise, in terms of local currency values, according to countries of destination and origin.

(vi) International balance of payments, including (1) trade in goods and services, (2) gold transactions, (3) known capital transactions, and (4) other items.

(vii) International investment position, *i.e.,* investments within the territories of the member owned abroad and investments abroad owned by persons in its territories so far as it is possible to furnish this information.

(viii) National income.
 (ix) Price indices, *i.e.,* indices of commodity prices in wholesale and re-tail markets and of export and import prices.
  (x) Buying and selling rates for foreign currencies.
 (xi) Exchange controls, *i.e.,* a comprehensive statement of exchange controls in effect at the time of assuming membership in the Fund and details of subsequent changes as they occur.
(xii) Where official clearing arrangements exist, details of amounts awaiting clearance in respect of commercial and financial trans-actions, and of the length of time during which such arrears have been outstanding.

(b) In requesting information the Fund shall take into consideration the varying ability of members to furnish the data requested. Members shall be under no obligation to furnish information in such detail that the affairs of individuals or corporations are disclosed. Members undertake, however, to fur-nish the desired information in as detailed and accurate a manner as is prac-ticable, and, so far as possible, to avoid mere estimates.

(c) The Fund may arrange to obtain further information by agreement with members. It shall act as a centre for the collection and exchange of information on monetary and financial problems, thus facilitating the preparation of studies designed to assist members in developing policies which further the purposes of the Fund.

Section 6. *Consultation between members regarding existing international agreements*

Where under this Agreement a member is authorized in the special or tempo-rary circumstances specified in the Agreement to maintain or establish restric-tions on exchange transactions, and there are other engagements between mem-bers entered into prior to this Agreement which conflict with the application of such restrictions, the parties to such engagements will consult with one another with a view to making such mutually acceptable adjustments as may be necessary. The provisions of this Article shall be without prejudice to the operation of Article VII, Section 5.

ARTICLE IX
STATUS, IMMUNITIES AND PRIVILEGES
Section 1. *Purposes of Article*

To enable the Fund to fulfill the functions with which it is entrusted, the status, immunities and privileges set forth in this Article shall be accorded to the Fund in the territories of each member.

Section 2. *Status of the Fund*

The Fund shall possess full juridical personality, and, in particular, the ca-pacity:
  (i) to contract;

Bretton Woods Agreements

Bretton Woods Agreements 347

ly>Woods Agreements* 347

(ii) to acquire and dispose of immovable and movable property;
(iii) to institute legal proceedings.

Section 3. *Immunity from judicial process*

The Fund, its property and its assets, wherever located and by whomsoever held, shall enjoy immunity from every form of judicial process except to the extent that it expressly waives its immunity for the purpose of any proceedings or by the terms of any contract.

Section 4. *Immunity from other action*

Property and assets of the Fund, wherever located and by whomsoever held, shall be immune from search, requisition, confiscation, expropriation or any other form of seizure by executive or legislative action.

Section 5. *Immunity of archives*

The archives of the Fund shall be inviolable.

Section 6. *Freedom of assets from restrictions*

To the extent necessary to carry out the operations provided for in this Agreement, all property and assets of the Fund shall be free from restrictions, regulations, controls and moratoria of any nature.

Section 7. *Privilege for communications*

The official communications of the Fund shall be accorded by members the same treatment as the official communications of other members.

Section 8. *Immunities and privileges of officers and employees*

All governors, executive directors, alternates, officers and employees of the Fund

(i) shall be immune from legal process with respect to acts performed by them in their official capacity except when the Fund waives this immunity.
(ii) not being local nationals, shall be granted the same immunities from immigration restrictions, alien registration requirements and national service obligations and the same facilities as regards exchange restrictions as are accorded by members to the representatives, officials, and employees of comparable rank of other members.
(iii) shall be granted the same treatment in respect of travelling facilities as is accorded by members to representatives, officials and employees of comparable rank of other members.

Section 9. *Immunities from taxation*

(a) The Fund, its assets, property, income and its operations and transactions authorized by this Agreement, shall be immune from all taxation and from all customs duties. The Fund shall also be immune from liability for the collection or payment of any tax or duty.

(b) No tax shall be levied on or in respect of salaries and emoluments paid by the Fund to executive directors, alternates, officers or employees of the Fund who are not local citizens, local subjects, or other local nationals.

(c) No taxation of any kind shall be levied on any obligation or security issued by the Fund, including any dividend or interest thereon, by whomsoever held

(i) which discriminates against such obligation or security solely because of its origin; or

(ii) if the sole jurisdictional basis for such taxation is the place or currency in which it is issued, made payable or paid, or the location of any office or place of business maintained by the Fund.

Section 10. *Application of Article*

Each member shall take such action as is necessary in its own territories for the purpose of making effective in terms of its own law the principles set forth in this Article and shall inform the Fund of the detailed action which it has taken.

ARTICLE X

RELATIONS WITH OTHER INTERNATIONAL ORGANIZATIONS

The Fund shall cooperate within the terms of this Agreement with any general international organization and with public international organizations having specialized responsibilities in related fields. Any arrangements for such cooperation which would involve a modification of any provision of this Agreement may be effected only after amendment to this Agreement under Article XVII.

ARTICLE XI

RELATIONS WITH NON-MEMBER COUNTRIES

Section 1. *Undertakings regarding relations with non-member countries*

Each member undertakes:

(i) Not to engage in, nor to permit any of its fiscal agencies referred to in Article V, Section 1, to engage in, any transactions with a non-member or with persons in a non-member's territories which would be contrary to the provisions of this Agreement or the purposes of the Fund;

(ii) Not to cooperate with a non-member or with persons in a non-member's territories in practices which would be contrary to the provisions of this Agreement or the purposes of the Fund; and

(iii) To cooperate with the Fund with a view to the application in its territories of appropriate measures to prevent transactions with non-members or with persons in their territories which would be contrary to the provisions of this Agreement or the purposes of the Fund.

Section 2. *Restrictions on transactions with non-member countries*

Nothing in this Agreement shall affect the right of any member to impose restrictions on exchange transactions with non-members or with persons in their territories unless the Fund finds that such restrictions prejudice the interests of members and are contrary to the purposes of the Fund.

ARTICLE XII

ORGANIZATION AND MANAGEMENT

Section 1. *Structure of the Fund*

The Fund shall have a Board of Governors, Executive Directors, a Managing Director and a staff.

Section 2. *Board of Governors*

(a) All powers of the Fund shall be vested in the Board of Governors, consisting of one governor and one alternate appointed by each member in such manner as it may determine. Each governor and each alternate shall serve for five years, subject to the pleasure of the member appointing him, and may be reappointed. No alternate may vote except in the absence of his principal. The Board shall select one of the governors as chairman.

(b) The Board of Governors may delegate to the Executive Directors authority to exercise any powers of the Board, except the power to:

(i) Admit new members and determine the conditions of their admission.

(ii) Approve a revision of quotas.

(iii) Approve a uniform change in the par value of the currencies of all members.

(iv) Make arrangements to cooperate with other international organizations (other than informal arrangements of a temporary or administrative character).

(v) Determine the distribution of the net income of the Fund.

(vi) Require a member to withdraw.

(vii) Decide to liquidate the Fund.

(viii) Decide appeals from interpretations of this Agreement given by the Executive Directors.

(c) The Board of Governors shall hold an annual meeting and such other meetings as may be provided for by the Board or called by the Executive Directors. Meetings of the Board shall be called by the Directors whenever requested by five members or by members having one quarter of the total voting power.

(d) A quorum for any meeting of the Board of Governors shall be a majority of the governors exercising not less than two-thirds of the total voting power.

(e) Each governor shall be entitled to cast the number of votes allotted under Section 5 of this Article to the member appointing him.

(f) The Board of Governors may by regulation establish a procedure whereby the Executive Directors, when they deem such action to be in the best interests of the Fund, may obtain a vote of the governors on a specific question without calling a meeting of the Board.

(g) The Board of Governors, and the Executive Directors to the extent authorized, may adopt such rules and regulations as may be necessary or appropriate to conduct the business of the Fund.

(h) Governors and alternates shall serve as such without compensation from the Fund, but the Fund shall pay them reasonable expenses incurred in attending meetings.

(i) The Board of Governors shall determine the remuneration to be paid to the Executive Directors and the salary and terms of the contract of service of the Managing Director.

Section 3. *Executive Directors*

(a) The Executive Directors shall be responsible for the conduct of the general operations of the Fund, and for this purpose shall exercise all the powers delegated to them by the Board of Governors.

(b) There shall be not less than twelve directors who need not be governors, and of whom

(i) Five shall be appointed by the five members having the largest quotas;

(ii) Not more than two shall be appointed when the provisions of (c) below apply;

(iii) Five shall be elected by the members not entitled to appoint directors, other than the American Republics; and

(iv) Two shall be elected by the American Republics not entitled to appoint directors.

For the purposes of this paragraph, members means governments of countries whose names are set forth in Schedule A, whether they become members in accordance with Article XX or in accordance with Article II, Section 2. When governments of other countries become members, the Board of Governors may, by a four-fifths majority of the total voting power, increase the number of directors to be elected.

(c) If, at the second regular election of directors and thereafter, the members entitled to appoint directors under (b) (i) above do not include the two members, the holdings of whose currencies by the Fund have been, on the average over the preceding two years, reduced below their quotas by the largest absolute amounts in terms of gold as a common denominator, either one or both of such members, as the case may be, shall be entitled to appoint a director.

(d) Subject to Article XX, Section 3 (b) elections of elective directors shall be conducted at intervals of two years in accordance with the provisions of Schedule C, supplemented by such regulations as the Fund deems appropriate. Whenever the Board of Governors increases the number of directors to be elected under (b) above, it shall issue regulations making appropriate changes in the proportion of votes required to elect directors under the provisions of Schedule C.

(e) Each director shall appoint an alternate with full power to act for him when he is not present. When the directors appointing them are present, alternates may participate in meetings but may not vote.

(f) Directors shall continue in office until their successors are appointed or elected. If the office of an elected director becomes vacant more than ninety days before the end of his term, another director shall be elected for the remainder of the term by the members who elected the former director. A majority of the votes cast shall be required for election. While the office remains vacant, the alternate of the former director shall exercise his powers, except that of appointing an alternate.

(g) The Executive Directors shall function in continuous session at the principal office of the Fund and shall meet as often as the business of the Fund may require.

(h) A quorum for any meeting of the Executive Directors shall be a majority of the directors representing not less than one-half of the voting power.

(i) Each appointed director shall be entitled to cast the number of votes allotted under Section 5 of this Article to the member appointing him. Each elected director shall be entitled to cast the number of votes which counted towards his election. When the provisions of Section 5 (b) of this Article are applicable, the votes which a director would otherwise be entitled to cast shall be increased or decreased correspondingly. All the votes which a director is entitled to cast shall be cast as a unit.

(j) The Board of Governors shall adopt regulations under which a member not entitled to appoint a director under (b) above may send a representative to attend any meeting of the Executive Directors when a request made by, or a matter particularly affecting, that member is under consideration.

(k) The Executive Directors may appoint such committees as they deem advisable. Membership of committees need not be limited to governors or directors or their alternates.

Section 4. *Managing Director and staff*

(a) The Executive Directors shall select a Managing Director who shall not be a governor or an executive director. The Managing Director shall be chairman of the Executive Directors, but shall have no vote except a deciding vote in case of an equal division. He may participate in meetings of the Board of Governors, but shall not vote at such meetings. The Managing Director shall cease to hold office when the Executive Directors so decide.

(b) The Managing Director shall be chief of the operating staff of the Fund and shall conduct, under the direction of the Executive Directors, the ordinary business of the Fund. Subject to the general control of the Executive Directors, he shall be responsible for the organization, appointment and dismissal of the staff of the Fund.

(c) The Managing Director and the staff of the Fund, in the discharge of their functions, shall owe their duty entirely to the Fund and to no other authority. Each member of the Fund shall respect the international character of this duty and shall refrain from all attempts to influence any of the staff in the discharge of his functions.

(d) In appointing the staff the Managing Director shall, subject to the paramount importance of securing the highest standards of efficiency and of technical competence, pay due regard to the importance of recruiting personnel on as wide a geographical basis as possible.

Section 5. *Voting*

(a) Each member shall have two hundred fifty votes plus one additional vote for each part of its quota equivalent to one hundred thousand United States dollars.

(b) Whenever voting is required under Article V, Section 4 or 5, each member shall have the number of votes to which it is entitled under (a) above, adjusted:

    (i) by the addition of one vote for the equivalent of each four hundred thousand United States dollars of net sales of its currency up to the date when the vote is taken, or

    (ii) by the subtraction of one vote for the equivalent of each four hundred thousand United States dollars of its net purchases of the currencies of other members up to the date when the vote is taken

provided, that neither net purchases nor net sales shall be deemed at any time to exceed an amount equal to the quota of the member involved.

(c) For the purpose of all computations under this Section, United States dollars shall be deemed to be of the weight and fineness in effect on July 1, 1944, adjusted for any uniform change under Article IV, Section 7, if a waiver is made under Section 8 (d) of that Article.

(d) Except as otherwise specifically provided, all decisions of the Fund shall be made by a majority of the votes cast.

Section 6. *Distribution of net income*

(a) The Board of Governors shall determine annually what part of the Fund's net income shall be placed to reserve and what part, if any, shall be distributed.

(b) If any distribution is made, there shall first be distributed a two percent non-cumulative payment to each member on the amount by which seventy-five percent of its quota exceeded the Fund's average holdings of its currency during that year. The balance shall be paid to all members in proportion to their quotas. Payments to each member shall be made in its own currency.

Section 7. *Publication of reports*

(a) The Fund shall publish an annual report containing an audited statement of its accounts, and shall issue, at intervals of three months or less, a summary statement of its transactions and its holdings of gold and currencies of members.

(b) The Fund may publish such other reports as it deems desirable for carrying out its purposes.

Section 8. *Communication of views to members*

The Fund shall at all times have the right to communicate its views informally to any member on any matter arising under this Agreement. The Fund may, by a two-thirds majority of the total voting power, decide to publish a report made to a member regarding its monetary or economic conditions and developments which directly tend to produce a serious disequilibrium in the international balance of payments of members. If the member is not entitled to appoint an executive director, it shall be entitled to representation in accordance with Section 3 (j) of this Article. The Fund shall not publish a report involving changes in the fundamental structure of the economic organization of members.

ARTICLE XIII
OFFICES AND DEPOSITORIES

Section 1. *Location of offices*

The principal office of the Fund shall be located in the territory of the member having the largest quota, and agencies or branch offices may be established in the territories of other members.

Section 2. *Depositories*

(a) Each member country shall designate its central bank as a depository for all the Fund's holdings of its currency, or if it has no central bank it shall designate such other institution as may be acceptable to the Fund.

(b) The Fund may hold other assets, including gold, in the depositories designated by the five members having the largest quotas and in such other designated depositories as the Fund may select. Initially, at least one-half of the holdings of the Fund shall be held in the depository designated by the member in whose territories the Fund has its principal office and at least forty percent shall be held in the depositories designated by the remaining four members referred to above. However, all transfers of gold by the Fund shall be made with due regard to the costs of transport and anticipated requirements of the Fund. In an emergency the Executive Directors may transfer all or any part of the Fund's gold holdings to any place where they can be adequately protected.

Section 3. *Guarantee of the Fund's assets*

Each member guarantees all assets of the Fund against loss resulting from failure or default on the part of the depository designated by it.

ARTICLE XIV
TRANSITIONAL PERIOD

Section 1. *Introduction*

The Fund is not intended to provide facilities for relief or reconstruction or to deal with international indebtedness arising out of the war.

Section 2. *Exchange restrictions*

In the post-war transitional period members may, notwithstanding the provisions of any other articles of this Agreement, maintain and adapt to changing circumstances (and, in the case of members whose territories have been occupied by the enemy, introduce where necessary) restrictions on payments and transfers for current international transactions. Members shall, however, have continuous regard in their foreign exchange policies to the purposes of the Fund; and, as soon as conditions permit, they shall take all possible measures to develop such commercial and financial arrangements with other members as will facilitate international payments and the maintenance of exchange stability. In particular, members shall withdraw restrictions maintained or imposed under this Section as soon as they are satisfied that they will be able, in the absence of such restrictions, to settle their balance of payments in a manner which will not unduly encumber their access to the resources of the Fund.

Section 3. *Notification to the Fund*

Each member shall notify the Fund before it becomes eligible under Article XX, Section 4 (c) or (d) to buy currency from the Fund, whether it intends to avail itself of the transitional arrangements in Section 2 of this Article, or whether it is prepared to accept the obligations of Article VIII, Sections 2, 3, and 4. A member availing itself of the transitional arrangements shall notify the Fund as soon thereafter as it is prepared to accept the above-mentioned obligations.

Section 4. *Action of the Fund relating to restrictions*

Not later than three years after the date on which the Fund begins operations and in each year thereafter, the Fund shall report on the restrictions still in force under Section 2 of this Article. Five years after the date on which the Fund begins operations, and in each year thereafter, any member still retaining any restrictions inconsistent with Article VIII, Sections 2, 3, or 4, shall consult the Fund as to their further retention. The Fund may, if it deems such action necessary in exceptional circumstances, make representations to any member that conditions are favorable for the withdrawal of any particular restriction, or for the general abandonment of restrictions, inconsistent with the provisions of any other articles of this Agreement. The member shall be given a suitable time to reply to such representations. If the Fund finds that the member persists in maintaining restrictions which are inconsistent with the purposes of the Fund, the member shall be subject to Article XV, Section 2 (a).

Section 5. *Nature of transitional period*

In its relations with members, the Fund shall recognize that the post-war transitional period will be one of change and adjustment and in making decisions on requests occasioned thereby which are presented by any member it shall give the member the benefit of any reasonable doubt.

ARTICLE XV
WITHDRAWAL FROM MEMBERSHIP

Section 1. *Right of members to withdraw*

Any member may withdraw from the Fund at any time by transmitting a notice in writing to the Fund at its principal office. Withdrawal shall become effective on the date such notice is received.

Section 2. *Compulsory withdrawal*

(a) If a member fails to fulfill any of its obligations under this Agreement, the Fund may declare the member ineligible to use the resources of the Fund. Nothing in this Section shall be deemed to limit the provisions of Article IV, Section 6, Article V, Section 5, or Article VI, Section 1.

(b) If, after the expiration of a reasonable period the member persists in its failure to fulfill any of its obligations under this Agreement, or a difference between a member and the Fund under Article IV, Section 6, continues, that member may be required to withdraw from membership in the Fund by a decision of the Board of Governors carried by a majority of the governors representing a majority of the total voting power.

(c) Regulations shall be adopted to ensure that before action is taken against any member under (a) or (b) above, the member shall be informed in reasonable time of the complaint against it and given an adequate opportunity for stating its case, both orally and in writing.

Section 3. *Settlement of accounts with members withdrawing*

When a member withdraws from the Fund, normal transactions of the Fund in its currency shall cease and settlement of all accounts between it and the Fund shall be made with reasonable despatch by agreement between it and the Fund. If agreement is not reached promptly, the provisions of Schedule D shall apply to the settlement of accounts.

ARTICLE XVI
EMERGENCY PROVISIONS

Section 1. *Temporary suspension*

(a) In the event of an emergency or the development of unforeseen circumstances threatening the operations of the Fund, the Executive Directors by unanimous vote may suspend for a period of not more than one hundred twenty days the operation of any of the following provisions:

    (i) Article IV, Sections 3 and 4 (b)
    (ii) Article V, Sections 2, 3, 7, 8 (a) and (f)
    (iii) Article VI, Section 2
    (iv) Article XI, Section 1

(b) Simultaneously with any decision to suspend the operation of any of the foregoing provisions, the Executive Directors shall call a meeting of the Board of Governors for the earliest practicable date.

(c) The Executive Directors may not extend any suspension beyond one hundred twenty days. Such suspension may be extended, however, for an additional period of not more than two hundred forty days, if the Board of Governors by a four-fifths majority of the total voting power so decides, but it may not be further extended except by amendment of this Agreement pursuant to Article XVII.

(d) The Executive Directors may, by a majority of the total voting power, terminate such suspension at any time.

Section 2. *Liquidation of the Fund*

(a) The Fund may not be liquidated except by decision of the Board of Governors. In an emergency, if the Executive Directors decide that liquidation of the Fund may be necessary, they may temporarily suspend all transactions, pending decision by the Board.

(b) If the Board of Governors decides to liquidate the Fund, the Fund shall forthwith cease to engage in any activities except those incidental to the orderly collection and liquidation of its assets and the settlement of its liabilities, and all obligations of members under this Agreement shall cease except those set out in this Article, in Article XVIII, paragraph (c), in Schedule D, paragraph 7, and in Schedule E.

(c) Liquidation shall be administered in accordance with the provisions of Schedule E.

ARTICLE XVII
AMENDMENTS

(a) Any proposal to introduce modifications in this Agreement, whether emanating from a member, a governor or the Executive Directors, shall be communicated to the chairman of the Board of Governors who shall bring the proposal before the Board. If the proposed amendment is approved by the Board the Fund shall, by circular letter or telegram, ask all members whether they accept the proposed amendment. When three-fifths of the members, having four-fifths of the total voting power, have accepted the proposed amendment, the Fund shall certify the fact by a formal communication addressed to all members.

(b) Notwithstanding (a) above, acceptance by all members is required in the case of any amendment modifying

(i) the right to withdraw from the Fund (Article XV, Section 1) ;
(ii) the provision that no change in a member's quota shall be made without its consent (Article III, Section 2) ;
(iii) the provision that no change may be made in the par value of a member's currency except on the proposal of that member (Article IV, Section 5 (b)).

(c) Amendments shall enter into force for all members three months after the date of the formal communication unless a shorter period is specified in the circular letter or telegram.

ARTICLE XVIII
INTERPRETATION

(a) Any question of interpretation of the provisions of this Agreement arising between any member and the Fund or between any members of the Fund shall be submitted to the Executive Directors for their decision. If the question particularly affects any member not entitled to appoint an executive director it shall be entitled to representation in accordance with Article XII, Section 3 (j).

(b) In any case where the Executive Directors have given a decision under (a) above, any member may require that the question be referred to the Board of Governors, whose decision shall be final. Pending the result of the reference to the Board the Fund may, so far as it deems necessary, act on the basis of the decision of the Executive Directors.

(c) Whenever a disagreement arises between the Fund and a member which has withdrawn, or between the Fund and any member during liquidation of the Fund, such disagreement shall be submitted to arbitration by a tribunal of three arbitrators, one appointed by the Fund, another by the member or withdrawing member and an umpire who, unless the parties otherwise agree, shall be appointed by the President of the Permanent Court of International Justice or such other authority as may have been prescribed by regulation adopted by the Fund. The umpire shall have full power to settle all questions of procedure in any case where the parties are in disagreement with respect thereto.

ARTICLE XIX
EXPLANATION OF TERMS

In interpreting the provisions of this Agreement the Fund and its members shall be guided by the following:

(a) A member's monetary reserves means its net official holdings of gold, of convertible currencies of other members, and of the currencies of such non-members as the Fund may specify.

(b) The official holdings of a member means central holdings (that is, the holdings of its Treasury, central bank, stabilization fund, or similar fiscal agency).

(c) The holdings of other official institutions or other banks within its territories may, in any particular case, be deemed by the Fund, after consultation with the member, to be official holdings to the extent that they are substantially in excess of working balances; provided that for the purpose of determining whether, in a particular case, holdings are in excess of working balances, there shall be deducted from such holdings amounts of currency due to official institutions and banks in the territories of members or non-members specified under (d) below.

(d) A member's holdings of convertible currencies means its holdings of the currencies of other members which are not availing themselves of the transitional arrangements under Article XIV, Section 2, together with its holdings of the currencies of such non-members as the Fund may from time to time specify. The term currency for this purpose includes without limitation coins, paper money, bank balances, bank acceptances, and government obligations issued with a maturity not exceeding twelve months.

(e) A member's monetary reserves shall be calculated by deducting from its central holdings the currency liabilities to the Treasuries, central banks, stabilization funds, or similar fiscal agencies of other members or non-members specified under (d) above, together with similar liabilities to other official institutions and other banks in the territories of members, or non-members specified under (d) above. To these net holdings shall be added the sums deemed to be official holdings of other official institutions and other banks under (c) above.

(f) The Fund's holdings of the currency of a member shall include any securities accepted by the Fund under Article III, Section 5.

(g) The Fund, after consultation with a member which is availing itself of the transitional arrangements under Article XIV, Section 2, may deem holdings of the currency of that member which carry specified rights of conversion into another currency or into gold to be holdings of convertible currency for the purpose of the calculation of monetary reserves.

(h) For the purpose of calculating gold subscriptions under Article III, Section 3, a member's net official holdings of gold and United States dollars shall consist of its official holdings of gold and United States currency after deducting central holdings of its currency by other countries and holdings of its currency by other official institutions and other banks if these holdings carry specified rights of conversion into gold or United States currency.

(i) Payments for current transactions means payments which are not for the purpose of transferring capital, and includes, without limitation:

(1) All payments due in connection with foreign trade, other current business, including services, and normal short-term banking and credit facilities;

(2) Payments due as interest on loans and as net income from other investments;

(3) Payments of moderate amount for amortization of loans or for depreciation of direct investments;

(4) Moderate remittances for family living expenses.

The Fund may, after consultation with the members concerned, determine whether certain specific transactions are to be considered current transactions or capital transactions.

ARTICLE XX

FINAL PROVISIONS

Section 1. *Entry into force*

This Agreement shall enter into force when it has been signed on behalf of governments having sixty-five percent of the total of the quotas set forth in Schedule A and when the instruments referred to in Section 2 (a) of this Article have been deposited on their behalf, but in no event shall this Agreement enter into force before May 1, 1945.

Section 2. *Signature*

(a) Each government on whose behalf this Agreement is signed shall de-

Bretton Woods Agreements

posit with the Government of the United States of America an instrument setting forth that it has accepted this Agreement in accordance with its law and has taken all steps necessary to enable it to carry out all of its obligations under Agreement.

(b) Each government shall become a member of the Fund as from the date of the deposit on its behalf of the instrument referred to in (a) above, except that no government shall become a member before this Agreement enters into force under Section 1 of this Article.

(c) The Government of the United States of America shall inform the governments of all countries whose names are set forth in Schedule A, and all governments whose membership is approved in accordance with Article II, Section 2, of all signatures of this Agreement and of the deposit of all instruments referred to in (a) above.

(d) At the time this Agreement is signed on its behalf, each government shall transmit to the Government of the United States of America one one-hundredth of one percent of its total subscription in gold or United States dollars for the purpose of meeting administrative expenses of the Fund. The Government of the United States of America shall hold such funds in a special deposit account and shall transmit them to the Board of Governors of the Fund when the initial meeting has been called under Section 3 of this Article. If this Agreement has not come into force by December 31, 1945, the Government of the United States of America shall return such funds to the governments that transmitted them.

(e) This Agreement shall remain open for signature at Washington on behalf of the governments of the countries whose names are set forth in Schedule A until December 31, 1945.

(f) After December 31, 1945, this Agreement shall be open for signature on behalf of the government of any country whose membership has been approved in accordance with Article II, Section 2.

(g) By their signature of this Agreement, all governments accept it both on their own behalf and in respect of all their colonies, overseas territories, all territories under their protection, suzerainty, or authority and all territories in respect of which they exercise a mandate.

(h) In the case of governments whose metropolitan territories have been under enemy occupation, the deposit of the instrument referred to in (a) above may be delayed until one hundred eighty days after the date on which these territories have been liberated. If, however, it is not deposited by any such government before the expiration of this period the signature affixed on behalf of that government shall become void and the portion of its subscription paid under (d) above shall be returned to it.

(i) Paragraphs (d) and (h) shall come into force with regard to each signatory government as from the date of its signature.

Section 3. *Inauguration of the Fund*

(a) As soon as this Agreement enters into force under Section 1 of this

Article, each member shall appoint a governor and the member having the largest quota shall call the first meeting of the Board of Governors.

(b) At the first meeting of the Board of Governors, arrangements shall be made for the selection of provisional executive directors. The governments of the five countries for which the largest quotas are set forth in Schedule A shall appoint provisional executive directors. If one or more of such governments have not become members, the executive directorships they would be entitled to fill shall remain vacant until they become members, or until January 1, 1946, whichever is the earlier. Seven provisional executive directors shall be elected in accordance with the provisions of Schedule C and shall remain in office until the date of the first regular election of executive directors which shall be held as soon as practicable after January 1, 1946.

(c) The Board of Governors may delegate to the provisional executive directors any powers except those which may not be delegated to the Executive Directors.

Section 4. *Initial determination of par values*

(a) When the Fund is of the opinion that it will shortly be in a position to begin exchange transactions, it shall so notify the members and shall request each member to communicate within thirty days the par value of its currency based on the rates of exchange prevailing on the sixtieth day before the entry into force of this Agreement. No member whose metropolitan territory has been occupied by the enemy shall be required to make such a communication while that territory is a theater of major hostilities or for such period thereafter as the Fund may determine. When such a member communicates the par value of its currency the provisions of (d) below shall apply.

(b) The par value communicated by a member whose metropolitan territory has not been occupied by the enemy shall be the par value of that member's currency for the purposes of this Agreement unless, within ninety days after the request referred to in (a) above has been received, (i) the member notifies the Fund that it regards the par value as unsatisfactory, or (ii) the Fund notifies the member that in its opinion the par value cannot be maintained without causing recourse to the Fund on the part of that member or others on a scale prejudicial to the Fund and to members. When notification is given under (i) or (ii) above, the Fund and the member shall, within a period determined by the Fund in the light of all relevant circumstances, agree upon a suitable par value for that currency. If the Fund and the member do not agree within the period so determined, the member shall be deemed to have withdrawn from the Fund on the date when the period expires.

(c) When the par value of a member's currency has been established under (b) above, either by the expiration of ninety days without notification, or by agreement after notification, the member shall be eligible to buy from the Fund the currencies of other members to the full extent permitted in this Agreement, provided that the Fund has begun exchange transactions.

(d) In the case of a member whose metropolitan territory has been occupied by the enemy, the provisions of (b) above shall apply, subject to the following modifications:

(i) The period of ninety days shall be extended so as to end on a date to be fixed by agreement between the Fund and the member.

(ii) Within the extended period the member may, if the Fund has begun exchange transactions, buy from the Fund with its currency the currencies of other members, but only under such conditions and in such amounts as may be prescribed by the Fund.

(iii) At any time before the date fixed under (i) above, changes may be made by agreement with the Fund in the par value communicated under (a) above.

(e) If a member whose metropolitan territory has been occupied by the enemy adopts a new monetary unit before the date to be fixed under (d) (i) above, the par value fixed by that member for the new unit shall be commmunicated to the Fund and the provisions of (d) above shall apply.

(f) Changes in par values agreed with the Fund under this Section shall not be taken into account in determining whether a proposed change falls within (i), (ii), or (iii) of Article IV, Section 5 (c).

(g) A member communicating to the Fund a par value for the currency of its metropolitan territory shall simultaneously communicate a value, in terms of that currency, for each separate currency, where such exists, in the territories in respect of which it has accepted this Agreement under Section 2 (g) of this Article, but no member shall be required to make a communication for the separate currency of a territory which has been occupied by the enemy while that territory is a theater of major hostilities or for such period thereafter as the Fund may determine. On the basis of the par value so communicated, the Fund shall compute the par value of each separate currency. A communication or notification to the Fund under (a), (b) or (d) above regarding the par value of a currency, shall also be deemed, unless the contrary is stated, to be a communication or notification regarding the par value of all the separate currencies referred to above. Any member may, however, make a communication or notification relating to the metropolitan or any of the separate currencies alone. If the member does so, the provisions of the preceding paragraphs (including (d) above, if a territory where a separate currency exists has been occupied by the enemy) shall apply to each of these currencies separately.

(h) The Fund shall begin exchange transactions at such date as it may determine after members having sixty-five percent of the total of the quotas set forth in Schedule A have become eligible, in accordance with the preceding paragraphs of this Section, to purchase the currencies of other members, but in no event until after major hostilities in Europe have ceased.

(i) The Fund may postpone exchange transactions with any member if its circumstances are such that, in the opinion of the Fund, they would lead to use of the resources of the Fund in a manner contrary to the purposes of this Agreement or prejudicial to the Fund or the members.

(j) The par values of the currencies of governments which indicate their desire to become members after December 31, 1945, shall be determined in accordance with the provisions of Article II, Section 2.

DONE at Washington, in a single copy which shall remain deposited in the archives of the Government of the United States of America, which shall transmit certified copies to all governments whose names are set forth in Schedule A and to all governments whose membership is approved in accordance with Article II, Section 2.

SCHEDULE A
QUOTAS

	(In millions of United States dollars)		(In millions of United States dollars)
Australia	200	India	400
Belgium	225	Iran	25
Bolivia	10	Iraq	8
Brazil	150	Liberia	.5
Canada	300	Luxembourg	10
Chile	50	Mexico	90
China	550	Netherlands	275
Colombia	50	New Zealand	50
Costa Rica	5	Nicaragua	2
Cuba	50	Norway	50
Czechoslovakia	125	Panama	.5
Denmark*	*	Paraguay	2
Dominican Republic	5	Peru	25
Ecuador	5	Philippine Commonwealth	15
Egypt	45	Poland	125
El Salvador	2.5	Union of South Africa	100
Ethiopia	6	Union of Soviet Socialist	
France	450	Republics	1200
Greece	40	United Kingdom	1300
Guatemala	5	United States	2750
Haiti	5	Uruguay	15
Honduras	2.5	Venezuela	15
Iceland	1	Yugoslavia	60

*The quota of Denmark shall be determined by the Fund after the Danish Government has declared its readiness to sign this Agreement but before signature takes place.

SCHEDULE B
PROVISIONS WITH RESPECT TO REPURCHASE BY A MEMBER OF ITS CURRENCY HELD BY THE FUND

1. In determining the extent to which repurchase of a member's currency from the Fund under Article V, Section 7 (b) shall be made with each type of monetary reserve, that is, with gold and with each convertible currency, the following rule, subject to 2 below, shall apply:

(a) If the member's monetary reserves have not increased during the year, the amount payable to the Fund shall be distributed among all types of reserves in proportion to the member's holdings thereof at the end of the year.

(b) If the member's monetary reserves have increased during the year, a part of the amount payable to the Fund equal to one-half of the increase shall be distributed among those types of reserves which have increased in proportion to the amount by which each of them has increased. The remainder of the sum payable to the Fund shall be distributed among all types of reserves in proportion to the member's remaining holdings thereof.

(c) If after all the repurchases required under Article V, Section 7 (b), had been made, the result would exceed any of the limits specified in Article V, Section 7 (c), the Fund shall require such repurchases to be made by the members proportionately in such manner that the limits will not be exceeded.

2. The Fund shall not acquire the currency of any non-member under Article V, Section 7 (b) and (c).

3. In calculating monetary reserves and the increase in monetary reserves during any year for the purpose of Article V, Section 7 (b) and (c), no account shall be taken, unless deductions have otherwise been made by the member for such holdings, of any increase in those monetary reserves which is due to currency previously inconvertible having become convertible during the year; or to holdings which are the proceeds of a long-term or medium-term loan contracted during the year; or to holdings which have been transferred or set aside for repayment of a loan during the subsequent year.

4. In the case of members whose metropolitan territories have been occupied by the enemy, gold newly produced during the five years after the entry into force of this Agreement from mines located within their metropolitan territories shall not be included in computations of their monetary reserves or of increases in their monetary reserves.

SCHEDULE C

ELECTION OF EXECUTIVE DIRECTORS

1. The election of the elective executive directors shall be by ballot of the governors eligible to vote under Article XII, Section 3 (b) (iii) and (iv).

2. In balloting for the five directors to be elected under Article XII, Section 3 (b) (iii), each of the governors eligible to vote shall cast for one person all of the votes to which he is entitled under Article XII, Section 5 (a). The five persons receiving the greatest number of votes shall be directors, provided that no person who received less than nineteen percent of the total number of votes that can be cast (eligible votes) shall be considered elected.

3. When five persons are not elected in the first ballot, a second ballot shall be held in which the person who received the lowest number of votes shall be ineligible for election and in which there shall vote only (a) those governors who voted in the first ballot for a person not elected, and (b) those governors whose votes for a person elected are deemed under 4 below to have raised the votes cast for that person above twenty percent of the eligible votes.

4. In determining whether the votes cast by a governor are to be deemed to have raised the total of any person above twenty percent of the eligible votes the twenty percent shall be deemed to include, first, the votes of the governor casting the largest number of votes for such person, then the votes of the governor casting the next largest number, and so on until twenty percent is reached.

5. Any governor part of whose votes must be counted in order to raise the total of any person above nineteen percent shall be considered as casting all of his votes for such person even if the total votes for such person thereby exceed twenty percent.

6. If, after the second ballot, five persons have not been elected, further ballots shall be held on the same principles until five persons have been elected, provided that after four persons are elected, the fifth may be elected by a simple majority of the remaining votes and shall be deemed to have been elected by all such votes.

7. The directors to be elected by the American Republics under Article XII, Section 3 (b) (iv) shall be elected as follows:

(a) Each of the directors shall be elected separately.

(b) In the election of the first director, each governor representing an American Republic eligible to participate in the election shall cast for one person all the votes to which he is entitled. The person receiving the largest number of votes shall be elected provided that he has received not less than forty-five percent of the total votes.

(c) If no person is elected on the first ballot, further ballots shall be held, in each of which the person receiving the lowest number of votes shall be eliminated, until one person receives a number of votes sufficient for election under (b) above.

(d) Governors whose votes contributed to the election of the first director shall take no part in the election of the second director.

(e) Persons who did not succeed in the first election shall not be ineligible for election as the second director.

(f) A majority of the votes which can be cast shall be required for election of the second director. If at the first ballot no person receives a majority, further ballots shall be held in each of which the person receiving the lowest number of votes shall be eliminated, until some person obtains a majority.

(g) The second director shall be deemed to have been elected by all the votes which could have been cast in the ballot securing his election.

SCHEDULE D
SETTLEMENT OF ACCOUNTS WITH MEMBERS WITHDRAWING

1. The Fund shall be obligated to pay to a member withdrawing an amount equal to its quota, plus any other amounts due to it from the Fund, less any amounts due to the Fund, including charges accruing after the date of its with-

drawal; but no payment shall be made until six months after the date of withdrawal. Payments shall be made in the currency of the withdrawing member.

2. If the Fund's holdings of the currency of the withdrawing member are not sufficient to pay the net amount due from the Fund, the balance shall be paid in gold, or in such other manner as may be agreed. If the Fund and the withdrawing member do not reach agreement within six months of the date of withdrawal, the currency in question held by the Fund shall be paid forthwith to the withdrawing member. Any balance due shall be paid in ten half-yearly installments during the ensuing five years. Each such installment shall be paid, at the option of the Fund, either in the currency of the withdrawing member acquired after its withdrawal or by the delivery of gold.

3. If the Fund fails to meet any installment which is due in accordance with the preceding paragraphs, the withdrawing member shall be entitled to require the Fund to pay the installment in any currency held by the Fund with the exception of any currency which has been declared scarce under Article VII, Section 3.

4. If the Fund's holdings of the currency of a withdrawing member exceed the amount due to it, and if agreement on the method of settling accounts is not reached within six months of the date of withdrawal, the former member shall be obligated to redeem such excess currency in gold or, at its option, in the currencies of members which at the time of redemption are convertible. Redemption shall be made at the parity existing at the time of withdrawal from the Fund. The withdrawing member shall complete redemption within five years of the date of withdrawal, or within such longer period as may be fixed by the Fund, but shall not be required to redeem in any half-yearly period more than one-tenth of the Fund's excess holdings of its currency at the date of withdrawal plus further acquisitions of the currency during such half-yearly period. If the withdrawing member does not fulfill this obligation, the Fund may in an orderly manner liquidate in any market the amount of currency which should have been redeemed.

5. Any member desiring to obtain the currency of a member which has withdrawn shall acquire it by purchase from the Fund, to the extent that such member has access to the resources of the Fund and that such currency is available under 4 above.

6. The withdrawing member guarantees the unrestricted use at all times of the currency disposed of under 4 and 5 above for the purchase of goods or for payment of sums due to it or to persons within its territories. It shall compensate the Fund for any loss resulting from the difference between the par value of its currency on the date of withdrawal and the value realized by the Fund on disposal under 4 and 5 above.

7. In the event of the Fund going into liquidation under Article XVI, Section 2, within six months of the date on which the member withdraws, the account between the Fund and that government shall be settled in accordance with Article XVI, Section 2, and Schedule E.

SCHEDULE E

ADMINISTRATION OF LIQUIDATION

1. In the event of liquidation the liabilities of the Fund other than the repayment of subscriptions shall have priority in the distribution of the assets of the Fund. In meeting each such liability the Fund shall use its assets in the following order:

(a) the currency in which the liability is payable;

(b) gold;

(c) all other currencies in proportion, so far as may be practicable, to the quotas of the members.

2. After the discharge of the Fund's liabilities in accordance with 1 above, the balance of the Fund's assets shall be distributed and apportioned as follows:

(a) The Fund shall distribute its holdings of gold among the members whose currencies are held by the Fund in amounts less than their quotas. These members shall share the gold so distributed in the proportions of the amounts by which their quotas exceed the Fund's holdings of their currencies.

(b) The Fund shall distribute to each member one-half the Fund's holdings of its currency but such distribution shall not exceed fifty percent of its quota.

(c) The Fund shall apportion the remainder of its holdings of each currency among all the members in proportion to the amounts due to each member after the distributions under (a) and (b) above.

3. Each member shall redeem the holdings of its currency apportioned to other members under 2 (c) above, and shall agree with the Fund within three months after a decision to liquidate upon an orderly procedure for such redemption.

4. If a member has not reached agreement with the Fund within the three-month period referred to in 3 above, the Fund shall use the currencies of other members apportioned to that member under 2 (c) above to redeem the currency of that member apportioned to other members. Each currency apportioned to a member which has not reached agreement shall be used, so far as possible, to redeem its currency apportioned to the members which have made agreements with the Fund under 3 above.

5. If a member has reached agreement with the Fund in accordance with 3 above, the Fund shall use the currencies of other members apportioned to that member under 2 (c) above to redeem the currency of that member apportioned to other members which have made agreements with the Fund under 3 above. Each amount so redeemed shall be redeemed in the currency of the member to which it was apportioned.

6. After carrying out the preceding paragraphs, the Fund shall pay to each member the remaining currencies held for its account.

7. Each member whose currency has been distributed to other members

under 6 above shall redeem such currency in gold or, at its option, in the currency of the member requesting redemption, or in such other manner as may be agreed between them. If the members involved do not otherwise agree, the member obligated to redeem shall complete redemption within five years of the date of distribution, but shall not be required to redeem in any half-yearly period more than one-tenth of the amount distributed to each other member. If the member does not fulfill this obligation, the amount of currency which should have been redeemed may be liquidated in an orderly manner in any market.

8. Each member whose currency has been distributed to other members under 6 above guarantees the unrestricted use of such currency at all times for the purchase of goods or for payment of sums due to it or to persons in its territories. Each member so obligated agrees to compensate other members for any loss resulting from the difference between the par value of its currency on the date of the decision to liquidate the Fund and the value realized by such members on disposal of its currency.

ARTICLES OF AGREEMENT OF THE INTERNATIONAL BANK FOR RECONSTRUCTION AND DEVELOPMENT

The Governments on whose behalf the present Agreement is signed agree as follows:

INTRODUCTORY ARTICLE

The International Bank for Reconstruction and Development is established and shall operate in accordance with the following provisions:

ARTICLE I

PURPOSES

The purposes of the Bank are:

(i) To assist in the reconstruction and development of territories of members by facilitating the investment of capital for productive purposes, including the restoration of economies destroyed or disrupted by war, the reconversion of productive facilities to peacetime needs and the encouragement of the development of productive facilities and resources in less developed countries.

(ii) To promote private foreign investment by means of guarantees or participations in loans and other investments made by private investors; and when private capital is not available on reasonable terms, to supplement private investment by providing, on suitable conditions, finance for productive purposes out of its own capital, funds raised by it and its other resources.

(iii) To promote the long-range balanced growth of international trade and the maintenance of equilibrium in balances of payments by encouraging international investment for the development of the productive resources of members, thereby assisting in raising productivity, the standard of living and conditions of labor in their territories.

(iv) To arrange the loans made or guaranteed by it in relation to international loans through other channels so that the more useful and urgent projects, large and small alike, will be dealt with first.

(v) To conduct its operations with due regard to the effect of international investment on business conditions in the territories of members and, in the immediate post-war years, to assist in bringing about a smooth transition from a wartime to a peacetime economy.

The Bank shall be guided in all its decisions by the purposes set forth above.

ARTICLE II
MEMBERSHIP IN AND CAPITAL OF THE BANK

Section 1. *Membership*

(a) The original members of the Bank shall be those members of the International Monetary Fund which accept membership in the Bank before the date specified in Article XI, Section 2 (e).

(b) Membership shall be open to other members of the Fund, at such times and in accordance with such terms as may be prescribed by the Bank.

Section 2. *Authorized capital*

(a) The authorized capital stock of the Bank shall be $10,000,000,000, in terms of United States dollars of the weight and fineness in effect on July 1, 1944. The capital stock shall be divided into 100,000 shares having a par value of $100,000 each, which shall be available for subscription only by members.

(b) The capital stock may be increased when the Bank deems it advisable by a three-fourths majority of the total voting power.

Section 3. *Subscription of shares*

(a) Each member shall subscribe shares of the capital stock of the Bank. The minimum number of shares to be subscribed by the original members shall be those set forth in Schedule A. The minimum number of shares to be subscribed by other members shall be determined by the Bank, which shall reserve a sufficient portion of its capital stock for subscription by such members.

(b) The Bank shall prescribe rules laying down the conditions under which members may subscribe shares of the authorized capital stock of the Bank in addition to their minimum subscriptions.

(c) If the authorized capital stock of the Bank is increased, each member shall have a reasonable opportunity to subscribe, under such conditions as the Bank shall decide, a proportion of the increase of stock equivalent to the proportion which its stock theretofore subscribed bears to the total capital stock of the Bank, but no member shall be obligated to subscribe any part of the increased capital.

Section 4. *Issue price of shares*

Shares included in the minimum subscriptions of original members shall be issued at par. Other shares shall be issued at par unless the Bank by a majority of the total voting power decides in special circumstances to issue them on other terms.

Section 5. *Division and calls of subscribed capital*

The subscription of each member shall be divided into two parts as follows:

(i) twenty percent shall be paid or subject to call under Section 7 (i) of this Article as needed by the Bank for its operations;

(ii) the remaining eighty percent shall be subject to call by the Bank only when required to meet obligations of the Bank created under Article IV, Sections 1 (a) (ii) and (iii).

Calls on unpaid subscriptions shall be uniform on all shares.

Section 6. *Limitation on liability*

Liability on shares shall be limited to the unpaid portion of the issue price of the shares.

Section 7. *Method of payment of subscriptions for shares*

Payment of subscriptions for shares shall be made in gold or United States dollars and in the currencies of the members as follows:

(i) under Section 5 (i) of this Article, two percent of the price of each share shall be payable in gold or United States dollars, and, when calls are made, the remaining eighteen percent shall be paid in the currency of the member;

(ii) when a call is made under Section 5 (ii) of this Article, payment may be made at the option of the member either in gold, in United States dollars or in the currency required to discharge the obligations of the Bank for the purpose for which the call is made;

(iii) when a member makes payments in any currency under (i) and (ii) above, such payments shall be made in amounts equal in value to the member's liability under the call. This liability shall be a proportionate part of the subscribed capital stock of the Bank as authorized and defined in Section 2 of this Article.

Section 8. *Time of payment of subscriptions*

(a) The two percent payable on each share in gold or United States dollars under Section 7 (i) of this Article, shall be paid within sixty days of the date on which the Bank begins operations, provided that

(i) any original member of the Bank whose metropolitan territory has suffered from enemy occupation or hostilities during the present war shall be granted the right to postpone payment of one-half percent until five years after that date;

(ii) an original member who cannot make such a payment because it has not recovered possession of its gold reserves which are still seized or immobilized as a result of the war may postpone all payment until such date as the Bank shall decide.

(b) The remainder of the price of each share payable under Section 7 (i) of this Article shall be paid as and when called by the Bank, provided that

(i) the Bank shall, within one year of its beginning operations, call not less than eight percent of the price of the share in addition to the payment of two percent referred to in (a) above;

(ii) not more than five percent of the price of the share shall be called in any period of three months.

Section 9. *Maintenance of value of certain currency holdings of the Bank*

(a) Whenever (i) the par value of a member's currency is reduced, or (ii) the foreign exchange value of a member's currency has, in the opinion of the Bank, depreciated to a significant extent within that member's territories, the member shall pay to the Bank within a reasonable time an additional amount of its own currency sufficient to maintain the value, as of the time of initial subscription, of the amount of the currency of such member which is held by the Bank and derived from currency originally paid in to the Bank by the member under Article II, Section 7 (i), from currency referred to in Article IV, Section 2 (b), or from any additional currency furnished under the provisions of the present paragraph, and which has not been repurchased by the member for gold or for the currency of any member which is acceptable to the Bank.

(b) Whenever the par value of a member's currency is increased, the Bank shall return to such member within a reasonable time an amount of that member's currency equal to the increase in the value of the amount of such currency described in (a) above.

(c) The provisions of the preceding paragraphs may be waived by the Bank when a uniform proportionate change in the par values of the currencies of all its members is made by the International Monetary Fund.

Section 10. *Restriction on disposal of shares*

Shares shall not be pledged or encumbered in any manner whatever and they shall be transferable only to the Bank.

ARTICLE III

GENERAL PROVISIONS RELATING TO LOANS AND GUARANTEES

Section 1. *Use of resources*

(a) The resources and the facilities of the Bank shall be used exclusively for the benefit of members with equitable consideration to projects for development and projects for reconstruction alike.

(b) For the purpose of facilitating the restoration and reconstruction of the economy of members whose metropolitan territories have suffered great devastation from enemy occupation or hostilities, the Bank, in determining the conditions and terms of loans made to such members, shall pay special regard to lightening the financial burden and expediting the completion of such restoration and reconstruction.

Section 2. *Dealings between members and the Bank*

Each member shall deal with the Bank only through its Treasury, central bank, stabilization fund or other similar fiscal agency, and the Bank shall deal with members only by or through the same agencies.

Section 3. *Limitations on guarantees and borrowings of the Bank*

The total amount outstanding of guarantees, participations in loans and direct loans made by the Bank shall not be increased at any time, if by such increase the total would exceed one hundred percent of the unimpaired subscribed capital, reserves and surplus of the Bank.

Section 4. *Conditions on which the Bank may guarantee or make loans*

The Bank may guarantee, participate in, or make loans to any member or any political sub-division thereof and any business, industrial, and agricultural enterprise in the territories of a member, subject to the following conditions:

(i) When the member in whose territories the project is located is not itself the borrower, the member or the central bank or some comparable agency of the member which is acceptable to the Bank, fully guarantees the repayment of the principal and the payment of interest and other charges on the loan.

(ii) The Bank is satisfied that in the prevailing market conditions the borrower would be unable otherwise to obtain the loan under conditions which in the opinion of the Bank are reasonable for the borrower.

(iii) A competent committee, as provided for in Article V, Section 7, has submitted a written report recommending the project after a careful study of the merits of the proposal.

(iv) In the opinion of the Bank the rate of interest and other charges are reasonable and such rate, charges and the schedule for repayment of principal are appropriate to the project.

(v) In making or guaranteeing a loan, the Bank shall pay due regard to the prospects that the borrower, and, if the borrower is not a member, that the guarantor, will be in position to meet its obligations under the loan; and the Bank shall act prudently in the interests both of the particular member in whose territories the project is located and of the members as a whole.

(vi) In guaranteeing a loan made by other investors, the Bank receives suitable compensation for its risk.

(vii) Loans made or guaranteed by the Bank shall, except in special circumstances, be for the purpose of specific projects of reconstruction or development.

Section 5. *Use of loans guaranteed, participated in or made by the Bank*

(a) The Bank shall impose no conditions that the proceeds of a loan shall be spent in the territories of any particular member or members.

(b) The Bank shall make arrangements to ensure that the proceeds of any loan are used only for the purposes for which the loan was granted, with due attention to considerations of economy and efficiency and without regard to political or other non-economic influences or considerations.

(c) In the case of loans made by the Bank, it shall open an account in the name of the borrower and the amount of the loan shall be credited to this account in the currency or currencies in which the loan is made. The borrower shall be permitted by the Bank to draw on this account only to meet expenses in connection with the project as they are actually incurred.

ARTICLE IV
OPERATIONS

Section 1. *Methods of making or facilitating loans*

(a) The Bank may make or facilitate loans which satisfy the general conditions of Article III in any of the following ways:

(i) By making or participating in direct loans out of its own funds corresponding to its unimpaired paid-up capital and surplus and, subject to Section 6 of this Article, to its reserves.

(ii) By making or participating in direct loans out of funds raised in the market of a member, or otherwise borrowed by the Bank.

(iii) By guaranteeing in whole or in part loans made by private investors through the usual investment channels.

(b) The Bank may borrow funds under (a) (ii) above or guarantee loans under (a) (iii) above only with the approval of the member in whose markets the funds are raised and the member in whose currency the loan is denominated, and only if those members agree that the proceeds may be exchanged for the currency of any other member without restriction.

Section 2. *Availability and transferability of currencies*

(a) Currencies paid into the Bank under Article II, Section 7 (i), shall be loaned only with the approval in each case of the member whose currency is involved; provided, however, that if necessary, after the Bank's subscribed capital has been entirely called, such currencies shall, without restriction by the members whose currencies are offered, be used or exchanged for the currencies required to meet contractual payments of interest, other charges or amortization on the Bank's own borrowings, or to meet the Bank's liabilities with respect to such contractual payments on loans guaranteed by the Bank.

(b) Currencies received by the Bank from borrowers or guarantors in payment on account of principal of direct loans made with currencies referred to in (a) above shall be exchanged for the currencies of other members or reloaned only with the approval in each case of the members whose currencies are involved; provided, however, that if necessary, after the Bank's subscribed capital has been entirely called, such currencies shall, without restriction by the members whose currencies are offered, be used or exchanged for the currencies required to meet contractual payments of interest, other charges or amortization on the Bank's own borrowings, or to meet the Bank's liabilities with respect to such contractual payments on loans guaranteed by the Bank.

(c) Currencies received by the Bank from borrowers or guarantors in payment on account of principal of direct loans made by the Bank under Section 1 (a) (ii) of this Article, shall be held and used, without restriction by the members, to make amortization payments, or to anticipate payment of or repurchase part or all of the Bank's own obligations.

(d) All other currencies available to the Bank, including those raised in the market or otherwise borrowed under Section 1 (a) (ii) of this Article, those obtained by the sale of gold, those received as payments of interest and other charges for direct loans made under Sections 1 (a) (i) and (ii), and those received as payments of commissions and other charges under Section 1 (a) (iii), shall be used or exchanged for other currencies or gold required in the operations of the Bank without restriction by the members whose currencies are offered.

(e) Currencies raised in the markets of members by borrowers on loans guaranteed by the Bank under Section 1 (a) (iii) of this Article, shall also be used or exchanged for other currencies without restriction by such members.

Section 3. *Provision of currencies for direct loans*

The following provisions shall apply to direct loans under Sections 1 (a) (i) and (ii) of this Article:

(a) The Bank shall furnish the borrower with such currencies of members, other than the member in whose territories the project is located, as are needed by the borrower for expenditures to be made in the territories of such other members to carry out the purposes of the loan.

(b) The Bank may, in exceptional circumstances when local currency required for the purposes of the loan cannot be raised by the borrower on reasonable terms, provide the borrower as part of the loan with an appropriate amount of that currency.

(c) The Bank, if the project gives rise indirectly to an increased need for foreign exchange by the member in whose territories the project is located, may in exceptional circumstances provide the borrower as part of the loan with an appropriate amount of gold or foreign exchange not in excess of the borrower's local expenditure in connection with the purposes of the loan.

(d) The Bank may, in exceptional circumstances, at the request of a member in whose territories a portion of the loan is spent, repurchase with gold or foreign exchange a part of that member's currency thus spent but in no case shall the part so repurchased exceed the amount by which the expenditure of the loan in those territories gives rise to an increased need for foreign exchange.

Section 4. *Payment provisions for direct loans*

Loan contracts under Section 1 (a) (i) or (ii) of this Article shall be made in accordance with the following payment provisions:

(a) The terms and conditions of interest and amortization payments, maturity and dates of payment of each loan shall be determined by the Bank. The Bank shall also determine the rate and any other terms and conditions of commission to be charged in connection with such loan.

In the case of loans made under Section 1 (a) (ii) of this Article during the first ten years of the Bank's operations, this rate of commission shall be not less than one percent per annum and not greater than one and one-half percent per annum, and shall be charged on the outstanding portion of any such loan. At the end of this period of ten years, the rate of commission may be reduced by the Bank with respect both to the outstanding portions of loans already made and to future loans, if the reserves accumulated by the Bank under Section 6 of this Article and out of other earnings are considered by it sufficient to justify a reduction. In the case of future loans the Bank shall also have discretion to increase the rate of commission beyond the above limit, if experience indicates that an increase is advisable.

(b) All loan contracts shall stipulate the currency or currencies in which payments under the contract shall be made to the Bank. At the option of the borrower, however, such payments may be made in gold, or subject to the agreement of the Bank, in the currency of a member other than that prescribed in the contract.

(i) In the case of loans made under Section 1 (a) (i) of this Article, the loan contracts shall provide that payments to the Bank of interest, other charges and amortization shall be made in the currency loaned, unless the member whose currency is loaned agrees that such payments shall be made in some other specified currency or currencies. These payments, subject to the provisions of Article II, Section 9 (c), shall be equivalent to the value of such contractual payments at the time the loans were made, in terms of a currency specified for the purpose by the Bank by a three-fourths majority of the total voting power.

(ii) In the case of loans made under Section 1 (a) (ii) of this Article, the total amount outstanding and payable to the Bank in any one currency shall at no time exceed the total amount of the outstanding borrowings made by the Bank under Section 1 (a) (ii) and payable in the same currency.

(c) If a member suffers from an acute exchange stringency, so that the service of any loan contracted by that member or guaranteed by it or by one of its agencies cannot be provided in the stipulated manner, the member concerned may apply to the Bank for a relaxation of the conditions of payment. If the Bank is satisfied that some relaxation is in the interests of the particular member and of the operations of the Bank and of its members as a whole, it may take action under either, or both, of the following paragraphs with respect to the whole, or part, of the annual service:

(i) The Bank may, in its discretion, make arrangements with the member concerned to accept service payments on the loan in the member's currency for periods not to exceed three years upon appropriate terms regarding the use of such currency and the maintenance of its foreign exchange value; and for the repurchase of such currency on appropriate terms.

(ii) The Bank may modify the terms of amortization or extend the life of the loan, or both.

Section 5. *Guarantees*

(a) In guaranteeing a loan placed through the usual investment channels, the Bank shall charge a guarantee commission payable periodically on the amount of the loan outstanding at a rate determined by the Bank. During the first ten years of the Bank's operations, this rate shall be not less than one percent per annum and not greater than one and one-half percent per annum. At the end of this period of ten years, the rate of commission may be reduced by the Bank with respect both to the outstanding portions of loans already guaranteed and to future loans if the reserves accumulated by the Bank under Section 6 of this Article and out of other earnings are considered by it sufficient to justify a reduction. In the case of future loans the Bank shall also have discretion to increase the rate of commission beyond the above limit, if experience indicates that an increase is advisable.

(b) Guarantee commissions shall be paid directly to the Bank by the borrower.

(c) Guarantees by the Bank shall provide that the Bank may terminate its liability with respect to interest if, upon default by the borrower and by the guarantor, if any, the Bank offers to purchase, at par and interest accrued to a date designated in the offer, the bonds or other obligations guaranteed.

(d) The Bank shall have power to determine any other terms and conditions of the guarantee.

Section 6. *Special reserve*

The amount of commissions received by the Bank under Sections 4 and 5 of this Article shall be set aside as a special reserve, which shall be kept available for meeting liabilities of the Bank in accordance with Section 7 of this Article. The special reserve shall be held in such liquid form, permitted under this Agreement, as the Executive Directors may decide.

Section 7. *Methods of meeting liabilities of the Bank in case of defaults*

In cases of default on loans made, participated in, or guaranteed by the Bank:

(a) The Bank shall make such arrangements as may be feasible to adjust the obligations under the loans, including arrangements under or analogous to those provided in Section 4 (c) of this Article.

(b) The payments in discharge of the Bank's liabilities on borrowings or guarantees under Sections 1 (a) (ii) and (iii) of this Article shall be charged:

    (i) first, against the special reserve provided in Section 6 of this Article.

    (ii) then, to the extent necessary and at the discretion of the Bank, against the other reserves, surplus and capital available to the Bank.

(c) Whenever necessary to meet contractual payments of interest, other charges or amortization on the Bank's own borrowings, or to meet the Bank's liabilities with respect to similar payments on loans guaranteed by it, the Bank may call an appropriate amount of the unpaid subscriptions of members in accordance with Article II, Sections 5 and 7. Moreover, if it believes that a default may be of long duration, the Bank may call an additional amount of such unpaid subscriptions not to exceed in any one year one percent of the total subscriptions of the members for the following purposes:

    (i) To redeem prior to maturity, or otherwise discharge its liability on, all or part of the outstanding principal of any loan guaranteed by it in respect of which the debtor is in default.

    (ii) To repurchase, or otherwise discharge its liability on, all or part of its own outstanding borrowings.

Section 8. *Miscellaneous operations*

In addition to the operations specified elsewhere in this Agreement, the Bank shall have the power:

    (i) To buy and sell securities it has issued and to buy and sell securities which it has guaranteed or in which it has invested, provided that the Bank shall obtain the approval of the member in whose territories the securities are to be bought or sold.

    (ii) To guarantee securities in which it has invested for the purpose of facilitating their sale.

    (iii) To borrow the currency of any member with the approval of that member.

    (iv) To buy and sell such other securities as the Directors by a three-fourths majority of the total voting power may deem proper for the investment of all or part of the special reserve under Section 6 of this Article.

In exercising the powers conferred by this Section, the Bank may deal with any person, partnership, association, corporation or other legal entity in the territories of any member.

Section 9. *Warning to be placed on securities*

Every security guaranteed or issued by the Bank shall bear on its face a conspicuous statement to the effect that it is not an obligation of any government unless expressly stated on the security.

Section 10. *Political activity prohibited*

The Bank and its officers shall not interfere in the political affairs of any member; nor shall they be influenced in their decisions by the political character of the member or members concerned. Only economic considerations shall be relevant to their decisions, and these considerations shall be weighed impartially in order to achieve the purposes stated in Article I.

ARTICLE V
ORGANIZATION AND MANAGEMENT

Section 1. *Structure of the Bank*

The Bank shall have a Board of Governors, Executive Directors, a President and such other officers and staff to perform such duties as the Bank may determine.

Section 2. *Board of Governors*

(a) All the powers of the Bank shall be vested in the Board of Governors consisting of one governor and one alternate appointed by each member in such manner as it may determine. Each governor and each alternate shall serve for five years, subject to the pleasure of the member appointing him, and may be reappointed. No alternate may vote except in the absence of his principal. The Board shall select one of the governors as Chairman.

(b) The Board of Governors may delegate to the Executive Directors authority to exercise any powers of the Board, except the power to:

(i) Admit new members and determine the conditions of their admission;

(ii) Increase or decrease the capital stock;

(iii) Suspend a member;

(iv) Decide appeals from interpretations of this Agreement given by the Executive Directors;

(v) Make arrangements to cooperate with other international organizations (other than informal arrangements of a temporary and administrative character);

(vi) Decide to suspend permanently the operations of the Bank and to distribute its assets;

(vii) Determine the distribution of the net income of the Bank.

(c) The Board of Governors shall hold an annual meeting and such other meetings as may be provided for by the Board or called by the Executive Directors. Meetings of the Board shall be called by the Directors whenever requested by five members or by members having one-quarter of the total voting power.

(d) A quorum for any meeting of the Board of Governors shall be a majority of the Governors, exercising not less than two-thirds of the total voting power.

(e) The Board of Governors may by regulation establish a procedure whereby the Executive Directors, when they deem such action to be in the best interests of the Bank, may obtain a vote of the Governors on a specific question without calling a meeting of the Board.

(f) The Board of Governors, and the Executive Directors to the extent authorized, may adopt such rules and regulations as may be necessary or appropriate to conduct the business of the Bank.

(g) Governors and alternates shall serve as such without compensation from the Bank, but the Bank shall pay them reasonable expenses incurred in attending meetings.

(h) The Board of Governors shall determine the remuneration to be paid to the Executive Directors and the salary and terms of the contract of service of the President.

Section 3. *Voting*

(a) Each member shall have two hundred fifty votes plus one additional vote for each share of stock held.

(b) Except as otherwise specifically provided, all matters before the Bank shall be decided by a majority of the votes cast.

Section 4. *Executive Directors*

(a) The Executive Directors shall be responsible for the conduct of the general operations of the Bank, and for this purpose, shall exercise all the powers delegated to them by the Board of Governors.

(b) There shall be twelve Executive Directors, who need not be governors, and of whom:

(i) five shall be appointed, one by each of the five members having the largest number of shares;

(ii) seven shall be elected according to Schedule B by all the Governors other than those appointed by the five members referred to in (i) above.

For the purpose of this paragraph, "members" means governments of countries whose names are set forth in Schedule A, whether they are original members or become members in accordance with Article II, Section 1 (b). When governments of other countries become members, the Board of Governors may, by a four-fifths majority of the total voting power, increase the total number of directors by increasing the number of directors to be elected.

Executive directors shall be appointed or elected every two years.

(c) Each executive director shall appoint an alternate with full power to act for him when he is not present. When the executive directors appointing them are present, alternates may participate on meetings but shall not vote.

(d) Directors shall continue in office until their successors are appointed or elected. If the office of an elected director becomes vacant more than ninety days before the end of his term, another director shall be elected for the remainder of the term by the governors who elected the former director. A majority of the votes cast shall be required for election. While the office remains vacant, the alternate of the former director shall exercise his powers, except that of appointing an alternate.

(e) The Executive Directors shall function in continuous session at the principal office of the Bank and shall meet as often as the business of the Bank may require.

(f) A quorum for any meeting of the Executive Directors shall be a majority of the Directors, exercising not less than one-half of the total voting power.

(g) Each appointed director shall be entitled to cast the number of votes allotted under Section 3 of this Article to the member appointing him. Each elected director shall be entitled to cast the number of votes which counted toward his election. All the votes which a director is entitled to cast shall be cast as a unit.

(h) The Board of Governors shall adopt regulations under which a member not entitled to appoint a director under (b) above may send a representative to attend any meeting of the Executive Directors when a request made by, or a matter particularly affecting, that member is under consideration.

(i) The Executive Directors may appoint such committees as they deem advisable. Membership of such committees need not be limited to governors or directors or their alternates.

Section 5. *President and staff*

(a) The Executive Directors shall select a President who shall not be a governor or an executive director or an alternate for either. The President shall be Chairman of the Executive Directors, but shall have no vote except a deciding vote in case of an equal division. He may participate in meetings of the Board of Governors, but shall not vote at such meetings. The President shall cease to hold office when the Executive Directors so decide.

(b) The President shall be chief of the operating staff of the Bank and shall conduct, under the direction of the Executive Directors, the ordinary business of the Bank. Subject to the general control of the Executive Directors, he shall be responsible for the organization, appointment and dismissal of the officers and staff.

(c) The President, officers and staff of the Bank, in the discharge of their offices, owe their duty entirely to the Bank and to no other authority. Each member of the Bank shall respect the international character of this duty and shall refrain from all attempts to influence any of them in the discharge of their duties.

(d) In appointing the officers and staff the President shall, subject to the paramount importance of securing the highest standards of efficiency and of technical competence, pay due regard to the importance of recruiting personnel on as wide a geographical basis as possible.

Section 6. *Advisory Council*

(a) There shall be an Advisory Council of not less than seven persons selected by the Board of Governors including representatives of banking, commercial, industrial, labor, and agricultural interests, and with as wide a national representation as possible. In those fields where specialized international organizations exist, the members of the Council representative of those fields shall be selected in agreement with such organizations. The Council shall advise the Bank on matters of general policy. The Council shall meet annually and on such other occasions as the Bank may request.

(b) Councillors shall serve for two years and may be reappointed. They shall be paid their reasonable expenses incurred on behalf of the Bank.

Section 7. *Loan committees*

The committees required to report on loans under Article III, Section 4, shall be appointed by the Bank. Each such committee shall include an expert selected by the governor representing the member in whose territories the project is located and one or more members of the technical staff of the Bank.

Section 8. *Relationship to other international organizations*

(a) The Bank, within the terms of this Agreement, shall cooperate with any general international organization and with public international organizations having specialized responsibilities in related fields. Any arrangements for such cooperation which would involve a modification of any provision of this Agreement may be effected only after amendment to this Agreement under Article VIII.

(b) In making decisions on applications for loans or guarantees relating to matters directly within the competence of any international organization of the types specified in the preceding paragraph and participated in primarily by members of the Bank, the Bank shall give consideration to the views and recommendations of such organization.

Section 9. *Location of offices*

(a) The principal office of the Bank shall be located in the territory of the member holding the greatest number of shares.

(b) The Bank may establish agencies or branch offices in the territories of any member of the Bank.

Section 10. *Regional offices and councils*

(a) The Bank may establish regional offices and determine the location of, and the areas to be covered by, each regional office.

(b) Each regional office shall be advised by a regional council representative of the entire area and selected in such manner as the Bank may decide.

Section 11. *Depositories*

(a) Each member shall designate its central bank as a depository for all the Bank's holdings of its currency or, if it has no central bank, it shall designate such other institution as may be acceptable to the Bank.

(b) The Bank may hold other assets, including gold, in depositories designated by the five members having the largest number of shares and in such other designated depositories as the Bank may select. Initially, at least one-half of the gold holdings of the Bank shall be held in the depository designated by the member in whose territory the Bank has its principal office, and at least forty percent shall be held in the depositories designated by the remaining four members referred to above, each of such depositories to hold, initially, not less than the amount of gold paid on the shares of the member designating it. However, all transfers of gold by the Bank shall be made with due regard to the costs of transport and anticipated requirements of the Bank. In an emergency the Executive Directors may transfer all or any part of the Bank's gold holdings to any place where they can be adequately protected.

Section 12. *Form of holdings of currency*

The Bank shall accept from any member, in place of any part of the member's currency, paid in to the Bank under Article II, Section 7 (i), or to meet amortization payments on loans made with such currency, and not needed by the Bank in its operations, notes or similar obligations issued by the Government of the member or the depository designated by such member, which shall be non-negotiable, non-interest-bearing and payable at their par value on demand by credit to the account of the Bank in the designated depository.

Section 13. *Publication of reports and provision of information*

(a) The Bank shall publish an annual report containing an audited statement of its accounts and shall circulate to members at intervals of three months or less a summary statement of its financial position and a profit and loss statement showing the results of its operations.

(b) The Bank may publish such other reports as it deems desirable to carry out its purposes.

(c) Copies of all reports, statements and publications made under this section shall be distributed to members.

Section 14. *Allocation of net income*

(a) The Board of Governors shall determine annually what part of the Bank's net income, after making provision for reserves, shall be allocated to surplus and what part, if any, shall be distributed.

(b) If any part is distributed, up to two percent non-cumulative shall be paid, as a first charge against the distribution for any year, to each member on the basis of the average amount of the loans outstanding during the year made under Article IV, Section 1 (a) (i), out of currency corresponding to its subscription. If two percent is paid as a first charge, any balance remaining to be distributed shall be paid to all members in proportion to their shares. Payments to each member shall be made in its own currency, or if that currency is not available in other currency acceptable to the member. If such payments are made in currencies other than the member's own currency, the transfer of the currency and its use by the receiving member after payment shall be without restriction by the members.

ARTICLE VI

WITHDRAWAL AND SUSPENSION OF MEMBERSHIP: SUSPENSION
OF OPERATIONS

Section 1. *Right of members to withdraw*

Any member may withdraw from the Bank at any time by transmitting a notice in writing to the Bank at its principal office. Withdrawal shall become effective on the date such notice is received.

Section 2. *Suspension of membership*

If a member fails to fulfill any of its obligations to the Bank, the Bank may suspend its membership by decision of a majority of the Governors, exercising a majority of the total voting power. The member so suspended shall automatically cease to be a member one year from the date of its suspension unless a decision is taken by the same majority to restore the member to good standing.

While under suspension, a member shall not be entitled to exercise any rights under this Agreement, except the right of withdrawal, but shall remain subject to all obligations.

Section 3. *Cessation of membership in International Monetary Fund*

Any member which ceases to be a member of the International Monetary Fund shall automatically cease after three months to be a member of the Bank unless the Bank by three-fourths of the total voting power has agreed to allow it to remain a member.

Section 4. *Settlement of accounts with governments ceasing to be members*

(a) When a government ceases to be a member, it shall remain liable for its direct obligations to the Bank and for its contingent liabilities to the Bank so long as any part of the loans or guarantees contracted before it ceased to be a member are outstanding; but it shall cease to incur liabilities with respect to loans and guarantees entered into thereafter by the Bank and to share either in the income or the expenses of the Bank.

(b) At the time a government ceases to be a member, the Bank shall arrange for the repurchase of its shares as a part of the settlement of accounts with such government in accordance with the provisions of (c) and (d) below. For this purpose the repurchase price of the shares shall be the value shown by the books of the Bank on the day the government ceases to be a member.

(c) The payment for shares repurchased by the Bank under this section shall be governed by the following conditions:

(i) Any amount due to the government for its shares shall be withheld so long as the government, its central bank or any of its agencies remains liable, as borrower or guarantor, to the Bank and such amount may, at the option of the Bank, be applied on any such liability as it matures. No amount shall be withheld on account of the liability of the government resulting from its subscription for shares under Article II, Section 5 (ii). In any event, no amount due to a member for its shares shall be paid until six months after the date upon which the government ceases to be a member.

(ii) Payments for shares may be made from time to time, upon their surrender by the government, to the extent by which the amount due as the repurchase price in (b) above exceeds the aggregate of liabilities on loans and guarantees in (c) (i) above until the former member has received the full repurchase price.

(iii) Payments shall be made in the currency of the country receiving payment or at the option of the Bank in gold.

(iv) If losses are sustained by the Bank on any guarantees, participations in loans, or loans which were outstanding on the date when the government ceased to be a member, and the amount of such losses exceeds the amount of the reserve provided against losses on the date when the government ceased to be a member, such government shall be obligated to repay upon demand the amount by which the repurchase price of its shares would have been reduced, if the losses had been taken into account when the repurchase price was determined. In addition, the former member government shall remain liable on any call for unpaid subscriptions under Article II, Section 5 (ii), to the extent that it would have been required to respond if the impairment of capital had occurred and the call had been made at the time the repurchase price of its shares was determined.

(d) If the Bank suspends permanently its operations under Section 5 (b) of this Article, within six months of the date upon which any government ceases to be a member, all rights of such government shall be determined by the provisions of Section 5 of this Article.

Section 5. *Suspension of operations and settlement of obligations*

(a) In an emergency the Executive Directors may suspend temporarily operations in respect of new loans and guarantees pending an opportunity for further consideration and action by the Board of Governors.

(b) The Bank may suspend permanently its operations in respect of new loans and guarantees by vote of a majority of the Governors, exercising a majority of the total voting power. After such suspension of operations the Bank shall forthwith cease all activities, except those incident to the orderly realization, conservation, and preservation of its assets and settlement of its obligations.

(c) The liability of all members for uncalled subscriptions to the capital stock of the Bank and in respect of the depreciation of their own currencies shall continue until all claims of creditors, including all contingent claims, shall have been discharged.

(d) All creditors holding direct claims shall be paid out of the assets of the Bank, and then out of payments to the Bank on calls on unpaid subscriptions. Before making any payments to creditors holding direct claims, the Executive Directors shall make such arrangements as are necessary, in their judgment, to insure a distribution to holders of contingent claims ratably with creditors holding direct claims.

(e) No distribution shall be made to members on account of their subscriptions to the capital stock of the Bank until

(i) all liabilities to creditors have been discharged or provided for, and

(ii) a majority of the Governors, exercising a majority of the total voting power, have decided to make a distribution.

(f) After a decision to make a distribution has been taken under (e) above, the Executive Directors may by a two-thirds majority vote make successive distributions of the assets of the Bank to members until all of the assets have been distributed. This distribution shall be subject to the prior settlement of all outstanding claims of the Bank against each member.

(g) Before any distribution of assets is made, the Executive Directors shall fix the proportionate share of each member according to the ratio of its shareholding to the total outstanding shares of the Bank.

(h) The Executive Directors shall value the assets to be distributed as at the date of distribution and then proceed to distribute in the following manner:

(i) There shall be paid to each member in its own obligations or those of its official agencies or legal entities within its territories, insofar as they are available for distribution, an amount equivalent in value to its proportionate share of the total amount to be distributed.

(ii) Any balance due to a member after payment has been made under (i) above shall be paid, in its own currency, insofar as it is held by the Bank, up to an amount equivalent in value to such balance.

(iii) Any balance due to a member after payment has been made under (i) and (ii) above shall be paid in gold or currency acceptable to the member, insofar as they are held by the Bank, up to an amount equivalent in value to such balance.

(iv) Any remaining assets held by the Bank after payments have been made to members under (i), (ii), and (iii) above shall be distributed *pro rata* among the members.

(i) Any member receiving assets distributed by the Bank in accordance with (h) above, shall enjoy the same rights with respect to such assets as the Bank enjoyed prior to their distribution.

ARTICLE VII
STATUS, IMMUNITIES AND PRIVILEGES

Section 1. *Purposes of Article*

To enable the Bank to fulfill the functions with which it is entrusted, the status, immunities and privileges set forth in this Article shall be accorded to the Bank in the territories of each member.

Section 2. *Status of the Bank*

The Bank shall possess full juridical personality, and, in particular, the capacity:

(i) to contract;
(ii) to acquire and dispose of immovable and movable property;
(iii) to institute legal proceedings.

Section 3. *Position of the Bank with regard to judicial process*

Actions may be brought against the Bank only in a court of competent jurisdiction in the territories of a member in which the Bank has an office, has appointed an agent for the purpose of accepting service or notice of process, or has issued or guaranteed securities. No actions shall, however, be brought by members or persons acting for or deriving claims from members. The property and assets of the Bank shall, wheresoever located and by whomsoever held, be immune from all forms of seizure, attachment or execution before the delivery of final judgment against the Bank.

Section 4. *Immunity of assets from seizure*

Property and assets of the Bank, wherever located and by whomsoever held, shall be immune from search, requisition, confiscation, expropriation or any other form of seizure by executive or legislative action.

Section 5. *Immunity of archives*

The archives of the Bank shall be inviolable.

Section 6. *Freedom of assets from restrictions*

To the extent necessary to carry out the operations provided for in this Agreement and subject to the provisions of this Agreement, all property and assets of the Bank shall be free from restrictions, regulations, controls and moratoria of any nature.

Section 7. *Privilege for communications*

The official communications of the Bank shall be accorded by each member the same treatment that it accords to the official communications of other members.

Section 8. *Immunities and privileges of officers and employees*

All governors, executive directors, alternates, officers and employees of the Bank

(i) shall be immune from legal process with respect to acts performed by them in their official capacity except when the Bank waives this immunity;

(ii) not being local nationals, shall be accorded the same immunities from immigration restrictions, alien registration requirements and national service obligations and the same facilities as regards exchange restrictions as are accorded by members to the representatives, officials, and employees of comparable rank of other members;

(iii) shall be granted the same treatment in respect of travelling facilities as is accorded by members to representatives, officials and employees of comparable rank of other members.

Section 9. *Immunities from taxation*

(a) The Bank, its assets, property, income and its operations and transactions authorized by this Agreement, shall be immune from all taxation and from all customs duties. The Bank shall also be immune from liability for the collection or payment of any tax or duty.

(b) No tax shall be levied on or in respect of salaries and emoluments paid by the Bank to executive directors, alternates, officials or employees of the Bank who are not local citizens, local subjects, or other local nationals.

(c) No taxation of any kind shall be levied on any obligation or security issued by the Bank (including any dividend or interest thereon) by whomsoever held —

>   (i) which discriminates against such obligation or security solely because it is issued by the Bank; or

>   (ii) if the sole jurisdictional basis for such taxation is the place or currency in which it is issued, made payable or paid, or the location of any office or place of business maintained by the Bank.

(d) No taxation of any kind shall be levied on any obligation or security guaranteed by the Bank (including any dividend or interest thereon) by whomsoever held —

>   (i) which discriminates against such obligation or security solely because it is guaranteed by the Bank; or

>   (ii) if the sole jurisdictional basis for such taxation is the location of any office or place of business maintained by the Bank.

Section 10. *Application of Article*

Each member shall take such action as is necessary in its own territories for the purpose of making effective in terms of its own law the principles set forth in this Article and shall inform the Bank of the detailed action which it has taken.

ARTICLE VIII

AMENDMENTS

(a) Any proposal to introduce modifications in this Agreement, whether emanating from a member, a governor or the Executive Directors, shall be communicated to the Chairman of the Board of Governors who shall bring the proposal before the Board. If the proposed amendment is approved by the Board the Bank shall, by circular letter or telegram, ask all members whether they accept the proposed amendment. When three-fifths of the members, having four-fifths of the total voting power, have accepted the proposed amendment, the Bank shall certify the fact by a formal communication addressed to all members.

(b) Notwithstanding (a) above, acceptance by all members is required in the case of any amendment modifying

>   (i) the right to withdraw from the Bank provided in Article VI, Section 1;

>   (ii) the right secured by Article II, Section 3 (c) ;

>   (iii) the limitation on liability provided in Article II, Section 6.

(c) Amendments shall enter into force for all members three months after the date of the formal communication unless a shorter period is specified in the circular letter or telegram.

ARTICLE IX

INTERPRETATION

(a) Any question of interpretation of the provisions of this Agreement arising between any member and the Bank or between any members of the Bank shall be submitted to the Executive Directors for their decision. If the question particularly affects any member not entitled to appoint an executive director, it shall be entitled to representation in accordance with Article V, Section 4 (h).

(b) In any case where the Executive Directors have given a decision under (a) above, any member may require that the question be referred to the Board of Governors, whose decision shall be final. Pending the result of the reference to the Board, the Bank may, so far as it deems necessary, act on the basis of the decision of the Executive Directors.

(c) Whenever a disagreement arises between the Bank and a country which has ceased to be a member, or between the Bank and any member during the permanent suspension of the Bank, such disagreement shall be submitted to arbitration by a tribunal of three arbitrators, one appointed by the Bank, another by the country involved and an umpire who, unless the parties otherwise agree, shall be appointed by the President of the Permanent Court of International Justice or such other authority as may have been prescribed by regulation adopted by the Bank. The umpire shall have full power to settle all questions of procedure in any case where the parties are in disagreement with respect thereto.

ARTICLE X

APPROVAL DEEMED GIVEN

Whenever the approval of any member is required before any act may be done by the Bank, except in Article VIII, approval shall be deemed to have been given unless the member presents an objection within such reasonable period as the Bank may fix in notifying the member of the proposed act.

ARTICLE XI

FINAL PROVISIONS

Section 1. *Entry into force*

This Agreement shall enter into force when it has been signed on behalf of governments whose minimum subscriptions comprise not less than sixty-five percent of the total subscriptions set forth in Schedule A and when the instruments referred to in Section 2 (a) of this Article have been deposited on their behalf, but in no event shall this Agreement enter into force before May 1, 1945.

Section 2. *Signature*

(a) Each government on whose behalf this Agreement is signed shall deposit with the Government of the United States of America an instrument setting forth that it has accepted this Agreement in accordance with its law and has taken all steps necessary to enable it to carry out all of its obligations under this Agreement.

(b) Each government shall become a member of the Bank as from the date of the deposit on its behalf of the instrument referred to in (a) above, except that no government shall become a member before this Agreement enters into force under Section 1 of this Article.

(c) The Government of the United States of America shall inform the governments of all countries whose names are set forth in Schedule A, and all governments whose membership is approved in accordance with Article II, Section 1 (b), of all signatures of this Agreement and of the deposit of all instruments referred to in (a) above.

(d) At the time this Agreement is signed on its behalf, each government shall transmit to the Government of the United States of America one one-hundredth of one percent of the price of each share in gold or United States dollars for the purpose of meeting administrative expenses of the Bank. This payment shall be credited on account of the payment to be made in accordance with Article II, Section 8 (a). The Government of the United States of America shall hold such funds in a special deposit account and shall transmit them to the Board of Governors of the Bank when the initial meeting has been called under Section 3 of this Article. If this Agreement has not come into force by December 31, 1945, the Government of the United States of America shall return such funds to the governments that transmitted them.

(e) This Agreement shall remain open for signature at Washington on behalf of the governments of the countries whose names are set forth in Schedule A until December 31, 1945.

(f) After December 31, 1945, this Agreement shall be open for signature on behalf of the government of any country whose membership has been approved in accordance with Article II, Section 1 (b).

(g) By their signature of this Agreement, all governments accept it both on their own behalf and in respect of all their colonies, overseas territories, all territories under their protection, suzerainty, or authority and all territories in respect of which they exercise a mandate.

(h) In the case of governments whose metropolitan territories have been under enemy occupation, the deposit of the instrument referred to in (a) above may be delayed until one hundred and eighty days after the date on which these territories have been liberated. If, however, it is not deposited by any such government before the expiration of this period, the signature affixed on behalf of that government shall become void and the portion of its subscription paid under (d) above shall be returned to it.

(i) Paragraphs (d) and (h) shall come into force with regard to each signatory government as from the date of its signature.

Section 3. *Inauguration of the Bank*

(a) As soon as this Agreement enters into force under Section 1 of this Article, each member shall appoint a governor and the member to whom the largest number of shares is allocated in Schedule A shall call the first meeting of the Board of Governors.

(b) At the first meeting of the Board of Governors, arrangements shall be made for the selection of provisional executive directors. The governments of the five countries, to which the largest number of shares are allocated in Schedule A, shall appoint provisional executive directors. If one or more of such governments have not become members, the executive directorships which they would be entitled to fill shall remain vacant until they become members, or until January 1, 1946, whichever is the earlier. Seven provisional executive directors shall be elected in accordance with the provisions of Schedule B and shall remain in office until the date of the first regular election of executive directors which shall be held as soon as practicable after January 1, 1946.

(c) The Board of Governors may delegate to the provisional executive directors any powers except those which may not be delegated to the Executive Directors.

(d) The Bank shall notify members when it is ready to commence operations.

DONE at Washington, in a single copy which shall remain deposited in the archives of the Government of the United States of America, which shall transmit certified copies to all governments whose names are set forth in Schedule A and to all governments whose membership is approved in accordance with Article II, Section 1 (b).

Appendix 2

FINANCIAL AGREEMENT BETWEEN THE GOVERNMENTS OF THE UNITED STATES AND THE UNITED KINGDOM

It is hereby agreed between the Government of the United States of America and the Government of the United Kingdom of Great Britain and Northern Ireland as follows: —

1. *Effective Date of the Agreement.*

The effective date of this Agreement shall be the date on which the Government of the United States notifies the Government of the United Kingdom that the Congress of the United States has made available the funds necessary to extend to the Government of the United Kingdom the line of credit in accordance with the provisions of this Agreement.

2. *Line of Credit.*

The Government of the United States will extend to the Government of the United Kingdom a line of credit of $3,750,000,000 which may be drawn upon at any time between the effective date of this Agreement and 31st December, 1951, inclusive.

3. *Purpose of the Line of Credit.*

The purpose of the line of credit is to facilitate purchases by the United Kingdom of goods and services in the United States, to assist the United Kingdom to meet transitional post-war deficits in its current balance of payments, to help the United Kingdom to maintain adequate reserves of gold and dollars and to assist the Government of the United Kingdom to assume the obligations of multilateral trade, as defined in this and other agreements.

4. *Amortisation and Interest.*

(i) The amount of the line of credit drawn by 31st December, 1951, shall be repaid in 50 annual instalments beginning on 31st December, 1951, with interest at the rate of 2 per cent. per annum.

Interest for the year 1951 shall be computed on the amount outstanding on 31st December, 1951, and for each year thereafter interest shall be computed on the amount outstanding on 1st January of each such year.

49 annual instalments of principal repayments and interest shall be equal, calculated at the rate of $31,823,000 for each $1,000,000,000 of the line of credit drawn by 31st December, 1951, and the fiftieth annual instalment shall be at the rate of $31,840,736.65 for each such $1,000,000,000.

Each instalment shall consist of the full amount of the interest due and the remainder of the instalment shall be the principal to be repaid in that year. Payments required by this section are subject to the provisions of Section 5.

(ii) The Government of the United Kingdom may accelerate repayment of the amount drawn under this line of credit.

5. *Waiver of Interest Payments.*

In any year in which the Government of the United Kingdom requests the Government of the United States to waive the amount of the interest due in the instalment of that year, the Government of the United States will grant the waiver if: —

(*a*) the Government of the United Kingdom finds that a waiver is necessary in view of the present and prospective conditions of international exchange and the level of its gold and foreign exchange reserves, *and*

(*b*) the International Monetary Fund certifies that the income of the United Kingdom from home-produced exports plus its net income from invisible current transactions in its balance of payments was on the average over the five preceding calendar years less than the average annual amount of United Kingdom imports during 1936–8 fixed at £866,000,000, as such figure may be adjusted for changes in the price level of these imports. Any amount in excess of £43,750,000 released or paid in any year on account of sterling balances accumulated to the credit of overseas governments, monetary authorities and banks before the effective date of this Agreement shall be regarded as a capital transaction and therefore shall not be included in the above calculation of the net income from invisible current transactions for that year. If waiver is requested for an interest payment prior to that due in 1955, the average income shall be computed for the calendar years from 1950 through the year preceding that in which the request is made.

6. *Relation of This Line of Credit to Other Obligations.*

(i) It is understood that any amounts required to discharge obligations of the United Kingdom to third countries outstanding on the effective date of this agreement will be found from resources other than this line of credit.

(ii) The Government of the United Kingdom will not arrange any long term loans from Governments within the British Commonwealth after 6th December, 1945 and before the end of 1951 on terms more favourable to the lender than the terms of this line of credit.

(iii) Waiver of interest will not be requested or allowed under Section 5 in any year unless the aggregate of the releases or payments in that year of sterling balances accumulated to the credit of overseas governments, monetary authorities and banks (except in the case of colonial dependencies) before the effective date of this agreement, is reduced proportionately, and unless interest payments due in that year on loans referred to in (ii) above are waived. The proportionate reduction of the releases or payments of sterling balances shall be calculated in relation to the aggregate released and paid in the most recent year in which waiver of interest was not requested.

(iv) The application of the principles set forth in this section shall be the subject of full consultation between the two Governments as occasion may arise.

7. *Sterling Area Exchange Arrangements.*

The Government of the United Kingdom will complete arrangements as early as practicable and in any case not later than one year after the effective date of this agreement, unless in exceptional cases a later date is agreed upon after consultation, under which immediately after the completion of such arrangements the sterling receipts from current transactions of all sterling area countries (apart from any receipts arising out of military expenditure by the Government of the United Kingdom prior to 31st December, 1948, to the extent to which they are treated by agreement with the countries concerned on the same basis as the balances accumulated during the war) will be freely available for current transactions in any currency area without discrimination with the result that any discrimination arising from the so-called sterling area dollar pool will be entirely removed and that each member of the sterling area will have its current sterling and dollar receipts at its free disposition for current transactions anywhere.

8. *Other Exchange Arrangements.*

(i) The Government of the United Kingdom agrees that after the effective date of this agreement it will not apply exchange controls in such a manner as to restrict

(*a*) payments or transfers in respect of products of the United States permitted to be imported into the United Kingdom or other current transactions between the two countries or

(*b*) the use of sterling balances to the credit of residents of the United States arising out of current transactions.

Nothing in this paragraph (i) shall affect the provisions of Article VII of the Articles of Agreement of the International Monetary Fund when those Articles have come into force.

(ii) The Governments of the United States and the United Kingdom agree that not later than one year after the effective date of this agreement, unless in exceptional cases a later date is agreed upon after consultation, they will impose no restrictions on payments and transfers for current transactions. The obligations of this paragraph (ii) shall not apply

(*a*) to balances of third countries and their nationals accumulated before this paragraph (ii) becomes effective; or (*b*) to restrictions imposed in conformity with the Articles of Agreement of the International Monetary Fund, provided that the Governments of the United Kingdom and the United States will not continue to invoke the provisions of Article XIV, Section 2 of those Articles after this paragraph (ii) becomes effective unless in exceptional cases after consultation they agree otherwise; or

(*c*) to restrictions imposed in connection with measures designed to uncover and dispose of assets of Germany and Japan.

(iii) This Section and Section 9 which are in anticipation of more comprehensive arrangements by multilateral agreement shall operate until 31st December, 1951.

9. *Import Arrangements.*

If either the Government of the United States or the Government of the United Kingdom imposes or maintains quantitative import restrictions, such restrictions shall be administered on a basis which does not discriminate against imports from the other country in respect of any product; provided that this undertaking shall not apply in cases in which

(*a*) its application would have the effect of preventing the country imposing such restrictions from utilizing, for the purchase of needed imports, inconvertible currencies accumulated up to 31st December, 1946; or

(*b*) there may be special necessity for the country imposing such restrictions to assist, by measures not involving a substantial departure from the general rule of non-discrimination, a country whose economy has been disrupted by war; or

(*c*) either Government imposes quantitative restrictions having equivalent effect to any exchange restrictions which that Government is authorised to impose in conformity with Article VII of the Articles of Agreement of the International Monetary Fund.

The provisions of this Section shall become effective as soon as practicable, but not later than 31st December, 1946.

10. *Accumulated Sterling Balances.*

(i) The Government of the United Kingdom intends to make agreements with the countries concerned, varying according to the circumstances of each case, for an early settlement covering the sterling balances accumulated by sterling area and other countries prior to such settlement (together with any future receipts arising out of military expenditure by the Government of the United Kingdom to the extent to which they are treated on the same basis by agreement with the countries concerned). The settlements with the sterling area countries will be on the basis of dividing these accumulated balances into three categories:

(*a*) balances to be released at once and convertible into any currency for current transactions;

(*b*) balances to be similarly released by instalments over a period of years beginning in 1951; and

(*c*) balances to be adjusted as a contribution to the settlement of war and post-war indebtedness and in recognition of the benefits which the countries concerned might be expected to gain from such a settlement.

The Government of the United Kingdom will make every endeavour to secure the early completion of these arrangements.

(ii) In consideration of the fact that an important purpose of the present line of credit is to promote the development of multilateral trade and facilitate its early resumption on a non-discriminatory basis, the Government of the United Kingdom agrees that any sterling balances released or otherwise available for current payments will, not later than one year after the effective date of this agreement, unless in special cases a later date is agreed upon after consultation, be freely available for current transactions in any currency area without discrimination.

11. *Definitions.*

For the purposes of this agreement:

(i) The term "current transactions" shall have the meaning prescribed in article XIX (*i*) of the Articles of Agreement of the International Monetary Fund.

(ii) The term "sterling area" means the United Kingdom and the other territories declared by the Defence (Finance) (Definition of Sterling Area) (No. 2) Order, 1944, to be included in the sterling area, namely "the following Territories excluding Canada and Newfoundland, that is to say;

(*a*) any Dominion,

(*b*) any other part of His Majesty's dominions,

(*c*) any territory in respect of which a mandate on behalf of the League of Nations has been accepted by His Majesty and is being exercised by His Majesty's Government in the United Kingdom, or in any Dominion,

(*d*) any British Protectorate or Protected State,

(*e*) Egypt, the Anglo-Egyptian Sudan and Iraq,

(*f*) Iceland and the Faroe Islands."

12. *Consultation on Agreement.*

Either Government shall be entitled to approach the other for a re-consideration of any of the provisions of this agreement, if in its opinion the prevailing conditions of international exchange justify such reconsideration with a view to agreeing upon modifications for presentation to their respective Legislatures.

Signed in duplicate at Washington, District of Columbia, this 6th day of December, 1945.

For the Government of the United States of America:
FRED M. VINSON,
Secretary of the Treasury of the United States of America.

For the Government of the United Kingdom of Great Britain and Northern Ireland:
HALIFAX,
His Majesty's Ambassador Extraordinary and
Plenipotentiary at Washington.

Appendix 3

PROPOSALS FOR CONSIDERATION BY AN INTERNATIONAL CONFERENCE ON TRADE AND EMPLOYMENT
(From *Proposals for Expansion of World Trade and Employment*)

A. NEED FOR INTERNATIONAL ECONOMIC COOPERATION

1. Collective measures to safeguard the peoples of the world against threats to peace and to reach just settlements of disputes among nations must be based not only on international machinery to deal directly with disputes and to prevent aggression, but also on economic cooperation among nations with the object of preventing and removing economic and social maladjustments, of achieving fairness and equity in economic relations between states, and of raising the level of economic well-being among all peoples.

2. Important contributions have already been made toward the attainment of these objectives. The Food and Agriculture Organization of the United Nations has been established. An International Monetary Fund to maintain reasonable exchange stability and facilitate adjustment in the balance of payments of member countries, and an International Bank for Reconstruction and Development to provide financial resources on a cooperative basis for those purposes are awaiting the action of governments required for their establishment.

3. In order to reach the objectives of the Atlantic Charter and Article VII of the mutual-aid agreements, it is essential that the cooperative economic measures already taken or recommended be supplemented by further measures dealing directly with trade barriers and discriminations which stand in the way of an expansion of multilateral trade and by an undertaking on the part of nations to seek full employment.

4. Cooperative action with respect to trade and employment is indispensable to the success of such other measures as those dealing with monetary and exchange stability and the flow of investment capital. Effective action in regard to employment and to trade barriers and discriminations must, therefore, be taken or the whole program of international economic cooperation will fail, and an economic environment conducive to the maintenance of peaceful international relations will not be created.

B. PROPOSALS CONCERNING EMPLOYMENT

Since high and stable levels of employment are a necessary condition for an enlarged volume of trade, and since problems of trade and employment are to be considered jointly at an international conference, the following propositions are advanced.

GOVERNING PRINCIPLES

1. It is recognized that:

   a. In all countries high and stable employment is a main condition for the attainment of satisfactory levels of living.

   b. The attainment of approximately full employment by the major industrial and trading nations, and its maintenance on a reasonably assured basis, are essential to the expansion of international trade on which the full prosperity of these and other nations depends; to the full realization of the objectives of all liberal international agreements in such fields as commercial policy, commodity problems, restrictive business practices, monetary stabilization, and investment; and, therefore, to the preservation of world peace and security.

2. Domestic programs to expand employment should be consistent with realization of the purposes of liberal international agreements and compatible with the economic well-being of other nations.

3. It is recognized that the adoption of the Bretton Woods Agreements and of measures to reduce restrictions on trade will contribute substantially to the maintenance of productive employment.

4. The United Nations have pledged, in the Charter of the United Nations Organization, to take joint and separate action in cooperation with the Organization to achieve the economic and social purposes of the United Nations, including higher standards of living, full employment, and conditions of economic and social progress and development.

EFFECTUATION OF AIMS

There should be an undertaking that:

1. Each of the signatory nations will take action designed to achieve and maintain full employment within its own jurisdiction, through measures appropriate to its political and economic institutions.

2. No nation will seek to maintain employment through measures which are likely to create unemployment in other countries or which are incompatible with international undertakings designed to promote an expanding volume of international trade and investment in accordance with comparative efficiencies of production.

3. Signatory nations will make arrangements, both individually and collaboratively under the general sponsorship of the Economic and Social Council of the United Nations Organization, for the collection, analysis, and exchange of information on employment problems, trends, and policies.

4. Signatory nations will, under the general sponsorship of the Economic and Social Council, consult regularly on employment problems and hold special conferences in case of threat of widespread unemployment.

C. Proposals Concerning an International Trade Organization

NEED FOR AN INTERNATIONAL TRADE ORGANIZATION

1. Measures designed to effect an expansion of trade are essential because of their direct contribution to maximum levels of employment, production and consumption. Since such expansion can only be attained by collective measures, in continuous operation and adaptable to economic changes, it is necessary to establish permanent machinery for international collaboration in matters affecting international commerce, with a view to continuous consultation, the provision of expert advice, the formulation of agreed policies, procedures and plans, and to the development of agreed rules of conduct in regard to matters affecting international trade.

2. It is accordingly proposed that there be created an International Trade Organization of the United Nations, the members of which would undertake to conduct their international commercial policies and relations in accordance with agreed principles to be set forth in the articles of the Organization. These principles, in order to make possible an effective expansion of world production, employment, exchange, and consumption, should:

  a. Provide an equitable basis for dealing with the problems of governmental measures affecting international trade;

  b. Provide for the curbing of restrictive trade practices resulting from private international business arrangements; and

  c. Govern the institution and operation of intergovernmental commodity arrangements.

PROPOSED INTERNATIONAL TRADE ORGANIZATION

There follows an outline of the principles which it is proposed should be incorporated in the articles of the Organization.

CHAPTER I

PURPOSES

The purposes of the Organization should be:

1. To promote international commercial cooperation by establishing machinery for consultation and collaboration among member governments regarding the solution of problems in the field of international commercial policies and relations.

2. To enable members to avoid recourse to measures destructive of world commerce by providing, on a reciprocal and mutually advantageous basis, expanding opportunities for their trade and economic development.

3. To facilitate access by all members, on equal terms, to the trade and to the raw materials of the world which are needed for their economic prosperity.

4. In general, to promote national and international action for the expansion of the production, exchange and consumption of goods, for the reduction of

tariffs and other trade barriers, and for the elimination of all forms of discriminatory treatment in international commerce; thus contributing to an expanding world economy, to the establishment and maintenance in all countries of high levels of employment and real income, and to the creation of economic conditions conducive to the maintenance of world peace.

CHAPTER II

MEMBERSHIP

The original members of the Organization should be those countries participating in the Conference on Trade and Employment which accept membership.

CHAPTER III

GENERAL COMMERCIAL POLICY

Section A. General Commercial Provisions

Members should undertake:

1. To accord to products imported from other members treatment no less favorable than that accorded to domestic products with regard to matters affecting the internal taxation and regulation of the trade in goods.

2. To provide, for products in transit through their territories, coming from or going to other members, freedom from customs and transit duties, from unreasonable transit charges, and from discriminatory treatment of all kinds.

3. To subscribe to a general definition of the circumstances under which antidumping and countervailing duties may properly be applied to products imported from other members.

4. To give effect, as soon as practicable, to agreed principles of tariff valuation designed to assure the use of true commercial values as a basis for assessing duties, and to cooperate with other members and with the Organization in working out internationally acceptable valuation procedures of a standardized character.

5. To give effect, as soon as practicable, to agreed principles looking toward the simplification of customs formalities with a view to eliminating unnecessary requirements which afford an indirect protection to domestic products.

6. To eliminate excessive requirements regarding marks of origin in so far as they affect products imported from other members.

7. To refrain from governmentally financed or organized boycotts or campaigns designed to discourage, directly or indirectly, importation or consumption of products of other members.

8. To provide for adequate publicity regarding laws and regulations affecting foreign trade, and to maintain or establish national tribunals of an independent character to review and correct administrative customs action.

9. To transmit to the Organization appropriate trade information and statistics.

10. To cooperate with the Organization and with other members in carrying out or implementing the articles of the Organization.

Section B. Tariffs and Preferences

1. *Import tariffs and preferences.* In the light of the principles set forth in Article VII of the mutual aid agreements, members should enter into arrangements for the substantial reduction of tariffs and for the elimination of tariff preferences, action for the elimination of tariff preferences being taken in conjunction with adequate measures for the substantial reduction of barriers to world trade, as part of the mutually advantageous arrangements contemplated in this document.

As an initial step in the process of eliminating tariff preferences it should be agreed that:

> *a.* Existing international commitments will not be permitted to stand in the way of action agreed upon with respect to tariff preferences.
>
> *b.* All negotiated reductions in most-favored-nation tariffs will operate automatically to reduce or eliminate margins of preference.
>
> *c.* Margins of preference on any product will in no case be increased and no new preferences will be introduced.

2. *Export tariffs and preferences.* Export duties should be open to negotiation in the same way as import duties. Members should undertake not to impose or maintain export duties which differentiate by reference to the destinations to which the goods are exported.

3. *Emergency action.* Commitments with regard to tariffs should permit countries to take temporary action to prevent sudden and widespread injury to the producers concerned. Undertakings for reducing tariffs should therefore contain an escape clause to cover such contingencies.

Section C. Quantitative Trade Restrictions

1. *General elimination of quantitative restrictions.* Except as provided for elsewhere in this Chapter, members should undertake not to maintain any quotas, embargoes, or other quantitative restrictions on their export or import trade with other members. This undertaking should not, however, apply to the following:

> *a.* Import and export prohibitions or restrictions, imposed during the early postwar transitional period, which are essential to (*a*) the efficient use of shipping space in short supply, (*b*) the equitable international distribution of products in short supply, or (*c*) the orderly liquidation of temporary surpluses of government stocks accumulated as a result of the war. Such prohibitions and restrictions should be removed not later than three years after the close of hostilities, but provision should be made whereby this period may be extended with the concurrence of the Organization.
>
> *b.* Export prohibitions or restrictions temporarily imposed to relieve conditions of distress in the exporting country caused by severe shortages of foodstuffs or other essential products.

c. Export prohibitions or restrictions necessary to the application of suitable standards for the classification and grading of commodities in international commerce.

d. Export or import quotas imposed under intergovernmental commodity agreements conforming to the principles set forth in Chapter V.

e. Import quotas on agricultural products, imported in any form, necessary to the enforcement of governmental measures which operate (*a*) to restrict the quantities of like domestic products which may be marketed or produced, or (*b*) to remove a temporary surplus of like domestic products by making such surpluses available to certain groups of domestic consumers free of charge or at prices below the current market level. Such quotas should not be more restrictive than necessary, should be removed as soon as they cease to be necessary for the purposes of this subparagraph, and should be made the subject of periodic consultation with the Organization. If such quotas are allocated among sources of supply, they should be allocated fairly, on the basis of imports during a previous representative period, account being taken in so far as practicable of any special factors which may have affected or which may be affecting the trade in the product concerned. Import quotas imposed under (*a*) of this subparagraph should not be such as would reduce imports relatively to domestic production as compared with the proportion prevailing in a previous representative period, account being taken in so far as practicable of any special factors which may have affected or which may be affecting the trade in the product concerned.

2. *Restrictions to safeguard the balance of payments.* Members confronted with an adverse balance of payments should be entitled to impose quantitative import restrictions as an aid to the restoration of equilibrium in the balance of payments. This provision should be operative under conditions and procedures to be agreed upon. These conditions and procedures

a. should set forth criteria and requirements in the light of which balance-of-payments restrictions might be imposed;

b. should, as regards the use of such restrictions in the post-war transitional period, be framed on principles which would be designed to promote the maximum development of multilateral trade during that period and which in no event would be more restrictive of such trade than the principles applicable, under Article XIV of the International Monetary Fund Agreement, to the use of exchange restrictions in the transitional period;

c. should provide for the determination of the transitional period for the purposes of subparagraph b, above, by a procedure analogous to that contained in Article XIV of the International Monetary Fund Agreement;

d. should provide for the full application of nondiscrimination in the use of such restrictions after the transitional period; and

e. should make appropriate provision for international consultation regarding balance-of-payments restrictions, whether imposed during the transitional period or thereafter.

3. *Equality of treatment.* Quantitative restrictions imposed on balance-of-payments grounds should be deemed nondiscriminatory if they are administered on a basis which does not discriminate among sources of supply in respect of any imported product.

a. In the case of restrictions imposed in the form of quotas, members imposing such quotas should publish the global amounts or values of the various products which will be permitted to be imported during a specified future period. Any allocation of such quotas among sources of supply should be based in so far as practicable upon the proportion of the total imports of the product in question supplied by the various member countries in a previous representative period, account being taken of any special factors which may have affected or which may be affecting the trade in that product.

b. In the case of restrictions not imposed in the form of quotas, the member imposing the restrictions should undertake to provide, upon the request of any other member having an interest in the product concerned, all relevant information as to the administration of the restriction, including information as to the import licenses granted over a past period and the distribution of such licenses among sources of supply.

c. Any member should be entitled to raise with the Organization the question as to whether another member was imposing balance-of-payments restrictions, whether in the form of quotas or otherwise, in a manner not in harmony with the guiding principles stated above or in a manner which unnecessarily injured its commerce, and the member imposing the restrictions should undertake in these circumstances to discuss the grounds on which it had acted.

4. *Inconvertible currencies.* The undertakings set forth in paragraph 3, above, should not apply in cases in which their application would have the effect of preventing a member from utilizing inconvertible currencies for buying needed imports.

5. *Scarce currencies and currencies of territories having a common quota in the Monetary Fund.* Members should not be precluded by this Section from applying quantitative restrictions *a)* in pursuance of action which they may take under Article VII of the International Monetary Fund Agreement, relating to scarce currencies, or *b)* in a manner designed to maintain the par value of the currencies of territories having a common quota in the Monetary Fund, in accordance with Article XX, Section 4 (g) of that Agreement.

6. *Application of quantitative restrictions by state-trading organizations.*

The provisions of this Section relating to quantitative restrictions on imports for balance-of-payments reasons should apply equally to the restriction of imports by state-trading organizations for the same reasons.

Section D. Subsidies

1. *Subsidies in general.* Subject to the provisions of paragraphs 2 and 3, below, members granting any subsidy which operates to increase exports or reduce imports should undertake to keep the Organization informed as to the extent and nature of the subsidy, as to the reason therefor and as to the probable effects on trade. They should also be prepared, in cases where, under procedures approved by the Organization, it is agreed that serious injury to international trade threatens to result from the operation of the subsidy, to discuss with other members or with the Organization possible limitations on the quantity of the domestic product subsidized. In this paragraph, the term "subsidy" includes any form of internal income or price support.

2. *Export subsidies.* Subject to the provisions of paragraph 3, below, members should undertake not to take any action which would result in the sale of a product in export markets at a price lower than the comparable price charged for the like product to buyers in the home market, due allowance being made for differences in conditions and terms of sale, for differences in taxation, and for other differences affecting price comparability. This undertaking should take effect, at latest, within 3 years of the establishment of the Organization. If at the end of that time any member considers itself unable to comply with the undertaking in respect of any particular commodity or commodities, it should inform the Organization, with an explanation of the reasons. It should then be decided by consultation among the interested members under procedures approved by the Organization whether there should be some further extension of time for the member desiring it in respect of the commodity or commodities concerned.

3. *Commodities in surplus supply.*

   a. When it is determined, in accordance with procedures approved by the Organization, that a commodity is, or is likely to become in burdensome world surplus, the members which are important producers or consumers of the commodity should agree to consult together with a view to promoting consumption increases, to promoting the reduction of production through the diversion of resources from uneconomic production, and to seeking, if necessary, the conclusion of an intergovernmental commodity arrangement in accordance with the principles of Chapter V.

   b. If, however, within a reasonable time to be agreed upon, such steps should fail of their object, the provisions of paragraphs 1 and 2, above, should cease to apply to such product until such time as it has been agreed under procedures approved by the Organization that those provisions should be reapplied to it.

   c. With regard to any export subsidies which may be imposed under subparagraph (*b*), no member should employ such subsidies so as to enlarge its share of the world market, as compared with the share prevailing in a previous representative period. The question as to what period would be representative in respect of the particular product concerned should be a subject for international consultation through the Organization.

Section E. State Trading

1. *Equality of treatment.* Members engaging in state trading in any form should accord equality of treatment to all other members. To this end, members should undertake that the foreign purchases and sales of their state-trading enterprises shall be influenced solely by commercial considerations, such as price, quality, marketability, transportation and terms of purchase or sale.

2. *State monopolies of individual products.* Members maintaining a state monopoly in respect of any product should undertake to negotiate, in the manner contemplated for tariffs, the maximum protective margin between the landed price of the product and the price at which the product (of whatever origin, domestic or foreign) is sold in the home market. Members newly establishing such monopolies should agree not to create protective margins greater than the tariffs which may have been negotiated in regard to those products. Unless the product is subject to rationing, the monopoly should offer for sale such quantities of the product as will be sufficient to satisfy the full domestic demand.

3. *Complete state monopolies of foreign trade.* As the counterpart of tariff reductions and other actions to encourage an expansion of multilateral trade by other members, members having a complete state monopoly of foreign trade should undertake to purchase annually from members, on the nondiscriminatory basis referred to in paragraph 1, above, products valued at not less than an aggregate amount to be agreed upon. This global purchase arrangement should be subject to periodic adjustment in consultation with the Organization.

Section F. Exchange Control

1. *Relation to the International Monetary Fund.* In order to avoid the imposition of trade restrictions and discriminations through exchange techniques, the members of the International Trade Organization should abide by the exchange principles established pursuant to the Articles of Agreement of the International Monetary Fund and for this reason it should be required that the Organization and the Fund have a common membership.

2. *Equality of exchange treatment.* Members maintaining or establishing exchange restrictions should undertake to accord to the trade of other members the equality of treatment with respect to all aspects of such restrictions required under the provisions of the Articles of Agreement of the International Monetary Fund or, in cases where the approval of the Fund is required, the equality of treatment prescribed by the Fund after consultation with the International Trade Organization.

Section G. General Exceptions

The undertakings in this Chapter should not be construed to prevent members from adopting or enforcing measures:

1. necessary to protect public morals;
2. necessary to protect human, animal or plant life or health;
3. relating to the traffic in arms, ammunition and implements of war, and, in exceptional circumstances, all other military supplies;
4. relating to the importation or exportation of gold or silver;
5. necessary to induce compliance with laws or regulations, such as those relating to customs enforcement, deceptive practices, and the protection of patents, trademarks and copyrights, which are not inconsistent with the purposes of the Organization;
6. relating to prison-made goods;
7. imposed for the protection of national treasures of artistic, historic or archaeological value;
8. undertaken in pursuance of obligations for the maintenance of peace and security; or
9. imposed, in exceptional cases, in accordance with a recommendation of the Organization formulated in accordance with criteria and procedures to be agreed upon.

Section H. Territorial Application of Chapter III

1. *Customs territories.* The provisions of Chapter III should apply to the customs territories of the members. If any member has more than one customs territory under its jurisdiction, each customs territory should be considered a separate member for the purpose of applying the provisions of Chapter III.

2. *Frontier traffic and customs unions.* The provisions of Chapter III should not prevent any member *a)* from according advantages to adjacent countries in order to facilitate frontier traffic or *b)* from joining a customs union, provided that such customs union meets certain agreed criteria. Members proposing to join a customs union should consult with the Organization and should make available to it such information as would enable it to make appropriate reports and recommendations.

CHAPTER IV

RESTRICTIVE BUSINESS PRACTICES

1. *Curbing of restrictive business practices.* There should be individual and concerted efforts by members of the Organization to curb those restrictive business practices in international trade (such as combinations or agreements to fix prices and terms of sale, divide markets or territories, limit production or exports, suppress technology or invention, exclude enterprises from particular fields, or boycott or discriminate against particular firms) which have the effect of frustrating the objectives of the Organization to promote expansion of production and trade, equal access to markets and raw materials, and the maintenance in all countries of high levels of employment and real income.

2. *Cooperation among members.* In order to achieve the purposes of paragraph 1, the Organization should be charged with the furtherance of this objective. The Organization should receive complaints from any member (or, with the permission of the member, from commercial enterprises within its jurisdiction who allege that their interests are affected), that the objectives of the Organization are being frustrated by a private international combination or agreement. The Organization should be empowered to call upon any member to provide information relevant to such a complaint; it should consider such data and, if warranted, make recommendations to the appropriate members for action in accordance with their respective laws and procedures; it should be empowered to request reports from members as to their actions in implementing such recommendations, and to report thereon. The Organization should also be authorized, within the scope of its subject matter, to conduct studies, to make recommendations concerning uniform national standards, and to call conferences of member states for purposes of general consultation.

3. *Continued effectiveness of national laws and regulations directed against restrictive business practices.* Any act or failure to act on the part of the Organization should not preclude any member from enforcing within its own jurisdiction any national statute or decree directed toward the elimination or prevention of restrictive business practices in international trade.

4. *Special enforcement arrangements.* It should be provided that members may, by mutual accord, cooperate in measures for the purpose of making more effective any remedial order which has been issued by a duly authorized agency of another member.

Chapter V
INTERGOVERNMENTAL COMMODITY ARRANGEMENTS

The production of, and trade in, primary commodities is exposed to certain difficulties different in character from those which generally exist in the case of manufactured goods; and these difficulties, if serious, may have such widespread repercussions as to prejudice the prospect of the general policy of economic expansion. Members should therefore agree upon the procedure which should be adopted to deal with such difficulties.

1. *Special commodity studies.*

    a. Special studies should be made in accordance with the procedure set forth in *b,* below, of the position of particular commodities of which excess supplies exist or are threatened, to the end that, if possible, consumption may be increased and the anticipated difficulties may thereby be averted.

    b. Members substantially interested in the production or consumption of a particular commodity should be entitled, if they consider that special difficulties exist or are expected to arise regarding that commodity, to ask that a special study of that commodity be made, and the Organization, if it finds that these representations are well founded, should invite the members principally concerned in the production or consumption of that commodity to appoint representatives to a Study Group to make a special study of that commodity.

2. *Intergovernmental commodity conferences.* If it is concluded, in the light of an investigation of the root causes of the problem, that measures for increasing the consumption of a commodity are unlikely to operate quickly enough to prevent excess supplies of the commodity from accumulating, the members may ask the Organization to convene an intergovernmental conference for the purpose of framing an intergovernmental commodity agreement for the commodity concerned.

3. *Objectives of intergovernmental commodity agreements.* It should be recognized that intergovernmental commodity agreements involving restrictions on production or trade would be justified in the circumstances stated in paragraph 2 above to achieve the following objectives:

   a. To enable member countries to find solutions to particular commodity problems without resorting to unilateral action that tends to shift the burden of their problems to other countries.

   b. To prevent or alleviate the serious economic problems which may arise when, owing to the difficulties of finding alternative employment, production adjustments cannot be effected by the free play of market forces as rapidly as the circumstances require.

   c. To provide a period of transition which will afford opportunities for the orderly solution of particular commodity_problems by agreement between member governments upon a program of over-all economic adjustments designed to promote a shift of resources and manpower out of over-expanded industries into new and productive occupations.

4. *Principles of intergovernmental commodity agreements.* Members should undertake to adhere to the following principles governing the institution of intergovernmental commodity agreements:

   a. Members having an interest in the production or consumption of any commodity for which an intergovernmental commodity agreement is proposed, should be entitled to participate in the consideration of the proposed agreement.

   b. Members should undertake not to enter into intergovernmental commodity agreements involving the limitation of production or exports or the allocation of markets, except after:

   1) Investigation by the Study Group of the root causes of the problem which gave rise to the proposal;

   2) Determination, in accordance with procedures approved by the Organization, either:

   a) that a burdensome surplus of the product concerned has developed or is developing in international trade and is accompanied by widespread distress to small producers accounting for a substantial proportion of the total output and that these conditions cannot be corrected by the normal play of competitive forces because, in the case of the product concerned, a substantial reduction of price leads neither to a significant increase in consumption nor to a significant decrease in production; or

b) that widespread unemployment, unrelated to general business conditions, has developed or is developing in respect of the industry concerned and that such unemployment cannot be corrected by the normal play of competitive forces rapidly enough to prevent widespread and undue hardship to workers because, in the case of the industry concerned, i) a substantial reduction of price does not lead to a significant increase in consumption but leads, instead, to the reduction of employment, and ii) the resulting unemployment cannot be remedied by normal processes of reallocation;

3) Formulation and adoption by members of a program of economic adjustment believed to be adequate to insure substantial progress toward solution of the problem within the time limits of the agreement.

c. Intergovernmental agreements involving the limitation of production or exports or the allocation of markets in respect of fabricated products should not be resorted to unless the Organization finds that exceptional circumstances justify such action. Such agreements should be subject to the principles set forth in this Chapter, and, in addition, to any other requirements which the Organization may establish.

5. *Operation of commodity agreements.* Members should undertake to adhere to the following principles governing the operation of intergovernmental commodity agreements:

a. The agreements should be open to accession by any member on terms not less favorable than those accorded to members parties thereto.

b. The members adhering to such agreements which are largely dependent for consumption on imports of the commodity involved should, in any determinations made relating to the regulation of prices, trade, stocks, or production, have together a voice equal to those largely interested in obtaining export markets for their production.

c. The agreements should, when necessary, contain provisions for assuring the availability of supplies adequate at all times for world consumption requirements at reasonable prices.

d. The agreements should, with due regard to the transitional need for preventing serious economic and social dislocation, make appropriate provision to afford increasing opportunities for satisfying world requirements from sources from which such requirements can be supplied most effectively.

6. *Termination and renewal of commodity agreements.* Intergovernmental commodity agreements should not remain initially in effect for more than five years. The renewal of an agreement should be subject to the principles governing new agreements set forth in paragraph 4, above, and to the additional principle that either *a*) substantial progress toward a solution of the underlying problem shall have been accomplished during the initial period of the agreement or that *b*) the renewed agreement is so revised as to be effective for this purpose.

7. *Review of commodity agreements.* Members should undertake to transmit to the Organization, for review, intergovernmental commodity agreements in which they now participate or in which they propose to participate in the future. Members should also transmit to the Organization appropriate information regarding the formulation, provisions and operation of such agreements.

8. *Publicity.* Full publicity should be given to any commodity agreement proposed or concluded, to the statements of considerations and objectives advanced by the proposing members, to the operation of the agreements, and to the nature and development of measures adopted to correct the underlying situation which gave rise to the agreement.

9. *Exceptions.* The provisions of Chapter V are not designed to cover international agreements relating to the protection of public morals; the protection of human, animal or plant life or health; the conservation of reserves of exhaustible natural resources; the control of international monopoly situations; or the equitable distribution of commodities in short supply. However, such agreements should not be used to accomplish results inconsistent with the objectives of Chapter IV or Chapter V. If any such agreement involves the restriction of production or of international trade, it should not be adopted unless authorized or provided for by a multilateral convention subscribed to by a substantial number of nations, or unless operated under the Organization.

CHAPTER VI

ORGANIZATION

Section A. Functions

The functions of the Organization should include the following:

1. To collect, analyze and publish information, regarding the operation of Chapter III, relating to general commercial policy, Chapter IV, relating to the prevention of restrictive business practices, and Chapter V, relating to intergovernmental commodity arrangements, or in general regarding international trade and commercial policy.

2. To provide technical assistance to members as may be required or appropriate under the provisions of Chapters III, IV and V.

3. To make recommendations to members regarding the operation of Chapters III, IV and V, including the following:

    a. Recommendations regarding the relaxation or removal of trade control measures permitted under Chapter III.

b. Recommendations as to measures for implementing the objectives with regard to restrictive private business practices, set forth in Chapter IV.

c. Recommendations regarding the application to commodity arrangements under consideration by members of the principles governing commodity arrangements set forth in Chapter V; and recommendations initiating proposals for new commodity arrangements, or proposing such modifications, including termination, of commodity arrangements already concluded, as may be deemed appropriate under the commodity principles or in the general interest.

d. Recommendations designed to promote the maximum obtainable consistency in the operation of Chapters III, IV and V and in other arrangements in the fields of general commercial policy, commodity arrangements and private business practices.

4. To interpret the provisions of Chapters III, IV and V, to consult with members regarding disputes growing out of the provisions of those Chapters, and to provide a mechanism for the settlement of such disputes.

5. In accordance with criteria and procedures to be agreed upon, to waive particular obligations of members, in exceptional circumstances.

6. To make recommendations for international agreements designed to improve the bases of trade and to assure just and equitable treatment for the enterprises, skills and capital brought from one country to another, including agreements on the treatment of foreign nationals and enterprises, on the treatment of commercial travelers, on commercial arbitration, and on the avoidance of double taxation.

7. Generally to perform any function appropriate to the purposes of the Organization.

Section B. Organs

The Organization should have as its principal organs: A Conference, an Executive Board, a Commercial Policy Commission, a Commission on Business Practices, a Commodity Commission, and a Secretariat.

Section C. The Conference

The Conference should have final authority to determine the policies of the Organization and to exercise the powers conferred upon the Organization.

1. *Membership.* All states members of the Organization should be members of the Conference.

2. *Voting.* Each member of the Conference should have one vote. Except as may be otherwise specifically provided for, decisions of the Conference should be reached by a simple majority vote. It may be desirable to provide for special voting arrangements with regard to the exercise of certain functions of the Organization.

3. *Sessions.* The Conference should meet at least once a year.

Section D. The Executive Board

The Executive Board should be authorized to take provisional decisions between meetings of the Conference and to exercise such powers as may be delegated to it by the Conference. The Conference should in general be authorized to delegate its powers to the Executive Board.

1. *Membership.* The Executive Board should consist of not more than eighteen member states, each of which should have one representative. Member states of chief economic importance should have permanent seats. The Conference should elect the states to fill the nonpermanent seats for 3-year terms, one-third of the nonpermanent members retiring every year. The number of nonpermanent seats should exceed the number of permanent seats, but the latter should not be fewer than one-third of the total number of seats.

2. *Voting and sessions.* The Executive Board should regulate its own procedure.

Section E. The Commissions

The Commission on Commercial Policy, the Commission on Business Practices and the Commodity Commission should be responsible to the Executive Board. Each Commission should be given as much initiative and independence of action as may be necessary for the effective discharge of its functions.

1. *Membership.* The Commissions should be composed of experts appointed by the Executive Board. The terms and other conditions of office of the members of the Commissions should be determined in accordance with regulations prescribed by the Conference. Such terms and conditions need not be uniform, but may vary from Commission to Commission. Pursuant to the reciprocal arrangements with other specialized international organizations contemplated in Section H, paragraph 2, of this Chapter, provision should be made for appropriate representation on the Commodity Commission of the Food and Agriculture Organization of the United Nations and of other specialized international organizations having an important interest in the commodity operations discussed in Chapter V.

2. *Chairmen.* The Chairmen of the Commissions should be nonvoting members of the Executive Board and should be permitted to participate, without vote, in the deliberations of the Conference.

3. *Voting and sessions.* Each Commission should regulate its own procedure, subject to any decisions made by the Executive Board.

4. *Functions.* The functions of the Commissions should include the following:

    a. The Commercial Policy Commission. The Commercial Policy Commission should:

        1) Review, and advise the Executive Board regarding, the operation of treaties, agreements, practices and policies affecting international trade.

        2) Investigate, and advise the Executive Board regarding, the economic

aspects of proposals to waive certain obligations of members in accordance with the provisions of paragraph 5, Section A, of this Chapter.

3) Investigate, and advise the Executive Board regarding, the economic aspects of proposed customs unions.

4) Develop and recommend to the Executive Board, for adoption by members of the Organization, cooperative projects of a technical nature in the field of commercial policy (e.g. standard bases and methods of determining dutiable value, uniform customs nomenclature, and standardization of statistical methods and nomenclature in foreign trade statistics).

5) Develop and recommend to the Executive Board additional programs designed to further the objectives of the Organization in the general field of commercial policy.

b. *The Commission on Business Practices.* The Commission on Business Practices should:

1) Inquire into activities on the part of private commercial enterprises which have the effect or purpose of restraining international trade, restricting access to international markets, or of fostering monopolistic controls in international trade.

2) Advise the Executive Board with regard to the recommendations which should be made to members in respect of business divestitures, reorganizations, dissolutions or other remedial actions.

3) Conduct investigations and make recommendations to the Executive Board looking to the promotion and adoption in all countries of codes of fair business practices designed to facilitate and enlarge the flow of international trade.

4) Advise the Executive Board as to the types of information which members should file with the Organization.

5) Facilitate appropriate intergovernmental arrangements for the international exchange of technological information, on a nondiscriminatory basis.

c. *The Commodity Commission.* The Commodity Commission should:

1) Investigate commodity problems, including the problem of an international buffer stocks organization or other arrangements which are proposed as a means of promoting solutions to commodity problems.

2) Make recommendations to the Executive Board on appropriate courses of action, including recommendations for the establishment of Study Groups for particular commodities. Such Study Groups should be established by the Executive Board, upon the recommendations of the Commodity Commission, for the purpose of investigating problems with respect to particular commodities. The Study Groups should be composed of repre-

sentatives of member governments invited to participate by the Executive Board and one or more representatives designated by the Commodity Commission.

3) Make recommendations to the Executive Board as to whether or not a particular commodity is in world surplus.

4) Make recommendations to the Executive Board as to whether an application made by a member for the convening of an intergovernmental conference should be granted.

5) Designate members of the Commission to participate in an advisory capacity in the formulation of intergovernmental commodity agreements.

6) Make recommendations to the Executive Board regarding the application of the commodity agreements under consideration by members.

7) Designate the Chairman and Secretary for any Commodity Council established to administer an intergovernmental commodity agreement.

8) Maintain continuous review of the conduct of the operations of intergovernmental commodity agreements in the light of the terms of the agreements, the commodity principles in Chapter V, and the general welfare; and make recommendations to the Executive Board with regard thereto.

Section F. Industrial and Mineral Unit

The Conference should create an Industrial and Mineral Unit responsible to the Executive Board. The Industrial and Mineral Unit should promote by technical assistance and other appropriate means the expansion of production and trade with regard to fabricated products and with regard to minerals and other primary commodities in respect of which such promotional activities are not under the jurisdiction of the Food and Agriculture Organization.

Section G. The Secretariat

The Secretariat, which should be divided into three or more offices, should serve all the organs of the Organization and the Commodity Councils established to administer specific commodity arrangements. It should be headed by a Director-General. Under his authority there should be three or more Deputy Directors-General each of whom should be in charge of an office. The Director-General, and on the advice of the Director-General, the Deputy Directors-General, should be appointed by the Conference upon the nomination of the Executive Board. The Director-General should be the chief administrative officer of the Organization and should be an *ex officio* member, without vote, of the Executive Board. Three Deputy Directors-General should be *ex officio* members of the three Commissions. The Director-General and the Deputy Directors-General should have the authority to initiate proposals for the consideration of any organ of the Organization.

Section H. Relations with Other Organizations

1. *Relations with the United Nations Organization.* The Organization should be brought into relationship with the United Nations Organization on terms to be determined by agreement between the Executive Board and the appropriate authorities of the United Nations Organization, subject to approval by the Conference.

2. *Relations with other specialized international organizations.* In order to provide for close cooperation between the Organization and other specialized international organizations with related responsibilities, the Executive Board, subject to the approval of the Conference, should be authorized to enter into agreements with the appropriate authorities of such organizations defining the distribution of responsibilities and methods of cooperation.

3. *Administrative arrangements.* The Director-General should be authorized, subject to the authority of the Conference or of the Executive Board, to enter into agreements with other international organizations for the maintenance of common services, for common arrangements in regard to recruitment, training, conditions of service, and other related matters, and for interchanges of staff.

BIBLIOGRAPHY

Adler, J. Hans. "United States Import Demand During the Interwar Period," *American Economic Review*, June 1945

Balogh, T. "The Foreign Balance and Full Employment," *Bulletin of the Oxford Institute of Statistics*, Vol. V, Supplement No. 5

——. "The International Aspects of Full Employment," in *The Economics of Full Employment*, Institute of Statistics, Oxford University, Blackwell & Mott, Oxford, 1945

Bank for International Settlements. *Fourth Annual Report*, Basle, 1934

Baykov, Alexander. *The Development of the Soviet Economic System*, Economic and Social Studies No. 5, National Institute of Economic and Social Research, Cambridge University Press, Cambridge (England), 1946

Beal, Edwin G. *See* Taeuber, Irene B.

Benham, Frederic. "The Muddle of the Thirties," *Political Science Quarterly*, December 1944

Beveridge, William H. *Full Employment in a Free Society*, Allen & Unwin, London, 1944

Black, J. D., and Tsou, J. S. "International Commodity Agreements," *Quarterly Journal of Economics*, August 1944

Bloomfield, Arthur I. *The British Balance of Payments Problem*, International Finance Section, Princeton University Press, Princeton, 1945

Brandt, Karl. *The Reconstruction of World Agriculture*, Norton, New York, 1945

Brown, A. J. "The Great Industrial Exporters," *Bulletin of International News*, March 3, 1945

——. *Industrialization and Trade: The Changing World Pattern and the Position of Britain*, Royal Institute of International Affairs, London, 1943

Brown, William Adams. *The International Gold Standard Reinterpreted, 1914–1934*, National Bureau of Economic Research, New York, 1940, Vol. I, Vol. II

Buchanan, Norman S. *International Investment and Domestic Welfare*, Holt, New York, 1945

Chalmers, Henry. "Current Trends in Foreign Trade Policies," *Foreign Commerce Weekly*, February 9, 16 and 23, 1946

Chase, Stuart. *Democracy Under Pressure*, Twentieth Century Fund, New York, 1945

Clark, Colin. *The Conditions of Economic Progress*, Macmillan, London, 1940

Cleland, W. Wendell. "A Population Plan for Egypt," in *Demographic Studies of Selected Areas of Rapid Growth*, Milbank Memorial Fund, New York, 1944

Cornfield, Jerome. "Employment Resulting From United States Exports, 1939," *Monthly Labor Review,* May 1945

Davis, Kingsley. "Demographic Fact and Policy in India," in *Demographic Studies of Selected Areas of Rapid Growth,* Milbank Memorial Fund, New York, 1944

de Vegh, Imre. "International Aspects of England's Reconstruction," *Proceedings of the Academy of Political Science,* January 1946

——. "Peace Aims, Capital Requirements, and International Lending," *American Economic Review,* May 1945

The Economist, May 26, 1945; June 2, 1945; June 9, 1945; June 23, 1945; July 7, 1945; August 18, 1945; August 25, 1945; September 15, 1945; October 20, 1945; "Second Thoughts," December 15, 1945; "The Trade Proposals," *ibid.;* "The Consequences," December 22, 1945

Efron, David. *See* Soule, George

Ellis, Howard S. *Exchange Control in Central Europe,* Harvard University Press, Cambridge (Mass.), 1941

Ellsworth, P. T. *Chile: An Economy in Transition,* Macmillan, New York, 1945

——. *International Economics,* Macmillan, New York, 1938

Ezekiel, Mordecai. "The Cobweb Theorem," *Quarterly Journal of Economics,* February 1938

Fabricant, Solomon. *Employment in Manufacturing, 1899–1939,* National Bureau of Economic Research, New York, 1942

Federal Reserve Bulletin, September 1945; April 1946; "The Foreign Loan Policy of the United States," March 1946

Fisher, Allan G. B. *The Clash of Progress and Security,* Macmillan, London, 1935

——. *Economic Progress and Social Security,* Macmillan, London, 1945

Fisk, Ysabel, and Rennie, Robert A. "Argentina in Crisis," *Foreign Policy Reports,* May 1, 1944

Florinsky, Michael T. "The Soviet Union and International Agreements," *Political Science Quarterly,* March 1946

Fong, H. D. *The Post-War Industrialization of China,* Planning Pamphlets, Nos. 12 and 13, National Planning Association, Washington, 1942

Frankel, H. "The Industrialization of Agricultural Countries," *Economic Journal,* June–September 1943

Gordon, Margaret S. *Barriers to World Trade,* Macmillan, New York, 1941

Gregory, T. E. *The Gold Standard and Its Future,* Methuen, London, 1932

Government of the United Kingdom. *Egyptian Foreign Exchange Requirements for 1945,* Egypt No. 1 (1945), British White Paper, Cmd. 6582

——. *Financial Agreement Between the Governments of the United States and the United Kingdom, Dated 6th December, 1945, Together With a Joint Statement Regarding Settlement for Lend-Lease, Reciprocal Aid, Surplus War Property and Claims,* British White Paper, Cmd. 6708

——. *Iraqi Foreign Exchange Requirements for 1945,* Iraq No. 1 (1945), British White Paper, Cmd. 6646

——. *Monetary Agreement Between the United Kingdom and Belgium*, Belgium No. 1 (1944), British White Paper, Cmd. 6557

——. *Statistical Material Presented During the Washington Negotiations*, British White Paper, Cmd. 6707, 1945

Haberler, Gottfried. "The Choice of Exchange Rates After the War," *American Economic Review*, June 1945

——. "Currency Depreciation and the International Monetary Fund," *Review of Economic Statistics*, November 1944

Hagerty, John J. "Wartime Shifts in Latin American Agriculture," *Foreign Agriculture*, May 1945

Hansen, Alvin H. *America's Role in the World Economy*, Norton, New York, 1945

——. "A Brief Note on 'Fundamental Disequilibrium,'" *Review of Economic Statistics*, November 1944

Hawtrey, R. G. *The Gold Standard in Theory and Practice*, Longmans, Green, London, 1939

Heimann, Eduard. "Developmental Schemes, Planning and Full Employment: The Economic Theory of the TVA," *International Post-War Problems*, January 1946

Hevesy, P. de. *World Wheat Planning and Economic Planning in General*, Oxford University Press, Oxford, 1940

Hilgerdt, Folke. "The Case for Multilateral Trade," *American Economic Review, Supplement*, March 1943

Hinshaw, Randall. "Foreign Investment and American Employment," *American Economic Review, Supplement*, May 1946

Hirschman, A. O. "The Commodity Structure of World Trade," *Quarterly Journal of Economics*, August 1943

——. *National Power and the Structure of Foreign Trade*, University of California Press, Berkeley, 1945

Hobhouse, L. T. *Liberalism*, Holt, New York, 1911

Holmes, Olive. "Anglo-American Caribbean Commission — Pattern for Colonial Cooperation," *Foreign Policy Reports*, December 15, 1944

Horton, Kathleen O., and Wilson, Thomas R. *Some Factors in Postwar Export Trade With British Empire*, Economic Series No. 39, Bureau of Foreign and Domestic Commerce, 1944

Innis, Harold A. "On the Economic Significance of Culture," *Journal of Economic History*, 1944

International Labor Office, *Intergovernmental Commodity Control Agreements*, Montreal, 1943

Keynes, J. M. *The Economic Consequences of the Peace*, Harcourt, Brace, New York, 1920

——. "The German Transfer Problem," *Economic Journal*, 1929

Kindersley, R. M. "British Oversea Investments," *Economic Journal*, 1939

Kiser, Clyde V. "The Demographic Position of Egypt," in *Demographic Studies of Selected Areas of Rapid Growth*, Milbank Memorial Fund, New York, 1944

Knorr, K. E. *Rubber After the War,* Food Research Institute, Stanford University, 1944

Lange, Oscar. *Price Flexibility and Employment,* Principia Press, Bloomington (Ind.), 1944

Lary, Hal B. "The Domestic Effects of Foreign Investment," *American Economic Review,* May 1946, pp. 672–86

Lary, Hal B., and Associates. *The United States in the World Economy,* Economic Series No. 23, Bureau of Foreign and Domestic Commerce, 1943

League of Nations. *Commercial Policy in the Post-War World,* Geneva, 1945. II.A.7

——. Report of the Delegation on Economic Depressions, Pt. II, *Economic Stability in the Post-War World,* Geneva, 1945.II.A.2

——. *Industrialization and Foreign Trade,* Geneva, 1945.II.A.10

——. *International Currency Experience,* Geneva, 1944.II.A.4

——. *Monthly Bulletin of Statistics,* September 1945

——. *The Network of World Trade,* Geneva, 1942.II.A.3

——. *Quantitative Trade Controls: Their Causes and Nature,* Geneva, 1943. II.A.5

——. *Review of World Trade, 1938,* Geneva, 1939.II.A.11

——. *Statistical Year-Book of the League of Nations, 1935–36,* Geneva, 1936.II.A.8

——. *Statistical Year-Book of the League of Nations, 1941–42,* Geneva, 1942.II.A.8

——. *The Transition From War to Peace Economy,* Geneva, 1943.II.A.3

——. *World Economic Survey, 1937–38,* Geneva, 1938.II.A.13

——. *World Economic Survey, 1942–44,* Geneva, 1945.II.A.4

Leontief, W. W. "Exports, Imports, Domestic Output and Employment," *Quarterly Journal of Economics,* February 1946

Leven, Maurice; Moulton, Harold G.; and Warburton, Clark. *America's Capacity to Consume,* The Brookings Institution, Washington, 1934

Lewis, Cleona. *Debtor and Creditor Countries: 1938, 1944,* The Brookings Institution, Washington, 1945

Lindberg, John. "Food Supply Under a Program of Freedom From Want," *Social Research,* May 1945

Lynd, Helen Merrell. *England in the Eighteen-Eighties,* Macmillan, New York, 1945

McClellan, Grant S. "Colonial Progress in Central Africa — Belgian Congo and French Equatorial Africa," *Foreign Policy Reports,* May 15, 1944

Machlup, Fritz. *International Trade and the National Income Multiplier,* Blakiston, Philadelphia, 1943

Mason, E. S. "The Future of Commodity Agreements," in *Food for the World,* Theodore W. Schultz (ed.), University of Chicago Press, Chicago, 1945

Moos, S. "The Foreign Trade of West-European Countries," *Bulletin of the Oxford Institute of Statistics,* January 13, 1945

Moulton, Harold G. *See* Leven, Maurice

Munzer, E. "Exports and National Income in Canada," *Canadian Journal of Economics and Political Science,* February 1945

National City Bank of New York. *Letter,* February 1945

National Institute of Economic and Social Research. *Trade Regulations and Commercial Policy of the United Kingdom,* Cambridge University Press, Cambridge (England), 1943

National Planning Association. Planning Pamphlets, Nos. 37–38, *America's New Opportunities in World Trade,* Washington, 1944

——. Planning Pamphlets, No. 15, *International Development Loans,* Washington, 1942

Ness, Norman T. *See* Soule, George

New York Herald Tribune, February 1, 1946

Notestein, Frank W. "Population — The Long View," in *Food for the World,* Theodore W. Schultz (ed.), University of Chicago Press, Chicago, 1945

——. "Problems of Policy in Relation to Areas of Heavy Population Pressure," in *Demographic Studies of Selected Areas of Rapid Growth,* Milbank Memorial Fund, New York, 1944

Notestein, Frank W., *et al. The Future Population of Europe and the Soviet Union,* League of Nations, Geneva, 1944.II.A.2

Nurkse, Ragnar. *Conditions of International Monetary Equilibrium,* International Finance Section, Princeton University, Princeton, 1945

PEP (Political and Economic Planning). *Economic Development in S.E. Europe,* London, 1945

Pigou, A. C. "The Foreign Exchanges," *Quarterly Journal of Economics,* 1922

Polanyi, Michael. *Full Employment and Free Trade,* Cambridge University Press, Cambridge (England), 1945

Purves, C. M. "Wartime Changes in World Food Production," *Foreign Agriculture,* January 1945

Rennie, Robert A. *See* Fisk, Ysabel

Robinson, Joan. *Economic Journal,* December 1945

Röpke, Wilhelm. *International Economic Disintegration,* Hodge, London, 1942

Rosenstein-Rodan, P. N. "The International Development of Economically Backward Areas," *International Affairs,* April 1944

——. "Problems of Industrialization of Eastern and Southeastern Europe," *Economic Journal,* June–September 1943

Sammons, Robert L. "International Investment Position of the United States," *Foreign Commerce Weekly,* January 27, 1945

Schultz, Theodore W. "Food and Agriculture in a Developing Economy," in *Food for the World,* T. W. Schultz (ed.), University of Chicago Press, Chicago, 1945

Smith, John S. "World Income From Shipping," *Foreign Commerce Weekly,* April 29, 1944

Soule, George; Efron, David; and Ness, Norman T. *Latin America in the Future World,* Rinehart, New York, 1945

Spengler, J. J. "Population and Per Capita Income," *Annals of the American Academy of Political and Social Science,* January 1945

Statistisches Reichsamt Internationale Uebersichten, *Statistisches Jahrbuch für das deutsche Reich, 1934*

Staley, Eugene. *War and the Private Investor,* Doubleday, New York, 1935

——. *World Economic Development,* International Labor Office, Montreal, 1944

Stinebower, Leroy D. *The Economic and Social Council,* Commission to Study the Organization of the Peace, New York, 1946

Stocking, George W., and Watkins, Myron W. *Cartels in Action,* Twentieth Century Fund, New York, 1946

Strausz-Hupé, Robert. *The Balance of Tomorrow,* Putnam's, New York, 1945

Sundbärg, Gustav. *Aperçus statistiques internationaux,* Norstedt, Stockholm, 1906

Taeuber, Irene B., and Beal, Edwin G. "The Dynamics of Population in Japan," in *Demographic Studies of Selected Areas of Rapid Growth,* Milbank Memorial Fund, New York, 1944

Tasca, Henry J. *World Trading Systems,* International Institute of Intellectual Cooperation, Paris, 1939

Tsou, J. S. *See* Black, J. D.

UNITED STATES GOVERNMENT

Bureau of the Census. *Statistical Abstract of the United States, 1936; 1943*

Bureau of Foreign and Domestic Commerce. "An Estimate of the Number of Persons Engaged in the Production, Distribution and Servicing of Goods for Export," January 10, 1939 (mimeographed)

——. *Foreign Commerce Weekly,* January 27, 1945

——. "Foreign Investment Experience of the United States, 1920–1940," March 19, 1945 (mimeographed)

——. "New Policy Statement by Export-Import Bank" (official announcement by the Bank), *Foreign Commerce Weekly,* September 29, 1945

——. *Survey of Current Business,* February 1945; February 1946

——. "United States Foreign Trade, 1941–44," 1945 (mimeographed)

——. Economic Series No. 23, *The United States in the World Economy,* 1943

Congress of the United States. United States Senate, 79th Cong., 1st sess., Committee on Finance, *Hearings on H.R. 3240,* "1945 Extension of the Reciprocal Trade Agreements Act," 1945

——. House Special Committee on Post-War Economic Policy and Planning, H.Rept. 541, 79th Cong., 1st sess., *The Post-War Foreign Economic Policy of the United States,* 1945

Department of State. *United States Department of State Bulletin,* May 30, 1944

——. Publication 1948, *Final Act and Section Reports,* United Nations Conference on Food and Agriculture, Section XXV, International Commodity Arrangements

——. *Final Act and Related Documents,* United Nations Monetary and Financial Conference, Bretton Woods, New Hampshire, July 1 to July 22, 1944

———. Publication 2411, *Proposals for Expansion of World Trade and Employment,* 1945

———. Publication 1880, Executive Agreement Series 276, *Reciprocal Trade Agreement and Supplemental Exchanges of Notes Between the United States of America and Uruguay,* 1943

President of the United States. *Twenty-First Report to Congress on Lend-Lease Operations,* Government Printing Office, 1946

Vegh, Imre de. *See* de Vegh, Imre

Viner, Jacob. *Trade Relations Between Free-Market and Controlled Economies,* League of Natons, Geneva, 1943.II.A.4

Warburton, Clark. *See* Leven, Maurice

Watkins, Myron W. *See* Stocking, George W.

Williams, John H. *Post-War Monetary Plans and Other Essays,* Knopf, New York, 1944, Pt. I

Wilson, Thomas R. *See* Horton, Kathleen O.

Wright, Quincy. "The Nature of History," App. IV, in *A Study of War,* University of Chicago Press, Chicago, 1942, Vol. I

INDEX

The designation (t) or (c) following a page number indicates the reference is to a table(t) or a chart(c).